Byzantium after the Nation

Byzantium after the Nation

The Problem of Continuity in Balkan Historiographies

Dimitris Stamatopoulos

CEU PRESS

Central European University Press

Budapest–Vienna–New York

Published in 2022 by
Central European University Press
Nádor utca 9, H-1051 Budapest, Hungary
Tel: +36-1-327-3138 or 327-3000
E-mail: *ceupress@press.ceu.edu*
Website: *www.ceupress.com*

ISBN 978-963-386-307-7 (hardback)
ISBN 978-963-386-308-4 (ebook)

Translation is based on Δημήτρης Α. Σταματόπουλος, *Το Βυζάντιο μετά το Έθνος: το πρόβλημα της συνέχειας στις Βαλκανικές Ιστοριογραφίες* (Athens: Alexandreia, 2009). Translated and published in English with the permission of Alexandreia Publications.

Library of Congress Cataloging-in-Publication Data

Names: Stamatopoulos, Dēmētrios, 1969– author.
Title: Byzantium after the nation : the problem of continuity in Balkan historiographies / Dimitris Stamatopoulos.
Other titles: Vyzantio meta to ethnos. English | Problem of continuity in Balkan historiographies
Description: Budapest ; New York : Central European University Press, 2022. | Includes bibliographical references and index.
Identifiers: LCCN 2021021758 (print) | LCCN 2021021759 (ebook) | ISBN 9789633863077 (hardback) | ISBN 9789633863084 (ebook)
Subjects: LCSH: Balkan Peninsula—Historiography. | Byzantine Empire—Historiography. | Historiography—Balkan Peninsula—History—19th century.
Classification: LCC DR34 .S7313 2022 (print) | LCC DR34 (ebook) | DDC 949.60072—dc23
LC record available at https://lccn.loc.gov/2021021758
LC ebook record available at https://lccn.loc.gov/2021021759

Contents

Transliterations

Cyrillic Alphabet [Russian/Bulgarian]	Latin Alphabet	Pronunciation
А а	A a	/a/
Б б	B b	/b/
В в	V v	/v/
Г г	G g	/g/
Д д	D d	/d/
Е е	E e	/e/
Ё ё (Russian)	Ë ë	/ö/
Ж ж	Zh zh	/zh/
З з	Z z	/z/
И и	I i	/i/
Й й	Y y	/y/
К к	K k	/k/
Л л	L l	/l/
М м	M m	/m/
Н н	N n	/n/
О о	O o	/o/
П п	P p	/p/
Р р	R r	/r/
С с	S s	/s/
Т т	T t	/t/
У у	U u	/u/
Ф ф	F f	/f/
Х х	H h	/h/
Ц ц	C c	/ts/
Ч ч	Ch ch	/tsh/
Ш ш	Sh sh	/sh/
Щ щ	Sht sht	/sht/
Ъ ъ (βουλγ.)	Â â	/â/
Ы ы (ρωσ.)	I i	/i/
Ь ь	’	/y/
Э э (ρωσ.)	E e	/e/
Ю ю	Yu yu	/ju/
Я я	Ya ya	/ja/

Turkish Alphabet Pronunciation	
A a	/a/
B b	/b/
C c	/dzh/
Ç ç	/tsh/
D d	/d/
E e	/e/
F f	/f/
G g	/g/
Ğ ğ	/γ/
H h	/h/
I ı	/ɯ/
İ i	/i/
J j	/zh/
K k	/k/
L l	/l/
M m	/m/
N n	/n/
O o	/o/
Ö ö	/œ/
P p	/p/
R r	/r/
S s	/s/
Ş ş	/sh/
T t	/t/
U u	/u/
Ü ü	/ü/
V v	/v/
Y y	/j/
Z z	/z/

Preface to the English Edition

More than ten years ago, in 2011, Diana Mishkova had invited me to present the Greek-language edition of my book Byzantium after the Nation at the Center for Advanced Study in Sofia before a group of doctoral candidates and young historians from across the Balkans. I was surprised by the discussion that followed. Although my work contains several innovative positions on nineteenth-century Balkan historiography, what above all drew the audience's attention was my view of Nicolae Iorga's thesis in Byzance après Byzance.

Iorga's influential work has in the last decades acquired the characteristics of a metonymy: reference to the work of the Romanian historian came to mean for many (including the students who were present at the lecture) an assumption that the multicultural societies of the present could find their counterpart in multicultural societies of the past.

Although today we are more suspicious of the ways in which the idealization of old empires can serve the ideological needs of modern postnational state integration, the need for a firm "scientific" reference made *Byzance après Byzance* the dominant historiographical perspective on how to understand the passage from the Middle Ages to modernity in Southeastern Europe.

Of course, in Greek historiography, the reference to "post-Byzantine times" has strong nationalist connotations, for self-evident reasons. But surely Romanian historians were responsible, to a large degree, for Byzantium's return to the discourse in the twentieth century, albeit for reasons directly linked to Western, and especially French, Byzantinology. Romanian historiography aligned itself with the critical view of French Orientalism toward the Ottoman Empire, and it was obvious that this attempt would find allies (in Greek historians) and opponents (in Turkish ones).

However, the game of reconstruction of medieval times became more complicated due to the involvement in the dissolution of the Ottoman Empire of Slavs and Albanians. The Balkan Great Ideas (and consequently the strategies of their national movements) turned not only against the Ottoman Empire but also against one another.

The main objective of this book, published in Greek in July 2009, was to show precisely that Nicolae Iorga's position, which in fact involves continuity between the Byzantine and Ottoman Empire, not only became a tool for his reconstruction of Romanian national historiography, but also was extensively discussed in nineteenth-century Istanbul by historians who wanted to challenge the predominant canon of their national history.[1]

Iorga's thesis about the continuity of empires in some way became an alternative to the Holy Grail of national historiographies, that is to say, the continuity of the nation, and it had as a political precondition the identification of national historians with the imperial model. Thus, the "imperial dimension" existed in the discussions of the nineteenth century, and despite its use by Iorga, this helps explain why it can now be used to recall "multicultural memories."

In the years following the publication of my book many of the topics that it had elaborated were also addressed by other historians: the ideology of religious, especially Christian, ecumenism; the significance of intellectuals like Konstantin Leont'ev who turned their contemporaries' attention to Byzantine studies; and the importance of the Byzantine past as a whole for the ideological reconstruction of Southeastern and European national identities at the turn of the nineteenth and the twentieth centuries.

However, the basic position of this book as described above seems to retain its epistemological value, perhaps because the method followed was not a general overview of works and writers of national historiographies, as would have been the case with a traditional treatment following the

1 Or what Stefan Berger defines as "master narrative." On the contrary, what we define here as "historiographical divergence" could be corresponded to the meta-narrative contest which "constitutes the format of the hegemonic political discourse and informs attitudes toward the neighbouring countries, competitors, and internal adversaries." Stefan Berger, *The Past as History*, 2.

History of Ideas, but, rather an intellectual history centered on a particular network of intellectuals active from the end of the nineteenth century to the beginning of the twentieth century in Ottoman Constantinople. So I decided that it would be worth circulating an English version.

In the intervening years, I was given the opportunity to revise parts of the monograph as a fellow of two important institutions of Advanced Studies: the Institute for Advanced Study at Princeton (2010-11) and the Institute of Advanced Studies at the University of Freiburg (2017-18), and also to discuss complicated aspects of Balkan historiography thanks to an invitation by Bernard Heyberger at the École des Hautes Études en Sciences Sociales, by Natalie Clayer at Center d'Études Turques, Ottomanes, Balkaniques et Centrasiatiques, by Hans-Christian Maner and Jan Kusber at the Johannes Gutenberg University of Mainz, and by Dimitri Gondicas at the Program in Hellenic Studies at Princeton University. I very much thank those colleagues who have been actively involved in this dialogue.

The person that brought the bulk of this very difficult task to fruition was a friend and translator, Diane Shugart, who somewhat tamed my harsh and dense text, which is not exactly what an English-speaking audience expects. I would therefore like to express my gratitude for her work. I also thank sincerely two friends who took over from her the work of editing (which was particularly difficult because it concerned two different phases of linguistic diligence): Alexander Patramanis and Iannis Carras. I am very grateful especially to Iannis because he did so amidst many professional and teaching duties.

I also thank the Central European University Press, which has taken on the revised version of the book in English, and especially Nóra Vörös, who helped considerably in solving critical issues concerning the publication.

Finally, a thought for my family who had witnessed the endless hours I wasted in front of a computer. Yet Roula, Katerina, and Hara were and are the main source of my happiness. That is why I dedicate this book to them.

Chapter I

Introduction

1. The Discipline of History: Canons and Divergences

This study is a comment on a phrase coined by Nicolae Iorga, "Byzantium after Byzantium"—which also became the title of one of his books.[1] By focusing on the interaction between the Moldavian and Wallachian princes and the Orthodox Church, Iorga sought to prove the survival of Byzantium's imperial and religious heritage during the period of Ottoman rule. This study—which uses the Romanian historian's work as paradigmatic with regard to its treatment of the Byzantine-Ottoman Middle Ages in shaping historiographical models of national continuity—attempts to explore the ways in which this thesis has been discussed by the respective historiographical canons in the Balkans in the transition from the nineteenth to the twentieth century. The solution Iorga proposed in the early 1930s, that is, to view the Ottoman Empire as a continuation of the Byzantine Empire, had been widely discussed in the late nineteenth century by intellectuals who could not (or would not) detach themselves from the imperial past. Iorga adopted this position because he sought to reconstruct the Romanian historiographical canon on the basis of its imperial heritage; for the nineteenth-century intelligentsia, it was an issue of "divergence" from the emerging national historiographical canon to which they were each subject.

By the national historiographical canon, what we mean is the prevalent model for resolving fundamental "ethnogenetic," and ultimately political, problems in compiling the respective national narratives in the

1 Iorga, *Byzance après Byzance,* first published in French in 1935.

Balkans.[2] We could define it as the sum of complementary narratives that progressively impose a dominant interpretative approach on the national past. Usually, the national historiographical canon's functionality corresponded to a legitimation of the nation's historical trajectory by the West and the imposition of a perceived linear development from cultural self-subsistence toward the creation of a nation state, and then finally a solid national identity around which the nation would coalesce. This constituted the broad outline. But the specific form which this dominant narrative approach would take reflected, to a large degree, the great strategic dilemmas that would emerge from the nation-building process. Balkan historiographies were rife with such examples: for instance, in the Greeks' case, Byzantium's legacy was directly linked to the irredentism of the Greek Orthodox populations in the Ottoman Empire; in the Romanians' case, the evacuation of the Danube limes with their sovereign rights in Transylvania but also with their dispersion in the lands of the Eastern Roman Empire; for the Bulgarian nationalism of the nineteenth century, Byzantium was a metonymy of the threat of Greek irredentism and the historical springboard of Phanariotism; and so on.

Naturally, priorities were always set according to the political agenda of the rival nationalisms. But this meant that the representational dynamic of the narratives was overdetermined again each time by a hierarchical ranking of the strategic problems that political or "spiritual" elites were called upon to resolve. From the moment that the West, influenced by the ideals of German Romanticism, revised its assessment of the European, and by extension Byzantine, Middle Ages, the linear emergence of the nation materialized by adopting schemes of continuity. Here we can briefly mention that in Greek historiography, approaching Byzantine history as the link between ancient and modern Greek culture provided an initial solution to the issue of continuity. Spyridon Zambelios (1815–1881), a radical nationalist intellectual from the Ionian Islands, and

2 For a brief overview of ethnogenetic theories in twentieth-century Balkan historiographies, see Vryonis, "*Prior tempore*," 189–220. Vryonis tends to describe these ethnogenetic theories as "contrived," which is somewhat inconsistent given his deliberate opposition to what he calls the "Fallmerayerism" of both Romilly Jenkins and Cyril Mango and their support for the discontinuity of Greek history. "... ethnogenetic theories may differ from what we call historical truth ... nonetheless they are an historical reality." (192). See a short description of this theoretical conflict in Liakos, "Hellenism," 217–22.

Konstantinos Paparrigopoulos (1815–1891), professor of Modern Greek History at the University of Athens, contributed to the idealization and primarily the Hellenization of the Byzantine Middle Ages, Zambelios by countering the Gibbonian heritage and Paparrigopoulos by following in the footsteps of Jules Michelet. Thus, Byzantium (in the context of the revival of Byzantine Studies in Europe), acquired positive connotations, and in the process shaped modern Greek identity. By contrast, in the case of the Serbs but mainly in that of the Bulgarians, Romanians, and Albanians, the Balkans' Byzantine past was denounced almost simultaneously with the Ottoman heritage. Their respective national identities took shape as a result of their secession from the Ottoman Empire and their shedding of Greek cultural influence.

Much has been said about how Zambelios and Paparrigopoulos contributed to establishing the scheme of continuity in Greek history. Perhaps the most critical theoretical contribution to the issue is the view that Byzantium's incorporation supplanted the "revival" model (that is, neo-Hellenism as a revival of ancient civilization) with the model of "continuity," and that a balance between the two was struck through the transformation of the meaning of "Hellenism" in Paparrigopoulos's work.[3]

Nonetheless, what constituted Byzantium for nineteenth-century scholars and the particular ways their perception was linked to the treatment of the imperial model are issues that have not been examined as thoroughly as they merit.[4] These included: whether the Byzantine Middle Ages were viewed differently in Greek lands in contrast to Constantinople; the ways in which the nineteenth-century Balkan nationalists and Russian scholars viewed Byzantium; how they invented their own Middle Ages (and, consequently, their own antiquity); and, chiefly, whether there were continuities or discontinuities in these approaches and in the ideological use to which the past was put.[5]

3 Liakos, "Pros episkevin," 171–99, and mainly 175–76, 179, 183–86. The argument is taken up anew in Sigalas, "Ellinismos," 3–70.

4 The most significant attempt at an overview of Greek scholars' views of Byzantium in the latter half of the nineteenth century can be found in Argyropoulos, *Intellectuels grecs*.

5 The use of the concept of "invention" recalls the great controversy between Constructivists/Modernists and Essentialists/Primordialists on the definition of nation. The literature is huge, but here we will suffice to mention how the concept is used by Eric J. Hobsbawm and Terence O. Ranger. (See the Introduction and Chapter 7 to Hobsbawm and Ranger, *Invention of Tradition*.)

While one might, thus, stereotypically describe the formation of the national historiographical canon in relation to Byzantium, the late nineteenth century provides examples of historiography that deviated from this—both in the Greek and in some other Balkan cases.[6] This study will analyze these divergences and insist on highlighting differences without overlooking similarities. And this is because differences indicate contrasts which contribute to the production of broader interpretive frameworks or deviant historiographical views whose adherence to the canons of their respective national historiography was and is open to dispute. If these declinations are not explored, then the different subjective aims cannot be examined: neither the relationship between interpretive schemes and political programs as reflections of Balkan national consciousness, nor the custodial position of Western academies (including Russia) in this "intellectual game." But the study of divergences can lead us to interesting conclusions about the final shaping of the canon, whose definitive form was crystallized by the national academies in the final decades of the nineteenth century.

It is interesting to note that these divergences appeared mainly in Constantinople in the works of writers who, despite having chosen a national identity, operated within an imperial environment that was trying to respond to the nationalisms threatening to undermine it through various ideological formations. Thus, the title of this work, *Byzance après la Nation*, does not relate only to the different historiographical approaches to Byzantium in the age of nationalisms but also to the imperial environment of Constantinople/Istanbul itself precisely during the period of the foundation of national states in the former territories of the Ottoman

It should be noted, however, that the use of constructivist methods is not necessarily associated with a modern conception of the nation, see for example, John Breuilly's criticism on Philip S. Gorski in Breuilly, "Changes in the Political Uses of the Nation," especially, 84. Gorski, proposing a discourse analysis inspired by Michel Foucault's work to deal with the issue of the Dutch uprising against the Habsburgs, argues for the existence of Dutch nationalism dating back to the seventeenth century. See Gorski, "Mosaic Moment." Breuilly's critique focuses on the fact that such a methodology can exacerbate the confusion between modern and non-modern, since premodern concepts are interpreted based on modern theoretical approaches.

6 The negotiation of the problem of the nation's incorporation into the West and its consequent detachment from the East was common to the national historiographical canons of the Balkans and contributed to the construction of a Eurocentric worldview. Nonetheless, the national historiographic canon may sometimes have achieved incorporation into the Western one through the development of anti-Western arguments. Often the road toward the West first passed through the East.

Empire and immediately afterwards. In brief, we could say that the meaning of *Byzantium after the Nation* relates to the following parallels:

> Byzantium as Constantinople (the spatial dimension): that is, Byzantium as a common political/cultural cradle for the development of divergent historiographies from those produced by the representatives of the national center.
>
> Byzantium as Middle Ages (the temporal dimension): that is, Byzantium as a common denominator for handling the problem of continuity in Balkan historiographies (by necessity, to some degree, as each respective national historiography had to face the challenge of inventing its own Middle Ages).

Through this double perspective and using as criteria whatever was produced about Byzantium, metaphorically and literally, some divergences from what we call the national historiographical canon will be studied. The approach will be comparative through a critical reading of the works of Manuel Gedeon, an intellectual identified with the policies of the Ecumenical Patriarchate for more than fifty years, Gavril Krâstevich, a "neo-Phanariot" leader of the Bulgarian community in Istanbul, and Şemseddin Sami, a member of the Ottoman bureaucracy involved in the formation of Albanian nationalism against the main representatives of their national historiographical canon like Constantine Paparrigopoulos and Spyridon Zambelios (Greek historiography), Marin Drinov (Bulgarian historiography), and Sami Frashëri (Albanian historiography), respectively. A note: Şemseddin Sami and Sami Frashëri are the same person; he participated in parallel literary traditions in the late nineteenth century: as Şemseddin Sami, a supporter of the Hamidian regime, he was the author of the first novel in the Ottoman literary history (*Taaşşuk-ı Talat ve Fitnat*, 1872), while as Sami Frashëri, one of the three famed Frashëri brothers, he was known as the founder of Albanian national historiography.

This does not mean that our comparative examination will be limited to the above historiographical confrontations; as long as the management of the national past's reconstruction was engaged with different academic networks, there were rival historiographical schools and a continuous re-evaluation of the nation's "friends" and "enemies." However, the analysis will insist on the above historiographical disputes because they were directly connected to the problem of the compatibility of the imperial with the national past. For the same reason, it was indispensable to include the Turkish case in our re-assessment of Balkan historiographies through a critical reading of the work of Ayşe Afet İnan and M. Fuad Köprülü based on their clash at the First Congress on Turkish History in 1932. Additionally, the Turkish case will be examined against the Romanian: the manner in which Nicolae Iorga "corrects" Xenopol's historiographical narrative to resolve the issue of continuity of the Romanian nation through the *Byzance après Byzance* scheme corresponds with Köprülü's failed and premature attempt to reconcile Turkish national identity with the Ottoman past.

Moreover, an extensive analysis of the works of writers inspired by the ideals of "religious ecumenism," such as the Russian Konstantin Leont'ev and the Bulgarian Marko Balabanov, will be attempted. While neither wrote purely historiographical works, their insistence on Byzantium's determining role in shaping the collective identity of the Slavic peoples directly influenced intellectual circles who subsequently occupied themselves with the problem of relations between the Slavs and Byzantium.[7] The works of Leont'ev and Balabanov will be compared to interesting "mutations" of their ideas: Leont'ev's work with the corresponding contribution of Ivan I. Sokolov on the issue of the meaning of "Byzantism/Byzantinism," and Balabanov's with the works of an important Serbian intellectual Stojan Novaković who had not yet embraced the ideals of religious ecumenism but, paradoxically, arrived at a number of similar conclusions. Additionally, along with the examination of Manuel Gedeon's work, the Ecumenical Patriarchate's Great Chartophylax, attempts by Greek Orthodox authors to write histories of the Ottoman Empire will be addressed.[8]

---

7 A characteristic example of this was the case of Dimitri Obolensky and the concept of the "Byzantine Commonwealth" he introduced. See Obolensky, *Byzantine Commonwealth.*

8 Generally speaking, the problem of historiography among the Slavs of the Western Balkans centered mostly on the relationship between West and East (given their location at its crossroads), rather than on their relationship with the imperial center, Constantinople. Thus, there does not

Similarly, just as we will explore the intricate paths of Orthodox ecumenism, we will also insist on some aspects of Pan-Islamic ideology, which was nevertheless the dominant imperial scheme in the Ottoman state during the reign of Abdul Hamid II. Dealing with some of the commonalities in the argumentation of Namık Kemal and Şemseddin Sami in the way they espouse Islamic culture mainly toward the West, one can discern a common way of perceiving the Byzantine imperial past.

A first observation which we could make from a comparative reading of above cases and their theoretical connotations is that the representatives of the historiographical divergences were inspired, for the most part, by a model of religious ecumenism shaped by late-nineteenth-century Istanbul. Analyzing the works of writers like Leont'ev and Balabanov, Şemseddin Sami and Namık Kemal, is crucial precisely because they constituted vital links in the formation of Constantinopolitan intellectual circles. Gedeon, then a young intellectual and personal friend of Balabanov, and Krâstevich, Balabanov's mentor, connected this model to the defense of a Pan-Orthodox ecumenism, while Şemseddin Sami as well as Namık Kemal and the group of the Young Ottomans linked it to the defense of a Pan-Islamic perspective. Twentieth-century authors like M. Fuad Köprülü and Nicolae Iorga were far removed from the ideological spirit of nineteenth-century Constantinople, yet an examination of their work is mandatory because they participated in a common discourse on the significance of the Byzantine (and, consequently, Ottoman) heritage in shaping the modern Balkans. Throughout the Balkan Peninsula, from the banks of the Danube River (Romania) to the massifs of Anatolia (Turkey), Byzantium once more became a reference point for organizing or adjusting national continuities. Even when the religious element receded from predominance and was accorded a more functional use by nationalism, studying the continuities and discontinuities between the Byzantine and Ottoman Empires would, as seen further on, provide the

---

seem to have been a representative of the Serbs, Croats, Slovenes, or Bosnians who adopted a historiographical form legitimizing religious ecumenism from the Empire's perspective. For an approach to the problem of the conflict between West and East in Croatian nationalism, see Sfetas, "Syniparxi kai sygrousi." See also Konstantakopoulou, *Politiki kai Mnimi*; Katsofska-Malogoudi, *Slavoi ton Balkanion*.

theoretical basis for conducting a dialogue between Balkan nationalisms and the colonial rationale of the West.

A second observation concerns the degree to which the Greek historiographical model of continuity suggested a "Balkanization" of the Balkans, in the sense of a canonical framework imposed against other Balkan historiographies in order to organize them along this basis[9] before the West invented what was awkwardly called "Balkanism."[10] Of course, the West was present in the Balkans regardless of Greek cultural influence. In the hegemonic scheme of continuity on which Greek nationalism was largely based, the Balkans responded with alternative models of origin (which the model of continuity can contain while not being identified with them). In the Greek case, the dominant historiographical model was mandated as continuity when Jacob Phillip Fallmerayer questioned the relationship between the modern and ancient Greeks; however, the existence of antiquity or its origins was never disputed per se.

Nevertheless, despite the attacks of the nineteenth-century European liberal intelligentsia, the model of continuity was not seriously challenged. As a result, the other Balkan historiographies not only had to construct forms of continuity but also had to invent equally important "ancestors"; if in the case of the Greeks, the sticking point was linking antiquity to modern times—that is, accommodating the medieval period—in most Balkan cases, the problem was the reconstruction of an antiquity that was not the equivalent of, but was certainly equal to, Greek antiquity. Invoking the glorious pasts of the ancient Thracians, Illyrians, Pelasgians, Dace-Getae, and later Macedonians, would resolve many of the problems of forging ethnic identities in the Balkans. Although managing the Middle Ages was often difficult (for instance, in the case of the Romanians or the Albanians), the prevalent tendency was to highlight this imaginary springboard for each respective nation whose surge could not be contained by the imperial shackles of the past: Roman, Byzantine, or Ottoman.

9 Spyros Vryonis appears to have reached the same conclusion while defending a different syllogism (See Vryonis, "*Prior tempore,*" 190). For a more detailed analysis of the ways in which Greek nationalism constructed its superiority complex over its Balkan neighbors, see Gounaris, *Ta Valkania ton Ellinon.*

10 Todorova, *Imagining the Balkans,* Mishkova, *Beyond Balkanism.*

2. The Problem of Continuity: Theories of Origin and Political Imperatives

One could say that among the examples to be studied, the Greek case represents the paradigm of the invention of continuity, while the Bulgarian the paradigm of the invention of origin—the intellectuals of the Bulgarian Renaissance "rediscovered" Paisius of Hilendar (Paisii Hilendarski) and his *Slavo-Bulgarian History* in the late nineteenth century, precisely as the debate on origin reached its peak. On the other hand, it could, of course, be argued that the Turkish and Albanian cases were a composite of the Greek and Bulgarian model even though their seminal point was set according to a constitutive discontinuity: the history of the Ottoman Empire. One might even make the same argument for the Greek and Bulgarian cases. But there is a fundamental difference. The issue of detachment from the Ottoman past in the Greek and Bulgarian cases was negotiated by historians, with the management of the Byzantine past as common denominator, albeit functioning in radically different ways. In the Turkish and Albanian cases, however, two fundamentally opposite historiographical approaches of continuity will be expressed simultaneously with regard to the acceptance or rejection of the Ottoman heritage.

Anthony D. Smith refers to a range of motifs through which various forms of origin are developed: the myth of origins, the myth of settlement and migration, the myth of genealogy, the myth of a heroic era, the myth of decline, and the myth of renaissance or rebirth. These constituted basic narratives on which national identities were built, space was nationalized, and, ultimately, political independence was sought for what had established itself as a "nation."[11]

Indeed, we find many of these motifs in the historiographical forms analyzed here. In each case, they appear to have served the models of continuity. Nonetheless, the encapsulation of these constitutive myths in order to support the narratives on which the nation's continuity was founded does not necessarily resolve the problem of the narratives' consolidation. The fact that in the late nineteenth century the ethnogenetic forms were predicated on the principles of positivist historiography and

11 Smith, *Myths and Memories*, 62–70.

simultaneously had to serve the goals of political romanticism created the prerequisites for the emergence of internal "rifts."[12]

Every form of continuity is marked by an internal rift. This consists in the declared discontinuity which it is called upon to manage. Positivist methodology is, by definition, forced to recognize this, regardless of whether the answer it will be called upon to offer is inscribed in a cultural (e.g., Paparrigopoulos), a racial (e.g., Drinov), or an origin-centric (e.g., Sami Frashëri) framework. The romantic canvas offers a way to transcend this via the prospect of organizing an "imagined community." But this does not mean the perceived discontinuity can be overlooked, especially when the problem of the hegemony of different proposals for the construction of this "imagined community" remains unresolved. This is the main reason the two predominant schools of thought on the interpretation of the nation—modernists/constructivists and primordialists/essentialists—encounter problems in coping with this issue of continuity. The former, by emphasizing the power of discourse, believe that it creates solid forms of continuity; the latter, by emphasizing the power of the "historical truth" cannot easily accept that factors such as imperial heritage, create prerequisites for a different approach to the historical path toward nationhood.

No historiographical approach can remain independent from the sociopolitical or even economic framework within which it is expressed. Thus, it was completely natural that Constantinople, as a peculiar space of political dominion, symbolic stature, and multicultural coexistence, would tend to produce different historical timelines from those produced by the national academies of newly formed Balkan states.

The issue of building networks must be examined within the broader framework of the shaping of an integral public sphere in Constantinople during the period of the Tanzimat.[13] The political dominance of the emerging urban bourgeois strata, the rise of "literate communities,"[14] and the common problems created by this reform project on the intellectual elite of each respective *millet* (or religious community) created the conditions for a common ground for dialogue centered on the problems of

12 On this topic, see Konstantopoulou, "Mnimi Ellis Skopetea," 27–40.

13 On the rise and fall of the civil public sphere, see Habermas, *Public Sphere.*

14 For one approach to the Greek case, see Exertzoglou, *Ethniki taftotita.*

national self-determination and its relationship to the empire's maintenance or dissolution.

At the same time, Constantinople developed a peculiar relationship with the European academies of both Central, Western, and Northern Europe (including Russia). This means that the production of any historiographical models should not depend solely on the imperial environment of the Ottoman capital but on its relationship to the ideological currents shaping European thinking at the time—Classicism, Romanticism, Positivism—and above all to ideological quests in the corresponding imperial environment of Russia (pro-Slav, pro-West).

In our opinion, this comparative approach can help contribute to an understanding of the development of historiographical models on two levels. First, on the level of the organization of networks of intellectuals both inside and outside the Ottoman Empire.[15] Second, the historiographical models can be viewed as cultural derivatives of the developments of two parallel, and not always contradictory, imperial discourses, the Russian and the Ottoman.[16] Certainly in the Greek, Romanian, and Turkish cases, the contribution of colonial imperial discourses was also remarkable and especially that of the defeated colonial partner: France.[17] Defeated by the English in North America and by the Germans in the heart of Europe, the French revolutionary tradition was transformed into a new type of imperial nationalism in the middle of the nineteenth century. We need to understand how Balkan historiographies (as well as national movements) dealt with the Western world's internal rifts, how they exploited the clashes between the Great Powers, and mainly, how they "exploited" the defeated colonialists. One of the main aims of the present work is to trace the effect of imperial nationalisms, either of the colonizing West or of the "resisisting" East, on the formation of the Balkan historiographical canons and divergences.

15 On the problem of organizing social networks and the conditions of reshaping these into power networks within the imperial environment, see Stamatopoulos, "From Machiavelli to the Sultans," 45–67.

16 In his seminal article "Back to the Future," A. G. Hopkins illustrates the progressive shift of historiographical focus from the national to the imperial.

17 Stamatopoulos, *Eastern Question*.

3. In the Shadow of the Empire

The clash of imperial discourses merits further theoretical elaboration. Even in the late nineteenth century, national discourses were defined by or against the imperial framework. The empires of Eastern and Southeastern Europe within which they developed naturally belong to the "old fashioned" continental empires; although the emergence of modernity (in practical terms, this is linked to the process of "Westernization" already underway in the Russian, Ottoman, and, of course, Habsburg Empires) in the Balkans was already a reality, this did not mean that individual or collective subjects were ready to adapt or even understand the difference between the organizational structures of modern and pre-modern types of states.[18]

This objective weakness of subjects to distinguish between "old" and "new" states, early modern and modern imperial forms, is very important in terms of how they perceived the restructuring of the time of nation. Nation-states envisaged their present and future on the basis of the imperial model (sometimes unaware of the differences between the two types), while empires tried to adapt to the new conditions by adopting different versions of nation-building procedures despite remaining multiethnic, multilingual, and multifaith. If the Greek and other Balkan states envisioned their expansion in terms of the imperial paradigm, the continental empires, oblivious of their approaching end, understood themselves through the prism of different models of nationalization. This is a point that deserves further consideration: the appearance of various versions of imperial nationalism in the continental empires was irrevocably linked to the problem of their recognition as equals in the eyes of the Western colonial world. The continental empires would seek recognition and equal status from the West, adopting in reality the Orientalist criteria projected upon them: cultural "difference" of which confession composed the core. Precisely at the time when, according to Edward Said, the dominant Orientalist paradigm was consolidated in the West, the empires of the east responded to Western Orientalism not only by adopting modernizing processes (that is, accepting their systemic inferiority) but also by

18 For this problem as it relates to the Greek case, see Kostis, "Formation of the State," 18–36, esp. 21–22.

glorifying that which made them autonomous and, thus, culturally equivalent entities, namely religion.[19]

Invoking religion was not related only to the issue of the reconstitution of these empires' legitimization in the eyes of their subjects. Naturally, the utility of instrumentalizing faith was obvious in both the case of Hamidian Pan-Islamism as well as in manufacturing the theory of the Third Rome in nineteenth-century Russia.[20] But by predicating imperial nationalism on cultural/religious "difference," the continental empires essentially sought equality and recognition from the West in a manner quite different from that chosen by the nations of Eastern and Southeastern Europe during the same period. The nations invoked the idea of temporal continuity as the foundation for their claims to space; the empires reflected on their (religious) ecumenism, a modern ecumenism, precisely to transcend the world's apportionment into nations. The nations of Eastern and Southeastern Europe sought equality with the West, promoting themselves as "collective subjects," whereas the empires promoted themselves as alternative "cultural paradigms."

This contradictory and intertwined ideological movement allowed a multitude of intellectuals who resisted or had yet to adapt to the logic of the nation-state to reorient their arguments in favor of the preservation of the empire to focus for the most part on a different perspective of time from that used by "organic intellectuals" of the nation-state. And this is the major problem regarding historiographical discourse that will be addressed here: the ways in which the continuity model was preserved within the framework of an empire rather than in its classical versions within national historiographies. Naturally, the problem of continuity was closely linked to the understanding of the nation as an essentialized collective subject. However, the incompatibility of the conceptualization of the nation as collective subject with the empire's ideological framework produced eccentric or divergent perceptions of national temporality.

The development of historiographical forms—particularly within the empire—that sought to provide options for the empire's survival often led to tension and even to a rift between the two models that we have

19 On this, see Stamatopoulos, "From the Vyzantism of Leont'ev," 329–48.

20 On the case of Hamidian Pan-Islamism, see Deringil, *Well-Protected Domains*. On the Third Rome idea, see Meyendorff, "Third Rome?"; and mainly, Rowland, "Moscow."

learned to handle homogenously in the processes of the "construction of the national time": the model of continuity and the model of origin.

Anchoring the historical rights of the nation in space and time presupposed the formulation of an originalist conceptualization that allegedly constituted the core of the continuity scheme. Nonetheless, the non-concentric handling of the phenomenon of nation-building—that is, from the empire's perspective—could have disintegrative consequences for the development of the continuity model. Let me remind the reader of the conceptualization of "nation" (*ethnos*) and "genos" (*millet*) in the work of Dimitrios Katartzis, one of the most prominent intellectuals of the Modern Greek Enlightenment, or Şemseddin Sami's definition of an "Ottoman identity" in the nineteenth century.[21] The extent to which forms of classical national historiography could trigger the conceptualization of continuity based on the origin model in order to invent a national antiquity, contriving a mythical Middle Ages—Christian or Islamic—as an imperial "living reality," could become a cause for restructuring the relationship of the nation with its antiquity: in other words, antiquity could be recast based on the image of the Middle Ages rather than vice versa. Even in the Greek case in which the Middle Ages were prematurely introduced (as compared to other Balkan historiographies) as part of a process of restoring a lost "intermediate" link necessary for continuity, we can diagnose a parallel "reconstruction" of Greek antiquity (especially in the work of Paparrigopoulos).

Balkan historians' invocation of Byzantium (or, better yet, any respective "medieval" period) to lend either a positive (the Greek and Romanian cases) or a negative sign (the Bulgarian, Albanian, and Turkish cases) in the building of the national canon reshaped the continuity perception. It did so by either by highlighting another origin that was more "compatible" with the imperial framework (Krâstevich) or by adopting a narrative that conflated the boundaries of the nation's history with the history of Christianity or Islam (Gedeon, Leont'ev, and Şemseddin Sami), or by subjugating the origin model to that of continuity, especially when

21 "By calling a Christian a 'Romios' (*Rum*), I mean the citizen of a nation . . . ," Katartzis, *Dokimia*, 44. See additionally Şemseddin Sami, *Kâmûs-ı Türkî*, 927. He defines Ottomanism either as the identity of the "Ottoman race and family" or as the identity of the subject of the Ottoman state. ("Osmanlilik-Osmanli kavim ve cinsine menusbiyet veya Devlet-i Osmanite'ye tab'iyet.")

seeking to preserve the empire's memory within the nation-state (Iorga and Köprülü). There is another important dimension: the dialogue and the process of recognition from the West's perspective. If the Balkan "reformers" were borrowing from the latter's Orientalist armory, the Occidentalist narratives invoking the Middle Ages aimed at legitimizing the East against the West.[22] Byzantium (and any medieval period), thus, operated as a point of escape from the impasse every Balkan nation faced when seeking to be evaluated as equal to Western states.[23]

As already noted, we should not forget that the form of continuity was not primarily invented to establish linear narratives but rather to resolve the thorny problems of discontinuity. All forms of continuity in reality accept the internal contradictions inherent to their logic.

It is assumed that all these alternative solutions were, for the most part, created on a double canvas: on one side, on a theoretical level, a type of romantic reconstruction of incompatible or even contradictory "narratives," and, on the other side, on a methodological level, a juxtaposition for an epistemologically rational, or rather a positivist interpretation, of historical sources. Both can be explained through the corresponding discussions taking place at that time in European historiography.

4. Describing the Network: The Ottoman Framework and Its Collapse

On April 5, 1925, which also happened to be Orthodox Good Saturday that year, Manuel Gedeon, writing from Athens where he had withdrawn after the end of the Asia Minor adventure, sent an interesting letter to Symeon, Bishop of Varna and Preslav.[24] Symeon held the title of Bishop from 1872, the year of the proclamation of the schism against the Bulgarian Exarchate on behalf of the Ecumenical Patriarchate, until his death in 1937.[25] This letter is held in the archives of the Bulgarian Academy of Sciences (Bâlgarska Akademiya na Naukite), along with the bishop's other

22 On the Bulgarian case, see, for example, Aretov, "Shto e Oksidentalizăm?," 123–30. See also Danova, "Otnovo za 'Oksidentalizma,'" 18–28, for an attempted comparison with the Greek case.

23 On the issue of the modern use of premodern motifs, see, among others, Duțu, *Political Models*, 109–10.

24 Bâlgarska Akademiya na Naukite (henceforth, BAN), file 144:1, no 291.

25 Markova, *Bâlgarskata ekzarhiya*.

personal files. Gedeon, "with great elation," learned via the Athenian press that while officiating services on March 25, "according to the Julian calendar," the Bishop had used the Greek language in addressing the flock who came from Odessa. Gedeon's jubilation was not prompted by patriotic satisfaction at Bulgarians' subordination to a Greek cultural and geographic space but rather by the glimmer of a revival of the once-solid Christian domain. The other source of Gedeon's joy was the news that an old friend from his Constantinople days was still alive:

> I was joyous that perhaps the only one from Halki Island, or in any case the oldest of the graduates, whose name I had first heard at the age of nine or ten because the all-holiness Symeon is, of course, the former Odysseas Papadopoulos [his secular name]. (BAN, file 144:1, no 291)

In some ways, the Theological School of Halki (Heybeliada) was the last laboratory for incubating a common Pan-Orthodox consciousness among the Greek and Bulgarian clergy staffing the Patriarchate of Constantinople.[26] Many years after writing this letter, Manuel Gedeon would publicly confess that he was an active opponent of the Schism, that is, the denouncement of the Bulgarian Exarchate's supporters by the Ecumenical Patriarchate and other Patriarchates in the Orthodox East. Gedeon views the loss of the world of a united Ecumenical Orthodoxy as a decisive factor in shaping his political awareness, as well as a primary driver of his historiographical studies aimed at highlighting the past of a united Orthodox *ecumene* either in the guise of the Byzantine Empire or as an Orthodox *millet* within the Ottoman Empire. As late as the mid-1920s, Gedeon continued to seek associates from that earlier period which, as Walter Benjamin's *angelus novus*, had banished to a distant past the wave of nationalism that dominated the nineteenth and twentieth centuries. Indeed, this was a period that had become quite difficult to recall.

Gedeon's letter to his old friend continues thus:

> Since 1872, when I witnessed the Schism, I've dreamt that one day, when this sad dissension has passed, we'll see the Bulgarian Exarch

26 Stavridis, *I Iera Theologiki Scholi*. For a Bulgarian perspective, see Balabanov, *Bâlgarskata koloniya*.

> officiating alongside all the Patriarchs of the Orthodox East. But I fear I may die before I have the chance to attend such a grand and devoted to the Almighty liturgy. (BAN, file 144:1, no 291)

Nonetheless, his desire to lift the consequences of the schism cannot overlook the stark reality: the decimation of the Orthodox world into national states and nation-oriented churches and, even more so, national identity supplanting of the dominant religious identity. However, from the wreckage of the Orthodox *ecumene* a new ideological ecumenism emerged that would attempt to reconnect these pieces:

> Perhaps there has been sufficient passage of time for the replacement of fratricidal rivalries and passions by Christian love, and the joining of brotherly hands, Greeks and Bulgarians, can work together against the various growing persecutors of the Christian Orthodox religion. (BAN, file 144:1, no 291).

This religious ecumenism is a child of modernity. Precisely for this reason, it does not set itself against the nation in order to negate it but rather transcends it: the power of religious awareness is exactly what will try to transcend the nationalist fragmentation of the modern world. But the routes followed by this process are many and varied. Someone may be able to trace common ideological trends among people in a shared network whose multiplicity must be seen as the basic reason for which its former members remained interested in defending those seemingly "old" values. Typically, Gedeon continues:

> If you order a response to this letter, please reply as to whether my old friend, Theodosius[27] (formerly Bishop of Skopje) is alive; perhaps none

27 Theodosius, a Bulgarian-speaking educated man, was born in the a village in the Nevrokop eparchy, just like his uncle Theodosius, a monk at the Monastery of Saint John (Timiou Prodromou) in Serres (1860–66 and 1870–85). His birth name was Vasil Iliev Gologanov. He had served as a church commissioner at Niš and a commissioner of the Bulgarian Exarchate at Constantinople. See Markova, *Bâlgarskata ekzarhiya*, 122, 123, 239, 329. Theodosius was enthroned as Metropolitan of Skopje under the Bulgarian Exarchate in 1887. See Gedeon, *Aposimeiomata Chronografou*, 330. On the other hand, Photios (Maniatis) had served as church representative in his neighborhood, Megalo Revma (Arnavutköy). During the patriarchal reign of Joachim II, the spiritual guide to

> of my old friends are alive and he may have died neglected, as did the former Bishop of Kozani, known to us as Photios, Metropolitan of Phillippopolis, who died alone and forgotten on the island of Aegina. (BAN, file 144:1, no 291)

In closing, the Grand Chartophylax of the Patriarchate conveyed his "wishes and regards," placing himself "at the disposal" of his respected friend—a display of almost religious obedience to the elderly cleric.

We do not know whether Symeon did finally respond to Gedeon, but a draft reply can be found in his archives. The draft is rambling, with self-imposed corrections (marked in the below excerpt by strikethrough) which are of greater importance than any reply that might in fact have been sent. The letter reads as follows:

> Dear Mr. M. Gedeon,
> I had never harbored the hope that I might be honored to receive correspondence from the diligent researcher and publisher ~~of letters and events~~ of important documents of the ~~Ecumenical~~ Patriarchate of Constantinople, which I had the honor to study and read to great benefit. I will attribute this honor to the news published in the Athenian press that I officiated at the feast of the Annunciation in the Greek language at a church in Varna. ~~It is true that for the first time this year, the services of the Annunciation were conducted in Greek in the city of Varna.~~ This ~~isn't entirely true~~ is true only as far as for the first time

---

Manuel Gedeon and a broad circle of lay people and members of the clergy, Photios had been Bishop of Eirinoupolis. In 1889, he moved to Phillippopolis (Plovdiv), where he served as Metropolitan for twenty-one years. In 1919, he was transferred to the See of Servia and Kozani, from which he stepped down voluntarily in March 1923 (see [Tsakopoulos], "Episcopal Catalogues," *Orthodoxia* 33 [1958], 35, 283, 421, and 34 [1959], 27–29). He fell out of favor during the patriarchy of Dionysius V (1887–1891) and was accused by the Patriarch himself of regularly conducting mixed marriages between Greek Orthodox and Catholic couples in his Stavrodromiou parish. According to Gedeon, Photios's protest that "my Lord . . . such marriages are quite rare," prompted the following outburst from Dionysius: "To whom are you saying this, eh? You wish to be unfaithful to your Patriarch, eh! You frequently marry our girls to Catholics; every day you wed Henrys, Laurences, Giuseppes, Thomases to Greek women who will lose their faith and nationality. How many millions of us are there for the Franks to take 100, 200, Orthodox women each year?" Photios's continued denial of these charges led the Patriarch to suspend him from the See of Eirinoupolis. The suspension was lifted after Dimitrios Paspalis, Nikolaos Psycharis, and Xenophon Zographos interceded with the Patriarch (see Gedeon, *Mneia pro emou*, 232–33, 236)

this year for the feast of the Annunciation, I ~~conducted~~ officiated the holy services in the church of the Panagia of Varna but only spoke a few lines in Greek: in Greek, two or three verses which I recalled ~~in~~ from my student years ~~in th~~ at the unforgettable Theological School at Halki. I would've conducted the entire service in Greek if ~~I had the bo~~ if I had had the service, and especially if I were not obligated to pay the heavy burden of emotions which reign ~~in the Greek countries~~ in Greece and Bulgaria. I would officiate in Greek if all the congregation that day had been Greek and if Greeks and Bulgarians ~~were not~~ did not believe that the use of one's language was for the others ~~a sin and error~~ an error of devotion. I've long held the belief that a prayer must be read in a language understood by the communicants. But this idea for many years has been considered ~~erroneous also by the~~ by the patriots of both sides erroneous and outdated which is why both use all means and methods possible not to allow their opponents to use their own language. Thus, the well of objection, struggle, and hate is bottomless.

It's not partiality but the truth that demands I say that you Greeks surpass us in this exclusion. If my memory does not fail me, the Greek churches and schools in Varna were made available to the Greeks much later than the Bulgarian schools and churches were placed under the jurisdiction of church or civil authorities.

We Greeks and Bulgarians fought amongst ourselves, defeating each other. The Bulgarians lost many places where Bulgarian nationals had resided who were Bulgarian-speaking ~~Gree~~ Romioi (e.g., Orthodox). You lost ~~Constantinople~~ the eternal dream of your ancestors, Constantinople, from where your fathers gave to other nations and to us Bulgarians the light of Christ, you lost Asia Minor, from where your ancestors raised ~~entire treasures~~ wealth and money and people to defend the center of Christian Hellenism. ~~You lost~~ You contributed to raising in your rear a friend who, sooner or later, will climb on your back. You lost, we also lost. But if ~~make a~~ compare damage, I am quite afraid that the harm done to you ~~is bigger and worse~~ are rather bigger and worse, just as your hopes were larger. (BAN, file 144:1, no 291, my translation)

This letter is not important primarily due to its mention of the losses suffered by one or the other side, or because it depicts the detachment from contemporary events of a man of the cloth, or even for its nostalgic reference to "unforgettable Halki," but rather due to the comparison prompted by the ideological and practical use of language by nationalist patriots on both sides. And it is important because the balance of losses reveals the inadmissible passion of Greek nationalism for Constantinople, projecting this as the desire of a man, Manouel Gedeon, who distanced himself to a substantial degree from the aims outlined by the official representative of the latter, that is, the Greek state.

But Constantinople—as well as Asia Minor, lost to the vision of the Megali Idea more recently—was identified precisely with the Christianization of the Roman Empire and a symbol of the Orthodox East against Western Catholicism (and its Protestant critics). This was an untamed enough ideological object which refused to submit completely to the needs and political designs of Greek nationalism. It is Constantinople that gives rise to divergent forms of historiographical discourse, "refusing" in a way to submit to the aggressive nationalists' demands.

Thus, the problem is how the issue of the Byzantine past was handled by the two sides of the old network that split in the wake of the Ottoman Empire's progressive dissolution—from Halki and Constantinople to Athens and Varna. There is no incident that illustrates this better than Symeon's self-censoring of the word "ecumenical" in describing the Patriarchate of Constantinople, even though he does choose the honorific plural. The unshakable reality of the national state not only imposes an official silence over banned issues such as the use of language, but it is also internalized by its subjects to such a degree that the simple composition of a text reflects those superimposed disciplines and politics.

This is why we shouldn't resort to a traditional history of ideas in order to ascertain influences, "transfusions" from the West's ideological armory, or their induction into broader theoretical or ideological trends, but rather see all of the above within the framework of shared ideological antagonisms and contradictions involving the members of this network of intellectuals. In other words, we should explore the conditions under which they were shaped as "intellectuals." In a way, we need to unfold the divergent ways—and what's interesting here is that it applies in all cases—in which they approached the past and the historiographical canon that was more or less shaped by their respective academic cultures through a common denominator—the management of the problem of giving priority to religion and, especially, the insistence on an imperial model that created ambiguous impressions as to whether it derived from the past or was a herald of the future.

Earlier we saw how Gedeon offered information on this network's extent, mainly through his association with certain clerics. In another text, Gedeon will offer even more salient information about the period of the schism: his good relationship with the important Bulgarian intellectual, writer, and journalist Marko Balabanov. Describing the political atmosphere immediately after the Schism and the desire of moderates on both sides to heal the wounds of the past, he writes:

> I assumed the task of writing in a pro-Orthodox spirit about a Greek newspaper named "Asia Minor," aiming to heal the Bulgarian Schism and cooperating with the legal expert Marko Balabanov. He made this friendly suggestion that we write in a spirit of Christian love; me in Missailides's *Asia Minor*, he in the Bulgarian newspaper *Vek*. Unfortunately, "Asia Minor" was left in the hands and editorship of a brute who destroyed it; I do not know how long Balabanov preserved *Vek*. He was a good friend exactly as a teacher at the Bulgarian school at Balat, and later the fourth Vice President of the Bulgarian Parliament, Petros (Petko) Slaveykov. (Gedeon, *Mneia*, 224–25)

Gedeon describes another network, this time of Bulgarian lay members with which he was associated and with whom he in some way coordinated his activity during this tense period. Of course, Gedeon is here writing sixty years after the fact, so it is natural that he let some things slip: Balabanov's newspaper *Vek* was published for two years, from 1874 to 1876, although he was also the publisher of *Chitalishte*, which was even more renowned among Constantinople's Bulgarian community. *Chitalishte* was launched in 1870, the first year the firman recognized the Bulgarian Exarchate and, like *Vek*, ceased publication in 1876 amid the Eastern Question crisis.

It is interesting that there is no reference in Balabanov's later writings to this peculiar relationship with opposing "moderates" like Gedeon. To some degree, this is logical. Having assumed senior posts in the newly formed Bulgarian state at a time when the events of 1870–1872 were a lot closer than they were to Symeon in 1925, it would be somewhat risky for him to have mentioned relationships whose very nature cast doubt on the historical possibility that was in fact realized (the formation of a national state), while also serving as reminders of a past history that everyone had sought to forget (the Empire's preservation).

Nonetheless, Balabanov dedicated a whole book to his spiritual and political mentor, Gavril Krâstevich, with whom he had been linked by 1871 after the convening of the great clergy-laity national assembly of supporters of the Bulgarian Exarchate in Istanbul. The national assembly's main purpose had been to draft the Exarchate's charter.[28]

Archival material in the repositories of the Bulgarian Academy of Sciences and the National Library in Sofia on Gedeon's correspondence with Balabanov—although there is no letter to or from either—proves his association and regular contacts with the same group of people that determined the historical course of the Ecumenical Patriarchate's Great Chartophylax. Symeon, as Bishop of Varna and Preslav,[29] as well as Bishop Theodosius of Skopje,[30] corresponded with Balabanov and maintained what seem to have been close relations through the early twentieth century.

But more important is the close relationship Balabanov maintained with Gedeon's mentor, Patriarch Joachim III. Shortly after Joachim's re-election to the patriarchal throne in October 1901, Balabanov also managed to be elected President of the Bulgarian national assembly.[31] This simultaneous rise of these two personalities to their respective posts may

---

28 Balabanov, *Krâstevich*. For an interpretative approach of the proceedings on the basis of the intra-communal relations of power, see Stamatopoulos, "Orthodox Millet," 243–70.

29 Narodna Biblioteka "Kiril i Metodiy Bâlgarski Istoricheski Arhiv" (henceforth NB-BIA), file 386, no 102. Symeon, Bishop of Varna and Prelsav, Shumen to Marko Balabanov, Istanbul, September 16, 1875, regarding the distribution of the newspaper *Vek* published by Balabanov (along with *Union Chrétien*). The letter also referred to the ban on marriage for clerics based on the Holy Synod's decisions.

30 NB-BIA, fil. 386, no 112. Theodosius, former Bishop of Skopje, Rila Monastery, to Marko Balabanov, Sofia, July 1, 1910. Theodosius informed Balabanov that Neophytos's election as his successor as Bishop of Skopje had been approved. The letter is quite personal as Theodosius conveyed his bitterness at being sidelined.

31 NB-BIA, file 386, no 9. Marko Balabanov, Sofia, to Patriarch Joachim III, Constantinople. Letter of gratitude in reply to a congratulatory note from Joachim preserved in the archives of the Bulgarian Academy of Sciences. See BIA, vol. 26:1, no 44. In this brief note, Joachim wrote: "H.E. Ivan Geov and new President of Parliament Mr. Balabanov, my warmest congratulations and blessings."

not have been coincidental and was linked to the new political landscape in Russian-Ottoman relations taking shape in the early part of the century.

In Bulgarian historiography, the members of this circle are described rather awkwardly: alternately as "moderates," "conservatives," and even as "Turkophiles" (or "Russophiles").[32] The cooperative spirit displayed toward the Patriarchate during the period of rising tensions, their privileged relations with sections of the Greek Orthodox elite, but mainly the adoption of some aspects of the Orthodox ecumenical ideology as inviolable principles for the Exarchate's structure—the 1871 National Assembly had a decisive role in this—rendered their incorporation into the dominant nineteenth-century narrative of a Bulgarian renaissance, or *Vâzrazhdane*, problematic.

In Rumen Daskalov's estimation, the appearance of historical works especially during the 1970s, including Zina Markova's superb monograph on the Bulgarian Exarchate, should be considered precisely part of an effort to legitimize references to these Bulgarians as a critical detachment from the common ground of official Bulgarian historiography, as this was renewed during the socialist period.[33] Bulgarian historians, however, despite having authored specialized essays on many of these individuals, rarely link their activities or ideological orientation to their Greek Orthodox associates.[34] In any case, the formation of such groups with uniform political and ideological characteristics (often stemming from shared material interests) is anticipated within the intellectual environment of the Tanzimat's Ottomanism and/or the Hamidian regime's Pan-Islamism.[35] It is, however, important to examine the ways in which the

---

32 See Markova, *Bâlgarskata Ekzarhiya*, 62 ("moderates"); Genchev, *Bâlgarskoto Vâzrazhdane*, 310 and Temelski, *Tsarkovno-Narodniyat Sâbor*, 9 ("Turkophiles"); and Todev, *Chomakov*, vol. I, 195 ("Russophiles").

33 Zechev, *Bâlgarskiyat Velikden*. See also Daskalov, *Making of a Nation*, 162–76. For an overview of Bulgarian historiography up to the socialist regime's collapse, see Todorova, "Bulgaria."

34 See, for example, Boneva, *Krâstevich*; Nazârska, "Krâstevich"; and Bozhinov, *Balabanov*.

35 Ellen Comisso suggested an interesting classification of the leaders of the nationalist groups (primarily intellectuals) in historical empires, with the examples of Austria–Hungary and Russia in mind: a) nationalists/revolutionaries, b) realists/compromisers, c) collaborators/imperial devotees, d) localists, and, e) "A-nationalists" in the sense that they are defined by interests or a form of solidarity that is not affiliated with anything than can be deemed "national." See Comisso, "Prisons of Nations," 138–46 and, especially, 144–49. Arguably the intellectuals studied here hover between the second and third categories.

members of this network sought to resolve the contradictions between the choice of national identification and the empire's preservation. And it would be a mistake to assume that the conciliatory manner in which the latter was viewed resulted from an unconditional defense of the former. If this were the case, we may have found simple political maneuvering and equivocation. The need to identify new historiographical forms, indeed ones that diverge from those crafted by the official national historiography, requires deeper interpretation.

Chapter II.

The Iconoclast Byzantium of Greek Nationalism

1. Manuel Gedeon's Perception of History

The question that is posed is whether one can detect, within this circle of intellectuals, any substantial divergence from the respective dominant historical narrative, particularly in relation to the two historical pillars of Christian Orthodox ecumenism through which it is fundamentally expressed: the Ottoman Empire (and consequently Byzantium) and, naturally, Russia.

This question could, of course, be posed differently: that is, if these divergences helped shape the canon, determining in some way the boundaries that should not be breached by any future historiographical effort.

I have interpreted earlier the fragmented way in which Gedeon approaches the restructuring of the historical past as stemming from Gedeon's psychological need not to uncover the dependence of his favorite "ethnarch" patriarchs, Joachim II and Joachim III, on Constantinople's powerful banking circle under Georgios Zarifis.[1] But his own relationship with historical discourse was mediated by his own dependence on Patriarch Joachim II: seventy-two pages into his *What I Witnessed* (*Mneia*) and having dedicated the greater part of the narrative to his predecessors as Great Chartophylax, Gedeon suddenly decides to reveal his "living sources," that is, the people providing him with information about life at the patriarchate in earlier centuries. Patriarch Joachim II is not merely prominent among these sources but is also the one who "ordered" Gedeon's writing of this work.

1 Stamatopoulos, "Gedeon," 377–87.

> Prominent among these, of course, is Patriarch Joachim II, to whom I owe the primary information about the Constantinople church's administration before the "General Regulations."[2] Joachim disapproved of the latter, telling me he had reasons for this. On the day when "canonical votes" [on the election of bishops] were being discussed, after describing the chapter on the patriarch's rights, he added this: "I tell you, my child, my ideas because you will write our history one day. I am old and will pass soon; you will live. I wish to be judged strictly but fairly in the fear of God." Fifty-nine years have since passed [the exchange described was in 1875, Gedeon is writing about it in 1934]. The venerable patriarch's worlds remain indelibly etched in my memory. (Gedeon, *Mneia*, 72)

This excerpt, which is somewhat lost in his massive work, clearly illustrates the commitment of the sum of his historical writing and research, linking it to his prominent position in the patriarchate's inner circle. Committed to writing the history of those who led the patriarchate for the better part of the nineteenth century, Gedeon becomes caught up in a far broader endeavor: describing the works and days of this elite would render his work a history that was never ethnocentric nor identified, at first glance, with the will of the Ottoman authority. From an uninterrupted seventy-year-long historiographical production, there emerges a history of the "Genos"—a massive body of information with fragmented character concerning a "collectivity" that the nineteenth century will find wavering between *millet* and *nation*: the Ottoman and the Western perception of the social organization's core.

Of course, Gedeon explains the fragmented way in which he offers information and sources as aimed at averting plagiarism:

My readers see that the references to sources are lumped together on a page but not under their names to the chagrin of plagiarists. I noted they copy Greek texts, without reference to the page or the source of the plundered work so that their readers will think them knowledgeable and widely read. (6)

---

2 The constitutional text on which the administration of the Ecumenical patriarchate was based from the Tanzimat reforms to the Asia Minor Catastrophe in 1922. For this issue, in greater extension, see Stamatopoulos, *Metarrithmisi kai Ekkosmikefsi*.

At least Gedeon hoped to force future plagiarists to expend the effort to find his source, "so they know what effort it takes to write a book."

But what treatment did Gedeon reserve for the representatives of Greek historiography?[3] His treatment of the work of Paparrigopoulos, whom he met during a trip to Athens in 1878,[4] was somewhat negative, at times sarcastic, while he appeared to show greater appreciation for Zambelios's work. Later, and after having withdrawn to Athens in the 1930s, when he was called upon to evaluate their work, he would observe that the "discovery" of the indivisible, trimillennial continuity of the Greek nation by both was delayed by at least fifty years:

> These essays—indeed those of older scholars and teachers of the nation—are always for the most part works that elevate the struggle to something divine, keeping high religious sentiment and fervor

3 Much can be said with regard to Gedeon's relationship to national ideology. According to his own testimony, Gedeon often toured the villages of the Astacus gulf (Nicomedia gulf, 1887), Proikonisia (1892), and the Dardanelles (1894), to study the locals' ethnic consciousness. In some cases, his descriptions tended to soften "problematic" aspects of his findings: "At Afthoni, ancient Aronnyn, I asked elderly locals, in their eighties, about their land's past. I heard a lot; two or three stopped talking in Greek. 'So, do you speak Bulgarian,' I asked. 'We speak Arvanitic,' they replied. 'So, are you Albanians,' I added. 'No, teacher. We are all Greek. We are not Albanian but we speak the language of our mothers.' All were conscious of their Greek origin, not just in the Proikonissi isles but in other parts that I visited. I admired their Christian patience with the bishops." See Gedeon, *Mneia*, 81–82. According to Gedeon, the Patriarchate regularly dispatched "high priests who were godless or shameless or truants or drunkards" to this province. Everywhere Gedeon visited, he asked locals two questions: "Are you dwindling or growing?" and "Is there a Greek consciousness among the peasants?" In his estimation, the population of the shores of Asia Minor had grown over the last century, and had preserved its Greek consciousness "with a whole variety of influences." Further afield, and faithful to the scheme of continuity between Byzantine "Hellenism" and modern Greeks, he based his argument on the family names of the populations of Mytilene, Trabzon, Gallipoli, and so on, in the seventeenth century. Nonetheless, another incident more clearly illustrates how he handled the issue of national self-determination. Referring to the abbot of the Karakalou Monastery at Mount Athos, Stephanos of Bitola, he says "The great 'patriots' accuse him of being a Bulgarian but they live outside of the monastery as "exokouritai." The fanaticized monks charge that he is the last of the Kollyvades (heretical monks of the late eighteenth century who claimed that the memorial services should be held on every single Saturday)." One could say that Gedeon had found in the abbot an alter ego as this is how he would describe himself in terms of his pro-Russian orientation as well as in relation to his obsessive defense of Orthodoxy. "Poor Stephanos", as he put it, pointed out that "if one sought to establish the nationality of Bitola's population on the basis of language, it is uncertain whether he would call every one of the Orthodox residents of the city: Albanian or Romanian, Bulgarian or Greek…" Nevertheless, according to Gedeon, he was "a strict monk, a good Christian and Greek." (90–91). In the above, it is worth noting the sarcastic reference to "patriots" and the quotation marks.

4 Ibid., 453.

> for our country. Preeminent in this are Spyridon Ioannis Zambelios for his "Byzantine Studies" and the preface to the "Demotic Songs of Greece," as well as Konstantinos Paparrigopoulos, author of the good "History of the Greek Nation." Both seek to show the continuity of the Greek race over four millennia as conceived and shown fifty years earlier by the physician Dimitrios Alexandridis, who published (in 1806 and 1807) Goldsmith's three-volume "History of Greece, From the Earliest Greek Years Through the Fall of Constantinople to the Ottomans." Spyridon P. Lambros followed in their footsteps and wrote the "History of Greece."[5] (Gedeon, *Mneia*, 459)

Additionally, there is evident sarcasm in his remark[6] that publication of Paparrigopoulos's *History*—a best seller in its time—was followed by a sharp drop in the prices of similar historical works by Dorotheos of Monemvasia[7] and Konstantinos Koumas.[8] These two documents, which he considered "panhellenic works" from which everyone learned the political history of the "Greek nation," saw their sales prices drop to one-fourth the original publication price as a result of this cut-throat competition.[9] But the "critical" approach to Paparrigopoulos' work is not just a metachronism; it refers back to Gedeon's commentaries in *Ecclesiastiki Alitheia* (Ecclesiastical Truth) in the 1880s.

Dimaras correctly notes that the critical way in which Gedeon positioned himself against Paparrigopoulos may suggest the Patriarchate's desire to distance itself from the choices made by the Greek state as expressed in the conflict between Charilaos Trikoupis and Joachim III.[10]

---

5 The work Gedeon is mentioning is Goldschmith, *History of Greece*. For an assessment of Dimitrios Alexandrides's edition of Oliver Goldsmith's work, see Tabaki, "Lumières néo-helléniques," 316–27, especially, 180. On the case of Spyridon Lambros, see Gazi, *Scientific National History*, 87–102

6 Gedeon, *Aposimeiomata*, 190, 338.

7 The reference is to Dorotheos, *Vivlion istorikon*.

8 Koumas, *Istoriai ton anthropinon prakseon*.

9 Before being "devalued," the price of the first was 40 gold francs and the price of the second was 160. See Gedeon, *Aposimeiomata*, 338. He makes another implicit and ambivalent reference to Paparrigopoulos in his article "Church and Science in the 18th Century," where Gedeon attacks the negative stance to Byzantium taken by Mihail Potlis, a professor of canonical law at the University of Athens. See Gedeon, *I pnevmatiki kinisi*, 97. He is referring to the phrase "armed book guardians" which Paparrigopoulos uses to describe the Byzantine scholars whom Potlis looks down on.

10 Dimaras, *Paparrigopoulos*, 319, 472. See also Demetrakopoulos, *Neoelliniki Dianoisi*. On the conflict between the Greek prime minister and the ecumenical patriarch, see Kofos, "Patriarch Joachim III."

Writing in *Ecclesiastiki Alitheia,* the official journal of the Ecumenical Patriarchate, Gedeon accused Paparrigopoulos of hastily "copying" some inaccuracies from the works of Skarlatos Vyzantios in order to expedite publication of his *History*'s fifth volume. He, thus, addressed him as "the historiographer K. Paparrigopoulos who committed numerous errors on the History of the Genos (Nation) after the Fall (of Constantinople)."[11]

Besides the different perception of the meaning of Genos, Gedeon's differentiation from Paparrigopoulos's historiographical scheme is not limited to his negative view of the latter's criticism of what he saw as the Patriarchate's inability to promote the Hellenization of the Balkan peoples in the eighteenth century. In other words, it was not limited to the years of Ottoman rule—which in any case, as will be examined further on, Gedeon viewed as a continuation of Byzantium—but to the Byzantine Empire itself and the manner in which Paparrigopoulos understood the inclusion of the "intermediate link" in the construction of the scheme of national continuity. Gedeon's disaffection with the way in which the national historiography handled its medieval period becomes evident through differing approaches to Iconoclasm, which by the nineteenth century, was considered a key issue in the internal evolution of Byzantine society and, ultimately, in its historiographical "Hellenization." In any case, for many historians, Iconoclasm was not simply the peak of religious conflict in Byzantium, it also paved the way for the clash between the Byzantine East and the Catholic West over leadership of the Christian world, and cultural influence over the delicate region of Eastern Europe.

On this point we can see below the substantive difference between Paparrigopoulos and Zambelios in their historiographical approach to Byzantium. Zambelios strikes a rather ambivalent stance on Iconoclasm (on the one hand calling it a "religious reform" but on the other viewing the defeat of the Iconoclasts as the climactic point of the process of Hellenization). Paparrigopoulos takes a clearly positive position, viewing Iconoclasm as a "reform" while in reality seeking the prerequisites for Byzantium's inclusion into the West's dominant narrative; in Byzantium, efforts to secularize the state preceded the Protestants' corresponding reform of

11 Gedeon, "Anekdota simeiomata," 606.

Catholic Rome by seven centuries. Cyril Mango was one of the first to highlight the importance of Paparrigopoulos's approach to Iconoclasm. Mango recognized that such an approach to Iconoclasm would create uneasiness in a modern historian trained to view it as "an Eastern movement" closer to Islam than to Western culture.[12]

2. A Periodization

The basic question posed by Gedeon concerns neither his pro-Russian inclinations nor the political tendencies of the circle he represented, but rather whether this peculiar political behavior—that is, identifying with the choices of the pro-Hamidian regime while also aligning with Russian political strategy—led to a different proposal for organizing the understanding of the past, especially Byzantium. If the prevalent tendency of Greek (Romantic) historiography had succeeded in the decades following the Crimean War in including Byzantium in the dominant national narrative, and if it did this in part to establish the relationship of the Greek state with whatever Constantinople represented, then the Patriarchate's "organic intellectuals" would also have to adopt similar arguments.

Nonetheless, patriarchal circles and Gedeon himself looked rather suspiciously at the sudden "upgrading" of the Byzantine Middle Ages. The fact that this reassessment of Byzantine history was a *sine qua non* for the challenge posed by national ideology to the Patriarchate of Constantinople's "ecumenical" nature was not the sole reason for this circumspection. The conceptualization of Byzantium and what it represented for the Patriarchate was far more important. For Greek nationalism, Byzantium was a link in seamless continuity of the historical advancement of a nation laying stake to the Empire's heritage. Gedeon's endeavor to write a history

12 Mango, "Byzantinism and Romantic Hellenism," 41. To understand Paparrigopoulos's choice we must thus look at it in relation to the conditions set by the opposing force: Fallmerayer's theory on the Slavicization of the Greek populations during the early centuries of the Byzantine era. Elli Skopetea identifies two very important points regarding this issue: the Austrian historian's anti-Byzantinism did not oppose the growth of Byzantine Studies in the West but rather presumed it—anti-Byzantinism is not incompatible with the incorporation of Byzantium's history into the Western narrative (Skopetea, *Fallmerayer*, 81)—and, secondly, that Fallmerayer viewed Iconoclasm as a prospect for Byzantium's internal evolution that did not in fact work out ("just like Paparrigopoulos!" as Skopetea noted [91]). For this same topic, see also Kitromilides, "Intellectual Content," 28n15, where a brief overview of Iconoclasm is also offered.

of the genos/millet elite was an attempt to document the continuity of the Byzantine and Ottoman past precisely in order to defend the Patriarchate's role within the Empire. In this respect, his history diverges from the national historiographic canon without, however, necessarily turning against it. But in order to succeed in meeting his basic aim, Gedeon had to defend the priority of the religious over the civil element, and this required more than his persistent citing of priests' biographical data and the topography of Byzantine churches.

All of his significant works (mainly collections of documents either on the Privileges or the Bulgarian Question) were written in the period 1909–10 with a clear political purpose. His works from this period aim primarily at proving that the Ottoman authorities' granting of the "Privileges" was the logical extension of the Church's more prominent role during Byzantine times.[13] This is why he dedicated the greater part of these works to showing how the Church achieved the extension of its jurisdiction and managed to curtail imperial interference in its internal affairs. Naturally, this renders Iconoclasm an element that is hard to manage; the Iconomacy's final conclusion theoretically legitimizes it. But the "corrections" to Paparrigopoulos were made in a different period from those marked by the crisis in relations between the Patriarchate and the Young Turks.

In broad terms, we can discern three major periods in Gedeon's work and political activity. The first spans early 1870 and the start of his journalistic activity and writing in various Constantinople daily and weekly newspapers (*Anatoli*, *Mikra Asia*, *Constantinopolis*, etc.), to his joining the staff of the Patriarchate's official journal, *Ecclesiastiki Alitheia*, up until his editorship of the paper in 1883. During this period, his participation in the founding and operation of the Association of Medieval Studies (later, Society of Medieval Studies) is especially significant, his involvement with the Byzantine past deepening and becoming more systematic.[14]

---

13 Recent historical research has shown that the awarding of privileges by the Ottoman state to religious functionaries of the millets occurred through *berats* [titles of privileges given to the lay or clerical officials on behalf of the Ottoman state] which, however, were intended to confer individual rights, which is to say that they did not necessarily presuppose recognition of the Orthodox or Armenian Patriarchates as institutionalized mechanisms of the Ottoman state or, to put it in modern terms, as public legal entities. On the question of progressive concessions of privileges to the Ecumenical Patriarchate, see Konortas, *Othomanikes theoriseis*, 123, 315–61.

14 Anestides, *I ethnarchiki paradosi*, 271–80. The founding of the Association of Medieval Studies

The second period of Gedeon's activities coincides with the period of the conflict between Joachim's supporters and opponents. While the first period of his journalistic and political career was marked by the upheavals and dramatic consequences of the Bulgarian Schism, the second was marked by the split within the patriarchal world along the axis of identification or not with Greek foreign policy. This phase ended with Joachim III's return to the patriarchal throne in 1901 and Gedeon's promotion to the position of his principal advisor. The rejection of ethnocentrism by the neo-Phanariot leaders and powerful bankers meant that a Romantic reconstitution of two then incompatible strategies—the defense of the Ottoman imperial model and the pro-Russian Pan-Orthodox policy—fell upon the shoulders of the Patriarchate's "organic intellectuals" like Gedeon.[15]

Before the Young Turk revolution, Gedeon's public interventions were essentially limited to the articles he wrote for *Ecclesiastiki Alitheia*. But the Young Turks' rise to power changed the political landscape: Joachim III no longer enjoyed the protection of the Hamidian regime, and the Privileges Question was raised anew. The period 1908–10 saw Gedeon politicized: on the orders of Joachim III and the Holy Synod, he published two major collections of patriarchal documents on the Bulgarian (1908) and the Privileges Question (1910), and three political pamphlets directly or indirectly touching on the latter (*The first rupture on the Privileges, Abbreviated Notations, Phases*).[16] It is interesting that these three pamphlets were not exclusively about the Patriarchate's history under the

should not be regarded as a supplementary move (as Anestides supposed), but as a counteraction to the operation of the Greek Literary Society of Constantinople, which was established in 1861. The prevalence of the nationalist and simultaneously "Classicist" Konstantinos Hercules Vasiadis in the Greek Literary Society after 1869–1870 led not only to the neo-Phanariots' expulsion from there but also to the rejection of the Byzantine Christian times: the idealization of the Classical Antiquity took place to the detriment of the Byzantine past. The founding of the Association of Medieval Studies must be seen in this light. "Exiled" from the Greek Literary Society of Constantinople, Byzantium found a roof with those specializing in its history: Gedeon, Papadopoulos-Vrettos, Moustoxidis, and others, who participated in the proceedings of the Association of Medieval Studies, trying to counter-balance the insistence of the society on the ancient classicist past (see also *Corrispondenza del Cavaliere Mustoxidi*).

15 On this issue, see below, as well as Stamatopoulos, "Hellenism versus Latinism," 79–106, and "Orthodox Millet," 201–47.

16 Gedeon was also involved in the publication of the former collections edited by the Patriarchate on both issues, see *Ekklisiastikon pronomion*; and *Eggrafa metaxi*.

Ottomans, but also contain references to its Byzantine past. This time, his preoccupation with Byzantium was not a conscious effort to distance himself from the dominant historiographical narrative of modern Greek nationalism, as was the case in the 1880s. Nonetheless, by invoking the historical depth of the Privileges against the authority of the Young Turks who disputed them, Gedeon raised the issue of the continuity of the two Empires, Byzantine and Ottoman. By necessity, the defense of the Privileges was framed by the identification with the imperial model at a time when it appeared to have reached its historical end. After 1910, Gedeon effectively fell silent. The progressive transformation of the Young Turks regime into authoritarianism and the death of Joachim III in October 1912 pushed him further into isolation and toward withdrawal until the events of the Asia Minor disaster.

The third major period took place in Athens. Seeing the coming catastrophe and having severed relations with the Patriarchate following Meletius Metaxakis's election as Ecumenical Patriarch, he left his beloved Constantinople.[17] In one way, his departure symbolized the absolute dominance of the model of the national state, even if this meant the definitive elimination of "Greater Hellenism" on which it had based its irredentist ideology. In this phase, and especially in the 1930s, Gedeon produced his most important autobiographical works. For this reason, and in the context of the reorganization of the national ideology taking place in the 1930s, Gedeon revised and reinterpreted Constantinople's past in the nineteenth century in an effort to render it compatible with the new ideological and political conditions. But, even so, these works remain valuable for the information they provide on this extremely interesting period.

We might summarize Manuel Gedeon's intellectual trajectory by viewing the Romantic endeavor to defend Orthodox ecumenism as its springboard and an attempt to legitimize the old "society of the Genos/Millet through the coordinates of the national ideology as revised by the Thirties' generation as its conclusion. This was a move from the Romanticism of Constantinople to the neo-Romanticism of Athens.

Judging the distinct mark made by Gedeon on the analysis of Iconoclasm requires a critical approach to the way the meaning of Byzantium

17 Nanakis, "I hireia tou Oikoumenikou thronou."

was invented in the works of Paparrigopoulos and Zambelios, and simultaneously an assessment of the ways iconoclasm fitted into the broader framework of their respective theoretical approaches. What will be attempted is not a general and comprehensive interpretation of the two basic historiographical works that marked the modern Greek perception of Byzantium but rather an appreciation of the empire's influence as depicted within each of these—that is, empire as memory, empire as political imperative, and empire as a theoretical canvas for the unfolding of the narrative of nation.

3. Zambelios's Transcendent Byzantium: From Aristotle to Hegel

Zambelios's endeavor is to reclaim history. To this extent, it constitutes the demand for a collective subject that is organized as a nation and seeks to manage the past. In Zambelios we have the subjective belief in the elevation of the individual to the collective: "The past! Alas! We allow foreigners to represent it under the prism of their biases and within their systems and interests."[18]

Time, historical and past, was reorganized as a political endeavor of self-determination in relation to the West ("foreigners"). The historical project was understood as a political action with immediate consequences for the manner in which it was redefined by a series of meanings devoid of semantic content (e.g., regeneration, race, mission, etc.). What guides history is its politico-ideological use, the "positivity" to seek "events" when there were no "occurrences." "Every nation today appears in the Courtyard of Civilization as equipped with a historical passport."[19]

Zambelios's instrumental approach to history was proclaimed, while the past was simultaneously juxtaposed to the present through a comparison of "truth" and "myths." "Truth" corresponds to historical reality, "myths" to the terms by which this was perceived, as imposed by the West.

Hellenism's historical course appears to be inspired by the Aristotelian structure: Monarchy, Aristocracy, and Democracy, and their deviations outline the foundation on which Zambelios was determined to organize

18 Zambelios, *Asmata Dimotika*, 7.
19 Zambelios, *Asmata Dimotika*, 8.

his arguments. In reality, the contribution of *Demotic Songs* was limited by the following questions that he poses in the introduction to this work. The variable that transforms the Aristotelian categories was religion, which, according to Zambelios, was itself transformable.

> What was the nature of the monarchy in its early years? What was its fate? Did it not suffer in the Middle Ages and how did it clash with Christianity? What powers were mobilized and it finally disappeared? What is the role of the aristocracy in antiquity and where must we seek it after the Embodiment? Was there a Byzantine aristocracy or not? And if there was, how was it divided and which of it was truly national, which not genuinely so.
>
> And democracy, the soul of the race, what happened to it? Was it lost with the flood of barbarians, or was it saved? If it was preserved, where did it seek a haven and how did it function? To what changes did it succumb and by what miracle was it handed down from one generation to the next?
>
> And religion, the main and almighty lever of Greek development, how was it transformed? Why did it appropriate all national elements and assimilate them in order to fight foreign insults and intrusions until it destroyed all enemies and rivals? (Zambelios, *Asmata Dimotika*, 10)

What Zambelios dubs "Greek history" was nothing but the interaction between those fundamental elements that were perceived not as political regimes but as reified and transcendent elements that shaped, through various combinations, their respective historical-political compositions. In each period, a different one of these elements dominates, some are subordinated, and some become latent.

Consequently, his reference to Aristotle was not accidental.[20] But the composite view apparently adopted by Zambelios was actually inspired by Machiavelli, and especially the *Discourses on the First Decade of Titus Livius*.[21] There was no transition or evolutionary course from monarchy to tyranny, from aristocracy to oligarchy, and finally from democracy to

---

20 Zambelios, *Asmata Dimotika*, 39–40.

21 Machiavelli, *Discourses*.

ochlocracy that paved the way for a new circle of internal change to the regime. On the contrary, the political elements to which Zambelios referred appear to have acted perpetually and concurrently, as in Rome. However, in the case of Rome ("the lofty republic of Rome," p. 57) monarchy appeared to constitute a fall of the democratic regime ("the law of decay," p. 57)—further proof that the republican vision was hardly alien to Zambelios. Conversely, in the Macedonians' case, the monarchy became in a way an organ of divine providence.[22] The Macedonian monarchy allied with the city-states' democratic factions to extend Hellenism (and democracy) to the East. (To be precise, the latter would surrender to the former.) But at the same time, Hellenism, in an attempt to forge West with East, shifts toward the East with the Macedonian conquest. "Greece, pardon the word, gets Orientalized."[23] In the same way the first Christian communities and monasteries are also "small, popular, and democratically-ruled entities" which, "paradoxically" in Zambelios's view, "comprise a small federal confederation" that coexists within an empire.[24]

For Zambelios, Byzantium was merely the outcome of a compromise between the monarchy, that is the Roman authority which retained control of political power but shifted the Empire's weight eastward, and the Church, which was not limited to representing the spiritual authority but Byzantine society as a whole.[25] To be precise, the four elements to which Zambelios refers to exist in pairs and are in perpetual competition:

> We thus say that two elements comprise Romaism: the Monarchy and, secondly, the Aristocracy. Two others comprise Hellenism, the Church and the People, of which the Church is primary and the People is secondary. . . . Apparently, these four elements work harmoniously and coexist fooling many observers; in reality they are divided into two rival classes, the two Roman elements on one side and the two Greek on the other. (Zambelios, *Asmata Dimotika*, 85–86)

22 The temporary suspension of the democratic regime in Athens by the Macedonian General Menyllos is presented as a necessary choice "since it (the democratic regime) had become tyrannical and oppressive." Machiavelli, *Discourses*, 48.

23 Zambelios, *Asmata Dimotika*, 45.

24 Zambelios, *Asmata Dimotika*, 70.

25 Zambelios, *Asmata Dimotika*, 79.

With this observation on the internal rivalry between the elements that comprise medieval Hellenism, and consequently Byzantium, Zambelios is both commenting on and correcting Polybius (as reflected by Machiavelli's *Titus Livius*), at least with regard to Byzantine history. If the grandeur of classical (imperial) Rome was due to the ideal mix of monarchist, aristocratic, and democratic elements, the corresponding mix achieved in the Byzantine Empire is comprised of these three elements plus religion. However, instead of seeing Byzantium as a continuation of the Roman Empire (which would be another way of legitimizing it), Zambelios interprets it through the prism of its continuous Hellenization: instead of considering Byzantium as the "New Rome," it is more appropriate to view it as the "New Athens" since Hellenism progressively supplanted the Latin element's dominant role in the new cultural mix. But achieving Hellenism's dominance (and by extension, the Church's and the people's) in the new regime required certain changes in the original form, changes resulting from its fierce rivalry with what Zambelios calls *Romaism*.

The Byzantine Empire (and thus the monarchy) found itself in perpetual opposition with the democratic element, which appeared to be the secret essence of Hellenism as well as of the Christianity which encapsulated the former (Hellenism).

> The Constantinople monarchy, from inception until the fourteenth century, with few exceptions, is so alien to its subjects' national inclinations that it doesn't shelter Hellenism except towards its end, and even then almost hastily and forcibly. Thus, there's a block between demos and king, a gap between Church and Court. (21)

The first compromise between Romaism and Hellenism occurred under Constantine the Great, but it did not last long.

As a result of this internal rivalry in Byzantium, one might identify two discrete strands in the history of Byzantium. One concerned the empire (which Zambelios called "Roman") and which was "foreign to the nation." The other concerned the common people and, thus, Hellenism. The latter was identified in reality with the history of the Church. When he mentioned the Church, Zambelios—and we must make special note here—was not referring to the Church as an institution or merely to the clergy but to a peculiar "unity" joining clergy and laity. In reality, the Church was identified almost completely with what we might call "society" (and everything it embraces) today. And if the criticism of religion in the West perceived it as an alienated version of the social sphere, Zambelios sought to lift the contradiction through the establishment of the "Olomeleia" (Plenary).[26] In other words, he sought to remove the fragmentation both of the historiographical prospects of Hellenism's evolution and the internal differentiations of the social structure in the various phases of its development.

Accordingly, Zambelios embraced the Empire's content while rejecting its form. It does not suffice to point out that this model proposed a "pro-democratic" reading of Greek history. This alone would not explain the reasons for his linking Christianity to democracy, nor his attempt to distinguish the meaning of Romaios (Roman) from Graecos (Greek). His project would not be understood if the former was identified with monarchy and the latter with republicanism, especially if we consider the evolution of his views in *Byzantine Studies.*

The motif of a "Republican Byzantium" (proposed by Hans-Georg Beck and renovated recently by Kaldellis) might be traced in some of the ambiguities of Zambelios's Byzantium at the middle of the nineteenth century. In the nineteenth century, generally Byzantium would be legitimized as a metonymy of monarchy, but for a liberal from the Ionian Islands, it was impossible for the medieval phase of Greek history to be described as completely authoritarian: Byzantium was an hybrid where the democratic tradition of Hellenism finally survived.

In Zambelios's Byzantium, democracy appeared in opposition to monarchy,[27] whereas aristocracy appeared split: secular aristocracy, that is, the aristocracy created by monarchy, was in decline, while clerical

26 See Skopetea, *Protypo vasileio,* 105–106n20. Liakos, "Pros kataskevin Olomeleias," 171–99.

27 On this very interesting discussion, see Kaldellis, *Byzantine Republic,* and its critique by Haldon, "Res publica Byzantina?" Many thanks also to Yannis Stouraitis who gave me his unpublished paper entitled "Is Byzantinism an Orientalism? Reflections on Byzantium's constructed identities and debated ideologies" which criticizes also Beck's "Republicanism" as a kind of neo-Gibbonism. On this issue we take seriously into consideration not only Zambelios's "pro-democratic" elaborations but also the transitional role of the French School of Byzantinists which reflected the work of Nicolae Iorga (see below) for re-legitimizing Byzantium as Rome of the East: transforming the old "negative" orientalism of Gibbon to a new "positive" one.

aristocracy was on the rise. Zambelios had then to resolve a problem of his own creation: the addition of religion to the triad of regimes that Hellenism experienced on its long journey turned his historiographical scheme into an anti-dialectic. Remember that Zambelios was attending courses by Hegel at Heidelberg; he would easily identify the Hegelian triadic dialectic with the theological trinity shape of Christianity. To this end, one of the primary elements in his historiographical hermeneutical approach had to be removed—and that element was the aristocracy. The political content of such a choice for a radical liberal writer of Ionian origin remains obvious.

Zambelios dedicated seven (!) chapters to banishing the aristocracy from his scheme. The aristocracy "not only holds a secondary position in relation to the other three, but in terms of historical truth it barely deserves to be considered an element."[28] He was, thus, left with the Monarchy, the Church, and the People: a (holy) trinity that appeared to be his theoretical springboard (Monarchy, Democracy, Aristocracy, plus Religion), but was not completely so. The monarchy's identification with Roman state authority seemed justifiable, although the imperial form here also differed substantively from the model of the monarchy of the Macedonian and Hellenistic times. But democracy's identification with the people, and religion's with the Church, was essentially the result of the dominance of Zambelios's third pole, the Holy Spirit, which sanctified the political elements in Hellenism. In fact, Zambelios's philosophical scheme silently shifted from essence to the collective subjects, from the political and metaphysical nature of the regime to the elements composing it. That is to say, a shift from an anti-dialectical Aristotelian triad (anti-dialectical due both to the circular transition of the regimes and the insertion of religion into the scheme) to a Hegelian dialectic (with the Aristocracy's transformation from an autonomous element to a property of the Monarchy or the Church, respectively).

Indeed, what happened to the aristocracy was in fact a process of transformation: while the artificial and manufactured (secular) aristocracy created by Constantine in the new capital quickly fell into decline and vanished without any trace of the old independent and self-regulated Western (Latin) aristocracy—indeed, it was transformed into an organ of

28 Zambelios, *Asmata Dimotika*, 86.

the "xenocracy"—a new aristocracy that emerged from one of the remaining elements of Zambelios's scheme: the Church. This new "national" aristocracy emerged from within the Church and through its clash with the Roman elements:

> The Church, precisely, in its persons, is but the national aristocracy in opposition to the foreign one. Constantine created in Byzantium a ridiculous aristocracy, while Hellenism counters the holy and virtuous aristocracy of Martyrdom and Apologia, supported on the firm ground of tribulation and faith. (Zambelios, *Asmata Dimotika*, 121)

In the clash of these two different "societies" within Byzantium, the "external"/foreign, headed by the secular emperor, and the "internal"/ national, under the spiritual ruler, the Patriarch, the aristocratic elements appeared to die and to be reborn as a "national" aristocracy within the ranks of the Orthodox clergy.

The issue of aristocracy was perhaps more important than the (alleged) clash between monarchy and democracy that distinguished the "democratic" *Demotic Songs* and the pro-monarchist *Byzantine Studies*. Already in his first work, Zambelios was prepared to acknowledge monarchy's significant role in Hellenism's renaissance:

> But because, and in contradistinction to aristocracy that to a large extent was but an offspring of the Byzantine body or a scion or even a part of it, monarchy modified and had a significant impact on medieval Hellenism, placing itself in direct relation to the national elements, that is the Church and the People. (112)

Despite being a foreign element, monarchy was submitted progressively to the law of "national growth." "For all these reasons, the monarchy rightly belongs to the history of Hellenism. At first, it dominates; later it is naturalized, and finally, shaped by us, it claims special enlightenment" (113).

Thus, the groundwork for "adapting" the Roman tradition's most important element to the Greek national narrative of continuity had already been laid in *Demotic Songs*. But even more interesting than the monarchy's "adaptation" was the aristocracy's disappearance and reemergence. In actual fact, by transforming the latter, Zambelios adopted a basic principle of the dialectic method: that one of the two antithetical poles was always stronger (in this instance, the Church, and through it Hellenism). This stronger pole determined the unfolding of the contradiction. The weaker pole, however, through its defeat, survived in the new synthesis. In this contradictory process, the "adaptation" of the weaker pole (i.e., the monarchy) was less salient than the "transformation" of the aristocracy imposed by the stronger pole, the Church.

By applying a modified Machiavellian interpretation to the history of medieval Hellenism, Zambelios drew a comparison with Romaism that was similar to Leont'ev's (see below). This was not an explicit comparison as, for example, someone could see in the case of Hellenism's sacred "mission" in the East. However, it was much more salient in the sense that the comparison had to prove the absorbing dynamic of Hellenism compared to the Latin West. This is why its "internal" evaluation had to smother what ancient Rome had historically been. The comparison had to be favorable not just in the eyes of the two civilizations but conversely through the existing self-value of Byzantine civilization. Zambelios did not shy away from using the word *Byzantium*, quite the contrary, as he considered Byzantium to be Greek.

Before moving to Paparrigopoulos's analysis of Byzantium, we need to focus on the manner in which Zambelios tried to establish the foundations of Hellenism's unity. Given that the Holy Trinity was the axis of his philosophical framework,[29] this unity of the three faces of God correspond to the three phases of Hellenism's growth. According to Zambelios, the internal unity of the trinitarian model is not only related to the space of the abstract and the metaphysical but to every aspect of material life. But this time instead of deriving the subjects from ideas, as in the case of the regimes—the people from democracy, the Church from religion—ideas are produced by the subjects of the triadic God. Father, Son, and Holy Spirit are transformed into Power (the monarchy's authority), Love (the Church as the body of Christ, "Law becomes Logos"), and Wisdom (the people's innate tendency to seek identity through tradition):

29 Ibid., 122–32.

that means a version of the Augustinian perception of the trinitarianism. Instead of innovating, as did other peoples who had nothing to lose, the Greek people had the advantage of turning to tradition, to "antiquity." But Zambelios's idealization of the doctrine would lead him to a contradiction: if the Church was a metonymy of the People, why did the Christian clergy reject the spiritual soul of the latter, that is, Hellenism?

Zambelios would seek to resolve this contradiction through the use of Hegelian dialectic of "the abstract and the concrete." But contrary to the radical Hegelian Left in Germany around this same period, which resolved the contradiction in favor of the "concrete," Zambelios would tilt the scales toward the "abstract" in order to deal with the problem of providing substance to the national subject.

In his view, the Church elaborated two versions of Christianity: the abstract and the concrete. The former is identified with the doctrine's theological elaboration and the latter with Christianity's spread to various peoples who comprehend it according to their respective spiritual states. In fact, the Fathers of the early centuries were not content with the latter but forged a theoretical elaboration according to which the "abstract" essence of religion suppressed differentiations of concrete societies: "in other words, was not Christianity the wisdom of one God and one History, objects themselves general, universal and abstract?"[30]

Zambelios's reference convinces us that he was not merely familiar with Hegel's work[31] (and obviously also with that of Herder) but perhaps even with the debates taking place at the time in Germany between left-wing and right-wing Hegelians. While he accepts the nucleus of Hegelian philosophy—indeed, its conservative version from the mid-nineteenth century—paradoxically, this was done against the grain of Hegel himself, because of Hegel's derogatory views of the Byzantine Empire. Hegel had joined Gibbon's camp. The serious consequences of this for the principal advocate of the Philosophy of History had to be answered through the development of a new Philosophy of History that would not simply substantialize the collective subject/ethnos but would do so using the same weapons, that is, dialectics.

30 Ibid., 140.

31 Argyropoulos, *Les intellectuels grecs*, 54–58.

What Zambelios was really attempting was a correction of Hegel based on the principles of Hegel's philosophy. Hegel believed that Christianity in Byzantium was an element in its decline because "it maintained an abstract and inert character, completely separated from the social body and its institutions; therefore religion has fallen into the hands of the mob."[32] According to Zambelios, Hegel's view was the result of a confusion:

> The sage conflates the element of the Church with the element of the People, he conflates Romaism with Hellenism, he misunderstands the eloquent historionomic nature of Theology, distorts Orthodoxy's mission, and finally attributes faults and weaknesses to the Greek clerical caste which the priests of our faith and the defenders of our homeland never had nor shared with the West (Zambelios, *Asmata Dimotika*, 141).

Beyond Zambelios's opinion on the issue of the role of the clergy—a new aristocracy, which we will return to later—we must carefully examine the issue of the functionality of triadic logic in his observations against Hegel. A prerequisite for the confusion is that Hegel did not take the component parts of Byzantium into account. "Romaism" and Hellenism, but especially clergy and laity were homogenized through the term "Byzantine society." Hegel made the mistake of turning himself upside-down. And this for Zambelios was an unforgiveable error.

Zambelios himself would use the Hegelian scheme to achieve the exact opposite: that is, not to incorporate Hellenism into history but to remove Hellenism from it. The "theological abstract" was nothing more than a way to substantiate the subject "Greek People," especially during medieval times, when

> Greece, after shattering the spark of antiquity, resorted as a whole to the mental pinnacles of Theology. . . . Then Divine Providence attached it to the land of the abstract just like the mother thrush attaches its nest on inaccessible cliffs to safeguard its hatchlings from the hawk's clutches. (Zambelios, *Asmata Dimotika*,)

32 Zambelios, *Asmata Dimotika*, 141. See Hegel, *Philosophy of History*, 355.

Orthodoxy was, thus, transformed into a "natural" religion for Hellenism, a "religion rather national than individual." It is at this point that he also constructed another differentiation from the West, where religion was a personal or individual choice—although since a comparison with Catholicism would not be particularly conducive to his argument, Zambelios used England and the United States as examples. Conversely, wherever Orthodoxy triumphed, it did so "via the idea of community." Orthodoxy and Hellenism intersect in the field of collective and transubstantiated unity, which is why "heresy" in terms of religious identity involved the heretic's expulsion from the national body. Zambelios erected his anti-Western scheme on the "essential," or as he calls it, the difference between a national and individual religion "that distinguishes Orthodoxy and Hellenism from the other European members" and does not even exclude Catholicism from the rule because Catholicism, despite being "an adherent of religious unity," was not identified with the "morale of a nation" or a specific race.

Here the arguments of many nineteenth-century scholars diverged as many identified Catholicism with Romanism. It is then curious that Zambelios avoided using this as an argument. Additionally, this flight toward the "abstract" created huge problems for the accommodation of the "concrete." For example, Zambelios rather awkwardly approached issues like the Church's rejection of the term "Hellene" or the rise of non-Greek Emperors to the Byzantine throne.[33]

If during the first period of Byzantine history the transformation of Zambelios's triadic scheme concerned the substitution of the ancient aristocracy by the new lay-national aristocracy, then in the second period (or, rather, the history of Medieval Hellenism), Zambelios saw an acute clash between the monarchy and the Church—a confrontation with manifest and latent effects on issues such as Iconoclasm, slavery, and the clash between the monarchy and the demes. Zambelios appears to have believed that this was fomented by the Church as he detected a preferential relationship between the Church and the Green demes: "Over time, the Church's power grew, for the more heretical views infiltrated the Court, the more the Church turned to the people, and, thus, threatened the monarchy."[34]

33 Zambelios, *Asmata Dimotika*, 207.

34 Zambelios, *Asmata Dimotika*, 242–48.

The Church's rise as a counterweight to the monarchy was effectively represented by the terms "social equality" or "instinctual isonomy," both coined by Zambelios.

In reality, Zambelios's *Demotic Songs* turned Hegel's own weapons against him. Zambelios attacked Hegel for embracing Gibbon yet used Hegel's methodology to prove his point. He began with Hegel's charge against Byzantium: namely the Christian religion's abstract character within Byzantium. And his appropriation of Hegel's method was not limited to the "continuity of the Greek spirit": if the old form did, indeed, survive in the newer ones, it would have to undergo a dialectic process that corresponds to the Hegelian paradigm. Zambelios's composition was, therefore, based on the Hegelian triadic method—or rather, the transformation of the Aristotelian triad (via the Holy Trinity) into a Hegelian triad via the "abstract-concrete" dialectic. By using the term "isonomy," which was of fundamental importance to understanding Hellenism's essence,[35] Zambelios sought to respond to Hegel's accusation that the nature of Christianity was theoretical-abstract, proving that "democracy" and "equality"—the culmination of the Absolute Spirit in history with the eruption of the French Revolution—were already contained within Byzantium's social formation because of the role of the "new national aristocracy," the Church.

> This society, under the sacred veil of the Eastern Church, dared what no other contemporary people conceived, and enjoyed, at the cost of sacrifice and blood, even for a moment, social isonomy on which all other freedoms depend, and without which progress cannot flourish. (Zambelios, *Asmata Dimotika*, 261)

Evidence that Zambelios developed his entire theoretical structure through the transformation of the Aristotelian model of three civil entities—and despite the conclusions of those juxtaposing the *Songs*' "democratic spirit" with the "pro-monarchy disposition" of the *Byzantine Studies*—is the fact that the monarchy was eventually considered to be beneficial to the formation of medieval Hellenism. Although

35 Koubourlis, *Formation*, 170–81.

Zambelios observed that the monarch "was split from national development," he immediately negated this point, expressing the view that both the Church's opposition to monarchy was positive as it strove "practically and spiritually in favor of freedom and enlightenment," and the monarchy's curtailment of the "potential political ambitions of the clergy" was useful" (262). He added that:

> It is certain that if the Greek and Christian democracies were left unlimited and without a secular leash they would go wild and rampant and thus move far and away from what is appropriate and eventually they would both end up in a bottomless and baneful abyss. (263)

Zambelios was not trying to remain neutral or show moderation. Neither was he only interested in emphasizing the idea of an unstable equilibrium between religious and political power as the ideal model for the coexistence of State and Church in the nineteenth century. Nor was he presenting balance-equivalence as a metaphor for the relationship between the two main figures of the Holy Trinity: the Father (State) and the Son (Church). Managing the relationship between monarchy and Church was necessary for the dialectic to work as it was only through the management of internal contradictions that he could claim that the gap between the abstract and the concrete had been lifted in the Greek case as well. The Absolute Spirit of History could unfold itself only through this confrontation.

4. Paparrigopoulos's Phanariot Byzantium and French Imperial Nationalism

Konstantinos T. Dimaras highlighted the Phanariot dimension in the work of Konstantinos Paparrigopoulos. His background, the trauma stemming from his father's persecution and his family's flight from Istanbul (and the burden of being an "*heterochthon*," which he carried for years) as well as his connections to other important Phanariot personalities in Greece (such as Rangavis, Soutsos, and Vyzantios) are all significant indications of this. At this point, of course, there is a "confusion" in Dimaras's work—judging the entire Phanariot class, which to a large degree identified with the preservation of Ottoman power, on the basis of the political and cultural behavior of the Phanariots who ended up in Greece.

Nonetheless, what is certain is that the Phanariot who migrated to Greece would want to imprint on the dominant national ideology the Byzantine imperial heritage that had sustained him in the Ottoman environment. In his critique of Jean Henri Abdolonyme Ubicini's article on Christians in the Ottoman Empire published in the *Journal des débats politiques et littéraires*,[36] Paparrigopoulos, writing in *Pandora* journal, noted:

> Mr. Ubicini does well to speak of the Phanariots' relics because this once great, wealthy, and robust class fell under the executioner's axe, the noble principle of liberty, created the conspiracy from which those relics evaded defeat, but the writer of the article remains on bended knee before Turkey in the face of them who massacred their parents. These relics were Dimitris Soutsos from Dacia, who fell with seven wounds after killing seven enemies; Negris, who died destitute on the Greek land for which he legislated and fought; Mavrokordatos, who gave outstanding service to Greece in the Parliament and in the army; and Rizos, one of the foremost ministers. And the Soutsos brothers, who brought honor to [the] Parnassos [Literary Society] and all mourned their passing from the earth leaving their parents' bones unburied as they fled to the beloved Greece of their dreams... (*Pandora*, vol. 4, issue 7 [July 1853], 203)

This tribute to the Phanariots who migrated to Greece highlighted the ideological power of Paparrigopoulos's argument on Byzantium's incorporation into modern Greek history.

The most significant of the personalities that appear to have had a definite influence on the "national historiographer" and whose experience included participation in the Ottoman administration was Paparrigopoulos's father-in-law Georgios Afthonidis. Afthonidis, the patriarch's celebrated secretary and legal counsel, was not forced to abandon Istanbul when the Greek Revolution erupted but rather many years later, in 1831, on the occasion of his clash with Alexandros Fotiades, a powerful Phanariot during the Patriarchy of Constantine I (1830–34). Afthonidis was not just an important lay officer of the Patriarchate but the "mouth through

36 *Journal des débats politiques et littéraires*, June 22, 1853.

which nine Patriarchs spoke,"[37] in the words of Konstantinos Kontogonis. For the first three decades of the nineteenth century, he was the Patriarchate's sole representative to the Sublime Porte. In January 1821, Patriarch Gregory V appointed him chief legal counsel.[38] But most significantly, Afthonidis drafted the Patriarchate's first administrative regulations (under Patriarch Agathangelos).[39] This text was never enacted even though his successor, Patriarch Constantine I, promised to uphold these rules. This early failed attempt at reform, before the start of Tanzimat, may have been the real reason Afthonidis left the Patriarchate.

If the Reformation was the link between Ottoman East and European West, then Byzantium's legitimation was first and foremost the legitimation of the "expatriate" imperial Phanariot in the newly formed Kingdom of Greece. But transforming a reference to Byzantium to the Great Idea, and indeed in its irredentist version, required more.[40]

As Dimaras correctly noted, Paparrigopoulos's ideas crystallized in the late 1840s. Nonetheless, this was not related, as one might have expected, to this period's key event, the 1848 revolution and its impact, especially in France. Dimaras somewhat guardedly considered Paparrigopoulos's historical endeavor to be politically motivated. Yet, this was not evident merely in issues related to the constitution or the expansion of the modern Greek kingdom but also in the broader framework defined by France's transition from Louis-Philippe to Napoleon III. Paradoxically, the Second Republic's transformation into the Second Empire had not yet been approached as a "material" prerequisite for the "pro-monarchist" criticism that, in 1852, Pararrigopoulos addressed to the "democratic" Zambelios. It was not primarily the intensely Francophile orientation of Paparrigopoulos's political mentor Ioannis Kolettis, prime minister of Greece for many years, that leads to such a conclusion, but more the channels of communication

37 Gedeon, *Aposimeiomata*, 57–58.

38 In practice this meant the conferring of the "exarchate" on the honoree, but in Aftonidis's case he was given the Geromerion Exarchy in Epirus. Ibid., 12–13.

39 The regulations included the introduction of the lay element in the Church's administrative affairs, the creation of a mixed clergy–lay committee, and issues related to the Patriarch's compensation by the Common Fund. See Gedeon, *Patriarchikis Istorias Mneia*, 19–22 and also Stamatopoulos, *Metarrhythmisi kai Ekkosmikefsi*, 40.

40 Here, too, we see Paparrigopoulos's problem with applying a consistent term to describe the Great Idea. See Skopetea, *Protypo vasileio*, 180–81.

between *Pandora*, a journal where Paparrigopoulos played a dominant role, and the circle of expatriate Phanariots, and its French counterparts, *Journal des débats* and *Revue des Deux Mondes*. This continuous dialogue took place with the full spectrum of politicized French scholars—and not just historians like Guizot, Michelet, and Tocqueville—but from the promonarchist Orleanists like Jean-Joseph-François Poujoulat to later establishment intellectuals of the Second Empire like Victor Duruy.

If 1848 was, for obvious reasons, the turning point, then the establishment of the Second Empire in 1851–52 touched off a series of discourses about the East, which, activated by the Crimean War as well as the "cultural imperialism" exercised by Napoleon III in its wake, redefined the relations between Catholic France and the nations of the Ottoman Empire.

We believe that the issue of the French intervention in the Ottoman East must be related to the formulation and transformation of the Great Idea from its cultural to its irredentist version. It has been correctly suggested that the shaping of the Great Idea should be linked to the reform process of the Ottoman Empire.[41] Incredibly, the common denominator in both processes, as far as the West's intervention is concerned—or rather the interaction with the French element, without seeking to underestimate Great Britain's role—remains in both cases unexplored. Édouard Driault, an apologist for the French interventions in the Balkans and the Ottoman East, was to make this link. At the precise moment when the Great Idea appeared near to completion with the conquest of Asia Minor, he reedited the eighth chapter of his book which he had titled "La France en Orient," dividing it into two chapters "La Grande Idée" and "La Réforme Turque."[42]

If there exists one reason for analyzing, albeit briefly, French influence in the Near East and the Balkans, it is precisely because we must

41 Panagiotopoulos, "Viomichaniki Epanastasi," 234–35n9. Alexis Politis aligned himself with Panagiotopoulos's view, claiming that Skopetea did not touch on this in her *To "Protypo vasileio" kai i Megali Idea*. Politis, *Romantika chronia*, 63n55. However, throughout her work (and not just in her first book), she showed particular insistence on the issue of the Balkan peoples' self-determination in the Ottoman East in relation to the role accorded them by the West or the role they sought from the West. If the Tanzimat or Western intervention seemed given then the formation of the Great Idea as a semantic form appeared as a self-evident process based on the inspiration of an overly Orientalist politician, Ioannis Kolettis.

42 Driault, *Grande Idée*, 113, 127.

examine the discussions on Byzantium that arose as the result of a process of national self-determination that struggled between the clashing rocks of two imperial discourses: the historiographical discourses produced in Constantinople that addressed the imperial ideologies of the Russian and Ottoman Empires (like Gedeon's work), and those produced in Athens, which addressed Napoleon's France and, later, Bismarck's Germany. This aimed at defining the root source of "imperial nationalism" rather than the enemy, which, before the Crimean War, was anyone obstructing the creation of a "Greek Eastern Empire," while afterwards it was Russianism, Pan-Slavism, and the Balkan Slavs.

Paparrigopoulos's responses to two articles published in the *Journal des débats* in 1852 and 1853 are well known. We have already mentioned his criticism of Ubicini's article. This had been preceded by the polemic against an article by Saint-Marc Girardin,[43] a hard-core classicist in the French Academy, upon the occasion of the publication of Jean-Joseph-François Poujoulat's book,[44] with whom he aligned to attack the Eastern Orthodox Church. Paparrigopoulos focused his defense here, concluding with his famous phrase about the missions that Hellenism had undertaken and would undertake in the last and final third of its historical trajectory: "There is in the East a nation . . ." This interesting closing remark—and this is perhaps the first time we find such a clear articulation of the Great Idea in his work—was not only in response to Girardin but also to Poujoulat, whose earlier works were familiar to Paparrigopoulos.[45] This political convergence of a hard-core Orleanist and a liberal democrat—Poujoulat was the lay representative at the 1848 Constitutional Assembly—may have been what worried Paparrigopoulos and prompted him to reply.

If in 1844 Kolettis's vision of the cultural missions to be undertaken by Greece in the east included France as an ally and cultural fount, in 1853, on the brink of the Crimean War, France appeared to cast doubt on Greece's role as mediator in relations between East and West—or at least raised stronger objections than had previously been the case.

43 Paparrigopoulos, "Anatoliki Orthodoxos Ekklisia," 162–74.

44 Poujoulat, *La France et la Russie*.

45 E.g., the book he coauthored with Joseph-François Michaud, *Histoire des croisades*.

5. France and Russia in Constantinople: Toward an Interpretation of the Great Idea

Paparrigopoulos does not seem to have read Poujoulat's pamphlet *La France et la Russie à Constantinople* when he wrote his vociferous critique of Girardin's article. Nonetheless, the pamphlet's rationale captures French hostility on the eve of the Crimean War toward the Ottoman Empire's Orthodox populations. Clearly, the French concern is not with faith but rather with how the Orthodox might react in the event of a war with Russia. Most of the pamphlet offers a historical overview of the French and Roman Catholic presence in the Holy Land. The author's main conclusion, as translated by Paparrigopoulos from Girardin's article, was that "The East cannot honorably fulfill its religious mandate and recover its proper status but only through Catholicism. There is also the nation destined under God to achieve this bright renewal, and this nation is France."

The only way to establish an aggressive version of the Great Idea was if its "civilizing" nature, as initially imprinted upon it by Kolettis in his parliamentary speech of 1844, was challenged or disputed. Poujoulat would henceforth try to conjoin the two Orthodox threats; the Russian (military) threat was tied by origin to the Greek (cultural) threat since the former's Orthodoxy derived from the latter's "schismatic" Church, severed from the body of the Catholic Church.[46] If Russia were to prevail in the East, this would mean a resurrection of the Byzantine Empire.[47] France's belittlement of the Orthodox element allowed it to assume the intermediary role potentially filled by Greek nationalism. But this strategy presupposed the collapse of the other pillar as well, namely, that the reforms that supposedly turned the Ottoman Empire toward the West would fail. "Yes, the Empire of Osman is dead!"[48] France's aspirations that the Otto-

46 "L'Église grecque, séparée du centre de la catholicité, enfanta ainsi l'Église russe," Poujoulat, *France et la Russie*, 86.

47 "Un Empire russe en Orient ce sera la résurrection de l'ancien Empire byzantin, moins le terrible voisinage des Turks et plus les forces incomparables des jeunes nations du nord" (97).

48 "Oui, l'Empire d'Osman est mort." And continues: "La réforme, don't presque toute la presse française caressait les chimériques perspectives, et dont nous signalions, il y a vingt ans, la périlleuse impuissance, a été pour la Turquie un remède héroique: du moment qu'elle ne la guérissait pas, elle devait la tuer" (102).

man Empire would willingly move toward the West were chimeric. The empire's peoples could only move toward the West if the French nation, largely through its Catholicism, were not only to assume the role of mediator but to establish itself in the East. This was the dilemma of the title *La France et la Russie à Constantinople*, which in fact was posited as *either* France or Russia in Constantinople.

Paparrigopoulos's intervention in response to the positions outlined by Poujoulat and Girardin is of interest for two reasons: first and foremost, because the specter of a French rivalry crystallized the Great Idea, leading to a gradual identification of its civilizational character with irredentism. Irredentism may have appeared to be in retreat after the Crimean adventure, and yet it would strengthen anti-Western reflexes. Greek nationalism understood the process of civilizing the East in exclusive terms. And it was precisely at this moment that it would try to establish, in an organized political fashion, the element of Orthodoxy as inextricable from the national identity (with whatever consequences that was to have on the role of the Patriarchate, the Bulgarian Question, and such like). This then provides a framework for interpreting Paparrigopoulos's defense of Orthodoxy from the attacks lobbed by Poujoulat and Girardin. Paparrigopoulos had not abandoned the position that just a few months earlier, as we will see below, prompted his criticism of Zambelios's reduction of nation to religion. Nonetheless, the role of Orthodoxy in the expansionist-civilizing mission of Hellenism was not negotiable.

Even the Great Idea—and the consequent need for Byzantium to become an object of renegotiation—should not then be seen as resulting solely from the emergence of "imperial nationalism" within the Greek kingdom, aiming at its capital's relocation from Athens to Constantinople (the "pro-Russian" version). Nor should it be seen solely as a consequence of Russia's possible establishment in Constantinople, that is, the Third Rome's occupation of the Second Rome (the "anti-Russian" version). But both of these two relatively utopian prospects have to be understood in relation to a very real possibility, namely that of imperial France gaining a foothold in Constantinople—something that a reading of the Tanzimat's second phase from the Hatt-ı Hümâyun forward, with the expansion of French political and cultural influence in the Empire, might easily point toward.[49] The Great Idea, by necessity, included an imperial dimension that treated as antagonistic to the imaginary dominance of Byzantium not only Moscow but also Paris. Two rival imperial discourses produced a complex politico-cultural nationalism. And this, in turn, sheds light on the other Balkan nationalisms and, in particular, the degree to which their national discourses depended on imperial ones.

6. Helleno-Ottomanism: The Response of Constantinople

The second reason Paparrigopoulos's clash with Poujoulat and Girardin remains significant relates to the Ottoman reforms. Paparrigopoulos's scheme—the gestation of which we see in Driault's defense of French foreign policy in the nineteenth century—had to be transformed. It was not enough to link the rise of the Great Idea as a civilizing mission to the corresponding Westernizing mission suggested by the Tanzimat reforms, even if someone was dealing the Ottoman Empire and the Greek Kingdom as a "closed system." In many ways, the West had already become part of the East, and the Great Idea could be seen as the Tanzimat reform's rival there. Inevitably, it acquires an ambivalent character: the reforms' success was compatible with the "civilizing" version, whereas the reforms' failure would be tantamount to highlighting the Greek state's version of irredentism. Both scenarios, as we know, unfolded over the next few years, albeit during different periods.

The foundation of the Greek Literary Society in September 1861 and the Medical Society earlier the same year, as well as the simultaneous establishment of the Educational Tuition Center (Ekpaidevtikon Frontistirion)—an experiment which ultimately failed—provided the spark for the development of academic activity which contributed, as has been aptly observed, to the organization of a vigorous "literate community."[50]

It has usually been maintained that the society's founding signified the establishment of an institutional producer of nationalist discourse which

49 As a part of this process, the nationalists of the Greek Literary Society of Constantinople came to terms with the antagonistic nature of the Second Empire's civilizing mission, especially through the founding of the Lycée de Galatasaray. See Stamatopoulos, "Hellenism versus Latinism," 92.

50 Exertzoglou, *Ethniki taftotita*. For the Ekpaidevtikon Frontistirion, see *Periodikon Ellinikou Filologikou Syllogou Konstantinoupoleos* [henceforth *PEFSK*] 4 (1871): 242–43.

contributed to the homogenization of Greek Orthodox educational activity in the empire, while also serving as a dynamic field of activity for the great bourgeois and Neo-Phanariot families.[51] These families, which frequently assumed the roles of "benefactors," "donors," and organizers of literary competitions on subjects dealing with various aspects of Greek culture, attempted in this manner to impose their social and cultural hegemony.

In accepting this (essentially correct) view, we should exercise some caution about whether there prevailed any sort of "unanimity" within the society concerning its real objectives. We have shown elsewhere that in the first decade of the society's long life, the discussions organized by various members were characterized by internal tensions, either concerning the rivalry between the offspring of powerful Neo-Phanariots in their attempts to rise to prominence in the production of intellectual discourse, or concerning deeper ideological-political differences between the leading men of the foundation.[52] The objectives of the representatives of the ideological current of "Helleno-Ottomanism,"[53] the members of Karatheodoris family, for example, did not always agree with those of the intellectuals belonging to radical ethnocentric circles, among whom Konstantinos Hercules Vasiadis or Xenophon Zographos could be considered as characteristic examples.

In trying to discover the ultimate ideological aims of this continuously expanding group of intellectuals (belonging to a variety of professions including many physicians, who also participated in the proceedings of the Medical Society, as well as teachers, bankers, clergymen, civil servants, etc.), it is not adequate to analyze their speeches, which were occasionally delivered from the society's rostrum. Nor is it sufficient to "decipher" the text of the proceedings, sometimes published in detail, at other times in summary form, in the society's journal.

An important variable in determining the degree of academic contact with or dependence on academic institutions abroad could be the

51 Under this term, all the families which replaced the old Phanariot aristocracy after the outbreak of the Greek revolution are included. The sources of their power should be traced more to the bureaucratic function than to entrepreneurial activities.

52 Stamatopoulos, "From Cratylus to Herder."

53 For the political-ideological current of Helleno-Ottomanism, namely, the strategic accordance of the Greeks of the Ottoman Empire with the undertaking of its rescue and protection, mainly from the threat of "Pan-Slavism," see Skopetea, *Protypo Vasileio*.

election of honorary members.[54] If the list of founding or corresponding members gives us a picture of the society's power relations, social composition, and ideological orientation(s), then the list of honorary members can provide clues as to the networks that the society, or at least some of its regular members, developed with European academies or universities, and consequently provides indications of the ideological selections that would ultimately characterize its activities. More specifically, we might investigate the nationality of the honorary members (academics or politicians from countries like England, France, Germany, and Russia), the academic achievements cited by the society in justifying their election, and most importantly, their position on the great ideological dilemmas of the nineteenth century over Romanticism or Classicism, Positivism or "Spiritualism."[55] Naturally, the common element of all elected members was their continuous occupation with various phases of the history of "Greek civilization" (if we may speak of a single, unified "Greek civilization"). However, the critical issue of continuity posed by nineteenth-century Romantic historiography, the choice between "ancients" or "moderns"[56] and the attitude toward what can be called "Modern" or "New" Hellenism and its relation to Byzantium, were pivotal questions for the future course of the society. The nomination of honorary members and their treatment of the above ideological dilemmas was certainly reflected in the internal ferment of the society.

However, the ideological strife between the representatives of Helleno-Ottomanism and the radical nationalists led to the use of motifs from the Romantic as well as from the classicist repertoire in a particular way, resulting from the fact that the problem of "continuity" assumed other dimensions within the framework of the Ottoman Empire. The problem was not only to determine the degree of continuity between "ancient"

54 For this issue, see Giannakopoulos, *Ellinikos Filologikos*, 56.

55 This ideological dipole was of course initially formulated by August Wilhelm Schlegel in his distinguished series of lectures, delivered in Berlin between 1801 and 1804, in which he juxtaposed the poetry of antiquity and modern poetry, associating "Romantic" with "progressive" and Christianity. See Minor, *Vorlesungen* vol. 1, 22. See also Eitner, *Neoclassicism and Romanticism*. In any case, the political-ideological use of both terms was altered throughout the nineteenth century from country to country, depending on the academic power relations prevailing at the time. For a comparative analysis of Romantic movements in the most important European countries, see Furst, *Romanticism in Perspective*.

56 For an extent analysis of this issue see Le Goff, *History and memory*.

and "modern" Greeks, but also whether or not to support the empire's political survival. For example, in a dispute between Helleno-Ottomanist Stephanos Karatheodoris and a radical nationalist, Hercules Vasiadis concerning the origin and nature of language, the former, a representative of the continuity of the imperial model (from Byzantium to the Ottomans), defended a model of coexistence of the Greek Orthodox populations within the context of Ottoman "multiculturalism." The latter, on the other hand, insisted on an idealized picture of Greek antiquity within which the contemporary reality could only be interpreted as the result of the sordid march of decline. The predilection of the newly established Greek nation-state for irredentist policies was a natural consequence of the second interpretation.[57]

Within this context, the orientation of intellectuals nominated for honorary membership in the society gained added importance. And it was amazing that the first man to have the honor of being elected an honorary member, at the end of 1862, was the French academician Saint-Marc Girardin. A relentless adversary of the Romantic Movement in France,[58] he succeeded to the chair of History at the Sorbonne immediately after the accession of Louis-Philippe to the French throne; not long afterward, enjoying the favor of the regime, he moved to the corresponding chair of poetry. In 1844, he became an academician and later, a member of the *Institut de France*. His royalist feelings (he was a fanatical Orleanist) and his opposition to the democratic regime were especially pronounced. Girardin's declared Philhellenism and his concomitant "classicism" functioned in a complementary fashion within this framework.[59] A conservative classicist of the *Académie française* (like those who had led J. P. Fallmerayer to construct his anti-classicist model against the dominant ideological trends of the

57 Stamatopoulos, "From Cratylus to Herder."

58 For an instructive presentation of the Romantic movement's reception by literary and academic circles in France at the beginning of the nineteenth century, see Lanyi, "Debates on Romanticism."

59 As the proceedings of the Association report characteristically puts it: "Remarkable were the reasons for which Mr. Girardin, analyzing a drama of Racine in 1855, was heard by his French audience to say: 'Greek antiquity is and will be the teacher of humanity; every science and art bring engraved in the name "Grèce"; all humanity, especially Frenchmen, ought to love and admire everything which bears the name of Grèce.' In response to his words, the audience called out 'Vive la Grèce.'" See *PEFSK* 1 (1863): 85n1. Girardin's most important work was a series of lectures, a sharp polemic against the Romantics, entitled *Cours de litterature dramatique, où, De l'usage des passions dans le drame* (Paris, 1843–1863).

Bavarian Academy, to recall Elli Skopetea)[60] with intense Philhellenist and royalist feelings, Girardin was perhaps the intellectual type to whose emergence the society would establish as exemplary within the Ottoman Empire.

As mentioned above, in addition to confronting Girardin over his comments regarding to the "schismatic" character of the Orthodox Church, the articles in *Pandora* gave Paparrigopoulos the chance to formulate a thesis on the historical mission of the Greek nation to civilize the East. In fact, the cultural version of the "Great Idea" (which arrived just as its military/irredentist version had failed with the Crimean War) was an ideological loan from the armory of French imperialist foreign policy in the Near East and also the first formulation of a dogma in which Hellenism would postulate its role as cultural bridge between the "civilized" West and the "barbarian" East; Hellenism should shed the light of Western civilization all over the peoples of the Balkans and the Ottoman Empire.[61]

However such a movement—the willingness of Catholic France to undertake a "civilizing mission" with any consequence which would entail the increase of the influence of the Second Empire within the Ottoman State (the unification of the Danubian Principalities, the extension of Catholicism into Orthodox Bulgarian populations, etc.)—would bring Hellenism into conflict with "Latinism," that is, with the French imperial nationalism. Nevertheless, while Greek nationalism made its choice concerning its stance vis-à-vis the (Latin) West, adopting dominant Romantic motifs (the sacred mission of the Nation, the existential collective subject), in Istanbul neither the *Megali Idea* nor Romanticism managed to prevail—up to the 1850s at least.

Consequently Girardin's election as the first honorary member of the Greek Literary Society symbolically declared the society's alienation from the main goals of Greek irredentism (for which the first issues of Paparrigopoulos's *History of the Greek Nation*, which appeared in the early 1860s, could be considered as its theoretical justification) as well as, paradoxically, from the ideological control the Ecumenical Patriarchate exercised

60 Skopetea, *Fallmerayer*, 19–25.

61 "Hellenism" as a term must be traced back to the works of Johann Gustav Droysen, *Geschichte Alexanders des Grossen*, and *Geschichte des Hellenismus*. The expansive foreign policy of the Prussian state at the beginning of the nineteenth century was legitimized by Alexander the Great's legend as the civilizer of the East. See, among others, Sigalas, "Hellénistes, hellénisme."

on the city's secular institutions and societies. Both of these components coincided absolutely with the political orientations of the dominant Neo-Phanariot bureaucratic stratum in this period.

Girardin was elected at the suggestion of the physician Alexandros Zoiros Pasha, who had studied in France and was one of the society's founding members.[62] In contrast, Vasiadis (who had studied in France as much as in Germany) attempted in various ways to demonstrate his disregard for the French academic without trying to prevent his election as an honorary member.[63] However, the next year he promoted the election of Abel-François Villemain.

If Girardin, a personal choice of Alexandros Zoiros, satisfied the anti-Romantic feelings of so many of the society's members, mainly powerful Neo-Phanariots, the election of Villemain appears to have been an attempt to introduce some kind of internal balance, especially with respect to supporters of the Herderian paradigm. Actually, Villemain's election was foreshadowed by the discussion that followed Zoiros's proposal concerning Girardin's *De l'usage des passions dans le drame.* Vasiadis observed, after Zoiros's extended presentation that up until the seventeenth century there had been great confusion about the definition of antiquity. It was then that the question of the precise distinction between the Ancients and Moderns, as well as the evaluation of their works, was first posited. Some writers claimed that the Ancients were superior to the Moderns, while others, like the important representative of the *Sturm und Drang* movement, August Wilhelm Schlegel, claimed the opposite. According to Vasiadis, the intervention of Villemain in this discussion proved decisive. Villemain established his textual analysis on the "historical" method, in contrast to the "philosophical" (or theological) method. Girardin actually was no more than a holdover from the "historical" method proposed by Villemain, although he attempted to relate it to the old philosophical hermeneutic tradition. Thus, through the election of honorary members,

62 Alexandros Zoiros succeeded in becoming a physician the following year (1863), while in 1864 he was elected fellow to the Chair of Pathology of the Military Medical Academy in Istanbul. Rallidis, "Alexandros."

63 Vasiadis studied literature at the University of Athens (1843) and medicine at the universities of Paris (1848–1857) and Berlin (1857–1859). While he had, therefore, great experience with French academic reality, he had also come into contact with the literate Germany of his age. Soulis, "Vasiadis."

the most influential modulators of the society's policies tried to strike new balances that would favor their choices in future.

Villemain certainly could not be considered a Romantic, nor could Vasiadis. In fact, in the mid-nineteenth century, the main issue was not the prevalence of Classicism or Romanticism as the dominant ideological current, but the combinations of different elements derived from both that served delicate ideological nuances: inclusion in the wave of political Romanticism (i.e., adherence to the irredentist visions of the nineteenth century)[64] did not necessarily mean adoption of the basic tenets of Romanticism as they had been formulated in the countries of Western Europe (mainly Germany, England, and France) at the turn of the eighteenth century.[65] Philipp August Böckh was perhaps the only newly elected honorary member whose work was clearly influenced by the Romantic movement, in particular by Herder and Hegel.[66]

Girardin's election was not accidental, signaling as it did a series of elections of honorary members sharing almost identical characteristics. Above all, they came from France; even when they were not French, they were members of the *Institut de France* and of the French Academy (usually, the *Académie des Inscriptions et Belles-Lettres*).[67]

64 Eleftheriadis, "Political Romanticism in Modern Greece."

65 From this point of view, one aspect of the discussion between Vasiadis and Zoiros is very interesting. In his initial speech, Zoiros, faithful to the basic principles of the classicist approach of Girardin, would evaluate Euripides's *Andromache* above that of Racine, confirming the supremacy of the Ancients over the Moderns. In contrast, Vasiadis defended the sublimity of Racine's *Andromache*: "[it] is superior to Euripides', because she remains to her death the faithful spouse of Hector and affectionate mother of Astyanax, and because she has not been twice wedded, like the Andromache of Euripides." Here once more Vasiadis chose to support one of the beloved patterns of Romantic discourse, identifying the Romantic with the Modern (A. G. Schlegel) in order to juxtapose both with the worship of classicist antiquity. However, when he was called to address the problem of the beginnings of language, he supported a model of the progressive decline of the ancient Greek language as it was developed through the centuries in both official and vernacular forms. Consequently, he unexpectedly combined the principles of political romanticism with a type of "linguistic classicism." Naturally, language cannot be assimilated into the "achievements" of ancient Greek culture: it retains its substance.

66 However, beyond the election of some intellectual of Romantic lineage (and who, for obvious reasons, was not entitled to membership of any of the French academic institutions), we can discern the interest on the part of Society's leaders during this period in electing members who were medieval scholars. In the case of Hase, for example, we have the public acknowledgement of an eminent Byzantinist (who edited the entries of a number of Greek authors in the collection of the *Historians of the Crusades*), while in the person of Miklosich the Association honored an outstanding Slavic medievalist.

67 Following the election of Girardin, the only honorary member elected in its first year of operation, the Society elected in 1863 four Frenchmen: Emile Egger (1813–1885: Institut de France, Acadé-

As we have already observed, improved relations with the French Academy took the form of institutionalized contacts between the Greek Literary Society and corresponding societies in Paris. However, this tempered extraversion had a reverse side expressed through a host of addresses characterized by anti-Western feelings and "Western-phobia." The fear that the "identity" of Hellenism could be threatened by Western permeation as well as the election to honorary membership of intellectuals who were guarded in their stance toward Christianity appear to have provoked a reaction from leading figures of the society.[68] And this political and theoretical problem was strongly connected with the relationship of Hellenism with "Latinism."

In one of his early discourses, the society's first chairman, Stephanos Karatheodoris, attempted to lend content to the significance of "moral character."[69] While the main subject in the first part of his address was the moral dimension of the individual character, at its conclusion Karatheodoris turned (as if he was a genuine partisan of Herderian ideas) to an analysis of the collective character of modern nations. If the moral character of individuals could be made virtuous by means of a "liberating education" (transmitting, according to Karatheodoris, unbiased knowledge of social relations) and the contribution of religious ethics, the character of nations depended on the totality of the individual moral beings it

mie des Inscriptions et Belles-Lettres), professor of Greek literature at the University of Paris; Carl Benedict Hase (1780–1864), a French Hellenist of German origin; *Charles-Marie-Wladimir Brunet De Presle* (1809–1875), well-known, inter alia, for his *Histoire et description de la Grèce* (1860) (see Politis, *Fauriel kai Brunet de Presle*); Abel-François Villemain (1790–1867: Académie française, Institut de France, Académie des Inscriptions et Belles-Lettres), French politician and man of letters; the Slovenian Franz von Miklosich (1813–1891), a noted philologist and Slavicist and member of the Institut de France and the Académie des Inscriptions et Belles-Lettres, and two Germans: the philologist Georg Curtius (1820–1885) and Philipp August Böckh (1785–1867), an ancient historian and one of the founders of modern classical philology. In addition, the English ambassador to Istanbul, Sir Henry Lytton Earle Bulwer, and the Orthodox archimandrite, Evgenios Xiropotaminos, who had sponsored a scholarship competition, were also elected honorary members. These elections occurred before September 1863, during the Society's second year of existence.

68 E.g., Gustave d'Eichthal, a well-known Gospel critic (who indeed, together with his letter to the Society, offered a series of his books, [see *PEFSK* 5 (1871): 77] or Littré, a Comptian positivist who became a target of harsh accusations from strict Catholics like Carné and Dupanloup, Bishop of Orleans, who denounced him in his *Avertissement à la jeunesse et aux pères de famille* as the chief of the French materialists. Littré finally managed to become a member of the French Academy, succeeding Villemain in 1871 (see Reichert, "Anti-Bonapartist Elections," 39n36). Victor Duruy could be included in the same category as long as his liberal educational reforms called forth the conservative reflexes of the Catholic Church.

69 *PEFSK* 1 (1863): 49–52.

encompassed. Karatheodoris had ultimately chosen a concept more positivist than the Herderian one for defining national character, notwithstanding that this was not his main goal.

"Our race (*genos*), however," he said, "[which] has already begun to rise to the moral horizon of civilized nations," has often been calumniated by representatives of the civilized world, because they, according to Karatheodoris, attribute to it the vile characteristics of certain individuals belonging to it. And this they do, he stresses, with excessive pride, "either because of the force, wealth or wisdom of their nation," without calculating how much their attitude aggrieves the objects of their criticism.

According to the Neo-Phanariot physician, such an attitude could be detected in the period of Roman domination, when, despite the existence of great personalities (such as Polybius, Plutarchos, or Panaitios, etc.) who were genuine admirers of the "Greek character," it remained for "scoundrels"[70] to shape the image of the subjugated Greeks with deprecatory appellations such as "Graeculus" and "Greaca fides," or expressions such as "Timeo Danaos et dona ferentes." Rome, while drawing from and employing the great wealth of knowledge and aesthetic forms of ancient Greece, contributed to the utmost in blackening the Greeks in perpetuity.

Karatheodoris made an interesting transition from the analysis of individual to the collective/national character, using it to defend the Greek race from deprecatory treatment by Western culture. It is obvious that he was anxious to obtain the equal inclusion of "our race" into Western culture.[71] If one of the basic concerns of the society's "literate community" was to create a framework for cross-cultural exchanges with Europe, the anti-Western stance (typified by the demonstration of anti-Roman spirit) on the part of some of its leaders was the means not to isolate it from the West but, on the contrary, to organize a discourse of equal inclusion among the ranks of advanced peoples. It is interesting that Karatheodoris's charge against the "Roman" (bearing in mind that the notion of "Roman" constituted a metonymy for that of

70 "... but some scoundrels, who may be found in all nations and among the Romans too, predominated in order to defile the totally immaculate character of our Race ..." *PEFSK* 1 (1863): 51.

71 Certainly, here he is not innovative as he repeats attitudes and behaviors already in use by the 1840s in Greece as well. See Skopetea, *Protypo Vasileio*, 163–70.

"Catholic"), and his effort to mitigate the contemptuous use of the name "Graikos"(Greek) by the West precisely by reducing the faults of individual characters to the ideal character-type of the Greek nation, shows that he was ready to make the jump to national self-determination and to abandon (provisionally) the unified community of the children of Abraham, which was the cultural essence of multinational Ottoman society. However, his interjection of religious-moral values and an unswerving loyalty to Ottoman power indicate that the "Roman" accusation as formulated by Karatheodoris was a presupposition necessary for the vindication of the Greek Orthodox as "Romioi."

Consequently, the defense of a term like Graikos/Greek no longer represented the viewpoint of a Westernized intellectual (such as Adamantios Korais), which entailed the acceptance of the prismatic view of Western culture as described above by the descendants and successors of the ancient Greeks and the rejection of medieval Byzantine heritage.[72] On the contrary, it was a claim for parity that imposed the acceptance of the superiority of Western culture at the technical/scientific level but mediated it through the realistic perspective of a Neo-Phanariot who claimed himself to be the successor of this "medieval" heritage.[73]

Karatheodoris's guarded stance toward the West was generalized to such a degree in succeeding years through presentations by other representatives of Helleno-Ottomanism (such as Gavril Sophocles[74] and the son of Stephanos Karatheodoris, Alexandros),[75] specifically in discussions that concerned the organization of Greek Orthodox schools in the Ottoman Empire, that Vasiadis, one of the pioneers of the Society's extrovert activities, was forced to maintain that "while in most respects we accept Europeanization, it is chiefly Hellenism that we accept. . . ."[76]

---

72 It is well known that Adamantios Korais has adopted the term "Greeks" (or Hellenes) as the name of his nation, rejecting contemporaneously the term "Romioi" which referred to the obscurantist past of the Byzantine Empire. See his *Dialogos dyo Graikon*.

73 Karatheodoris's attitude can be considered formal for whoever claims that there was an equivalent preparedness for confrontation on the part of the West through the prism of political pragmatism: we recall the corresponding case of another representative of the classic Phanariot world, Dimitrakis Katartzis, who tried to delimit the identity of Romios in juxtaposition not only with the "irrational" East but also with Western influences (especially in literature), Katartzis, *Δοκίμια*, 42–73.

74 Stamatopoulos, "Neophanariotes kai Romantismos" 41–55.

75 Stamatopoulos, "From Cratylus to Herder."

76 Cited by? Stamatopoulos, "Neophanariotes," 41–51.

The two main ideological currents of Helleno-Ottomanism and Greek nationalism met in taking an ambivalent stance vis-à-vis the "West." While recognizing that it provided the spark for the intellectual growth of the "East," they were very cautious about accommodating themselves to its *Weltanschauung*. But a careful observer cannot help but notice that the "golden age" of Helleno-Ottomanism was connected with the intensification of French influence in the Ottoman Empire (for reasons explained above), with the corresponding retreat of the influence of Russian foreign policy, and that it derived its support from an Anglo-French formula for promoting reforms that would neutralize the growth of new centrifugal tendencies.

It is very interesting that France, instead of being considered a gateway to Europeanization, is treated as Europe's springboard to the East. But here the problem is more that of the role of Hellenism than one of European infiltration, i.e., whether it would retain its monopoly on the spread of European conquests in the East. While this represents a radical differentiation in relation to the Enlightenment period, there is also a significant resemblance: the resemblance is the continuing belief that *ex occidente lux*, while the differentiation lies in the fact that other populations of the Ottoman East should become participants in European culture without the mediation, and hence the preferential position, of the Greeks within the Western imagination. This phenomenon had already appeared in pronounced form in the case of the Ottomans and Bulgarians. But paradoxically, refusing to "Europeanize" also meant rejecting the constitutive principles of Ottomanism.

7. Heretical Byzantium in *The History of the Greek Nation*

Hellenism's sacred mission suggested by Paparrigopoulos was not inspired so much by divine Providence as by an attempt to supplant the West in its civilizational and, therefore, imperialist version. This constitutes the reasons why the positivist/historicist structure of Paparrigopoulos's work should not be confused with Zambelios's Romantic structure. The critical point is not acceptance of the scheme of continuity but mainly the way in which it accommodated discontinuity.[77]

77 The acceptance of turning points and ruptures in History and indeed the fact that the nation was

By 1853, in the abridged version of *The History of the Greek Nation*, Paparrigopoulos comprehensively summarized his views on how Hellenism, in its centuries-long journey through history, coped with foreign domination. Roman domination was handled through the superiority of Greek education (and, implicitly, language's important role in this).[78] On the contrary, the preservation of its faith saved the Greek nation during the years of Ottoman rule.[79] Paparrigopoulos's judgment had two prerequisites: one implicit and one explicit. In both cases, he admitted that the means for the Greek nation's survival were accepted by each respective conqueror. They were not imposed upon the conqueror but rather chosen by him: the Romans because they had begun to share in Greek education before their conquest; the Ottomans, and particularly Mehmed II the Conqueror, through the horizontal organization of the *millet* system provided through Islam. The latter prerequisite for Paparrigopoulos's argument is not explicitly stated but can be derived; the springboard for the new phase in the dynamic rebirth of the substantialized subject is its conquests in the previous phase.

Byzantium and religion were inextricable. Thus, the question of how the Eastern Roman Empire, as Paparrigopoulos described it early on in his writings, was gradually Hellenized remained central. The answer was not as "easy" to formulate as in Zambelios's case. Paparrigopoulos could not resort to a "philosophical" approach to the issue. And even though his approach was not philosophical, it can claim to have been dialectic. This meant that Paparrigopoulos realized that Hellenism and Christianity coexisted inside Byzantium in a contradictory manner. The initial solution he adopted encapsulated Hellenism mainly through the philosophical and theognostic means provided by language.

But this solution did not suffice to explain the process of Byzantium's Hellenization for one simple reason: language may have been the solution to the problem of continuity in the case of the Roman conquest, which

---

not a reified collectivity that expresses its dominance in space and time, but rather a body for the legitimation of political power, did not automatically render a historiographer anti-nationalist.

78 "What saved the Greek nation is its exceptional diligence with the arts and letters." Paparrigopoulos, *Istoria tou Ellinikou Ethnous [I proti morfi: 1853]*, 89.

79 "What ultimately saved the Greek nation was its loyal devotion to its fathers' faith." Paparrigopoulos, *Istoria tou Ellinikou Ethnous [I proti morfi: 1853]*, 119.

meant that it was hard to re-employ it to Hellenize something that had already, to whatever degree, been "Hellenized."

This occurred through the history of the Ecumenical Councils and the way they occasionally resolved the appearance of "heresies" and "heresiarchs." But while the doctrine—in other words, the Council's verdict—crystallized and institutionalized the Christian element, how might one identify the reappearance of Hellenism? The answer that provided was precisely through the heresies themselves.

From the moment that Paparrigopoulos commenced his discussion of the issue of internal religious clashes, starting with the condemnation of Arianism by the first Ecumenical Council, it became clear that "heresies" sprang from an important legacy of Greek intellectual thought: philosophical examination. Even if this did not emerge in Arius's case—Paparrigopoulos openly supported a theological approach and embraced Arius's condemnation, clearly positioning himself in favor of the Athanasius's solution of an "Homoousian" Father and Son—there were some elements confirmative of the above. For one, in the table of contents, the chapter on Arianism was titled "Hellenism's Great Reaction," while Paparrigopoulos acknowledged that the Arianist heresy originated within the segment of Late Roman society that sought compromise between Christians and idolaters.[80] From this perspective, it is not accidental that Arianism emerged not at the imperial center but in Alexandria ("not only the commercial, but also the political and moral capital of Hellenism"). The same, of course, could not be said about Nestorius and his followers roughly a century later.

Indeed, in the second volume of his work (the eighth book), Paparrigopoulos observed that Arianism should be viewed as the result of neo-Platonism's impact on the core of the Christian doctrine. Arius himself claimed to have studied under Porphyry.[81] In his view, however, neo-Platonism and Christianity had a fundamental similarity: the triadic doctrine, albeit, in the former, in its more "philosophical" form. As such, the Holy Trinity of Father, Son, and Holy Spirit corresponds to the neo-Platonists The One, The Mind, The Soul.[82] While acknowledging that

80 Paparrigopoulos, *Istoria tou Ellinikou Ethnous,* vol. 2, 565.

81 Ibid., vol. 2, 574.

82 Ibid., vol. 2, 566.

disputing Arius's *homoousion* of the Father and Son threatened the very foundations of the Christian religion,[83] Paparrigopoulos's discussion of the similarities between neo-Platonism and Christianity should be read as a belated comment on Zambelios's historiographical/philosophical scheme. According to Paparrigopoulos, the imperial center was susceptible to accepting the heretics' views. As examples of this, he cited Constantine the Great, who in his waning years made concessions to Arius's followers,[84] and Theodosius II's favoring of the Nestorians. Noting that the Eastern clergy was more susceptible to heresies than the Western clergy, Paparrigopoulos attributed the apparent paradox to philosophy's dissemination in the empire's eastern provinces.[85]

At this point, it is worth observing that Paparrigopoulos' and Gibbon's respective approaches to heresies differ substantially. Gibbon supposedly contributed to the formation of the image of a mystical Byzantium, despotic and dark, yet Paparrigopoulos found no objection to this. As discussed below, he adopted Gibbon's secular interpretation, correlating Iconoclasm with the Reformation in its entirety. But when Gibbon described the salient issues raised during the confrontations with the early heretics, he adopted the perspective of a devout Christian. For example, Gibbon also noted the Platonic origin of the concept of the *homoousion* that marked the confrontation between Arius and Athanasius.[86] His description censured the former's views, and he devoted thirty-three pages(!) to praising the latter, with whom he seems to have identified.[87] In reality, the narrative structure of Paparrigopoulos's corresponding chapter on the confrontation between Arius and Athanasius was inspired by the third volume of Gibbon's *History*.

Nonetheless, there is an essential difference between these two narratives: the source of the heretical ideas. Both writers made reference to

83 Ibid., vol. 2, 601–602.

84 Ibid., vol 2, 625–26.

85 Ibid., vol. 2, 754.

86 Gibbon, *Decline and Fall*, vol. 3, 7.

87 Ibid., vol. 3, 38–61. Gibbon did the same with other contemporary heresies that misinterpreted the meaning of the *homoousion*, the Tritheists and the Sabellians. Accordingly, he noted: "When the mysteries of the Christian faith were dangerously exposed to public debate, it can be seen that human faculties proved capable of creating three discrete, albeit incomplete, systems for understanding the Holy Trinity's nature and it was proven that none of these three systems, clearly and absolutely, managed to escape heresy and error...." Vol. 3, 18–20.

the Platonic origin of the idea of the *homoousion* but in a different perspective. Gibbon used it to explain why Arius's ideas proved so attractive to the Greek populations in the East,[88] while Paparrigopoulos used it as a reminder that the neo-Platonic elaboration springs from the grand Ancient Greek philosophical tradition. The difference in their narratives stems from the role Gibbon attributed to the Jewish community of Alexandria in the adoption of Platonism (or at least some of it).[89] Gibbon obviously viewed the East as the source of heresies mainly because of the influence of Judaism's aniconic monotheism. By contrast, Paparrigopoulos treated its philosophical quests, even if they led to heretic beliefs, as the surviving spirit of Ancient Greece. Gibbon described Arianism (and other early Christian heresies) as a result of the infusion of Hellenism and Judaism in order to juxtapose the East to the West of the Roman state. In Paparrigopoulos's view, Arianism was the effect of the neo-Platonic influence on nascent Christianity.

This divergence is important because it is directly linked to the issue of continuity. For Paparrigopoulos, taking a positive stance on the issue of early heretics was essential to his reinterpretation of Byzantium because it restored Ancient Greek culture's status within Byzantium. But, to this end, he had to distance himself from the "theologian-centric" views adopted by Gibbon, the opponent of Byzantine *superstitiousness*.[90]

Gibbon classified heresies into early and later based on their respective focus on the *Homoousion* and the *Incarnation*. This shift in his work pointed to the East's growing importance within Byzantium. Conversely, in Paparrigopoulos's narrative, this distinction was blunted. In broad

88 He noted: "The eparchies of Egypt and Asia that cultivated the language and customs of the Greeks were deeply soaked in the poison of the Arian confrontation. The familiar study of the Platonic system, a vain and controversial stance, an excessive and flexible idiom, supplied the clergy and the people of the East with an inexhaustible flow of words and distinctions, and in the midst of these violent confrontations, they easily forgot that philosophy introduces doubt, while religion imposes submission." (Vol. 3, 27).

89 Vol. 3, 9. Of course, according to Gibbon, the "Hellenized" Jews committed a distortion.

90 There are some delicate twists in these arguments. For example, Gibbon considered the "intrepid" (vol. 3, 22) Athanasius as the primary advocate of the "homoousion", while for Paparrigopoulos he was "was one of the best examples of Hellenism's moral renaissance just completed" (vol. 2, 568). Paparrigopoulos thus blurred the line that Gibbons had painstaking drawn in to juxtapose the Greek East with the Latin West. Paparrigopoulos's methodology did not only demystify Byzantium, but also wherever this was needed Gibbon's own methodology.

terms, he saw all heresies before the fourth Ecumenical Council of Chalcedon (451)—that is, those of Arius, Nestorius, and Eutyches—as merely the reinstatement of one and the same issue: the dispute over the divine nature of Christ.

At the end of his eighth book, Paparrigopoulos repeated his entire scheme for Hellenizing Byzantium. The Roman Emperors' domination was steadily undermined by a plethora of elements that represented Hellenism, from the Church itself and the institution of the Ecumenical Councils (which he viewed as the Roman monarchy's rivals) to the Pandidakterion (Constantinople's University) and the linguistic Hellenization of the state. Given, however, his belief that the heresies were a product of the Ancient Greek philosophical tradition, he appeared to perceive the Hellenization process as an internal dialectical clash in which the ancient world's elements were not obliterated by Christianity's "overhaul" but left traces through the arrangements made by the Ecumenical Councils. Paparrigopoulos definitely aligned himself with the doctrine rather than the heresy, and he could not do otherwise.[91] The heresy resulted from the philosophical examination of the divine which inevitably led to a questioning of the "incarnate economy," in other words, the doctrine's very foundation for Christ as both man and God. Paparrigopoulos states this succinctly but without adopting the position of Christian zealots. On the contrary:

> Yes, the heresies didn't dare, as far as we know, to state bluntly that the Saviour was human but because their interpretations all entail that subversive conclusion, peaceful coexistence between themselves and Orthodoxy was impossible. The time for religious intolerance had not yet arrived. (Paparrigopoulos, *Istoria tou Ellinikou Ethnous*, vol. 3, 24)

---

91 Although he is often prone to statements like "God knows how much the monarchs were pressured by mobs and monks to repeatedly issue laws against the Nationals" (Paparrigopoulos, *Istoria tou Ellinikou Ethnous*, vol. 3, 17), in the end he condemned the heretics (Nestorians and Monophysites) as collaborators of "our bitterest opponents," in the belief that a compromise between the Orthodox and heretic Christianity of the East was impossible after the Sixth Ecumenical Council of 680, mainly because the heresies had lost any sense of their philosophical quest after the seventh century. Ibid., 344–45. In other words, he chided the heretics not for clashing with the Orthodox doctrine but because their association with the barbarians had weakened their ideological foundations. And although this issue was concluded with the Sixth Ecumenical Council, another one was required, albeit to vindicate the wrong side through the condemnation of Iconoclasm.

This excerpt is exceptionally interesting as it clearly highlights Paparrigopoulos's view that all heresies in Byzantium had a common foundation. His reference to religious tolerance (18–19) is also interesting as it indicates the side he chose to defend, just as he had done before when he had treated the principle of "freedom of consciousness," a principle that had allegedly been introduced by Constantine the Great's administration as a policy of neutrality between the two contending parts.[92] According to Paparrigopoulos, Byzantium paid dearly for this internal rift as the "desperate" heretics were forced to cooperate with the Persian invaders (Nestorians) and the Muslims (Monophysites) in conquering Syria, Palestine, and Egypt. The damage to the state was more moral than material, such as the closing of the great Greek schools in these areas:

> The intellectual bond between National and Christian Hellenism was thus broken both in Europe and Asia . . . What Julian had desired and Gregory Nazianzen had deflected with exasperation, unfortunately happened in the end. Christian Hellenism was deprived, for many centuries, of Ancient Hellenism's traditions, sentiments and convictions. (vol. 3, 25)

Conversely, Paparrigopoulos's affinity for the Monophysitist heretics of the Empire did not automatically assume a friendly stance toward Islam. Citing Jules Barthélemy Saint-Hilaire's recently published *Mahomet et le Coran*, he shows that he completely understood the dogmatic affinity between the religion introduced by Mohammed and Monophysitism. ("Mohammed rejected the mystery of the Trinity because, in a word, it ran counter to the unity of God and because as an *in actu* it was not compatible with the mission of this new prophet.")[93] Nonetheless, he kept his distance from Barthélemy Saint-Hilaire's position that the tough battle between Islam and Christianity was not a direct consequence of the Koran's doctrine but that was attributable from the start to political interest. He did not seem to agree with Barthélemy Saint-Hilaire's view that the Koran declared Muslim's religious tolerance toward Christians and

92 Naturally, one of the first examples of the Christians' merciless persecution of the "pagans" was none other than Hypatia. Paparrigopoulos, *Istoria tou Ellinikou Ethnous*, vol. 3, 19.

93 Paparrigopoulos, *Istoria tou Ellinikou Ethnous*, vol. 3., 286.

Jews. Conversely, Paparrigopoulos embraced the view of the English historian William Muir (*Life of Mahomet and History of Islam*) that religious tolerance was "initially a principle unknown *to* the Muslim world" while Islamic justice's rulings on polygamy, divorce, and slavery undermined "public morals." Paparrigopoulos further believed in a fundamental difference between Christianity and Islam: the former was intensely cosmopolitan and suited to more culturally-developed societies, whereas Islam, as a religion, was more suited to "less–culturally developed nations." This is why the Greek nation was the only one that resisted its spread in contrast to Asian nations like Persia and India or to African nations.[94] Paparrigopoulos's view on Islam clearly shows the Orientalist prerequisites of his continuity scheme. Even when resorting to Byzantium's heretical tradition to prove its compatibility with the West, he was reluctant to disturb the established boundaries that separate West and East.

Paparrigopoulos's orientalist preference to heretics was exactly the proof of his devotion to ancient rationalism. Paparrigopoulos finally believed that heretics' persecution had led to an alienation from the spirit of Hellenism. Medieval Hellenism, as a result of the synthesis of national and Christian Hellenism, suffered from a lack of love for the fatherland. To a certain extent, the "religious feeling" that ran through Hellenism compensated this lack but at the same time it led to tribulations (superstition, the bolstering of monasticism, etc.). When dealing with the era of Iconoclasm, which was the apex of the Empire's Hellenization process and at the same time the epitome of the arguments against heresies in Byzantium (in the sense that the inability to depict the divine corresponded to a specific understanding of the Son's nature as both Human and God), Paparrigopoulos adopted a very interesting position: the Iconoclast Emperors, especially the Isaurians, inaugurated a massive reform seven centuries before the Protestant Reformation in Western Europe.

Paparrigopoulos sought to curtail the negative effects of "religious feeling" by counterposing a "patriotic" one (". . . neither a nation without a religion can exist nor a religion without a nation can be preserved. . . .").[95] But how could one evaluate the Iconoclasm, that is, the state's attempt to

94 Paparrigopoulos, *Istoria tou Ellinikou Ethnous*, vol. 3, 292

95 Ibid., vol. III., 30.

control the centrifugal forces of the Church and the abusive aspects of Orthodox worship, without considering the legacy of the censured heretics of the fourth and fifth centuries?

8. Iconoclasm as a Conspiracy of the Monarchy

Iconoclasm is widely considered to have been a key period for the interpretation of all Byzantine history. It marked, among other things, the end of the war against "heresies," the end of the Ecumenical Councils, the origin of the schism with the West, the beginning of Byzantium's civilizing work in the Slav world, and, primarily, the start of a new period many historians have approached as the "Hellenization" of the Roman period with regard to the Empire's civil identity. Thus, all nineteenth-century historians and scholars seeking to take a position against Byzantium had to reckon with Iconoclasm.

Zambelios also viewed Iconoclasm within the framework of bolstering the Byzantine Emperor's "absolutism." For Zambelios, Iconoclasm only appeared to be a religious issue. In actual fact, it was a political issue that could result in the curtailment of the absolutism that peaked during Justinian's reign. The Roman monarchy in Constantinople had "forgotten" the tradition of "Latin liberty" found back in Rome. Understandably, deme and Church resistance continuously escalated. The monarchy responded with the Iconoclasm. Yet, in Zambelios's view, Iconoclasm, which marked the collapse of "Romanism" and the dominance of "Hellenism," was merely the result of an "abominable plan" aimed at "sowing discord" between the clergy and the people. This "malicious religious reform" was nothing but a contrivance by those in power aimed at weakening the other two members of the Holy Trinity. And the pretext for this was: "the alleged abusiveness of the worship of divine images."[96]

Iconoclasm was, thus, a heresy fomented by "malignant" Emperors starting with Leo III the Isaurian. When analyzing the basic coordinates along which Zambelios perceived Byzantium, we referred to an excerpt from Hegel's *Philosophy of History* in which Hegel clearly followed Gibbon. This excerpt was also cited by Zambelios. But further along in the

96 Zambelios, *Asmata Dimotika*, 301.

same text, Hegel refered to Leo as "brave"![97] Hegel juxtaposed the mystical and superstitious Byzantium with the historical trajectory of the West, comparing the Seventh Ecumenical Council that vindicated Iconolatry with the Council of Frankfurt in 794, which censured "the superstitions of the Greeks."

Hegel obviously took a positive approach to Iconoclasm, forcing Zambelios to believe that a defense of Byzantium against the Gibbonians required its irrevocable condemnation.[98] Hegel's ghost thus continued to torment Zambelios on this issue as well. Interpreting Iconoclasm as a heresy fanned by Byzantine absolutism could provide a belated response to Hegel-Gibbon on this point. At the same time, Zambelios's anti-absolutist interpretation of Iconoclasm ran counter "to chronicles at that time." As a matter of methodology, Zambelios approached Byzantine chroniclers critically, and this methodology differentiated him from Gedeon who approached Iconoclasm historically.

Zambelios's reading of Iconoclasm is also interesting as he attempted to juxtapose it to Hellenism. In his view, Leo III the Isaurian was responsible for the destruction of the university at Constantinople (Pandidakterion) by fire.

> The most sacred relics of the Church and ethnicism were kept in this building as instruments of enlightenment ... from the start, Leo tried in every way possible into lure into malignant views the teachers of the nation and the scientists, but science was inseparable already from Orthodoxy and ethnicism, so the disease-wicked failed. (Zambelios, *Asmata Dimotika*, 305)

The fanatic and heretical Emperor's rage was unleashed on the one institution that had provided refuge in the sacred "relics of antiquity."

Zambelios also found a way to handle the problem of discontinuity: for him, the link between Hellenism and Christianity had already been

97 "The brave Emperor Leo the Isaurian in particular, persecuted images with the greatest obstinacy, and in the year 754, image-worship was declared by a Council to be an invention of the devil. Nevertheless, in the year 787 the Empress Irene had it restored under the authority of a Nicene Council, and the Empress Theodora definitively established it...", see Hegel, *The Philosophy of History*, 357.

98 Ibid., 358.

forged by the Fathers in the early Christian centuries. Iconoclasm aimed to create a rift between these two elements, hence his reference to efforts to sow discord between Church and people.

Zambelios correctly understood that the removing of icons and the banning of the worship of saints' relics targeted the clergy's intermediary role in Byzantine society. Disparaging the material depictions of religion would lead to a similar devaluation of the clergy's role and the concomitant severing of its ties "with the lower strata." The same holds for the persecution of monasticism as well. The Church was on the receiving end of an all-out attack by the monarchy.[99]

As previously mentioned, Zambelios consigned Iconoclasm and the Seventh Ecumenical Council to the long list of heresies that shook Byzantium: the "rabid Iconoclasts" were censured and damned alongside Arius, Macedonius, Nestorius, Eytyches, and Dioscorus. But while linking Iconoclasm to the heresies and to Julian[100] would allow one to consider it to be a remnant of the ancient world (as in Paparrigopoulos's case), Zambelios argued the opposite. Denigrating Iconoclasm was necessary for him in order to establish a different scheme of continuity leading back to antiquity; in spite of his subtle statements on the issue of the restoration and worship of icons, his ulterior goal was to link Iconolatry with ancient idolatry. Showing no inferiority complex toward the West, he wrote: "Some northerners are heretics worshipping the Ancient Greeks, albeit idol-worshippers. The younger ones were defamed as worshipping icons and praying to wooden effigies. And those looking but not seeing don't realize that the Greek spirit is by nature disposed towards symbols."[101]

---

99 Zambelios's descriptions of atrocities against iconolaters were vivid, especially when compared to his references to the tribulations of the early Christians at the hands of Roman authorities (see ibid., 308–9). Of course it becomes evident here that Zambelios was following in the footsteps of the Iconolatric chroniclers like the self-declared historian Theophanes, setting aside his self-proclaimed critical stance to their work.

100 Citing Constantine Copronymus's *Novella on relics and invocation of the saints*, which among others bans the use of the word "saint", Zambelios added: "The Apostles should be referred to as simply Peter, Paul, Jacob; the Despotis Christos [Almighty Christ] as a common man and not as the son of God, and the Theotokos [Mother of God] as Christotokos [Mother of Christ] or addressed as only Maria. This and other things were reminders of Arius's and the violator Julian's wrath plagued the Church and the country." Zambelios, *Asmata Dimotika*, 310.

101 Zambelios, *Asmata Dimotika*, 312.

In order to justify the continuity between the Ancient Greeks and the new "idol-worshippers" (we should not neglect that this was a frequent accusation made by Islam against medieval Christianity), Zambelios resorted to the distinction he had already made between an individual and a national religion. Both Ancient Greek religion and Orthodoxy fall under the rubric of national religion, making the use of symbols necessary and required. Zambelios predicated the continuity between Antiquity and the Middle Ages or Ancient and Medieval Hellenism on this relationship at the religious level: "Greece must write the history of restoration in gold letters. For, if Marathon and Salamis saved Ancient Greece, [the Council of] Nicaea saved modern Greece."[102]

As in the clash between the Roman Empire and Hellenism, with the latter proving the stronger pole in the antithesis, the clash between monarchy and Church ended with the latter victorious. Nonetheless, in Iconoclasm's wake, the Church's evident hostility toward anything reminiscent of Ancient Greek culture created a theoretical problem for Zambelios. How could he establish the concept of continuity when the successor denies his ancestors' political/cultural legacies?

This was resolved by identifying an internal contradiction within the ancestor. Isolating an excerpt on Platonic ideas in the work of John Italus—which, in actual fact, is a treatise against the Ancient Greeks' legacy in its entirety—Zambelios finds an opportunity to distinguish two schools of thought within this heritage, the Platonic and the Aristotelian: "The class of the Educated has always been always divided into two conflicting sides. The Platonists fortify heresy, innovation, foreignism; the Aristotelians, many of whom are sage and respected Fathers, faithfully follow the line etched by Orthodoxy.... Platonic cosmopolitanism proved redundant and detrimental to Christian universality and often openly plots against established doctrines and accepted traditions. Aristotelianism conversely helped the nation, and the Clergy borrowed from it the necessary reasoning and dialectic forces to destroy the continuously emerging heresies."[103]

As a result, (Aristotelian) philosophy became a tool against the heresies, while (Platonic) cosmopolitanism tended to reinforce them. These

102 Ibid.

103 Ibid., 316–17.

two schools of thought continued to clash in Byzantium. This is why the Church's conflict with some *Hellenists* (read: Platonists) who found refuge in the palace should not be seen as a complete rejection on the part of the Church, of Ancient Greek civilization. Zambelios's position may have been inspired by the way the Church had adopted Aristotelianism as the dominant ideology during the Ottoman Middle Ages. But what is important is that, on the one hand, this ideology was completely compatible with the Aristotelian trinity as a theoretical point of departure for his analysis and, on the other, it paved the way for a positivist historionomic approach to the phenomenon of modern Hellenism: "From the theological level, the *genos* is moved to the popular stage; it becomes, so to speak, historicized, positivized, laicized, and concerned with its worldly life."[104]

The turning point of Iconoclasm was decisive for the historical trajectory of Medieval Hellenism as it marked the moment of the ultimate internal conflict that would establish the principle of continuity between Ancient and Medieval Hellenism. It is also so vitally important that it divided the medieval period in two: ancient medievalism and new medievalism. Rupture, yet at the same time, continuity. The end of Iconoclasm constituted the establishment of New Hellenism.

9. Iconoclasm as Reformation

The same year that Zambelios released his *Demotic Songs*, Paparrigopoulos reviewed it in *Pandora*, the journal where he served as a member of the editorial board.[105] The critique focused on the period of Iconoclasm, yet the reasons for this seemingly paradoxical choice remain obscure to this date. Why did Paparrigopoulos focus on this point? As a result of the fact that he understood that Zambelios's entire scheme of continuity hinged upon the interpretation of this period? This he sought to subvert in order to reinstate the scheme of continuity. Was Paparrigopoulos motivated by the fact that, according to Zambelios's version, Christianity could be embraced by and reimprinted onto the Greek national narrative, whereas Byzantium, as an imperial political concept, could not?

104 Ibid.
105 Paparrigopoulos, "Bibliografia," 397–403.

Zambelios legitimized Byzantium as an inextricable part of Hellenism's (medieval) history, but not as an empire. And this led Paparrigopoulos to make use of the monarchy as the means to counter Zambelios's argument.

In the long introduction to Zambelios's review, that is, before he came to the crux of his critique, Paparrigopoulos characteristically tried to outline the arguments for the political, and not merely scientific, nature of his engagement with the *History of the Greek Nation* by recalling that Fallmerayer himself had raised this political dimension in his *The Slavic Element in Greece* by posing some important dilemmas for the West. The political dilemmas posed by doubting the continuity of the Greek nation can be summarized as follows:

1. The need for Europe to stop believing that the existence of a Greece is now possible and to leave this game to children and scholasticists.
2. The need for Europe, if it does not wish to be seen as ridiculous, to stop fantasizing about the rise of the great Eastern state with Byzantium as the capital.
3. The need for Europe, with regards to the Christian populations between Istros [the Danube river delta] and Tainaron [the Southern Peloponnese], to not forget that these tribes amalgamate dead elements that cannot be revived with the breath of an outsider spirit. (Paparrigopoulos, "Bibliografia," 398)

If these were the political dilemmas outlined by a theory disputing continuity in Greek history, they should have been taken into consideration by any theory expressed in support of continuity. Therefore, if there was a criterion of "political correctness" in Zambelios's approach, it would be judged by whether it addressed these dilemmas, especially the second. According to Paparrigopoulos, Zambelios's work was a definite contribution in this direction. In his view, Zambelios was not attempting to prove the Greek nation's survival through the Middle Ages in a negative fashion (by countering arguments for Slavicization as well as Albanization of the ancient Greek populations) but in a positive way (by highlighting substantive aspects of the "moral, political, and intellectual life" of Medieval Hellenism). Paparrigopoulos also seems to have taken a positive view of

Zambelios's effort to go against the tide of prevalent European thought at the time and present the debates about dogmatic issues in Byzantiumas as a sign of cultural vitality, rather than as a sign of obscurantism.

Yet, Paparrigopoulos seems to have taken the second dilemma set by Fallmerayer's intervention particularly seriously. Whereas the solution of Helleno-Christianism sufficed for Zambelios, Paparrigopoulos needed to inscribe the irredentist characteristics of the Great Idea onto his project. According to Paparrigopoulos, Zambelios's excessive eagerness to defend religious doctrine led him to downgrade part of "our political history." The Iconoclast Emperors were unfairly treated in Zambelios's assessments given that they had contributed to the Byzantine state's political restructuring.

But what is the cause of Zambelios's unfairness? Was the fact that he took the chroniclers at face value? They were contemporaries of the emperors but had joined the ranks of the rival camp. Paparrigopoulos noted:

> In the words of these chroniclers, it is not stated that almost all the Iconoclasts were rulers at war, unmatched in their courage, admirable for their prowess at internal administration, virtuous in their private lives, for the most part, and indeed, the latter, avid protectors of the sciences and letters. (Paparrigopoulos, "Bibliografia," 400)

Paparrigopoulos raised an issue that Zambelios had purportedly resolved: the objective use of the source material. But the problem in Zambelios differs from the one we will examine in Gedeon later on in this book. Whereas Gedeon assumed he had to resort to the testimonies of the Iconophile chroniclers, Zambelios was supposedly concerned with the objectivity of his sources (as also in *Byzantine Studies*). According to Paparrigopoulos, Zambelios's "schizophrenic" approach to the sources—he theoretically declared that he used them in an objective manner, but in practice, he identified with the perspective of the narrative they provided—stemmed from a fundamental methodological choice: Zambelios's reduction of the nation to religion.[106] Here too we find a positivist Paparrigopoulos that flies in the face of the perfunctory labeling of him

106 Koubourlis correctly noted that this criticism pushed Zambelios toward a "secularized" look at Byzantine history in his subsequent work, *Byzantine Studies*. Koubourlis, *Formation*, 290–93.

as a Romantic. In their review of Dimaras's *Paparrigopoulos*, Georgios Veloudis and Elli Skopetea had identified Paparrigopoulos as the first representative of Historicism in Greek historiography.[107]

But how did the historicist Paparrigopoulos demolish Zambelios's Romantic model? He trained his fire on its Hegelian structure. In other word, he targeted the ways in which the Roman survived in the context of monarchy even up until its collapse. He thus created a dilemma around the definition of the people: if we accept that the monarchy survived as a Roman institution, no one could honestly argue for Byzantium's Hellenization. It is small wonder then that the treatment of this dilemma was the starting point for Zambelios's *Byzantine Studies*, published a few years later.

Indeed, Paparrigopoulos's criticisms of Zambelios[108] in 1852 were the theoretical springboard for the tenth volume of his *History*, which was dedicated in its entirety to Iconoclasm. This time Paparrigopoulos would not content himself with highlighting the positive characteristics of the Iconoclast Emperors' political administration but would define the entire period of Iconoclasm as a "Reformation." Here, too, Paparrigopoulos followed Gibbon who believed that the efforts of the "brave" Iconoclast Emperors to lift Byzantium out of the "long night of superstition" heralded, in a way, the sixteenth-century Reformation, when "liberty and knowledge spread through all aspects of human life."[109] This time he did not need to reverse Gibbon's line of argumentation—it had already taken

107 In *Protypo Vasileio*, Skopetea refers to the paradox of a "Romantic's" recognition as a national historiographer after the end of the period of Romanticism. See also Veloudis, *Fallmerayer*.

108 In an article published in the same issue of *Pandora* and immediately after Paparrigopoulos's book review, Papadopoulos-Vrettos underscored, albeit sympathetically, the most problematic element of Zambelios's attempt at narrating the history of Medieval Hellenism: "... and wishing to always appear, to the extent my meager abilities allow, beneficial to my fellow Hellenes, I hasten to correct a very important bibliographic error of S. Zambelios; and I say *very important* error because correcting it will destroy from its foundations an entire chapter of his treatise." What was this error? That "(his) apparently total reverence and piety offers a *religious* explanation of the eve of the Greek race's rebirth and attributes Greece's liberation from the [Ottoman] yoke to the Holy Mother of God" (author's emphasis). Papadopoulos-Vrettos referred to Zambelios's use of an excerpt from Elias Miniatis's work. See Papadopoulos-Vrettos, "Bibliographic observations," 403–406. Of import here is the theoretical position taken rather than the example cited.

109 Gibbon, however, did not abandon his interpretation of the Reformation as the result of the "West's strength in spurning the ghosts that dominate the sick and servile weakness of the Greeks." See Gibbon, *Decline and Fall*, vol. 6, 186–87.

a secular turn. Thus Paparrigopoulos did not limit his analysis to a single Iconoclast Emperor like Theophilos (829–645),[110] who already enjoyed favorable reports from the Iconolatric chroniclers (". . . he was an iconomach but for political reasons, not by conscience . . . ") but would focus on the first generation of Iconoclast kings like Leo III, the Isaurian and his son Constantine V, who were iconoclasts by conscience.[111]

In the third volume of his *History of the Greek Nation* (book ten),[112] Paparrigopoulos would attempt to highlight the Isaurian dynasty's work as the last significant effort to restructure the Byzantine state before it entered the phase of irreversible decline. It may not be an exaggeration to mention that the way Paparrigopoulos presented the Isaurians seems to have been the ideal model on the basis of which he defended the institution of the Byzantine monarchy. To this end, however, he had first to adopt a secular perspective.

Indeed, the tenth book of Paparrigopoulos's *History* begins with a direct attack on what he calls the "ineptitudes" of Byzantine monasticism and its aberrant turns to superstition and religious fanaticism.[113] He believed that Leo II did not seek confrontation but was forced into it by an already existing clash between the Iconoclast minority and Iconolatric majority. He, therefore, found a historical opportunity to restructure the state and limit the powers of the Church, and especially the monks.

Paparrigopoulos had already criticized Zambelios for viewing Iconoclasm as an attempt by the monarchy to divide clergy and people with the ultimate goal of limiting the clergy's authority. But what did this interpretation of Iconoclasm as "Reformation" actually mean? While Paparrigopoulos had forced Zambelios to abandon the reduction of the nation to religion outlined earlier, he himself approached the period—and essentially of all of Byzantine history—from a "religious" perspective; having forced Zambelios to reconsider whether Iconoclasm was a conspiracy by the monarchy, Paparrigopoulos conceptualized it in a way that effectively accepted that what was at stake in this confrontation was the authority of Byzantine absolutism.

110 Paparrigopoulos, "Oi teleftaioi Eikonomachoi," 15–21, 65–71, 130–37, 175–82.
111 Paparrigopoulos, "Oi teleftaioi Eikonomachoi," 176.
112 Paparrigopoulos, *Istoria tou Ellinikou Ethnous*, vol. 3.
113 Paparrigopoulos, *Istoria tou Ellinikou Ethnous*, 406–409.

Does this mean that Zambelios was deconstructed for no good reason? Rather the contrary. The difference between the two viewpoints was in their handling of the West. Zambelios's Hegelian scheme did not simply place Greek history outside History but also in juxtaposition to the West. Conversely, Paparrigopoulos's scheme is beset by the anxiety of inscribing Greek history into European history. This is the reason he demolished the self-referential scheme devised by Zambelios. And he did not attempt this by relating the two sides in a "positive" manner but rather in an "apophatic" way. For example, he did not compare the two cases at the level of the Renaissance or the Enlightenment, but at the level of the ending of the Middle Ages, to the extent that the eruption of religious wars in the West signified.

Paparrigopoulos was occupied with the following question: what engendered the emergence in the West of the "wonderful civilization of modern times" despite the fact that both the West and the East had witnessed the manifestation of heresies and great misunderstandings in the interpretation of the Gospel. For Paparrigopoulos, the key to interpreting the different path followed by the West was the religious Reformation that took place in the sixteenth century. Long before Max Weber's *Protestant Ethic*, and in the footsteps of Thomas Babington Macauley's analysis of this historic event, he observed that ". . . while the countries accepting reform—north Germany, England, North America—continued advancing in the field of culture and to this day are leaders in this, those countries remaining under Papal dominance—Southern Germany, Italy, Spain, and South America—rather lost, by and large, their edge, declined or even withered, like Spain."[114]

10. Gedeon's Medieval Hellenism: The Zambelios–Paparrigopoulos Scheme and the Ottoman Divergence

On October 15, 1873, Gedeon delivered the opening speech at the newly formed Society of Medieval Studies. His lecture was published in the Constantinople daily *Chronos* and reprinted in Athens the following year as the first part of his *Medieval Anthology*.[115] The focus on the lecture's

114 Paparrigopoulos, *Istoria tou Ellinikou Ethnous*, vol. 3, 416. France was the only one among the Catholic countries that could be excluded from the rule. And yet in France the authority of the Catholic Church had already been severely curtailed.

115 Gedeon, *Mesaionika Analekta*, 3–32.

published version was not accidental because there was a fundamental difference between the delivered speech (aside from any "corrections" made in the interim): the references or "notes." Indeed, these annotations seem more important to the lecture's basic corpus because they reveal the "rifts" that were to emerge in Gedeon's historiographic perception later on. Naturally, the footnotes were added for the text's published version as is evident from the references to issues that emerged after Patriarch Joachim II's second rise to the patriarchal throne.

Reconstructing the political context for the text remains important for deciphering it. As of September 30 of the same year, Patriarch Anthimus VI, a member of the Mousouros family (and Stefan Vogoridi's former protégé), resigned. This opened the way for Joachim II's return and re-enthronement on November 23rd.[116] The Society's launch, thus, coincided with a critical period of intra-patriarchal conflict. Gedeon's initiative in founding this association must be linked to the comeback of the man he described as his spiritual mentor. The new patriarch's rise was, of course, the work of his political patrons—the group of bankers led by Georgios Zarifis and Christakis Zographos.

It is worth focusing attention on this seminal text for Gedeon's "career" in the Patriarchate as it appears to reflect the basic parameters of this political juncture. The lecture unfolded along two axes. First, it explicitly adopted the arguments of Greek Romantic nationalism on the issue of Byzantium's Hellenic identity. Second, it periodized the Greek Middle Ages, as Gedeon called this period. Typically, with regard to the first, the text featured numerous references and excerpts from the works of Paparrigopoulos (who was described as a "sage"), Zambelios, Sathas, and other European medievalists such as Amédée Thierry.

The issue of periodization that Gedeon broached deserves some interest. But what did he consider *medieval*? Oddly, in Gedeon's view, the term did not shed its negative connotations even when included in the historiographic narrative that legitimized continuity. The Middle Ages were "a period of darkness and devious days" with which every nation had to cope within its historical trajectory.[117] The idea that "each nation experi-

116 Stamatopoulos, "Orthodox Millet," 243–70.
117 Gedeon, *Mesaionika Analekta*, 6.

enced its own Middle Ages" allowed him to make yet another interesting statement: "The Middle Ages in general, in the opinion of other historians, ended at the time of the French Revolution in 1789, which is when the Greek Middle Ages end too."

These "Enlightenment legacies" reappear in Gedeon's subsequent work.[118] This is paradoxical because he did not seem to realize the contradiction of a "dark Middle Ages" that extended across the entire "lower years"—as he called Ottoman rule—and the cultural achievements of "medieval Hellenism" during the same period.

For him, the medieval period should be divided into three subperiods: ". . . the Hellenism after the fall, the Hellenism before the fall, or the Byzantine Middle Ages, whose beginning we set around the ninth century and which paves the way, so to speak, for the Hellenization of the state and spans the fourth to the ninth centuries."[119]

Gedeon consequently proposed a tripartite scheme for understanding medieval Hellenism comprised of a) the period from the fourth century to the ninth, during which the "Graeco-Roman" state was progressively Hellenized; b) the period spanning the ninth century to 1453, during which he considered as defining for the state's Hellenic character and its corresponding abandonment of its "Graeco-Roman" traits;[120] and, c) the third period that extended from the fall of Constantinople to 1789, the year of the French Revolution (given that for obvious reasons it was difficult for him to make direct reference to the 1821 Greek Revolution here). He considered this period "transitional" for the formation of neo-Hellenism, as Hellenism "lives . . . under the scepter of another religion, or even under a foreign rule, and under the roof of the Orthodox Church. . . ."

If the extension of the Greek Middle Ages to 1789 by the Ecumenical Patriarchate's future Great Chartophylax seems surprising, the attempt to insinuate the "homogeneity" of the Ottoman dynasty with its Byzantine-origin subjects is an even greater counterbalance.

118 See Iliou, "Pothos Martyriou," 267–84, in which Gedeon appears as the defender of a "rational religious position."

119 Gedeon, *Mesaionika Analekta*, 7.

120 According to Paparrigopoulos, Zenon the Isaurian (474–491) should be considered Byzantium's first "Greek" Emperor. Paparrigopoulos, *Istoria tou Ellinikou Ethnous*, vol. 3, 35–36.

For Gedeon, the importance of understanding medieval Hellenism—a task to be undertaken by society as a whole—was obvious given the "paradox of knowing your ancestors' (i.e., Ancient Greeks') days and deeds while ignoring those of our fathers whose sons we are." He described the Hellenization process in the Byzantine Empire's first phase in detail, offering many examples (from the Pandidakterion of Constantinople through the Hellenization of names and legislation). It is also interesting that he believed the terms "Hellene" and "ethnism" were legitimized during the second phase of medieval Hellenism's growth, although he did not distinguish whether this happened before or after the Frankish conquest of Constantinople.

He sought the causes of Constantinople's fall to the Ottomans in the decline of the "moral and material forces of the nation," the decrease in the Greek population, the empire's incompetence in negotiations with the pope, the peaking of "religious doctrine" (does he perhaps mean Hesychasm?), and the simultaneous deadening of religious sentiment.

Here, Gedeon did something particularly interesting that is common among several nineteenth-century writers: he discussed the historical problem of the extent to which the Byzantine Empire contributed to the West's evolution, if at all. Byzantium's legitimization, as it was well known, depended on the compatibility of its values with those of the West European civilization. He attempted to establish this link in a similar way to the basic coordinates of Paparrigopoulos's scheme:

> If, Gentlemen, in every nation, to the extent that for every nation there are four vital cultural elements—religion, science, art, and law—it is needless to point out that without Leo the Isaurian and Constantine V, Luther and Calvin, Zwingli and Melanchthon would be nothing or, at best, god-mongering sellers of indulgences and sly Franciscans. [But] without Fotios and Neilos Doxapatris, Pachymeris and Acropolites, Fournis and Kavasilas, Mark of Ephesus and Scholarios, the sixteenth-century reformists among whom, as is known, there were the Greeks, Melanchthon and Martinus Crusius may have been deprived of the weapons they bore in their brave struggle against the supercilious and despotic Rome.... (Gedeon, *Mesaionika Analekta*, 11–12)

Gedeon's turn of phrase is not impressive for his positive stance toward the great leaders of the Protestant Reformation, but mainly for his paradoxical perspective, that is, for an advocate of Orthodoxy.[121] His acknowledgment of the Iconoclast Emperors' positive role in this process—which, of course, bore the influence of Paparrigopoulos—were undermined by his reference to the great leaders of the Christian Orthodox world who were responsible for the schism with the Catholic West (e.g., Photios) and its deepening by the movement of Hesychasm (e.g., Kavasilas). In one way, the superficial acceptance of Paparrigopoulos's thesis allowed Gedeon to desecularize it.

After raising the same issue for the Byzantine jurists as he had already done for iconomach Emperors and the spiritual leaders of orthodoxy during the years of "decline," Gedeon pointed out that without them, "West and East, North and South would lack aspects of their civilization. For where else have the art and science, philosophy and the letters been preserved other than Byzantium?"

It is not simply that Byzantium's immigrant scholars contributed to the emergence of the renaissance, but that the very survival of the "nations" in the West was due to Byzantine Hellenism's resistance to Arab and Seljuk raiders. Gedeon referred to a French historian (whom he did not cite but may quite possibly have been Amédée Thierry) to pass the following judgement: Byzantium constituted a part of the West from the moment it halted the biggest attacks from the East at a time when the West was making the transition from the Middle Ages to modern times.

Which "nations" benefited from Byzantium's halting, even if temporarily, Asian barbarism? "The Germanic and in general the Western world that had trained the barbarian kings; the Ottomans and their rival Arabs who abolished the political state [Byzantine Hellenism] to which alone

121 However, we should not overlook the fact that one of Gedeon's most important works in the 1870s was his attempt to cleanse Cyril I Lucaris of any shadow of cooperation with the Protestants (Gedeon, *Kyrillos Loukaris*). This work (which follows the footsteps of Markos Renieris and Sophocles K. Oikonomou), although also published as a book in 1876, had first appeared as a series of newspaper articles in Omonoia in 1870. Even here, however, and taking the occasion of the defense of the Orthodox Church as catholic, he maintained that its universality was due to the fact that it "submits to truth and piety all people, favouring neither Scythians nor Greeks, distinguishing neither among peoples nor among races" (23).

they owe the intellectual brilliance and glory of Baghdad, Salerno, Cordoba; the Slavs, and finally, the Greeks."[122]

Employing the dominant paradigm constructed by Paparrigopoulos and Zambelios, Gedeon argued that religious sentiment and the broader role played by Orthodoxy contributed to Hellenism's survival as an "ethnicity" under Ottoman rule. And the reason should be obvious. At the same time, he recalled the work of historians like Thierry, George Finlay, and others, with the aim of supporting the scheme of the continuity of ancient and modern Hellenism as well as emphasizing the need for studying the medieval period, whether Byzantine or Ottoman. Nonetheless, he persisted on the point of the medieval Hellenism's privileged position regarding the Church, especially after the Fall of Constantinople. "What the land was for Antaeus, this Church and faith is for Hellenism." Indeed, Gedeon cited the work of "the celebrated expatriate Byzantinist" Zambelios to praise the Church's role and argue that "just as before, so after the Fall, it continues to contain and encompass the entire political, social, and intellectual life of our nation."[123]

For Gedeon, this argument was no reason for rejecting the Ottoman period but the opposite: it was a reason for incorporating it into the narrative of national continuity through the normalization of relations between conquerors and Hellenism. Hellenism did not simply survive within the structure provided by the Church, but what is more, the Ottoman state, and most notably Mehmed the Conqueror also adopted certain fundamental principles from the Greek *volksgeist*. Naturally, the Phanariot and neo-Phanariot families played a decisive role in the formulation of this argument. Indeed, Gedeon unabashedly stated that "many, after the conqueror, Sultans spoke in Greek and proclaimed it the official language of the state." Obviously, this was not just about the nation's survival within the Church, albeit within a foreign and hostile environment, but was nonetheless a step short of claiming that the Ottoman Empire

122 Gedeon, *Mesaionika Analekta*, 13.

123 Gedeon, *Mesaionika Analekta*, n17. The excerpt from Zambelios's notes that "the different phases in our Church…its course, its adventures, its blessings, may never be detached from our *genos*; for us, that is the law and the sole philosophical authority that regulates these faces of the Hellenic character within the embrace of this Orthodoxy, the Greek individual receives its first social and grammatological expression."

could have been compatible with Hellenism had it not been already Hellenized itself.

It is therefore obvious that Gedeon—and the majority of his published works support this argument—was not only interested in a Hellenized Byzantium but in a Hellenized Ottoman Empire (and, indeed, at the level of governance, not just cultural dominance). Here, one can see a definite and substantial divergence from the "Zambelios–Paparrigopoulos" scheme.

Having proved the Hellenization of Byzantium on the basis of the Hellenization of the names chosen by Byzantine scholars (for example, Nikolaos Chalkokondyles to Laonikos Chalkokondyles), Gedeon vividly described the Greek influences on Ottoman governance.

> Also, during this specific period, that is in the years after the Fall, it is worth noting the clearly observable impact of Hellenism on all who ruled. Mehmed II The Conqueror, the greatest king of the time, had an acute and political mentality, in his worldly mission, to the favor of the survival of our nation as provided by divine providence, something we have supported elsewhere, admittedly communicated in Greek; he employed Greek staff including his secretary Critobulus from Imbros, known by his Greek name, and the coins were stamped by his name. The pen of a Greek, and specifically that of Critobulus, who mimicked the writing style of Thucydides, narrated his deeds with the same care as if they were those of Phocas or Tzimiskes or other Greeks . . . Greeks also conducted the political and military affairs of the state in which the Grand Vezier Mesih (or Misac), of Palaiologean descent, and Amirouzis excelled, and later a long series of interpreters including the families of Kallimachis and Mavrokordatos, Nikousios and Mavrogenis, Soutsos and Aristarchis who with their political acuity and devotion to the throne of Sultan Fatih rescued the government from dire situations and freed the country through virtue in order to deliver it to their offspring, as the Olympian orator would have put it. Many, after the conqueror, Sultans spoke in Greek and proclaimed it the official language of the state. (Gedeon, *Mesaionika Analekta*, 18–19)

Accordingly, Byzantium not only saved Europe from the Seljuks (and the Arabs), but also favored the Ottomans' rise—as well as that of the

Germans, Slavs, and Greeks. While Byzantium was the bulwark against the East's expansion, as a cultural heritage it was itself transformed into its opposite: it becomes a Hellenized Ottoman Orient.

Finally, and despite its implicit reference to a "free homeland" (possibly the new Greek state), Gedeon emphasized the Phanariots' and neo-Phanariots' loyalty toward Ottoman authority. These contradictions in Gedeon's line of thought could not coexist if he had not adopted the position of continuity between Byzantium and the Ottoman Empire, a position that would quickly prove to have manifest consequences at the political level.

11. Footnotes: The Denunciation of Helleno-Orthodoxy

As mentioned earlier, this especially salient text for Gedeon's "academic" and political career should be evaluated based on its footnotes and annotations rather than on the main text itself. In the first, and lengthiest part, Gedeon outlined his views on the Schism's political context, that is, the Ecumenical Patriarchate's denunciation of the Bulgarian Exarchate two years earlier, in 1872. Gedeon seized the opportunity for some more general theoretical observations which objectively placed him on the side of the Schism's opponents—a position he would defend throughout his life.

Based on an analysis of the main text, one would expect Gedeon to have adopted a national historiographical narrative that was compatible with Paparrigopoulos's (or at least Zambelios's) scheme. In fact, he did the unexpected. Gedeon denounced the use of the term "Helleno-Orthodoxy" and its instigators as being synonymous with ethno-racism ("ethno-phyletism"). What could the term Helleno-Orthodoxy connote other than the dissolution of the Christian world by all manner of emerging nationalisms?

> . . . ridiculous are those who coined the terms Helleno-Orthodoxy, etc. As if the Church could ever be dismembered into so many names as there are races and into so many Orthodoxies as there are leaves and flowers . . . As if the Orthodox Church that the twelfth article of the credo defined as one, holy, universal, and apostolic Church did not exist. (Gedeon, *Mesaionika Analekta*, 25)

Gedeon believed that adopting such an "ethnophyletist" view actually constituted a "Judaic" influence. He also seems to have been in agreement with the notion of the chosen people, the core of many nineteenth-century nationalisms. Like all who fought the schism, his primary aim was to avoid a clash between the Greeks and Bulgarians that would inevitably undermine the Pan-Orthodox strategy that the Patriarchate would not abandon until the 1870s—and certainly had not been abandoned by the lay–clergy group led by Joachim II with whom Gedeon was allied. But his dissent on the issue of nationalism should not be examined only through the prism of the Patriarchate's internal disputes. It has also to be understood as a position adopted by someone who shared the Empire's perspective. This required the defense of religious ecumenism. Conversely, the instrumentalization of religion by nationalism was more than evident to this major intellectual of the nineteenth-century Patriarchate. Characteristically, Gedeon noted that "this very exclusionary spirit [of "Helleno-Orthodoxy"] produces a sort of potentially religious reverence toward ethnicism and not toward the Orthodox faith, that facilitates the growth of ethnicist sentiments and the weakening of the religious ones, as current events attest."[124]

But perhaps the most interesting aspect of his attack on "Helleno-Orthodoxy" remains that it appeared to make a clear reference to Helleno-Christianism, the term Zambelios introduced into the armory of Greek nationalism in 1852. Thus, even when using Zambelios against Paparrigopoulos, Gedeon was fully aware that the history of the *Genos* to which he was devoted did not correspond precisely with the new Greek historiography's invention of the totality of the nation.

12. Byzantium as a Metaphor: Greeks and Slavs

Gedeon did not explicitly dispute the model of the nation's continuity, although he rarely refered to Greek antiquity, which did not seem to interest him particularly. He was interested in reconstituting the continuity of Byzantine Hellenism with the Hellenism of the Ottoman Empire. Gedeon mentioned "Byzantine Greeks" and approached the Late

---

124 Gedeon, *Mesaionika Analekta*, 26.

Byzantine period as Greek. His early work "The Church's Work in the Adventures of Our Nation"[125] is vital for understanding his ideological bent. In Gedeon's own words, this text was intended as a section of a book to be titled "Greeks and Slavs," which "was a part of my medieval research as was my treatise, 'The Woman in the Iconoclast Discord,' which was published in the journal *Ecclesiastiki Alitheia*."[126] Although we know he never managed to publish this book, both texts must be examined within the framework of a comprehensive approach to Byzantium and its history. The first text was a peculiar allegorical "metaphor" on ways to improve the relationship between the Patriarchate and the Bulgarian Exarchate as this relationship had developed during the crucial 1880s, and the second a critical intervention in the reception of Byzantium by contemporary Greek historiography.

The Church's Work concerned Patriarch Nicholas I Mystikos's mediation between Romanos I Lekapenos (mentor of the then-minor Constantine VII Porphyrogenitus) and Tsar Symeon when he reached the walls of Constantinople in September 914. In letters to the Bulgarian king published by Mai and Migne and reprinted in the *Corpus Fontium Historiae Byzantinae*,[127] we see how Nicholas must have contributed to the peace reached between "Romanos and the rebellious Symeon."[128] The allegorical message of this reminder in the 1880s was quite clear: the Church, as usual, played the same role of peacemaker as it would now in the conflict between Greeks and Slavs (specifically, Bulgarians) in the Balkans. Nicholas's advice to the Bulgarian Tsar was similar to the style of counseling taken by the Great Church with the Bulgarians, at least as described by Gedeon:

> The beatific Patriarch's letters to Symeon, written, as he mentions in the fifth of them, not in ink but in tears, takes Symeon to task for annulling previous agreements and tries to reinstate the Bulgarian ruler to the path of political virtue and honesty . . . the good Patriarch

125 Gedeon, "To ergon tis ekklisias," 636–39.

126 Gedeon, "To ergon tis ekklisias," 639.

127 Mai, *Scriptorum veterum*, vol. 10; Migne, *Patrologiae cursus completus*, 163; Nicholas Mystikos, *Letters*, 26–80, 92–214.

128 Testimonies of chroniclers like Cedrenus, Logothetis, and especially Leo Grammaticus suggest direct mediation.

> advises this beloved son of Christ not to leave the name of a tyrant as his legacy. (*Ecclesiastiki Alitheia*, 3 [1883], 638)

Gedeon's text, of course, did not lack references to the "barbarian" invader and his ilk: "In the rest of this letter, the Patriarch expounds disadvantageous hostility between Greeks and Bulgarians, and eventually bows to the savage leader . . . " He also wrote: "How did the Bulgarian ruler respond, the heir of a vicious king, who called one of the good Byzantine Emperors a leather-eater?"

Symeon viewed Nicholas with disdain. In Nicholas's tenth letter, we learn that Symeon had called the Byzantine Patriarch a "moron." Yet, Nicholas persisted with his peacemaking interventions, a fact that further elevated him in Gedeon's estimation. Of course, his own descriptions of the Patriarch took on the character of ideological normalization; Gedeon mentioned that Nicholas advised Symeon not to gloat over his victories against the Byzantine troops and reminded him that the Bulgarians were "slaves of darkness and deception before we Orthodox Greeks taught them the true faith."[129]

Nonetheless, while the purpose of Gedeon's "translation" of Nicholas's words in the context of the national Romantic paradigm of the nineteenth century is clear, his goal was different: to suggest the Church as the only organization that could intercede to blunt the clashes between national (or ethnic) groups. While he admitted that Symeon eventually retreated from Constantinople's walls in exchange for financial gains (the amount or value is not made clear by the Byzantine chroniclers), he insisted that "the peace between Greeks and Bulgarians is the result of the Church's saving intervention on behalf of the state." The volume of the correspondence "sways" Symeon, who writes back that he would like to meet with the Patriarch. "Thus the Patriarch's victory is assured, while Nicholas thanks but also counsels and recommends."

129 Naturally, in all his correspondence, Nicholas referred to "*Romaics* and Bulgarians," "*Romaic* authority," "*Romaic* monarchy," etc. Nowhere did he mention "Orthodox Greeks." Also interesting is the fact that when *reasoning* with Symeon, Nicholas often used as an example the fate of the Persians in their clash with the Byzantine Empire in previous centuries. The issue of the Persians as opponents of Byzantium as well as Ancient Greek city-states would be utilized ideologically by various writers, from Leont'ev to Köprülü, as will be seen further on.

Gedeon's decision to use this incident as an example is not coincidental for another reason: Symeon's arrival at the walls of the New Rome was the Bulgarians' last attempt to take Constantinople. The dream of conquest was revived by the Bulgarian nationalists, who saw the establishment of the Bulgarian Exarchate in the Ottoman capital as a direct demand for not only ecclesiastical autonomy but also leadership over the Ecumenical Patriarchate.

That Christian love prevailed in a world of harsh state interests constituted the essence of an ecumenical discourse that emerged as the dominant narrative of the Great Church. Within this framework, national differences were recognized. The Christian Ecumene as conceived by the nineteenth century did not deny the validity of nations. This was not a crucible that integrated nations in a unified political/cultural community as was the eighteenth-century *millet*.

The Christian Ecumene emerged as a transcendent authority within which disputes were resolved through the Church's intervention, but whose axis has shifted from the religious to the national body. Yet, at the moment when the Middle Ages were being transformed through the emergence of nations, and despite the fact that they could not argue against this process, the defenders of the ecumenical model sought to preserve the predominance of the religious over the secular. This contradiction, which did not seem to have been apparent to them, is, from the point of view of Constantinople, the point on which they grounded their entire ideological structure. And this is evident in all of Gedeon's historiographical endeavors, especially during the second period when he would be called on to manage the Byzantine past as a basis for the securing of the patriarchal "privileges."

It is, however, certain that Gedeon was fully aware of the internal diversity of the Rum *millet* and the Greek Orthodox element's dominant position within it. Gedeon juxtaposed the meanings of the Romios (Rum) and the Hellene, believing them to have overlapped. In a very important article in the journal *Ecclesiastiki Alitheia* in which he presented unpublished material from the Patriarchal Archives on the growth of the Patriarchate's debt and the consequent intervention in the Patriarchate's internal affairs by the Ottoman authorities or the laity, he pointed out:

> The ugliness to which the Patriarchs fell prey arose and developed outside the Church hierarchy in the fold of a diverse community that presented itself to the authorities as a homogenous whole and race under the name of Rum. Greek or Bulgarian, Slav or Arab, Albanian or Armenian, whatever Orthodox populations were included in the ethnological family of the Romioi, either through their wealth or relations with the authorities, not only aspire to, but demand to become involved with the church administration in order to impose their will on it (*Ecclesiastiki Alitheia* [1880], 65).

This excerpt reveals Gedeon's broader world view. The term *Romios* did not necessarily represent a homogenizing cultural melting pot in which various ethnic groups lost their respective characteristics. Nonetheless, the choice of Ottoman authority to project "Greek identity" tended to render the Romioi a single "ethnological family." But no matter what relationship existed between the "civil society (*koinonia politike*) of the Greeks," to recall Katartzis and the ethnoglossic groups comprising it, for Gedeon it was the leadership of the "Church administration" that seems to have been at stake. This seems to be resisting efforts by financially and socially powerful members of the lay strata to seize it.

Gedeon therefore projected the form through which he established his political activity and scientific interventions at the end of the nineteenth century across the entire history of the Rum millet. By highlighting the history of the *millet/genos*, he addressed not only the issue of normative ethics (so that past mistakes were not repeated) but also the issue of political practice, with the aim of subordinating the lay element to the Church hierarchy's priorities, thereby preserving the latter's privileges.[130] This is very important because the re-establishment of the dominance of the Church over the nation's "civil society" in the late nineteenth century was itself a deviation from the canon of producing national ideology (and national history). The treatment of this issue by Zambelios and Paparrigopoulos proves that the Helleno-Christian ideal did not reserve a leadership role for the Church's representatives on the canvas of the nation—just a relationship of subordination.[131]

---

130 *Ecclesiastiki Alitheia*, 1 (1880), 65.

131 The canon seems to have forced Gedeon to correct himself. While, at the beginning of the text, he included the interference of powerful Greeks in the Patriarchate's internal affairs and described var-

13. The Iconoclast Byzantium and the Break from Greek Historiography

In order to explore the extent to which the ecumenical structure Gedeon represents was compatible with the model of the Greek national narrative, we need to pay attention to the Gedeon of the 1880s (and not the early-twentieth-century Gedeon speaking about his old self).

If there was one thing that Gedeon repeated systematically during his long presence in the Patriarchate's intellectual life, it was the reconstitution of the Orthodox *millet*. From the very moment that he was appointed editor of the journal *Ecclesiastiki Alitheia*, he systematically published historical documents from the patriarchal archives about either Phanariot society or patriarchal activities (often in response to criticisms about particular persons). His work essentially aimed at salvaging the *millet*'s reputation. This unavoidably leads to the question: was the memory of the Orthodox *millet/genos* being identified with that of the "nation"? The normalization of his work in the latter half of the 1930s is not particularly helpful on this point. We need to take a more careful look at some of his intercessions during his tenure as editor of *Ecclesiastiki Alitheia*. Let us look at some of his writings, specifically a series of articles he wrote in 1883, one year after becoming editor, under the title "Woman in the Iconoclast Discord."

The series was ostensibly about the role of the great Byzantine empresses like Zoe and Irene during Iconoclasm. But Gedeon, somewhat unexpectedly, launched a direct attack on Konstantinos Paparrigopoulos.[132] We reiterate: the works of Konstantinos Paparrigopoulos and Spyridon Zambelios constructed the dominant narrative of the continuity of Greek

ious instances of divergence (for example, the disfigurement of Joasaph I Kokkas by the Sultan for not approving the wedding of the Protovestiarios, or highest financial officer, from Trebizond and the imposition of the *peşkeş*, or gift, as a result of his fall from the patriarchal throne and his succession by Raphael I, a Serb), Gedeon returned to the issue of interference to make the following correction, perhaps out of a feeling of guilt for his earlier observation: "At the beginning of this article, we showed that responsibility for these unfortunate affairs could not be placed on either our leaders or the Greek race, who exclusively bear the title of Romios which in later years was expanded. Our claim was based on what history attested. See *Ecclesiastiki Alitheia* 1 (1880), 66. As to whether the accusations against Raphael I the Serb for the institutionalization of the *peşkeş* constitute proof of a clash among ethnic groups in a pre-modern environment, see also Chassiotis, *Apo tin "Anarrosin"*.

132 *Ecclesiastiki Alitheia* 3 (1883), 277–81, esp. 279.

history from antiquity to modern times on the basis of the idea of "Helleno-Christianism." Their major contribution was the incorporation of Byzantium into this narrative. Byzantium was no longer the obscurantist and despotic Eastern state rejected with great aversion by the representatives of the European (mainly French) Enlightenment. It was a glorious moment of "ecumenization" of the Ancient Greek spirit within, of course, the Roman civil structure, with Christianity as the agent for cleansing its pagan origins. Recalling the impact of German Romanticism on the re-legitimization of "dark" medieval times may be considered superfluous. But from the moment Byzantium was included in the national narrative, wouldn't this fact suffice to make the project totally acceptable by the patriarchal world—the natural successor of the Byzantine Empire within the Ottoman Empire? However, the Patriarchate and the world of the Helleno-Ottoman bankers and traders rejected Byzantium's incorporation into the dominant Greek nationalist narrative, and not only because of the grandiose ambitions of the Greek state against the Ottoman Empire.

Gedeon attacked Paparrigopoulos using the pretext of the Greek historian's description of an incident involving the Patriarch Tarasios's attempt to convene the Seventh Ecumenical Council in Constantinople, although it eventually took place in Bithynia's Nicaea.[133] Paparrigopoulos believed the Iconoclasts would have the majority in Constantinople and that Tarasios was forced to peacefully dissolve that Council. He underlined that on that day, it was unequivocally proved that the supporters of the Reformation were "materially and morally" far more powerful, regardless of Patriarch Tarasios's stature. Paparrigopoulos supported this position by offering an excerpt written by the chronicler Theophanes.

According to Paparrigopoulos, Theophanes, while a supporter of the Iconolaters, was forced to accept the reformers' "moderate" and positive disposition given that even though they had the upper hand at the Council, they did not try to force decisions. But Gedeon interpreted the passage differently as he deemed that "the bright Theophanes is slandered by Paparrigopoulos."[134] This is because Theophanes mentioned something

133 Paparrigopoulos, *Istoria tou Ellinikou Ethnous*, vol. 3, 552.
134 *Ecclesiastiki Alitheia* 3 (1883), 279.

that Paparrigopoulos omits: that the Iconoclast soldiers "unsheathed their swords" and threatened the lives of the Patriarch and senior clergy, so this conclave was not exactly peaceful.

Of course, Gedeon's attack on Paparrigopoulos was not only a result of Paparrigopoulos's supposed misreading of Theophanes. The chronicler was a contemporary of the events he described and a very important source whose importance Paparrigopoulos acknowledged in various points of his *History*. But the problem with Theophanes—as with Cedrenus or Nikephoros and the other chroniclers of those times—was that they were aligned with the Iconolaters and were prejudiced against their enemies.

The attack launched by the Gedeon concerned Paparrigopoulos's critical stance on—or distortion of—Theophanes's text. But in reality, Gedeon appears to have a problem with Paparrigopoulos's overall interpretation of this period. As has been seen, Paparrigopoulos showed greater leniency toward the Iconoclast Emperors Leo III and his son Constantine V. He believed that their bad image, especially Constantine's, was the result of Iconoclast chroniclers like Theophanes and Nikephoros. But in addition, we have also seen that Paparrigopoulos's basic position on Iconoclasm was encapsulated in the term he used to describe it: Reformation.

Paparrigopoulos claimed that if further proof of the Reformation's necessity was required, it would focus on the state's desperate condition in the wake of Empress Irene's attempt to reverse the work of Leo III and Constantine V.[135] Obviously, this is not about restoring images. If the restoration of images as institutionalized by the Seventh Ecumenical Council did not in any way offend the basic principles of the Reformation, then what exactly does Papaprigopoulos mean by this term?

> Reforms, imposing a daring hand on all those faults that undermine the material, moral, and intellectual strength of society, attempted, as it seems, aside from the banning of icons and the restriction of the use of holy relics, to curb the number of monasteries and impose a levy on church and monastic estates, to remove the clergy from public education, abolish serfdom, limit slavery, establish religious tolerance

135 Paparrigopoulos, *Istoria tou Ellinikou Ethnous*, vol. III.,, 539–41.

> (especially towards marriage and, occasionally, to the icons' issue) and not content with this, to legislate and rule in a way that sought to form a new society, on the basis of noble and nation-centered dispositions. (Paparrigopoulos, *Istoria tou Ellinikou Ethnous*, vol. 3, 418–19)

To state the obvious, the Byzantium that the Isaurians envisaged was not exactly that which a man of the Patriarchate such as Gedeon would have dreamt of.

Paparrigopoulos's interpretation of Iconoclasm as Reformation actually corresponded to a comprehensive reinterpretation of Byzantine history: Paparrigopoulos, for obvious reasons, could not do more than this since on the icon issue, what he described as reform constituted no more than the need to make Byzantium palatable to the West. But such a perspective would retroactively have vindicated Iconoclasm—not only on the issue of the icons but with regard to the hegemonic role accorded to the clergy in Byzantine society after the Seventh Ecumenical Council—and this could not be acceptable to the Patriarchate. This was especially true given that what Paparrigopoulos dubs "reform" was in many ways similar to what the Ottoman Empire tried to enforce during the Tanzimat. This was the reason it was necessary to emphasize that the insistence on pursuing Pan-Orthodox policies had as a consequence moderate openings toward the Slav Orthodox churches and also set as a prerequisite the *millet* form of internal administration in which the Orthodox clergy preserved its privileged position over the lay element.

The interpretation of Byzantium proposed by Greek "Romantic" nationalism could not be accepted even though the Romantic paradigm was adopted in the re-reading of history from the *millet*'s perspective. Paparrigopoulos's Byzantium differed from Gedeon's: whereas the former sought to erase the West's negative connotations, the latter understood the Byzantine tradition in the resolution imposed by the ending of Iconoclasm, which was symbolically associated with the primacy accorded to the clergy and particularly its more advanced segment, monasticism.

Of course, Gedeon consistently condemned heresies in his work. In his inaugural speech at the Pavlos Antoniades School in 1877, he presented the Greek people, or more precisely the Greek "*genos*/millet," as the historical servant of Christianity.

> Open the holy scripts and memoirs of the lives of saints, flip through our national history from Christ to the present day and each page teaches us nothing but that over the long period of eighteen-hundred years, our people, the Greek *genos,* which in precious blood supported the seven-pillared Church, a structure established by the God-man savior through his death at horrific Golgotha, this Greek *genos* painted the Church's untainted vestment with blood so that Arians and Macedonians and Slav Bogomils sought to rip the Lord's cloth. The instigators of all there is through its (god-spoken) language trumpeted the Councils and displayed as trophies its curses against schisms and heresies. (Gedeon, *Logos Eisagogikos,* 5)

On the other hand, Gedeon's ambition of achieving historical objectivity often forced him to detach himself from the judgments of the Byzantine chroniclers, especially on some surprising issues such as that of Julian the Apostate. In a series of articles for *Ecclesiastiki Alitheia,* he commented on Archmandrite Philaretos Vafiades's (and later Bishop of Melnik) newly published *Ecclestiastic History* (which took an anti-Joachimist line). With regards to Julian, he commented:

> From the fourth century until the present, the chroniclers' fanaticism rabidly opposed the early Emperors of the Eastern state through cursing and the use of harsh expressions, a disgusting mass was compiled against Julian the Apostate. Not content with attaching the appellations of Apostate and Violator, Symeon the Metaphrast, Cedrenus, Manassis, Theophanes, Amartolos called him a believer of many faiths, deaf, faith-changer, deadly, vain, evil, infected, sacrilegious, demonic, hated by god, atheist, miserable, cruel, unmasked, sinful, hedonistic, irreverent, inert, dabbling in magic, disrespectful, god-bashing, Idololatric, clay-covered "whose impiety has shaken the world"; the charming Amartolos even euphemizes his name, *eidolianos* [idol in Greek; Julian is Ioulianos]. We do not wish to say anything now, but reason dictates that we "say that the Apostate was judged very harshly and cruelly. In his private life, he was virtuous. He loathed profligacy, the opulence of the Byzantine palace, and maliciousness; he disliked the large entourage of eunuchs as being a student of our history,

> he knows the awful damage caused through their influence, in the philosopher Emperor . . . No one denies that the Apostate has often taken inappropriate action, perhaps exceeding his authorities out of Christian zeal . . . (*Ecclesiastiki Alitheia* 4, [1884], 153).

Gedeon's critique of Julian was similar in structure to Paparrigopoulos's judgement of the iconomachic Emperors. An Emperor whose rejection was based on Orthodox Christian morals was restored in the reader's conscience. But it was particularly interesting that Gedeon denied this "restoration" for the advocates of the "Monophysitist" version of Christianity while accepting it for the emperor identified with idolatry's return. For him, the return to the Ancient Greek world did not harbor as many dangers as subjugating religion to the state, as heralded by the iconomachic Emperors.[136]

14. Byzantium as a Metonymy: The Church and the Ottoman State

Gedeon's second period, which as we seen above was marked by severe tensions between Patriarch Joachim's supporters and his opponents, focused on history: patriarchal biographies, historical documents on the Patriarchate's Byzantine and especially Ottoman periods, and even the histories of Constantinople's churches. This preoccupation with history at times seems to have been an outlet, if not an escape, from harsh political realities for a man who experienced events at the Patriarchate in a dramatic manner. However, in this period's last phase, during Joachim III's second reign and especially after the Young Turks' Revolution, Gedeon composed and published a series of works that were intensely political.

The first of these was published on January 1, 1908 (that is, before the Young Turk revolution) and was a collection of documents on the Bulgarian Question—a work whose publication was no doubt prompted by the persecution of the Greek populations in Eastern Rumelia and cities around the Black Sea. Three more works followed in 1909 and 1910, respectively, each dealing with the key issue of "privileges" accorded by the Sublime Porte to the Ecumenical Patriarchate. The *Brief Note* (1909)

136 See also Zambelios, *Asmata Dimotika*, 99–102.

and especially *Official Correspondence* and the *Phases of the Church Question* (1910) were apologetic. And while the first two titles were published with "the blessing and urging of His All Holiness Ecumenical Patriarch Joachim III," the third appears to have been Gedeon's personal initiative[137] and contained a theoretical legitimization of the archival material (authentic or not) edited by Gedeon in the first two titles.

In these works, Gedeon made extensive reference to the Byzantine period and relations between Church and state, using metonymic motifs to directly or indirectly approach the major political problem of the time: the Young Turks' challenge of the privileges of the Ecumenical Patriarchate. For Gedeon, the dilemma of whether the Patriarchate should "preserve or rebuild" the privileges was moot.[138] In discussing the issue at the level of Church–state relations, he raised, perhaps more vehemently than ever before, the issue of continuity between the Byzantine and Ottoman Empires.

In *Brief Note*, Gedeon made a substantive distinction between "privileges" and "rights," a distinction that was fundamental for his political project.[139] The distinction seems to have been at the expense of the privileges and, to a considerable extent, was aligned with the political orientation of the Patriarchs Joachim II and Joachim III. "Privileges" qua historical remnants were destined to eclipse. By contrast, rights were "sound and immutable," (11) although they were limited to the freedom to worship. At this level, the first "continuity" between the Byzantine and Ottoman periods was identified:

> The study of history reveals that the Church enjoyed [the freedom of worship] from the times of Constantine—who was equal to apostles—to the collapse of the Byzantine Empire. During this period, the Church was self-governed, set laws and institutions for the faithful to live by and to organize the relations amongst themselves, their rank, secular and spiritual authorities and God. (Gedeon, *Vracheia simeiosis*, 12)

137 See Gedeon's introduction to *Phases*, 5.

138 See Konortas, "I exelixi ton 'ekklisiastikon' veration kai to Pronomiako zitima," 259–86, on Metropolitan Leontios of Larissa's supposed *berat* (tax exemption). This was published by Gedeon in *Vracheia simeiosis peri ton ekklesiastikon imon dikaion*, 66–72.

139 Gedeon, *Vracheia simeiosis*, 8–10.

By invoking Mattheos Vlastaris's *Constitution*, Gedeon attempted to ground the state's "eudemonia" on "the dual nature of man": king and patriarch qua personifications of secular and spiritual authority should be in "unanimity and harmony" for the state's good.

His analysis of the "rights" enjoyed by the Church under the Byzantine Emperors concentrated on the Orthodox clergy's jurisdictions (which concerned mainly misdemeanors committed by the clergy), the right to freely practice Christian worship, the jurisdictions granted on matters of family law, and the right to maintain charities and schools.[140]

According to Gedeon, the only Emperors who tried to challenge the Church's right to organize education were the Iconoclasts: they sought to "secularize" education and make it "God-free", while, according to Balsamon, the Iconoclasts' insistence that the state be made responsible for supervising and running schools "infuriated" the people.[141] But the Iconoclast period was only an exception to the rule. And the rule in Byzantium, according to Gedeon, was the recognition of the Church's autonomy by the secular authorities, although he had to admit they often interfered, for example in patriarchal elections. But even when individuals paid the price, "the institutions were preserved."

The Ottoman Empire only wanted to preserve ("almost") the equality in the relationship between secular and religious power that existed in Byzantium. A constitutive continuity between the two empires, thus, existed, although the examples Gedeon employed as illustration of this, for example, Omar's *ahidnâme* after conquering Jerusalem, were more relevant to Arab Islam than to Ottoman.

Gedeon's *Brief Note* did not aim at reaffirming the issue of continuity between the Byzantine and Ottoman Empires but actually organized a set of rules governing the relationship between the state and the Church, which Byzantium supposedly represents—rules which should be followed by a Muslim state such as the Ottoman Empire. Given the privileges, it was even more necessary than before for the Ottoman Empire to commit to past precedent. Where its own past offered insufficient precedent,

140 See Gedeon's views on the existence of "a great ecumenical school" in Constantinople as well as on the establishment of a university after the final restoration of the icons by the Emperors Michael and Theodora, and the foundation of a new university a century later. Ibid., 37.

141 Ibid., 39.

for obvious reasons it was necessary to reconstruct the Ottoman Empire's relationship with Byzantium, a relationship that was being jeopardized by the ideologies of Pan-Islamism and Pan-Turkism. If reference to Byzantium established a metonymic relationship between the Byzantine and Ottoman pasts, a reminder of the Iconoclast Emperors' role constituted a reference point for any potentially similar behavior toward the Great Church of Christ on the part of the Young Turk administration.[142]

Paradoxically, while this was the spirit that permeated the works commissioned by Joachim (*Brief Note* and *Correspondence*), its theoretical legitimization in the *Phases* diverged from the rule.

The problem posed by Gedeon's analysis was that if the issue raised was not patriarchal "rights" but the participation or interference by the lay (or imperial) element in the institution of the Church, then things were reversed: Byzantium could be seen as a negative example of continuous interference while the Ottoman period could be seen as a rather idyllic one for the internal affairs of the Church.

> The rivalry between the secular and the divine authority, that is, the State and the Church, in common parlance, seems to have been spawned by Constantine the Great, who convened the First Council of Nicaea to end the religious discord, as he assumed for himself, according to the Roman doctrine, the right to manage issues of faith since the Roman Caesars treated this doctrine as imperishable. (Gedeon, *Ai Phaseis*, 6–7)

Censuring such behavior was, for Gedeon, an inviolable condition for the defense of the Christian Church against both those who shared the same faith and those of different faiths.

> No matter what the historiographer Eusebius Pamphili (of Caesarea) had in mind in seeking to vindicate Constantine, it seems to me groundless as that is the spirit of the Roman caesarocracy. (7)

142 Gedeon, *Ai Phaseis tou par'imin ekklesiastikou zitimatos*, 18–19, for the passage on the Iconoclast Emperors' policies and the Church's resistance to reform, and parallels to resistance in the context of similar conditions in Gedeon's time ("today").

According to Gedeon, the "caesarocracy" was founded on the fact that in "old Rome," the Emperors were both High Priests and Kings. For Constantine and his successors, it was very hard to shed the title of Pontifex Maximus, which perpetuated the conflation of secular Christian authority with religious authority. No attempt was made to delineate authorities until after Gratian (375–383), and during the reign of Ambrosius of Mediolanum (374–397), and, especially, under his successor Theodosius I the Great. Gedeon drew a parallel between Ambrosius's resistance to Valentinian's order, at the instigation of his mother Justina, to cede two churches to the Arians and "the resistance by the Church today in our issue," clearly alluding to the Bulgarian Exarchate's claims to a number of churches. Gratian's renunciation of the title of Pontifex Maximus and Theodosius the Great's acknowledgment of the discrete roles of Emperor and High Priest formed the model for the coexistence of the two authorities in Byzantium.

In Gedeon's view, the key to understanding the way in which the issue of Church–state relations was resolved was Byzantium's "Hellenization." This helped transcend the blurred boundaries between the Pontifex Maximus and imperial power and, consequently, allowed the relationship between the Emperor and the Patriarch to be understood as coequal. It is interesting that Gedeon did not miss the opportunity to retroactively attack Theoklitos Pharmakides, the main instigator of the establishment of a nationalized Church in Greece, who, in his *Synodic Volume or about Truth*, argued that the state model was predominant in Byzantine history and insisted that it was founded during the reign of Constantine.[143]

In fact, the point of contention Pharmakides had been forced to deal with by his main opponent, Konstantinos Oikonomos, who wanted to preserve the organic relations between the Greek Autocephalous Church and the "Mother Church," the Ecumenical Patriarchate: should the coexistence of civil and religious society be resolved by the latter's subordination to the former (as Pharmakides, contended) or was "the Church not a state within a state but a soul within a body" (as Konstantinos Oikonomos argued)? Gedeon's goal to ensure that the pattern established by nation-states that had emerged from the empire's gradual dissolution was

143 Gedeon, *Ai Phaseis*, 11n9.

not repeated made him turn to the ideological armory of those opposing a state-centered approach to the Church. However, they—in particular, Paparrigopoulos— were also the same who had legitimized Iconoclasm, the period that had altered Byzantium's character.

Nonetheless, while Gedeon's position on the supposedly harmonious relationship between Church and state in Byzantium was outlined in absolute terms, his subsequent narrative suggested the opposite. Gedeon recalled a succession of crises between these two institutions following Iconoclasm. A series of interferences in the Church's internal affairs were described, from Nikephoros Phokas to Alexios I Komnenos[144] and Andronikos Palaiologos, that Gedeon's historiographical consciousness cannot mute. And while in theory Gedeon sought to legitimize the existence of "privileges" or "rights," in reality, his historical review proved that issues like the adjudication of cases involving the clergy had always been a source of conflict between Church and state.

It is also interesting that when his narrative reached the period of Ottoman rule, in which he took for granted the Sultans' (especially Mehmed the Conqueror's) respect for "privileges," he tried to transform the relative disadvantage of the Church's claims—that is, the lack of recognition of legal public entities—into an advantage. Indeed, the Ottoman state accepted the privileges by awarding *berats* without this preventing it from waiving its trust toward particular persons while preserving the privileges of the institutions themselves:

> We know of examples of Muslim leaders who interfered unlawfully, and the state respected the Church administration's law-abiding resistance. This may have inflicted damages, many not one, on those clerics who resisted the unlawful decrees of the secular authorities. And yet their rage fell upon the shoulders of individuals and not holy institutions. (Gedeon, *Ai Phaseis*, 52)

For Gedeon, the Phanariot period contributed to the expansion of rights since they worked "for their own material gain." Indeed, from the time of Patriarch Samuel I (Hançerli) in the late eighteenth century

144 See also Gedeon, *I proti peri*.

to Gregory V's successive patriarchies in the early nineteenth century, Gedeon identified a broadening of the Church's jurisdiction, including not only the adjudication of cases between Christians, clergy and/or the laity, but even Muslim suits against Christians and disputes over trade.

Conversely, during the nineteenth century, Gedeon observed two attempts by the Ottoman state to interfere in the internal affairs of the Church, although one could, in actual fact, refer to these examples of interference as "reforms" in the context of the Tanzimat. These reforms aimed chiefly at institutionalizing lay involvement in the Patriarchate's administration and the patriarch's election. Gedeon considered these reforms unacceptable because they undermined the "ancient regime" of the Church, an order that rested on the two pillars of Gerontism and of the guilds. Gedeon usually tried to interpret such developments through a recourse to conspiracy theories, for example as a consequence of Napoleon III's politics. Yet, in this work, for the first time, he lay the blame on direct interference by the Ottoman state apparatus, even naming specific persons such as Sultan Abdülmecid,[145] and in several instances, the Great Vizier Âli Pasha (72). He saw the culmination of this interference in the issue of the firman of 1870 allowing the establishment of the Bulgarian Exarchate (74).

In this political text written in 1910 under intense pressure from the Young Turks administration to have the "privileges of the Great Church" abolished, Gedeon appeared to opt for a break with the Ottoman past, unlike his earlier writings. Was his aim a "nationalization" of the millet and correspondingly a nationalized reading of the Ottoman past? In fact, the opposite seems to have been more likely. Gedeon criticized the nineteenth-century period of reforms, drawing an image of a mythologized Ottoman past in which the Church managed to retain its power within the state despite obstacles and difficulties. The nostalgia-filled descriptions of patriarchal enthronements constitute a typical example of this idealization.[146]

But the Patriarchate and the Rum millet were not alone in reacting to the Ottoman state's dissolution. All ethnic/religious groups of the empire

145 Even if Gedeon did so indirectly. See Gedeon, *Ai Phaseis*, 61–67. For example, he considered unacceptable the guidelines sent by the Sublime Porte, under the aegis of the Sultan, by which the National Assembly of 1858–1860 was convened.

146 Gedeon, *Ai Phaseis*, 69.

recognized as millet by the Ottoman authorities reacted also: "neither Armenians, nor Bulgarians, nor Christians of another denomination, nor Israelites approved in any way the change or weakening of the privileges they had been granted." According to Gedeon, the Iconoclasts' rationale was being revived once more through the Young Turks' interference.

15. Ecumenism as a Romantic Reconstruction

Gedeon chose to use the Byzantine past, as metonym or as metaphor, either to support the clergy's primacy in safeguarding the unity of the Orthodox ecumene, or to legitimize through history the privileges that were under attack due to successive mutations of Ottoman imperial ideology. Under these circumstances, rejecting a Westernized Byzantium compatible with the Tanzimat reforms and their successive transformations seemed natural. But the question remains whether in his perception of Byzantium through the prism of Greek Romantic nationalism, Gedeon was also rejecting Romanticism as a broader ideological current for comprehending the contemporary world?

If we followed the positivist and rationalist account of Gedeon provided by Philipos Iliou, we might perhaps answer this question affirmatively.[147] Gedeon's methodology in terms of his "objective" use of sources was up to the standards of nineteenth-century historical Positivism. But if we look more carefully at the broader ideological project that he was committed to, the defense of Orthodox ecumenicity, then our conclusion might be different. To proceed with our analysis, we need to clarify the ecumenist ideology, especially as our position that it sheltered a Romantic reconstruction of mutually exclusive strategies can be applied to other defenders of the imperial scheme examined in this book (Gedeon, Krâstevich, Leont'ev, and the early Şemseddin Sami).

The Christian Ecumene was the natural seamless domain of the Patriarchate's ideological influence up until the collapse of the empire, even though the schism with the Western world and Rome led to its identification with the Orthodox Christian East. The Byzantine Empire's succession by the Ottomans in the Balkans and Middle East changed the

147 Iliou, "Pothos Martyriou."

Patriarchates rules of operation without, however, forcing it to shed its fundamental right to invoke ecumenicity—namely, the ideological and political unity of the Orthodox flock of the now Ottoman East. And this can, of course, be accounted for by the fact that, ultimately, ecumenicity corresponded to an imperial state structure, it was, in other words, the cultural crystallization by means of which the Empire apprehended its relationship with space and time. The Christian Ecumene provided the connecting link between linguistically and ethnically diverse populations, completing the periphery's control by the center—a fundamental ingredient of any imperial political structure.

This political and cultural function, which can be traced historically, was also absolutely vital within the Ottoman Empire. The only instance in which ecumenicity was challenged was not by the Catholic and Protestant West, which had followed a different course, but by Russia. The ideology of a Third Rome accompanying the shift of the Russian Empire's center of gravity from Kiev to Moscow not only raised the issue of the recognition of church independence but also of the founding of a new patriarchate that would represent the millions of Orthodox in the Russian north.[148]

An effort was made to preserve this arrangement in the Patriarchate's relationship with the new autocephalous churches that emerged during the course of the nineteenth century as a result of national revolutions in the Balkans. Indeed, the crisis in relations with the Greek Autocephalous Church ended in 1850, with latter's formal plea for recognition, while the proposed resolution of the Bulgarian case was based on the concept of an "Exarchate"—that is, the founding of a church organization spiritually dependent on the Patriarchate.

The Greek and Serb national revolutions in the nineteenth century and the developing nationalist movements of Romanians, Bulgarians, and Albanians created the circumstances for the splintering of the unified orthodox ecumene represented by the Patriarchate within the framework

148 The Patriarchate of Constantinople under Jeremiah II the Great had indeed recognized the Moscow Bishopric as a patriarchate, although it ranked it fifth in the hierarchy, not only under Constantinople but also below the Orthodox Patriarchates of Alexandria, Jerusalem, and Antioch. The effort to balance relations between the two Orthodox worlds seemed the only way for the Orthodox world to appear united. But from the moment that the Patriarchate remained the highest authority from which any new church organization drew legitimacy, the principle of ecumenism (ecumenicity) could theoretically be preserved.

of the Ottoman Empire.[149] The Orthodox Ecumene's breakup found its counterpart in the splintering of the Orthodox millet. Thus, it should not be a surprise that the religious question of the Patriarchate's relations with the new churches reflected a severe political problem: the dilemma over the preservation of the Ottoman Empire itself, given that the Orthodox populations comprised the overwhelming majority of non-Muslims in its European territories.

Crucially, this dramatic moment—essentially, the long nineteenth century—in which individual and social subjects had to deal with the dilemma of founding new national states or maintaining old imperial structures (as if these state forms could be compatible with the principle of national self-determination), heralded the rethinking of the basic components of the ideology of ecumenism.

Preserving the Ottoman Empire meant identifying with ideological projects like Ottomanism and Pan-Islamism.[150] Preserving the Orthodox *Ecumene* meant maintaining the bonds of the Ottoman Empire's orthodox populations with the Slavs in the Balkans and Russia. These two projects, which, in middle of the nineteenth century seemed mutually exclusive, by its end appeared compatible under certain conditions.[151]

Indeed, Joachim's second term (1901–1912) was very important for solidifying the ecumenical structure. For the first time after the adoption of the General Regulations, a Patriarch was to remain on his throne for eleven years and, indeed, until his death. Joachim enjoyed the respect not only of the Greek, Austrian, and Russian Embassies but of the Hamidian regime as well. His good relations with the Hamidian regime were presumed: since his enthronement in 1878, he had had the favor of Georgios Zarifis, the Sultan's personal banker who was highly influential in Constantinople's financial circles in the late nineteenth century. Drawing upon Konstantinos Spanoudis's now classic treatise [152] on Joachim's second patriarchy, which began in 1901, it might seem easy to conclude that Leonidas

149 Kitromilides, "Imagined Communities," 149–92.

150 The notion that the Christian ecumene was established as a counterpart to the Islamic ummah is interesting, to say the least. It is outlined by Charisios Vamvakas, a Greek member of the Ottoman Parliament in 1910. See Skopetea, "Oi Ellines," 25. See also Anagnostopoulou, "Millet, Genos, Ethnos," 37–55.

151 Stamatopoulos, "Orthodox Millet," 201–24.

152 Spanoudis, *Istorikes selides*.

Zarifis, Georgios's son, continued to support Joachim unconditionally, and that the Patriarch's relationship with the Zarifis family remained unbroken. So, emphasizing the link between the Patriarchate's ecumenical ideology (as it crystallized between and during this great Patriarch's reigns), and the dominant ideology of the Hamidian regime, seems reasonable. Nonetheless, a number of logical inconsistencies can be detected.

It would be somewhat risky to claim that the ecumenical ideology derives from a relatively limited period at the Ottoman Empire's end. A timeline is, of course, necessary to avoid the generalizations inherent in adopting a fundamental "antinomy between Orthodoxy and Nationalism."[153] Indeed, the existence of a fundamental antinomy would make it hard to explore the complexity of their relations in the nineteenth century. This applies to both nationalist projects' instrumentalization of Orthodoxy and to the Orthodox clergy's equivalent effort to maintain either within the empire or within nation-states, the privilege of political intervention which they had attained in earlier centuries.

Nonetheless, the Pan-Orthodox dimension constituted a basic characteristic of ecumenical ideology. As such, the invocation of Orthodox unity did not concern only populations inside the Ottoman Empire's borders but also the Orthodox populations of Southeastern Europe as well as the Middle East. The Orthodox world could not exclude the Slavic Orthodox, especially the Russian Orthodox. Consequently, a genealogical examination of the Orthodox world might simulate the Ummah,[154] but it would rather focus on the rivalry within it, that is, the struggle for its leadership between Constantinople and Moscow. The ideology of ecumenism, therefore, could not be interpreted solely as an intellectual endeavor during the Pan-Islamic period. We must also trace its formation back in time to the end of the Greek War of Independence and the Treaty of Hünkâr İskelesi (when Russia strengthened its foothold inside the Empire) but mainly after the end of the Crimean War and the formation of a group of clergy with Pan-Orthodox orientations under Joachim II (to which Joachim III also belonged).[155]

153 Kitromilides, "Imagined Communities."

154 Even such a Turkish nationalist as Ziya Gökalp made the distinction between Islamic and Christian Ummah when attempting to analyze the gradual transition from religious consciousness to national self-determination. See Gökalp, *Principles of Turkism*, 90.

155 Georgios Zarifis's involvement in the Patriarchate's inner workings dates from the 1850s. He and

Another logical inconsistency in the view that ecumenism was merely a version of the dominant state ideology concerned its audience. The function ecumenism served within the dominant political framework was not self-evident, unlike in the case of Pan-Islamism which served as a strategic project for preserving the empire through its large Muslim populations. The invocation of Orthodox ecumenism did not necessarily aim at those Orthodox who remained within the empire, given that the circle of national movements in the Orthodox Balkans had virtually closed. The possibility that it may have been directed at the Greeks within the Empire seems meaningless, for this would imply that it sought to convey latent irredentist messages; after all, there were strong ethnocentric circles in Constantinople and other cities who could do this more effectively.

If the ecumenical ideology corresponded to the needs of a state ideology such as Pan-Islamism, its purpose was not to undermine the Ottoman state's unity but rather to marginalize those political circles threatening it. Ecumenism had to be understood as the strategic marginalization of extreme nationalists, not just the Bulgarians or Romanians but Greeks as well. This is the reason its emergence as the main element in patriarchal ideology should be sought in the era before the Hamidian regime.

For events leading to the Schism of 1872, adequate explanation has been proffered as to why traditional factions of the Patriarchate conceded to a solution pushed by nationalist hardliners.[156] This could be regarded as schismatic in the proclamation of Exarchate supporters as well as in the denunciation of the heresy of "ethno-phyletism."[157] It would also become evident in the adoption of selected extreme nationalist arguments against the Bulgarians that would allow for Joachim II's triumphal return to the patriarchal throne the following year (1873). His return, however, was not

Christakis Zographos (both formerly pro-Russian) succeeded Ioannis Psycharis, the (formerly pro-French) Chios bey, as leaders of an interest group. The clergy was represented in the group by then-Metropolitan Joachim of Cyzicus and later Patriarch Joachim II, mentor of Joachim III. The ideological consolidation of ecumenism also involved the fraction of clergy under the pro-Russian Patriarch Gregory VI, protégé of the Grand Logothete Nikolaos Aristarchis. Intellectuals among the clergy from both these groups helped shape the ecumenical ideology, most notably Philotheos Vryennios from the first group and Efstathios Kleovoulos from the second. See Stamatopoulos, *Metarrhythmisi kai Ekkosmikefsi*.

156 Stamatopoulos, "Bulgarian Schism," 105–25.

157 Stamatopoulos, *Metarrhythmisi kai Ekkosmikefsi*, 325–44, 360–67.

marked by a tough stance against the Bulgarians or Russia, as some of his late supporters might have expected. Quite the contrary: he followed an overtly pro-Russian policy until his death in 1878. The patriarchy of his protégé, Joachim III, was merely a continuation of this policy, that is, a peculiar combination of a Pan-Orthodox and, thus, pro-Slav policy, who enjoyed the simultaneous political support of the Ottoman state. This group's political orientation would be confirmed by its opponents: the Greek state's irredentist foreign policy and, domestically, the fierce opposition mounted by the Greek Embassy of Constantinople and the radical nationalists grouped around the newspaper *Neologos* who stood against the possibility that Joachim would return to the patriarchal throne.

The two inconsistencies in interpreting ecumenism as a product of state ideology described above can be summarized as follows: first, underestimating a factor like the Pan-Orthodox dimension; and second, overlooking the internal tensions within the Patriarchate and consequently lacking comprehension of the different versions of the dominant discourse employed by rival factions. But the true dimensions of these inconsistencies may have been even greater. With regard to the first, while ecumenism was a hegemonic strategy for dealing with the arguments of Bulgarian and Romanian nationalism, it also constituted an attempt to marginalize the extreme ethnocentric elements in the Greek Orthodox community. The question that needs to be addressed is why ecumenism appeared as an alternate version of nationalism.

I believe this occurred precisely because it reproduced a dominant Romantic motif—the unification of two mutually exclusive projects. It resulted from the management of two fundamental strategies' split—Pan-Orthodox and imperial—by building a monist structure of ideologization and idealization of the millet's past.

Here we should take a moment to explain the meaning of Romanticism, the problem of its theoretical definition as greater than that of ecumenism given that it constitutes an inextricable part of the entire European philosophical tradition.

From Arthur Lovejoy to Isaiah Berlin, there have been attempts to offer a comprehensive definition of all ideological or artistic currents dubbed Romantic in Western Europe (Germany, England, France). This theoretical weakness led to attempts at comparative analyses, with Lilian

R. Furst's work playing a principal role.[158] Nonetheless, the dominant view was that this was an essentially literary or artistic movement of the European center until the 1820s, when it was transported to the periphery in the 1830s where it dominated until the 1880s as political Romanticism (primarily through the effects of German Romanticism and the successful political endeavor of German unification).

Specialized research on this issue suggests that purely Romantic motifs are rare in peripheral literatures, especially those of the Balkans' (where it was more common to find a blend of Romantic and Classicist motifs). Undoubtedly, Romanticism played a definitive role in the political expression of peripheral nationalisms, although its influence varied. Consistent elements running through the predominant narratives in Balkan historiographies included the construction of schemes of historical continuity; the mythologization of the past and the reification of collective subjects in a way that was similar to the reification of individuals and their passions and sentiments.

Nonetheless, Romantic motifs should not be unilaterally linked to nationalism. As Michael Löwy's analyses show,[159] Romanticism infiltrated the critical ideological movements of the nineteenth century to such an extent that their messianic character can be attributed to its influence. If we wanted to codify the Romantic motif—beyond or including its different manifestations in literature and politics, or as a trend in nationalism or socialism in the European center and periphery—we would say that that it appealed to a typically lost unity. This is the reason for nostalgia being key to its comprehension. The appeal to unity can be seen as a critique of the long Cartesian tradition that split the world in two: reason and passions, *res extensa* and *res cogitans*, nature and humankind, and, ultimately, subject and object. The romantic heritage should not be reduced to the *volksgeist* philosophy heralded in the late eighteenth century by the works of Herder, Fichte, Hegel and Hölderlin but can be traced back to a monistic Spinozian perception of the world.

158 For the difficulties in "defining Romanticism," see Berlin, *Roots of Romanticism*. See also Lovejoy, "Meaning of Romanticism," and *Revolt against Dualism*; Furst, *Romanticism in Perspective*; and Löwy and Sayre, *Revolt and Melancholy*.

159 Löwy and Sayre, *Revolt and Melancholy*.

Clashes between the advocates and the opponents of the Romantic paradigm were the order of the day in many discussions among the members of the Greek Literary Society in Constantinople.[160] Nevertheless, the dominant paradigm of "political Romanticism" or "Romantic nationalism" does not seem to have had a direct impact on the representatives of the radical nationalists, as might have been expected. Broadly speaking, Romantic ideals among the neo-Phanariots and Greek Orthodox scholars were accepted warily because these challenged the widely accepted nineteenth-century rules of civic ethos formation and led to the legitimation of irredentist visions. As we noticed above, the Greek Literary Society's first honorary membership was conferred on Saint-Marc Girardin, a staunch critic of the French Romantics who had been targeted by Paparrigopoulos's criticism a few years earlier.[161] Even Vasiadis, one of the Society's most prominent founders and a representative of its radical ethnocentric current, despite his selective use of Herder, chose a blend of Romantic and Classical patterns in his indirect defense of the continuity of the Greek ethnos.[162]

Although the Romantic motifs were exorcised from the secular political field, they do appear to have drastically influenced how the intellectuals defending the Patriarchate's role in the new era understood the past and the future of the Genos—the Orthodox millet. Thus, the issue of unity in space and time promoted by the Romantic ideal corresponded to an attempt to verify the Patriarchate's primacy in an inexorably fragmented space (in other words, from the Pan-Orthodox perspective) and a corresponding effort to understand the transition from the Byzantine to the Ottoman Empire as smooth.[163]

Manuel Gedeon's work has become a reference point for examining these two versions of the ecumenical scheme (pan-Orthodox and imperial) and the ways in which these were accommodated by the Patriarchate in the transition from the nineteenth to the twentieth century.

---

160 See Stamatopoulos, "From Cratylus to Herder," 254–64.

161 Stamatopoulos, "Neophanariotes," 41–55. On his disagreement with Victor Hugo, see for example, Labitte "Ecrivains critiques."

162 Stamatopoulos, "From Cratylus to Herder," 256–58.

163 The legitimation of the "privileges" supposedly granted by the Conqueror to Gennadius II Scholarios, Patriarch of Constantinople, was a key point for understanding the Patriarchate's position in the Empire, whose unity the Patriarchate defended to the degree that the Empire guaranteed these privileges.

In his *What I Witnessed*, Gedeon employed this phrase to describe Joachim III whom he served with devotion for many years: "He was an Ecumenical Patriarch, he was a Greek Patriarch."[164]

Many of these identifications of the ecumenical ideology with versions of Greek nationalism stemmed from some excerpts from Gedeon's work. Yet, both the phrase quoted above and other references that appear to support the view of the millet's "Hellenization" must be examined with a critical eye. The above work, like Gedeon's other works, was published in Athens after he had left the Patriarchate and Constantinople in the 1930s, at a time when Greece's national ideology was undergoing a fundamental review that included a debate on the Byzantine question. Gedeon as a source must, therefore, be examined against the period in which he was writing: Gedeon in the 1930s was, for obvious reasons, trying to soften ecumenism's anti-nationalist dimension.[165]

Even so, one can find indisputable evidence of Joachim III's pro-Russian—Pan-Orthodox—orientation during both his Patriarchies. Any analysis that portrays him solely as a product of Pan-Islamic policy underestimates this dimension. The Orthodox Ecumene did not necessarily seek to simulate the Islamic Ummah but to bridge the gap that separated it from the Orthodox Slavs. Gedeon typically wrote: "I was a friend of the Russians [read: Pro-Russian Patriarchs], like Joachim II and Joachim II."[166] This statement may be considered quite revealing of ecumenism's Pan-Orthodox content.

Another incident suggests that this stance reflected the attitude of the Patriarchate's entire leadership and not just the Patriarch's personal obsession.[167] In 1906, amid the Macedonian Struggle, Joachim commissioned a committee to publish political articles. At one of its meetings, the Patriarch began outlining his views on the need for articles censuring

164 Gedeon, *Mneia*, 263.

165 Chrysanthos Philipidis, later Metropolitan of Trebizond, shed light on the difference between Gedeon in the 1930s and Gedeon as editor of *Ecclesiastiki Alitheia*, of which Phlipides was appointed archivist and co-editor by Joachim. In his memoirs, he noted that Gedeon was "a difficult colleague but adapted to reality." See *Ecclesiastiki Alitheia* 1 (1880), LVI. Gedeon's adaptation to reality was not painless and his resistance can be detected in references to ecumenism's Pan-Orthodox character in his later works.

166 Gedeon, *Mneia*, 224.

167 Ibid., 252–53.

the Bulgarian priests "because they had been ordained by defrocked and excommunicated priests, and the Bulgarian people must be informed because its priests are no longer members of the priesthood, thus the people are neither baptized nor wed because the priests were ordained by people who were not members of the priesthood." Noting the incident, Gedeon also commented on Joachim: "Occasionally Joachim thought of things that had not taken place and made up irrational judgements." Indeed, in the ensuing discussion, Gedeon expressed the opinion that such an article could not be published in the Patriarchate's official paper, *Ecclesiastiki Alitheia*, as it deviated from orthodox dogma.

> Your All Holiness. The Patriarchate's official newspaper cannot support such teaching that is alien or foreign to the official doctrine. Who teaches that defrocking waives priesthood? That is not waived by either defrocking or excommunication or even marriage after ordainment. Priesthood, Your All Holiness, is ineradicable.

Archimandrite Kallinikos Delikanis echoed Gedeon's views. Asked by the Patriarch to explain "why the Church defrocks," Gedeon replied: "I do not know why it defrocks. Nor has any Ecumenical Council removed the priesthood from those it has excommunicated itself nor has Your All Holiness in the past insisted on the notion that defrocking removes the priesthood." Joachim accepted Gedeon's syllogism.

What is interesting about this incident is not that Joachim softened his position toward the Bulgarians, but that these old opponents of the schism and supporters of the Pan-Orthodox current completely controlled the ideological orientation of the patriarchal leadership. Especially interesting was the fact that the Pan-Orthodox current had as its basis a clergy-centric interpretation—if the priesthood was ineradicable, then the schism was essentially meaningless.

To make this historicist reading of a Romantic argument more readily understood it is worth mentioning another incident from Gedeon's autobiographical notes that may be considered fairly typical of the Patriarchate's ideological orientation.

The Patriarchy of Dionysius V (1887–1891) took place between Joachim III's two patriarchies during which the—according to Joachim's supporters, disastrous—decision was taken to close Christian churches in the fall of 1890. Gedeon managed to win Dionysius's trust and keep his post as director of *Ecclesiastiki Alitheia*. By his own admission, the patriarch was neither pro-Russian nor pro-Greek. According to Gedeon, Dionysius remained loyal to Ottoman legality and, indeed, at the height of the Privileges issue—that is, during the period when Orthodox churches were closed on the Ecumenical Council's orders—he had an open communication channel with the Sublime Porte.

The incident described below took place during Dionysius's term.[168] The Phanariot Greek politician and diplomat Alexandros Rizos Rangavis asked the Patriarch to certify his family's "imperial line of descent" so his daughter could be wed to a Russian count who insisted that his wife must be of imperial lineage. Dionysius sought Gedeon's opinion, who replied:

"My Despot, old phanariots told me that the line of Rizos comes from their fathers and the line of Rangavis from their mothers. Therefore, there are others as well like Neroulos Rizos or Manen Rizos, the doctor. Now, they want, I heard, the Patriarchate to certify their imperial lineage. But is it in our interest to certify imaginary lineages?"

To which Dionysius replied: "Take away this family tree . . . and relieve me of this annoyance. . . . The Patriarchate will not be turned into a marriage brokerage!"

Gedeon, thus, undertook the task of writing an expert opinion which stated that there was no evidence of any imperial lineage in the Ragavi family.

It is interesting that the Patriarchate, the true heir of the imperial heritage in a manner of speaking, refused to certify the "fake" connection to its medieval past that the nascent Greek state's envoy was so anxious to establish. The Patriarchate's relationship to Byzantium was quite different to that being constructed by the emergent Greek national irredentism. Rangavis's reason for requesting certification of "imperial lineage"—marriage to a Russian aristocrat—should be considered even more interesting. If the canceled match recalled Zoe–Sofia Paleologue's wedding to Ivan III the Great on which the Russian imperial ideology of a Third Rome was based, we might claim that, once again, the Patriarchate not only reserved the

168 Gedeon, *Mneia,* 231–32.

monopoly over the ideological use of the Byzantine past but also sought to ensure the unity of the orthodox Ecumene, not certifying fake aristocratic lineage but acting as an intermediary between the Greeks and Russians.

In summary, we might say that the Patriarchate's invocation of an Orthodox ecumene that had taken shape in the nineteenth century assumed the form of a modern ideology whose functionality was to offset threats to the unity of the Orthodox flock and, by extension, to the imperial unity posed by national irredentist visions in the Balkans. In the context of the Tanzimat, which triggered a secularization process, the ecumenist ideology was closely associated with the argument that the clergy must retain the dominant role it occupied in the Orthodox millet and with models of patriarchal centralization as expressed by Gregory VI, Joachim II, and Joachim III.

Of course, we must emphasize that during Joachim's first period of dominance, the demand for the unity of the Pan-Orthodox and Imperial dimensions acquired a utopian character in reality. Conversely, in his second patriarchy, it seems that the utopian character of the ecumenical composition was taken for granted, and yet the new geopolitical conditions—peace signed between Russia and the Ottoman Empire in 1894, Greece's defeat in the 1897 war, and the concomitant collapse of the irredentist visions of the Great Idea—allowed the deployment of the Patriarchate's new ecumenical ideology. Manuel Gedeon and his work consequently played a catalytic role in the theoretical crystallization of a new hegemonic discourse.

16. Histories of the Ottoman Empire

In the fifth and final volume of his *History of the Greek Nation*, Paparrigopoulos described Ottoman rule and offered his views as to whether the Fall of Constantinople could have been averted. He believed that not only could the West have prevented Southeastern Europe's conquest by the Turks but that it could have also helped found a Christian state to succeed the Byzantine one in these areas. As with his views of heresies as central to Hellenism's survival within Byzantium, where he rushed to assuage any suspicions religious readers might have had, Paparrigopoulos was quick to add that such a new state would not have become puppet of "the high priest of Rome." Nonetheless, the new state could have been a very interesting combination of the "ancient" and "modern" worlds, the worlds of Orthodoxy and Catholicism; in other words, it could have operated as an interesting experiment where the schism's removal would not be considered in both religious and cultural terms.

> We claim that Western Europe committed a huge mistake by not trying to topple Ottoman rule in order to found a large and strong Christian state in the East, a state that feels the need to come to terms with the Orthodox Church, to respect the peculiarities of its native populations, to incorporate them in the army and administration, and transmit to them the spirit of modern civilization while also benefiting from their experience of governance and intellectual traditions. From such a combination there would be a gradual union of the ancient and modern worlds, a state that the native monarchy in Constantinople strove for one thousand years to shape but failed as a result of continual opposition which, paradoxically, included Western Europe from the eleventh century onwards. (Paparrigopoulos, *Istoria tou Ellinikou Ethnous*, vol. 5, 473.)

The symbolic confrontation between Paparrigopoulos and Gedeon was not exhausted in an a posteriori identification with the Iconoclasts' or the Iconolaters' arguments, respectively. On the contrary, it extended to an equally critical Byzantine dispute directly linked to their assessments of what they believed the Ottoman Empire had been—the battle between Unionists and Anti-Unionists. Paparrigopoulos's identification with Unionist arguments went beyond averting the danger of Byzantium's collapse. Resorting to the West's arms would not just have been a solution of convenience. It would have constituted a great opportunity to overcome the Schism between East and West. This was also an opportunity for Paparrigopoulos to express the view that Byzantium had tried to resolve this immense problem internally. Indeed, Paparrigopoulos argued that the Church of Constantinople represented the Byzantine imperial heritage within the Ottoman Empire.[169]

169 Paparrigopoulos simultaneously adopted two positions on the Patriarchate of Constantinople's position within the Ottoman Empire. Neither necessarily contradicted his overall structure. These views were at the core of the "traditional" and "modern" historiographical interpretations of the Ottoman

Gedeon, therefore, had more reasons than Dimaras assumed to attack Paparrigopoulos over the fifth volume of his *History*. The belated alignment with the positions of the Unionists or the Anti-Unionists concealed a fundamental difference in how they perceived "continuity." Paparrigopoulos's scheme posited the continuity of the nation between two empires, with the transitional phase between the two perceived as catastrophe, as a "discontinuity." Conversely, in Gedeon the problem is shifted: continuity existed not in the sense of the nation's survival in a different state structure but rather as the continuity of the two empires. The transition between the two empires is viewed as smooth rather than catastrophic. And this, Gedeon's position, was already made manifest in his opening lecture at the Association of Medieval Studies conference.

The Ottomans' arrival was understood in one case as a catastrophe and in the other as divine providence.[170] In reality, what distinguished these two approaches was, for the most part, their interpretation of the Ottoman Empire's essence. Gedeon was not the only Greek Orthodox of the Ottoman state to confront this problem. In the last quarter of the nineteenth century, several *Histories of the Ottoman Empire* were published after years of being overshadowed by the works of Hammer and Zinkeisen.[171] These *Tales* were published mainly as teaching aids for Greek Orthodox communities, and it is worth briefly examining three of these.

Empire. On one hand, therefore, Paparrigopoulos saw the Patriarch as an "ethnarch" Through the privileges he won from the Sublime Porte, "the Patriarch became, as the Ottoman government said, an 'ethnarch,' the supreme church but also largely political authority of the nation." Having made the mistranslation of *milletbaşi* to *ethnarch*, he added: "And because then, and until the end, no ethnic distinction was made against non-Muslim subjects but everyone was called Romaioi, the Patriarchate's authority extended throughout the Orthodox Christian world of the East, not only over the Greeks but also to the Albanians, Bulgarians, Serbs, and other Slavs, and the Armenians." Paparrigopoulos, *Istoria tou Ellinikou Ethnous*, vol. 5, 510. Thus, by covering the full spectrum of interpretations of the terms *millet* and *nation*, Paparrigopoulos really assumed the position of a "national" historiographer. Just as he described the millet as supranational, he subordinated it to the "national" supervision of the patriarchate. From this perspective, he expressed another view on the Patriarchate's role as the continuation of the Byzantine imperial heritage, a view that was to be reproduced in a partially altered form by contemporary Greek historiography. "In general, the office of the head of the Church, after the fall, enjoyed, at least *superficially/in terms of its external characteristics*, a status similar or even higher than it enjoyed during the Byzantine Empire, as Meletius Mitrou pointed out in the eighteenth century. But even in earlier times, patriarchal history affirmed that people worshipped the patriarch as supreme ruler and king." (510). On the relationship between imperial and Church ideology before the Fall of Constantinople, see Kiousopoulou, *Vasilefs h Oikonomos*.

170 Argyriou, *Exégèses grecques*; Kariotoglou, *Islam kai christianiki chrismologia*.

171 Hammer-Purgstall, *Geschichte des osmanischen Reiches*. The work was translated several times

In 1874, in Izmir (Smyrna), the first volume of a *History of the Ottoman Empire* by the brothers Minas and Christos Hamoudopoulos was published.[172] Minas later moved to Thessaloniki where he became the director of *Ecclesiastiki Alitheia* until May 1883, when he was replaced by Gedeon.[173] This change of guard—from the more "ethnocentric" investigator of history from Smyrna to the more "ecumenist" rival from Constantinople—was prompted by personal rivalries as well as the political line of the Patriarchate's official newspaper, and it foreshadowed the impending clash over the Privileges Question.

In their introduction, the Hamoudopoulos brothers stated that they had undertaken this task because there was no Greek-language history of the "Ottoman state," whose fortunes were so entwined with that of the Greeks. The Hamoudopoulos brothers were aware of European scholars' works on the Ottoman state, including those by Hammer,[174] and perhaps even a planned Greek translation which had been in the works since 1870. Addressing a Greek readership, however, the Hamoudopouloses departed from the usual timeline of these works, which began with Osman as the start of the Ottoman dynasty, as they believed the late Byzantine state should be examined in tandem, because the reasons for [ottoman] dominance and the end of the Byzantine monarchy, which the Ottomans succeeded, lay in the detailed examination of events that had taken place since the beginning of the tenth century and the appearance of the Osmanlı (i.e., *Oghuz Turks*).[175]

The Hamoudopoulos brothers began their *History* with a review of the Turks' origins. Similarly to Paparrigopoulos, they approached the mythological genealogies with caution and identified the Turkish progenitor with Herodotus's Targitaos and Japeth's son Thergama (Togarmah) from *Genesis*. While they felt obliged to mention the old Western tradition (Aeneas Sylvius) that identified the Turks with the Trojans (with Teucer and Hector as their supposed genarchs), they were inclined to identify the Turks

into English and French. Its translation into Greek triggered the publication of numerous history sourcebooks. Zinkeisen, *Geschichte des osmanischen Reiches*.

172 Chamoudopoulos and Chamoudopoulos, *Istoria tis Othomanikis Aftokratorias*, vol. I.

173 *Ecclesiastiki Alitheia*, 1 (1880), XXIII.

174 Indeed, they cited as their main sources the following works: Byzantine Chroniclers, Hammer's *History*, but also Ottoman histories such as Lufti Efendi's, Ahmed Cevdet Pasha's *Tarih-i-Cevdet*, and Hayrullah Efendi's, *Devlet-i-Aliyeyi Osmaniye tarihi*.

175 Chamoudopoulos and Chamoudopoulos, *Istoria tis Othomanikis Aftokratorias*, A–B.

with either the Tatars from the Volga or the Mongol tribes of Central Asia. Their critiques stemmed from this position as they distanced themselves from Byzantine writers such as Chalkokondyles who identified the Turks with peoples like the Persians, Hungarians, Scythians, and Parthians.[176]

But the reference to the Turks' distant future and their excursus through various theories seeking to find the cradle of their civilization provides the Hamoudopoulos brothers with the pretext for discussing the earliest relations between Greeks and Turks, relations which they date back to Alexander the Great. "When the Greeks, fulfilling their great mission, conquered Asia and civilized it, on the Sogdia steppes, in the Turan desert, they came across the ancestors of the Turks who tried to halt the great Greek hero's victorious march."[177]

According to this approach, the Turks did not emerge in the eleventh century but constituted a part of Greek antiquity as rivals of the Macedonians. Before appearing as Oghuz, Seljuk, or Ottoman, they had existed as Sodgians. Their clash with the Macedonians, however, did not take place so much on a military but rather on a cultural level. Greeks and Romans were the nations chosen by divine Providence in antiquity to achieve its goals: "for both, their mission was to conquer and via conquest to unite." The Roman conquest, however, would appear to have had an exclusively "material" nature. Conversely, the Greek conquest was "immaterial" and "intellectual," something to which the Hamoudopoulos brothers attributed Alexander's benevolent civilizing of conquered peoples. It was under Macedonian influence that the Sogdians, "the Ottomans' ancestors," abandoned barbarian customs such as throwing the sick to the dogs and the forced starvation of those over the age of seventy.

The Byzantine Empire was to have a similar civilizing effect on the Turkish tribes within its reach. The Hamoudopouloses dedicated a large part of the first volume—chapters six through twelve—to Byzantium's waning centuries, with frequent reference to Paparrigopoulos's work (as well as to Zambelios's), completely adopting the scheme of Iconoclasm as reform.[178] In their narrative, the transition from Byzantine to Ottoman rule was not smooth. Hellenism was the last driving force for defending

176 Ibid., 2–3.
177 Ibid., 7.
178 Ibid., 144–45.

the Byzantine monarchy against the Turkish threat, as in Zambelios's scheme. And if in the end Hellenism did not succeed, this was due to "wounds" delivered by the West, just as had been the case in Paparrigopoulos's scheme.[179]

A few years later, Georgios Katselidis published a *Concise History of the Ottoman Empire* in Athens.[180] This volume by the former publisher of the patriarchal newspaper *Omonoia* was released with permission from the Ottoman Ministry of Public Education and the Patriarchate's Central Education Committee "for use in schools."[181] Katselidis was, of course, aware of the translation of Hammer's work, but he considered it too unwieldy due to its size and too expensive for pupils attending Greek Orthodox schools. While claiming to have taken it into account in writing his own work, Katselidis nonetheless admitted that his main reference was the far more concise *History* written by Louis Charles Collas.[182] He also asked Greek readers for their indulgence and reminded them that "the book was published in Turkey about Turkey, where there is censorship which was exercised energetically at the time of approval, due to which the final version of the book hardly looks like the submitted manuscript."

In his narrative, Katselidis categorized the Turks as Tatars. He briefly described their clashes with the "Graeco-Roman Empire" and organized his narrative around the most significant sultans. The person-centric narrative allowed him to refer to a series of anecdotal incidents that in the spirit of the times made it more suitable for textbook use. He did not neglect to emphasize issues like Mehmed II's granting of "privileges" to the "Greeks,"[183] or the organization of the Janissaries' battalions. The "Greeks" had the right of self-organization in communities and of maintaining "their own militia," the Armatoloi. Although their "privileges" were occasionally threatened, they were never abolished "thanks to the prudence and modesty of the state's wise counsel" (25).

Katselidis somewhat abruptly switched to the Ottoman Empire's "Classical period," the rule of Selim I and Süleyman I (to whom he

179 Ibid., 147.
180 Katselidis, *Epitomos Istoria*.
181 See Stamatopoulos, *Metarrhythmisi kai Ekkosmikefsi*.
182 Collas, *Histoire de l'Empire Ottoman*.
183 Katselidis, *Epitomos Istoria*, 21–22.

dedicated paeans) and to the largely failed reform attempts of the early nineteenth-century sultans (Selim III and Mahmoud II) without any detailed reference to what is usually described as the empire's "Revolution." Yet, he immediately followed this with a chapter on the Greek Revolution (75–85), which may be considered rather odd for a book destined to be used as a textbook in the Ottoman Empire and submitted to the censors for approval. Of course, he counterbalanced this by following chapter with one on the dismantling of the Janissaries and the origins of the Tanzimat reforms. This may have been the reason for the book's eventual publication in Athens.

One year later, the Patriarchate's Central Education Committee approved the publication of another *Concise Ottoman History* written by Ioannis P. Miliopoulos, a member of the Translators' Bureau and a "book reviewer of the Ottoman Customs Service," the censorship agency to which Katselidis implicitly but unmistakably referred.[184] Indeed, Miliopoulos's book also gained approval from the Ministry of Public Education.

In the introduction, Miliopoulos laid out his intent in writing the book: "Ottoman history, since it was our destiny to be linked to this state, *comprising with the Turks of one and the same people*, benefits equally the Greeks as it does the Turks" [emphasis added]. And to prevent any doubts, he added: "Political, social, ethical, spiritual, commercial bonds, bonds of morals and traditions, always linked both peoples."[185]

Miliopoulos saw the need for mandatory teaching of Ottoman history in schools, by analogy to the gradual shift from the voluntary to mandatory teaching of the Ottoman language. He openly defended the assimilatory effect of teaching Ottoman to an inherently multiethnic and multilingual society, by citing the benefits reaped by Greeks who spoke Turkish.

> The idea that the learning of this language is useless and insurmountably difficult, due to lack of vowels, has eclipsed not only among the literate youth but the majority of the national population. Nowadays, things have fortunately changed since we have identified our destiny

184 Miliopoulos, *Epitomi tis Othomanikis Historias.*

185 Ibid., ii.

> and our political and private interests with theirs and live under the aegis of people-loving and holy rulers, like the respectable Emperor Abdoul Hamid Khan II, and enjoy his care and protection, we ought, out of necessity, to learn the language of our rulers. The learning of this language, as history testifies, has offered to our fellow subjects great political service and excellent future [career] prospects (Miliopoulos, *Epitomi tis Othomanikis Historias*, ii–iii).

Professional ambitions and prospects of social mobility were not the only reasons Miliopoulos advocated the mandatory teaching of the Ottoman language in schools. A mix of Arabic, Persian, and Tatar, the Ottoman language had been used to record many "legacies" of world culture.

> [It] has picked up the sweetest honey from the most beautiful flowers, all the beauty of these three languages. Some of the "jewels" of world civilization, poetry as well as important treatises on history, philosophy, and ethics, are written in the Ottoman language.[186]

But there were even more pressing and important reasons. A sequence of historical events, clashes, alliances, and especially institutions, civil and political, brought together "both [peoples] in one body, one home and one interest."[187] The political agenda behind his writing of the *Concise History* is now more than clear.

Similar to Katselidis, Miliopoulos believed that the only "complete" and "perfect" history of the Ottoman Empire was the one which had been written "in German," that is, Hammer's. And like Katselidis, he found it too *cumbersome and expensive* to be taught in schools. Miliopoulos stated that his own book was based mainly on the works of Ottoman writers, without mentioning specific writers as the Hamoudopoulos brothers had done.

It is not essential to analyze the body of Miliopoulos' work. His political aim, inscribed at it was in the Hamidian version of the Greek–Ottoman paradigm, was outlined clearly in his introduction rather than

186 Miliopoulos himself had published Greek–Turkish and Turkish–Greek dialogues and extracts from Turkish and Greek poetry, writings on philosophy, etc.

187 Miliopoulos, *Epitomi tis Othomanikis Historias*, iv.

concealed in the narrative, as was (for obvious reasons) the case with Katselidis. But it is worth noting an element that could become a measure for comparison with the other histories of the Ottoman Empire examined here: Miliopoulos's handling of the issue of the Ottomans' origin. While he too ventured back to Herodotus (Targitaos) and the Bible (Thergama), connecting the Turks to the Trojans and repeating the mistakes of Byzantine writers, he outlined a novel theory not dissimilar to the Kemalist historians of the 1930s, as we examine below. "We reject the opinion of many earlier writers that the Turks are part of the Mongol race as they belong to the Caucasian race but are not included in its Indo-German subcategory as they constitute their own branch."[188]

Even at the level of managing the Ottoman past, organic intellectuals of the Greek Orthodox community adopted all possible positions on a spectrum of political goals, from the most ethnocentric (such as the Hamoudopoulos brothers and Katselidis) to the identification with the attempt to salvage the empire (such as Miliopoulos). This review contributes to our understanding of Gedeon's position on this spectrum: Gedeon and the Patriarchate seem to have identified with Miliopoulos's political orientation. But Gedeon never resorted to a theory of origins to solve the problem of shared interests with the Ottoman state. Gedeon's endeavor was far more refined, precisely because he wanted it to be hegemonic in the face of ethnocentric readings and interpretations of the Ottoman past.

188 Ibid., 13.

Chapter III

The "Medieval Antiquity" of Bulgarian Historiography

1. The Canon of Bulgarian Historiography: The Origin Model

It is widely known that there is a Promethean moment in Bulgarian historiography: the publication of Paisi's *Slavo-Bulgarian History*, which he wrote on Mount Athos in 1762,[1] that is, almost simultaneously with the origin of what we call the Neo-Hellenic Enlightenment. This work, however, was not published until 1844 and then only in Budapest, although by that time it circulated widely as a manuscript.[2] Yet even twenty-five years after its publication, its influence had been negligible in shaping the modern Bulgarian national consciousness.

As with the political sanctification of Rigas Ferraios and Adamantios Korais in Greece around roughly the same period, this nineteenth-century innovative figure came into the limelight at a time of internal strife among the generation of intellectuals representing the spiritual movement of the Bulgarian renaissance. In fact, at the risk of sounding foolish, the discovery of Paisius may be considered more important than the discovery of the importance of Bulgaria's medieval past by him.

Gavril Krâstevich, one of the most powerful Bulgarian neo-Phanariots in Constantinople, was the first to make extensive references to Paisius in an 1859 article published in his magazine. However, it was the Bulgarian historian Marin Drinov who has, for the most part, been viewed as

1 For a description of the intellectual environment in which Paisius's work was published, see Genchev, *Bâlgarskoto Vâzrazhdane*, 86–92.

2 On this issue, see Konstantakopoulou, *I Elliniki glossa sta Balkania*, 123n2; Aretov, *Natsionalna Mitologiya*, 122–23; and others. On the circulation of the manuscript of *Slavo-Bulgarian History*, see Economou, *Paisiou Hilandarinou*, 36–40.

the scholar who in 1871 brought Paisius to the attention of the Bulgarian intelligentsia.[3] Prior to that, Yuriy Venelin's work had been the most consistent reference for those who sought a scientific approach to the Bulgarians' past.[4] But from the Bulgarian perspective, the element of the national historical "self-determination" was something that was missing.

Nonetheless, Krâstevich and Drinov engaged in a vicious theoretical and historiographical clash from 1869 to 1873 when, apparently unbeknownst to each other, they simultaneously published histories of the Bulgarian people.[5] Krâstevich's *History*[6] was published in Constantinople in 1869 by the *Makedoniya* newspaper press, and Drinov's *History*[7] was published in Prague in April of that year. The *Makedoniya* newspaper was published in Istanbul by Petko Slaveykov, by his own admission a friend of Manuel Gedeon, while Prague was one of the educational centers of the rising "Pan-Slavist" intelligentsia. What was important in this dispute, whose content we will examine later in this chapter, was not just their differences, but also the common denominator on which their historiographical attempts at what we would describe as a model of origin was built.

This discussion shifted Bulgarian historiography from Venelin and the model of origin to Paisius and the model of continuity, and simultaneously imposed Drinov's views as the prevalent canon of Bulgarian historiography for the next several years.[8] Drinov, of course, "discovered" Paisius before Krâstevich's history was published. As previously mentioned, Krâstevich also referenced the monk, who was vital in arguing Bulgarian history's Slavicization. It is interesting, however, that this disagreement created the rule for understanding the Bulgarians' national development, a rule which remains prevalent to this day: the Proto-Bulgarian element

3 See Drinov, "Otec Paisi." See also Moser, *Bulgarian Literature*, 43; Sampimon, *Becoming Bulgarian*, 21–24; and Aretov, *Bâlgarskoto Vâzrazhdane*, 61–62. As Drinov attests, Paisius's work was known among many Russian Slavologists and Bulgarians in Russia, such as Mazurkevich, Venelin, Bodjanski, Aprilov, and Toshkovich, but only a few, such as Rakovski and Lamanski, paid any attention to his writings.

4 For example, see Clark, "Serbia and the Bulgarian Revival," 141–62.

5 See Krâstevich, *Drinovâta kritika*, 3.

6 Krâstevich, *Istoriya Bâlgarska*, vol. 1.

7 Marin Drinov, "Pogled vârhu proizhozhdaneto na bâlgarskiya narod," 43–122.

8 It seems that Drinov's form may have been consolidated when it was adopted by the Czech historian Konstantin Jireček for *Istoriya na Bâlgarite*.

that sprang from the dissolution of the Black Bulgarian state below the Volga was absorbed or assimilated by the Slavic populations settled in the Balkans south of the Danube.[9] This canon was largely reminiscent of the same course followed in the ethnogenetic evolution of the Slavicized Varangians and the German-weaned Franks. This normalized relations with the Russians on a cultural level—a relationship that many Bulgarians in the nineteenth century did not take for granted—and reiterated a motif that Western historiography had already classified.

In general, what we must observe about the differentiation in the orientation of Bulgarian historiography is that the turn toward the Bulgarians' Slavic past went hand-in-hand with the Bulgarian state's dependence on Russia. Conversely, the periods of disengagement from Russian foreign policy bolstered alternative historiographical approaches that reinforced the importance of the "Proto-Bulgarian" or "Thracian" pasts.[10] There was an open clash between scholars educated in Russia and those who had studied in Greece like Raino Popovich and Neofit Rilski. Rilski typically expressed his frustration with the "Odessians," the Bulgarians who studied in Russian universities. In 1860, the clash between these two camps acquired political overtones.

Nikolay Aretov outlined four currents in managing the issue of Bulgarian antiquity, viewed as "communication strategies" for the induction of the Bulgarian national narrative into European culture. These currents determined the variances in welcoming foreign literatures, which was the topic of his analysis. The first current was, of course, the one advocated by Paisius's *Slavo-Bulgarian History*. Aretov described this as an attempt at reconciling the emerging national identity with the tradition of an Orthodox Christian world in whose dissolution Paisius had participated. Paisius placed the Bulgarians within the Bible's system of coordinates and attempted to establish their national identity in terms of the Noah myth.

---

9 Jireček, *Istoriya na Bâlgarite*, 84–104.

10 From this perspective, it is hardly accidental that the "Iranian theory" appeared prominently in Bulgarian historiography in the 1990s, especially in the public sphere. The "Iranian theory" is a variation on the old "Thracian" theory, which minimizes the Slavic dimension of the Bulgarians' origin but especially the Turkish origin. "Indo-Europeanism," thus, served as a refuge from the threat of "Slavic" and "Turkish" origins. Prominent historians such as Georgi Bakalov and Bozhidar Dimitrov support this view, although Dimitrov, similarly to Petâr Dobrev, places definite priority on the "Proto-Bulgarian" past over the Slavic. See, among others, Dimitrov, *Bâlgarite*.

The second current, described as a "renaissance," looked toward a reading of antiquity that was in fact fabricated. In some cases, there was an effort to highlight elements common to the Slavo-Bulgarian people and to classical antiquity. The representatives of the first two currents actually sought connections to the fundamental motifs of Western European culture, the natural heir of ancient civilization and the Christian tradition.

The third current was rooted in the Slavic community and insisted on reconstructing Slavic antiquity. For a number of reasons, some of which were "obvious," as Aretov noted, this was the prevalent current and was approached as such by later historians and scholars.

The fourth current was represented by Georgi Rakovski, who insisted on the Indo-European roots of the Bulgarian *ethnos* and offered his own model for restoring it to the map of world civilizations, in direct conflict with all the other currents.

Aretov viewed Krâstevich and the *Bulgarian History* he published in 1871 as the result of a rather "weakly expressed understanding" of the Bulgarians' origins rather than a "current" of thought, such as those outlined above. Furthermore, this was an "understanding" that had been censured since Vasil Aprilov, even before it had been refuted with the "scientific" arguments of Marin Drinov.[11]

Nonetheless, Krâstevich's clash with Drinov was pivotal in the construction of the Bulgarian national narrative's prevalent canon. In a way, Krâstevich served as the internal opposing force, something underscored by Bulgarian nationalism's awkward approach to the Proto-Bulgarian past.[12] The reason for this was that in contrast with other theoretical currents, Krâstevich's did not appear to involve a narrative about the Bulgarian nation's "antiquity" (*Antichnost*) compatible with the corresponding narratives of how it was understood in the Western imagination, which in turn determined the conditions for its induction into the Western world. On the contrary, at first glance, Krâstevich appeared to legitimize the Ottoman Empire's preservation and, in particular, to adopt a Western-inspired theory of origin that definitively placed the Bulgarians in the

11 Aretov, *Bâlgarskoto Vâzrazhdane*, 17–18.

12 Aretov correctly describes these currents as "identification models" containing different "versions of the national myth" that took disparate approaches to "deep wounds" in the national consciousness. Ibid., 16.

Eastern sphere.[13] But this theory of origin also constituted the answer to early Bulgarian historiography's problem of disengaging from the "commitments" implied by its inclusion in the Orthodox millet. And for this reason, prior to any evaluation of the Krâstevich-Drinov dispute, an examination of the theories of origin of the Bulgarian people since the beginning of Bulgarian historiography remains essential.

2. Bulgarians: Vandals, Illyrians, or Macedonians?

Paisius of Hilendar's work did not constitute a complete break with the intellectuals of a uniform (mainly Slavic) Orthodox World, even though its fierce disagreement with Ottoman and particularly the Greek scholars triggered a narrative of (at least somewhat) national self-determination. Paisius commenced his narrative from the narrative of the flood in Genesis. Noah and his descendants served as the imaginary springboard for the Slavic, and by extension Bulgarian, nation. "Japeth had a son whose name was Mosoch. It was his tribe and race from which our Slavic ethnos stems and it was named the race and ethnos of Mosoch."[14] The Bulgarians' Slavic origins were mediated by the evolution of Noah's descendants, and this cosmos seems to have remained inscribed in the world of the Bible.

Paisius's work was influenced by several of the older Western historians such as Mauro Urbini (*Il Regno degli Slavi*, 1601), and Cesare Baronio (*Annales ecclesiastici*, 1589).[15] Raia Zaimova notes that the Hilandrian monk's work outlined three basic theories of origin derived from Western scholarly works of the preceding centuries. The first linked the Bulgarians to Scythia. The second located them around the Volga, from which their name derived. This was sometimes referred to as the "Sarmatian" or "Volgic" theory and was adopted by Baronio who cited Byzantine chronographers like Theophanes and Skylitzes. The third theory linked the Bulgarians to Scandinavia from which they supposedly came to Thrace. This

13 In other words, we see the opposite of the arguments posited by Ivaylo Ditchev who claimed that the Proto-Bulgarian past contributed to the alienation of the Byzantine and Ottoman heritage from the contemporary collective Bulgarian imaginary. Ditchev, "Eros of Identity," 243.

14 Economou, *Paisiou Hilandarinou*, 55. Japeth's sixth son was named Mosoch or Mesech and was identified as the Slavs' ancestor. See Aretov, *Bâlgarskoto Vâzrazhdane*, 21.

15 Genchev, *Bâlgarskoto Vâzrazhdane*, 88.

was the "Vandal" theory embraced by Urbini.[16] Yet, whether one adopted the Gothic ("Vandals") or Turkish/Scythian ("Sarmatians") versions, one could not avoid classifying the Bulgarians in the barbarian world, and, indeed, in the world of the East.

This issue does not seem to have escaped Paisius's contemporaries' attention. Consequently, a connection legitimized in the Western imaginary, that is either Ancient Greek or Roman, had to be found.

Two parallel attempts were made to define the Bulgarians' relationship with history. The first, *Zografska Historija* (History of the Monastery of Zographou), was anonymous and written during Paisius's time. The second, which was the most significant, was Spiridon Gabrovski's *Concise History of the Slavo-Bulgarian People* written in 1792.[17] Scholars highlight its relationship with *Slavo-Bulgarian History* as well as with the *History of the Monastery of Zographou.*[18]

In contrast to Paisius and the anonymous author of *Zografska Historija*, Gabrovski introduced a line of "Illyrian and Bulgarian" kings prior to the era of Alexander the Great into his narrative. These were no doubt borrowed from folk traditions such as the "Illyrian" songs or literary works like the Bulgarian King Lando VI in Ioannis Zonaras. Gabrovski commenced his narrative in the third century, inspired by the Cyrenaic philosopher Euhemerus (*Holy Inscription*), who claimed that the gods were merely former kings or heroes who were deified posthumously because of their achievements. As Aretov notes, from one perspective, this constitutes a reversal: while Euhemerus actually deconstructed the old myths that had been fraying during the Hellenistic Era, Gabrovski attempted to construct a new national mythology or to attribute new functions to mythological elements found in folklore.[19]

---

16 Zaimova, "Po vâprosa." Paisius's reference to Biblical events suggests his familiarity with the Innocent Guizel's *Synopsis*, which was first printed in 1674. This very popular text was reprinted several times, and it also adopted the Sarmatian theory. Paisius combined Urbini's "Vandal" theory with the Sarmatian theory from *Synopsis*, which was based on the etymologies of Biblical names such as Mosoch/Mesech. See Aretov, *Bâlgarskoto Vâzrazhdane.* Also, Chanev, *Bâlgarskata Istoricheska knizhnina*, 57

17 Aretov, *Natsionalna Mitologiya*, 123.

18 Genchev, *Bâlgarskoto Vâzrazhdane*, 110.

19 Aretov, *Bâlgarskoto Vâzrazhdane*, 26. Paparrigopoulos used the reference to Euhemerus to raise the issue of the ancient myths' interpretation. Paparrigopoulos did not deem Euhemerus's views worthy of comment, yet he believed that the citation set off a trend for scientifically explaining ancient

While early Bulgarian antiquity was established through the Bible, a new timeline was sought in Greco-Roman antiquity for the "Illyrian" stage that followed.[20] Like Paisius, Gabrovski used the Kievan *Synopsis* to identify the Bulgarians ("Illyrians") through Alexander the Great. Alexander defeated Perun, the Illyrians' king[21] (to whom Philip II was subjugated) and became head "of the entire Illyrian army and Perun's two sons . . . and set off for the world war." Following his successful Asian campaign, he settled in Babylon "and gives them Macedonia, his home, and gives them a papyrus on which is written in gold letters 'a strong and undefeated people'. Additionally, he cedes to them the royal titles for their great bravery and glorious victory."[22]

It remains curious that the first act inducting the Bulgarians into Greco-Roman antiquity was an act of concession by the victor (Alexander the Great) toward the defeated (Illyrians). Throughout the nineteenth century, all Bulgarians attempting a similar endeavor found it easier to identify the victor (Macedonians) with the defeated (Illyrians) rather than accept this ritualized scene of succession. In any case, the reference to Alexander the Great and the Macedonians was a constant for organizing related structures throughout the Bulgarian renaissance.

For example, Trifonov commented on this story about Alexander the Great translated in the early nineteenth century in Pleven:

> To understand what fascinates Pleven's writers Spas Hristov and Lazar Dimitrov, we not only need to keep in mind their tendency toward

myths that resulted in a number of important nineteenth-century works, such as George Grote's *A History of Greece*, and *Griechische Mythologie und Antiquitaten*. Paparrigopoulos shared Grote's view that ancient rituals like the mysteries of Eleusis and Samothrace were non-orgiastic, thus not Oriental. But he was mainly interested in Grote's distancing from an allegorical interpretation of ancient myths; the gods were not embodiments of natural elements or moral principles but understood as persons "reflecting real human life." In a way, Grote was a belated vindication of Euhemerus. See Paparrigopoulos, *Istoria tou Ellinikou Ethnous*, vol. 1, 36–56.

20 In Gabrovski's *History*, the Bulgarian past was frequently correlated with ancient Rome, most notably with the reference to Emperor Traianus's war with Dicephalus, "the King of the Slavs," and the Daco-Gatae. According to Gabrovski, "the Roman victory was due to the fact that Traianus's army included many secret Christians." See Aretov, *Bâlgarskoto Vâzrazhdane*, 28.

21 This may be the Triballi king, Syrmus, whom Alexander tried to subjugate before his campaign against the Persians. See Strabo, *Geography*, 3.8. In Strabo, the Triballi were referred to as a Thracian tribe, but other authors such as Stephanus of Byzantium considered them Illyrians.

22 The reference is included in Aretov, *Bâlgarskoto Vâzrazhdane*, 27.

> fiction but also the translators' utter certainty that Alexander the Great's Macedonians were ancestors of the present-day Macedonians, that is Bulgarians, while the Persians the great king battled were Turks. Since they knew that today's Persians are Muslims, which for them is equal to Turks, the translators considered that the old Persians were too. For this reason, it was pleasurable for them to read that the Macedonians once defeated the Turks, and since they bore in mind the saying that "where water once flowed, it will flow again," they believed that time will again come when the Bulgarians will defeat the Turks. (Trifonov, *Istoriya na grad Pleven*, 91–92)

In the case of the Pleven writers, it was not only the establishing of common origins between Bulgarians and Macedonians that was important, but also the fact that this was done on an axis defining East and West, where religious identity, despite its utilitarian role for emerging nationalisms, remained strong. But the inability to disengage from religion highlights another, deeper weakness: the detachment from the imperial vision. Whether the subjects chose religion as determining their ethnic identity or whether the induction into Christianity or Islam would postpone the empire's dissolution was still at stake. A solution like the expression of a theory of origin might easily have followed either path.

3. Drinov's History: The Slavicization of Bulgarians

Marin Stoyanov Drinov (known in Russia as Marin Stepanovich Drinov) was perhaps the most emblematic nineteenth-century Slavistic scholar. Born in 1838 in the northern Thracian town of Panagyurishte, he studied History and Philology at the universities of Kiev and Moscow. By the end of the 1860s, he had started writing articles for such Bulgarian periodicals as *Narodnost*, *Makedoniya*, and *Pravo*. In 1869, the year he published the work on the Bulgarians' origins that we will be examining, he also published a "History of the Bulgarian Church,"[23] which provided the theoretical foundation for the Bulgarian nationalists' demands for an independent exarchate. This work was translated into Russian in 1870 and

23 Drinov, "Istoricheski Pregled," 9–165.

published in *Pravoslavnoe Obozrenie* (Orthodox review). Also in 1869, Drinov co-founded the Bulgarian Literary Society with Borislav Stoyanov, Rayko Zhinzifov, and Georgi Bonchev in Brăila. The society later became the Bulgarian Academy of Sciences.[24] Over the next few years, Drinov published several articles in the society's journal. In 1871, he published a new treatise on the relations between Bulgaria and the patriarchate and two years later, in 1873, he published an essay on the growing Slavic presence in the Balkans from the third century to the seventh. In 1873, he was also a reader in Slavistics at the University of Kharkiv, which is worth noting as it was in the region of this city, near the Lower Volga, that Black Bulgaria had flourished. In 1876, he submitted his doctoral dissertation titled *Southern Slavs and Byzantium in the 10th Century*. In it, he examined the first phases of the Serbs' and Croats' settlement in the Balkans.

From 1877 to 1878, Drinov was the head of the Ministry for Education and Spiritual Affairs of the newly formed Bulgarian Principality (under Russian administration). He was among the drafters of the Târnovo Constitution and those who supported Sofia's selection over Târnovo, favored by Austria, as the new capital of the new Bulgarian state established under the Treaty of San Stefano. From 1881 until his death on February 28, 1906, he lived in Kharkiv. His collected works[25] were published in 1909 by his intellectual offspring, the Bulgarian Literary Society.

It is evident that having built a career as a professional historian within the Russian academic milieu, and owing much of his political career to Russian support, Drinov would find it almost impossible to distance himself from an academic orientation that did not establish the historical underpinnings of the close relationship shared by the Bulgarian and Russian peoples.[26] Reducing this to a common Slavic past and a few words

---

24 The Bulgarian Literary Society (*Bâlgarsko Knyizhevno Druzhstvo*) launched its official journal a year after its founding in 1870. In 1878, the society relocated from Brăila to Sofia and was renamed Bulgarian Academy of Sciences (Bâlgarska Akademiya na Haukite) in 1911. Drinov served as the society's first president, and Ivan Geshov was the first president of the Academy.

25 Zlatarski, *Writings of Drinov*. Drinov's works would be reprinted in 1971 as *M.S. Drinov Izbrani Sâchinenia* (Selected writings), edited by Ivan Duychev.

26 He was not the only representative of the Slavophile-Russophile secretariat. B. Petkov and N. Daskalov (both of them had contributed to the translation of the works of Yuriy Venelin) ,Vasil Aprilov "Bâlgarskite Knizhitsi ili na koe slavyansko pleme prinadlezhi kirilovskata azbuka" [Bulgarian pamphlets, or to which Slavic tribe the Cyrillic alphabet belongs] (1841), and D. I. Ilovajski ("Za Slavyanskoto proizhozhdenie na Dunavskite Bâlgari" [On the Slavic origins of the Danubian Bul-

about the Bulgarians' Slavic origins resolved many scientific/theoretical problems, but it mainly resolved political ones. The Russian–Turkish War of 1877–78 and the founding of the independent Bulgarian Principality following Russia's catalytic intervention politically capped this process.

Nevertheless, one could easily ask whether the Bulgarians were Slavs. The obvious answer was not a given in the mid-nineteenth century. Theories of "Thracian" or "Volgic/Sarmatian" origins were as widespread as views of the Bulgarians' Slavic origins. Supporters of the first theory included foreign writers like Johann Gatterer,[27] Joachim Lelevel,[28] and A. D. Chertkov.[29] This school of thought supported the theory that the modern Bulgarians were descended from the Balkans' ancient inhabitants, the Thraco-Illyrians. This view was adopted by prominent Bulgarian intellectuals like Petâr Beron[30] and, as already mentioned, Georgi Rakovski.[31] The Thracian origin theory resolved issues linked to the Bulgarian nationalist movement's political claims during this period.

---

garians] (1875) should be mentioned. Certainly, the main representative of the idea of Slavic unity in Russia during this period was Rayko Zhinzifov, a prominent member of the Bulgarian community. However, the peak of the pro-Russian period was marked by the publication of Todor Burmov's essay, "Brachko obyasnenie na Bâlgarin kâm bratyata mu Bâlgare" [A brotherly explanation of a Bulgarian to his fellow Bulgarians], published anonymously in Bucharest in 1876. The essay goes as far as claiming that the Bulgarians would have nothing to lose if they suddenly became citizens of the great Russian Empire and accepted Russian as the official language. However, there were also instances of Bulgarians who stayed in Russia but never completed their studies at Russian universities, never assimilated into Russian society, and expressed strongly anti-Russian views. Examples include Georgi Rakovski and Lyuben Karavelov.

27 Gatterer, *Synchronistische tabellen*, vol. 1, 12.

28 Lelevel, *Histoire de Pologne.*

29 Chertkov, *O perevode Manassiinoi letopisi.*

30 Petâr Beron (1799–1871) expresses similar ideas in the 1850s and 1860s, especially in his *Slavyanska Filosofiya* [Slavic Philosophy] and *Panepistimiya* [Panepisteme]. His main work, *Origine de l'unique couple humain*, was published in France. Beron studied philosophy at Heidelberg and became a doctor of medicine in Munich where he followed Schelling's lectures. He studied ancient and modern Greek, Latin, German, and French. Acquainted with Hegelian philosophy, he tried to create something similar in *Panepisteme* in which the "theoretical" and "empirical" would comprise a uniform whole. As Atanas Stamatov correctly observes, at the time when post-Hegelian philosophy in Europe was abandoning its efforts to create holistic philosophical structures, Beron was doing the opposite in the "European periphery" despite spending most of his life at European universities. See Stamatov and Raychena, "Paradoxes," 6–7. This was an attempt to combine theoretical philosophy's heritage with a new version of empiricism, Positivism. We find this pattern repeated in several Balkan intellectuals, including the Greek Literary Society of Constantinople: unravelling at the center parallels a desire in the periphery to achieve restoration.

31 Rakovski, *Pokzalech ili râkovodstvo*; *Nekoliko pechi*; and *Bâlgarska starina*. See also Rakovski, *Avtobiografiya i memoari* and Traikov, *Rakovski.*

If origin could be established on the principle of autochthony, it would be easier to express claims to the state that corresponded to the places settled by the ancient Thracians. At the same time, this also solved the problem of creating a Bulgarian antiquity, albeit not as brilliant as Greek antiquity but chronologically contemporary to it. Indeed, in an intriguing way, this antiquity met the challenge of the major political issue at stake at the time: the demand to disengage the Thracian-Bulgarian people from Greek cultural influences.

On the opposing side were several variations of the view that the Bulgarians must be considered descendants of the combination of races under Asparuh, who moved between the Lower Volga and the Danube after the dissolution of Great (or Black) Bulgaria. Such proponents included European writers like Johann Thunmann,[32] Johann Christian Engel,[33] Jovan Rajić,[34] and others. This camp also included a writer who cannot be overlooked: Yuriy Venelin.[35] The theory of the Bulgarians' "Volgic" origin had also been adopted by a major personality of the Bulgarian renaissance: Krâstevich. While he outlined this position in an article published in 1858–59 in *Bâlgarski Knizhitsi*, he never returned to it. Still, this fact renders the simultaneous publication of the separate histories written by Drinov and Krâstevich even more significant.

3.1 The two discontinuities

Drinov's *A Look into the Origins of the Bulgarian People and the Beginnings of Bulgarian History* offers an overview of the Balkan peninsula's demographic evolution from Late Antiquity forward and, thus, constitutes a description of events leading up to Asparuh's founding of the first Bulgarian kingdom.[36] Drinov dedicated the final chapter to responding

32 Thunmann, *Untersuchungen*.

33 Engel, *Geschichte des ungarischen Reichs, I. Bulgarien, Pannonien*.

34 Rajić, *Istorija raznih slavjanskih narodov*.

35 Venelin, *Drevnie i nyneshnie bolgare*, vol. 1. He has been described as the man "who died after resurrecting the Bulgarian nation."

36 Drinov, "Pogled," 43–122. The table of contents reads: 1. The Balkan peninsula's ancient inhabitants. The gradual reduction of their population. The abandonment of the Balkan peninsula in the 5th century AD. 2. The settlement of new populations in the Balkan peninsula. Slavs: geographic review of their intermingling in the 6th and 7th centuries. 3. The arrival of Asparuh's tribes, the founding of the Bulgarian kingdom, the beginnings of the modern Bulgarian people. The Helleni-

to the basic arguments of the Thraco-Ilyrian and Volgic theories. He focused mainly on the latter, which Felix Kanitz had brought back to the fore. Drinov was aware of Krâstevich's views but was not able to criticize them because Krâstevich had not attempted to substantiate them.

Before turning to the origins of his contemporary Bulgarians—and while referencing the Balkans' medieval past—Drinov approached the question of the origins of the Bulgarians' great rivals, the Greeks.

The origin issue in the Greek case cast doubt on the issue of continuity. Interestingly, the adoption of Fallmerayer's position by a Bulgarian historian shifted the center of Bulgarian historiography from the origin model to the continuity model, a process that can be followed more closely.

Drinov's insistence on highlighting the discontinuity in the Greek example is required—although it did create contradictions—to offset the evident vacuum in Bulgarian national development, especially in the Ottoman Empire's waning centuries. In his essay on Paisius of Hilendar, Drinov dealt extensively with the issue of discontinuity in Bulgarian history. He attempted to limit this to the eighteenth century in the belief that the sense of "Bulgarianness" had not yet emerged in the first centuries of the Ottoman conquest. He wrote:

> We can say that the first half of the previous [eighteenth] century was the blackest period in the history of our people. As harsh as Bulgarians' economic situation was in the fifteenth sixteenth, and seventeenth centuries, as oppressed as they were, they had not yet lost their popular spirit, they had not neglected that they too were one of the world's peoples with a past and a history. Memories of this historical past still survived among Bulgarians, and it was the "guardian angel" of Bulgarian ethnicity [nardnost] in such catastrophic circumstances of existence . . . The Bulgarian world presents a completely different image from the start of the eighteenth century. There is not a single reassuring characteristic on which the weary gaze can rest. The popular spirit is not visible anywhere. This is not the space to detail the causes that brought our people to this disastrous condition in the

zation of some Slavic tribes with the arrivals of the modern Greeks. 4. Some more arguments that corroborate the above-mentioned view on the origins of our people. 5. Brief review of the theories on the origins of our people.

> eighteenth century. We want only to note that those who see in this a negligible Bulgarian popular character, a supposed absence of a long historical tradition, are mistaken. (Drinov, "Otec Paisi," 163)

Drinov avoided extensive reference to the "causes" of this spiritual and by extension "national" underdevelopment, described in bleak terms to emphasize Paisius's decisive role, but he did mention one, which he perhaps considered the most salient:

> We now have in our hands sufficient proof that this fact was preceded by a long and persistent battle by the Bulgarians who, only after the total destruction of their natural strength, were subjugated to their fatal destiny. The Phanariots swooped like black crows onto the exhausted hero and plucked out his soul.[37] Our people were, thus, dead from the beginning of the eighteenth century. The Bulgarians no longer existed as a people, it was a mass of oppressed, choked, destroyed individuals. The word itself, people [narod], in Old Bulgarian had been lost and replaced by the word "hora" [humans], which is borrowed from the Greek language [hora or land, horiatis or peasant] and means inhabitants of the countryside condemned to all types of heavy labor and tribulations. Indeed, only such Bulgarians remained during that period. If someone managed to stand on his own feet and create a more humane urban life, he was no longer a Bulgarians but a Greek. This was because the Bulgarian was not suited to the urban life, that was a privilege solely of the Greeks.... (Drinov, "Otec Paisi," 163–64.)

Of course, the "Phanariots" to whom Drinov referred were not the ordinary lay members staffing the state apparatus, but the clergy, mainly those at the Phanar, whom he discussed in his text on the Bulgarian Church. The Byzantine Empire's heirs continued behaving toward the

37 This was not the first time Drinov would take such a harsh position toward the Phanariots. He similarly denounced them in an 1866 article titled "The Phanariots and Jesuits Provoke Fear for Our Ethnicity," in which, according to Aretov, he introduced the new idea of identifying Phanariotism with the Inquisition—an idea often repeated in the works of Bulgarians with Russian ties and linked to Western anti-Inquisition motifs in the translated prose works of the 1860s and 1870s. See Aretov, *Bâlgarskoto Vâzrazhdane*, 27.

Slavic races just as its political leaders had done. Fallmerayer, however, offered an excellent opportunity to undermine the pursuit of continuity: at the very moment of the Byzantines' absolute dominance, there was a rift with the Ancient Greek past at a racial level.

Detached from the "objectivity" of Western European historians' analysis, Drinov's argument adopted the racial relationship between Bulgarians and Slavs that settled the Greek peninsula in the fifth and sixth centuries, and approached them as victims of a forced Hellenization at the cultural level, which had halted their historical development. Slavs and Albanians disrupted the relationship between modern and Ancient Greeks at the cost of their own national identity.

Drinov offered a detailed description of the efforts of Byzantine Emperors, from Michael III to Constantine VII Porphyrogenitus, to impose their control on the Slavs in the Peloponnese. He wrote:

> Thus ended the struggle which lasted three centuries. The mainland Greeks and Peloponnesian Slavs, cut off from their brothers and united under the authority of a powerful kingdom, were weakened by the protracted armed clashes and subjugated to Byzantium. (Drinov, "Pogled," 91)

Indeed, Drinov went even further as he describes the Slavs' position in ethnic terms: when Constantine VII Porphyrogenitus subordinated the last two races, the Ezeritai and the Melingoi, he agreed to their request not to be highly taxed because he feared they would join forces with the other Slavs and push for the Peloponnese to secede from the rest of the empire.[38] The other Slavs in the Peloponnese followed a different historical path from their "brother" Bulgarians who, having accepted Christianity and the alphabet from Cyril and Methodius, managed to survive ethnically because they were able to record their language in writing. Conversely, the Byzantine Empire's Slavs were forced to adopt the Greek alphabet and, by extension, the Greek language. Their Hellenization was a given, which was proved by the sources: all references to them end in the eleventh century. The second wave of Slavic "incursions" in the fourteenth

38 Ibid., 90.

and fifteenth centuries completed de-Hellenization at the same time as the Albanians were being Hellenized:

> And, thus, the Slavs and Albanians, Hellenized by the Byzantines,[39] were the ancestors of today's Greeks in the Hellenic kingdom and in Thessaly . . . the modern Greeks were neither pure nor descendants of the Ancient Greeks . . . A people of Slavic and Albanian origin now lives in place of the Ancient Greeks. (Drinov, "Pogled," 92)

This position did not imply the "brothering" of two neighboring peoples with the same origin.

Fallmerayer's retrospective vindication—he was essentially unrecognized at his death in 1861—by necessity rested on a contradiction in which the racial perception of the nation superseded the cultural perception. But Drinov's aim was not to argue the discontinuity of the Greek nation through a successful Hellenization but to raise the issue of the Greeks' privileged relationship with the West:

> Fallmerayer's discovery seemed to frighten the Greeks, who believed they were the pure descendants of the victors at Salamis and Marathon and that the blood of Pericles and Aristotle still flows in their blood. This also discomfited the European philhellenes . . . In the end, the best philhellenes had to accept the truth in his work and his great abilities. (93)

39 The Byzantines were also touched by the Slavic wave. If the philhellenic line was to emphasize the Thracian underpinnings in Bulgarian culture and relations with Greek culture, the Slavophiles' intentions were often expressed by the tendency to conceal the Slavic origin of popular figures in Byzantine history. These include Velissarios and a handful of emperors like Justin I, Justinian, or Basil I, the Macedonian. Similar opinions were expressed by Vasil Aprilov in *Bâlgarski Knizhitsi* who says about Justinian: "He was the nephew of Justin from Ohrid. His name was *Uprauda*, which was translated as 'Justinian' when he became Roman Emperor. [Of course, *Uprauda* does not correspond perfectly with Justinian who had, in any case, initially adopted the name Roman Petrus Sabbatius and was later given Justinian by his uncle, the Emperor Justin]. His father was Istok, and his sister was Beglitsa, which was translated as Vigilantsia [which was actually his mother's name]. Subsequently, Velissarios, derived from German, is the name of a village near Ohrid," is mentioned by Aretov in *Bâlgarskoto Vâzrazhdane* (59). In *Pogled,* Drinov also adopted the theory of the Bulgarian origins of Justinian (527–567) and Basil I (867–886), although in neither case did this suggest Byzantium's complete Slavicization. This would constitute a *de facto* eradication of the conflict with Greek nationalism.

Indeed, he even cited the Scottish historian George Finlay, who could hardly be accused of having been biased against the Greeks, as "understanding that Fallmerayer's opponents have been defeated."[40]

The Bulgarians' Slavic origin was, therefore, not merely a scientific issue but was indirectly related to the biggest strike against the model of continuity that Greek nationalism had imposed as the dominant historiographical paradigm in the Balkans. This was the only possible option to offset the Bulgarian nation's structural "discontinuity" during Ottoman rule. Disputing the Slavic origin would create a huge problem in developing an argument against Greek cultural dominance—a problem that would become even larger in the version of Proto-Bulgarian origin since this even cast doubt on the possibility of a break from the Ottoman Empire.

3.2 The critique of alternative origin models

The basic theories of the Bulgarians' origin had been outlined by the late eighteenth century and embraced by distinguished writers, but adopting one or the other in the nineteenth century was not merely an issue of literary quests. Drinov dedicated the final section of his study to refuting these.

The "Thracian" theory claimed the Bulgarians were descended from the ancient Thraco-Illyrians. The ideological prerequisites for adopting this theory will be analyzed below, especially in Rakovski's case. Here we are interested in the basic points against which Drinov trained his polemic. The para-etymological interpretation of some ancient Thracian tribes as Slavic and the opinion that the massive Thraco-Illyrian substrata could not have simply disappeared was a basic pillar on which this theory rested; in the worst case scenario, the substrata intermixed with the Balkan foreigners. Drinov found it easy to respond to this type of argument:

> This is how weak the first pillar of the Thracian theory is: based on five or six names,[41] and controversial ones at that, you cannot conclude that the Thraco-Illyrian people, which included more than forty

40 Ibid., 93. See also Skopetea, *Fallmerayer.*

41 He is referring to tribal names such as Triballi, Koreli, Krobyzi, and Bessi which the supporters of the Thracian theory have linked etymologically to the Slavic tongue.

> tribes, we repeat cannot be concluded based on such a weak claim that the Thraco-Illyrians are Slavs. Conversely, there are many strong arguments that prove they are not. Today, we know for a fact that the Albanian language was not the language of the ancient Illyrians[42] who belonged to the same tribe as the Thracians. And no one can say that the Thracian tongue has disappeared; there still remains some words which in no way resemble Slavic words. (Drinov, "Pogled," 110)

Aside from the scientific weakness of the arguments, he raised another issue which is of a political nature: the Thraco-Illyrian past could not be easily monopolized by the Bulgarians even if there had been some mixing of the ancient Thracians with the foreign Slavs south of the Danube. But this concerned the second pillar of the Thracian theory: if the Bulgarians were not descended from the Thraco-Illyrians, then what became of them? Here Drinov argued that the gradual decline of their population was a result of foreign interventions—something which, admittedly, he carried out with less scientific clarity than his etymological observations. Macedonians (notwithstanding the fact that he described them as "brothers" of the Thraco-Illyrians), Romans, and the Great Migration of Peoples (Huns, Ostrogoths, Visigoths) in the fourth and fifth centuries, completed overwhelming and successive strikes against the Thraco-Illyrians whose population was reduced.[43] But this applied not only to them. According to Drinov, the Slavs themselves participated in the decrease of the Thraco-Illyrian population:

> The Slavs also destroyed many Thraco-Illyrians in battles, as Procopius attests, or enslaved them. . . . Taking into account all these misfortunes and the destruction of the Thracian people, we do not believe asking what happened to the ancient Thracians is a valid question. We wonder more how it can be that one million of them managed to preserve and today survive with the name Albanian among those living in the Balkan peninsula. (113–14)

42 Here he cited J. G. Hahn's *Albanesische Studien*, vol. 1, Vienna, 1853.

43 Ibid., 111–13.

The loss of the Thraco-Illyrian past also meant the loss of "Bulgarian antiquity," as Georgi Rakovski attempted to introduce it in his work of the same titled published in Bucharest in 1865. The Bulgarians had to settle for arriving in the Balkans in the Christian era, either as Slavs or Proto-Bulgarians. But it seemed inconsequential for Drinov if the Bulgarians' presence as Slavs contributed to the deconstruction of the Greek ethnogenetic model.

On the other hand, the Volgic variations on the theory also had to be countered as Drinov appeared to consider these far more dangerous than the Thraco-Illyrian version largely because of their objective historical foundation. Asparuh and his hordes not only existed but were responsible for the founding of the first Bulgarian kingdom in the Balkans. Drinov would need to resort to rational thinking rather than rely on historical sources, something that was further complicated by the several variations on the Volgic theory.

For Drinov, the issue was directly linked to the size of the Bulgarian population in the Balkans. (Krâstevich used the same argument, but for different reasons.) This was a matter of common sense: if the Bulgarian population in the Balkans was as significant and extensive as described forty years earlier by Yuriy Venelin[44] or even in the 1840s by Pavel Šafárik[45] and Ami Boué,[46] then these millions of Bulgarians could not be descended from a small nomadic tribe that arrived at some point from the Volga to the Danube. Drinov used the issue of discontinuity to attempt to explain the misperceptions of many eighteenth-century and early nineteenth-century writers; but he added the Hellenization process that the Slavs underwent on the Greek mainland as well as the Serbification of the Western eparchies of present-day Bulgaria and Northern Macedonia and the Magyarification, mainly through the conversion to Catholicism, of many

44 In *Drevnie i nyneshnie bolgare*, Venelin expressed the opinion that the Bulgarians were the most important people of the Balkan peninsula.

45 In 1824, three years before Venelin, Šafárik estimated the Bulgarian population at 600,000 in his classic work *Geschichte der slawischen Sprache* published in Budapest. In a later work, *Slovanský naropodis*, which was published in Prague in 1849, he revised that number to 3,000,000. On Šafárik and his relationship to Bulgarian nationalism, see Danova, "Otnovo za Šafárik," 323–34.

46 Ami Boué estimated the number of Bulgarians at 4.5 million. See Boué, *La Turquie d'Europe*, vol. 2, 5. See below also.

Bulgarians in the Vidin[47] province to the causes of the Bulgarian population's decline.

Drinov concluded:

> Through these testimonies on the size of our people's population and its historical evolution, we would ask readers to bear in mind what we have said about the size of Asparuh's horde. Is it possible that our people is descended from such a small group, whose number may have been less than 100,000 people? This is the main deception of those writers who accept Asparuh's Bulgarians as the ancestors of today's Bulgarians. (117)

As previously noted, there were several variations of the Volgic theory which posited that today's Bulgarians descend from the hordes of Asparuh, who lived with his brothers somewhere along the Volga before arriving in the Lower Danube. This shared basic supposition did not, however, denote complete agreement between the Bulgarian writers who advocated this position.

Johann Thunmann (1746–78) was the first to examine this issue. In Leipzig in 1774, he published his *Untersuchungen über die Geschichte der östlich-europäischen Völker*, in which he claimed that the Volga Bulgarians were of Tatar (thus Altaic) origin.[48] Roughly two decades after Thunmann's work was published, Johann Christian Engel published his *Geschichte von Bulgarien* (Vienna, 1796), in which he discussed the Bulgarians' origins at length.[49] Engel believed Asparuh roamed the region between the Dnieper and Dniester rivers with his horde before leading them to the Balkans, where he took Lower Moesia and Little Scythia from the Byzantine Empire, founding the first Bulgarian kingdom there. Asparuh's horde mixed with the indigenous population, but according to Engel, this process did not result in the conquerors' assimilation but in the gradual reinforcement of the Tatar element which was dominant. Thus, in Engel's opinion, the Bulgarian people traced their origins to Asparuh's horde.

47 Drinov, "Pogled," 115–16.

48 "...und die alten Wallachen und ihre Brüder, die Bulgaren, scheinen in der That ein türkisches Volk gewesen zu seyn . . . " Thunmann, *Untersuchungen*, 116.

49 Engel, *Geschichte von Bulgarien*.

Engel knew that the language of the modern Bulgarians had similarities to the Slavic language, but this problem was easily overcome. He explained the similarities based on the climate, the influence of time, and the intermixing of Asparuh's horde with the Slavs.[50] Engel did not dispute this mix but simply understood it erratically, concluding that the Tatar element became stronger through its intermixing with other peoples (the Slavs).

Drinov did not delve deeply into Engel's theory, although he did dispute Engel's credibility as a historian based on his use of historical sources.[51] He did not spend any time on Thunmann's speculation on the Proto-Bulgarians' possible Tatar roots. But what he did find problematic in the expression of this theory was the lapse in logic given the differences in the size of the horde and Bulgarian populations:

> Let's suppose [Engel] has a hazy notion of the numerous Slavic tribes that Asparuh encounters in the Balkans. Bear in mind that his history was written at the end of the last century, when the prevalent belief was that our people numbered fewer than a half-million. Given this, it is not strange that Engel concluded that today's Bulgarians are the enslaved descendants of Asparuh's hordes or, as he comments, enslaved Tatars. (Drinov, "Pogled," 119)

Venelin's theory, which was first presented in Urbini's work,[52] received the same treatment from Drinov. Venelin's theory had also inspired Paisius and had been adopted by Jovan Rajić in the early eighteenth century.[53] Paradoxically, Venelin aimed to counter Engel's claim that the Bulgarians were enslaved Tatars. However, by adopting the position that Asparuh and his horde had to be considered the modern Bulgarians' ancestors, he committed the same error as his opponent. According to Drinov, Venelin could not counter Engel by reversing his theory because he fell into the same logical inconsistency.

50 Drinov, "Pogled," 118.

51 For example, Engel identified Ogglon, where the chroniclers Theophanes and Nikephoros had claimed that Asparuh's horde settled before arriving in the Balkans as located in Lower Moesia rather than in Bessarabia—where Drinov believed the site was in fact located. See Drinov, "Pogled," 119.

52 Urbini, *Il Regno degli Slavi*.

53 Rajić, *Istorija raznih slavjanskih narodov*.

> Like Engel, [Venelin] also considered Asparuh and his horde to be the ancestors of today's Bulgarians. He could not estimate either the number of Asparuh's horde or the significance of the settlement in the Balkan peninsula of so many Slavic tribes. Thus, though his theory countered Engel's, it was rooted in the same deceit. It only differed from Engel's in terms of research methodology. Engel started from the Volga's Bulgarians and after concluding they were of Tatar origin, arrived at today's Bulgarians to conclude that as their genuine descendants, they must have had the same origin, that is, Tatar. Venelin proceeded backward: he started from today's Bulgarians and, after determining that they were pure Slavs, shifted to the Volga Bulgarians as the ancestors of today's and concluded they too were pure Slavs. (Drinov, "Pogled," 120)

Venelin's last position deserves special attention because, as we shall see, it was the last point conceded by Krâstevich in his dispute with Drinov on the issue of the Bulgarians' origin. In order to resolve the contradiction in the position that the Bulgarians were Huns (Tatars, in this case), he adopted the even odder view that the Huns were Slavs. However, when Drinov wrote these lines, he probably could not have imagined that these positions would be adopted by a distinguished Bulgarian intellectual.

Drinov battled Venelin—and, unknowingly at the time, Krâstevich also—by identifying with Pavel Šafárik's views.[54] Writing in the 1830s,[55] Šafárik had claimed a Finnic origin for the Proto-Bulgarians. But he put things in proper order:

> Asparuh's horde was not numerous or courageous or skilled in the martial arts. It invaded the land of the peaceful Slavs and managed to dominate them completely. But because it settled quickly among them, it was forced to adopt their language, customs, and traditions, and to completely alter its Ural-Finnic ethnicity to Slavic. This is why the Slavs had to take from their conquerors the name which they bear to this day, that is, Bulgars. (Šafárik, *Slovanské starožitnosti*, vol 1, 4n39)

54 Czech Slavic scholars like Pavel Šafárik and Konstantin Jireček were very influential in shaping the intellectual milieu of numerous Bulgarian thinkers from Marin Drinov to Ivan Dobrovsky.

55 Šafárik, *Slovanské starožitnosti*.

Drinov was satisfied with Šafárik's ordering of events. The Proto-Bulgarians must, indeed, be considered of Altaic (and specifically Finnic) origin, whose settlement in a different geographic environment with a dominant Slavic population forced them into gradual slavification. As a result of its adoption by Drinov, Šafárik's position became the prevalent canon on which the problem of the Bulgarians' origin was resolved. But it is interesting is that the problem's resolution was combined with an assumption of the Bulgarians' position vis-a-vis the clash between East and West. The Slavic "East" should not be identified with the corresponding Turkish "East"; this Slavic East should be seen differently by the West than despotic Asia. Drinov noted:

> Most contemporary scientists accept, like Šafárik, that the Volga Bulgarians were a Finnic race, but few of them have a correct understanding of the relationship between those Bulgarians and the ethnicity of today's Bulgarians. Now only the Slavic writers understand the relationship as outlined by Šafárik, while for non-Slavic scientists, this obvious truth remains unproven to date. And to date, French and German bibliographies contain texts about our people that repeat Engel's deceit with the sole exception that he considered the Bulgarians to be enslaved Tatars while these new texts view them as enslaved Finns. (Drinov, *Pogled*, 121–22)

This inability of Western—that is, non-Slavic—writers to understand the Bulgarians' historical path definitely corresponded to a lack of willingness to make the distinction between the Slavic and Turkish East, or better yet, to recognize the Slavic nations of Eastern and Southeastern Europe as equals in the circle of European nations. Drinov was referring to specific writers like Felix Kanitz,[56] who reproduced the erroneous logic regarding the Bulgarian Slavs' ancestry, something he considered unacceptable four decades after Šafárik's theory had been published.

56 Kanitz's article "Bulgarische Fragmente" prompted Drinov to write his short treatise. But similar views had also been expressed by writers like Guillaume Lejean (*Ethnographie de la Turquie d'Europe*) and Dora D'Istria ("La nationalité bulgare").

4. Krâstevich's Thesis: The Bulgarians Are Huns (The Positive Use of Byzantine Chronography)

The same year that Drinov published *Pogled,* Gavril Krâstevich was publishing the first volume of his *Bâlgarska Istoriya*. Krâstevich was probably the most "establishment" Bulgarian of his time. Born 1817 in Kotel, Bulgaria—the hometown of Sophronius, Bishop of Vratsa, and the Vogoridi family— Krâstevich as a youth was taken under the wing of Stefan Vogoridi. He completed his encyclical studies (1831–35) at the famed Rayno Popovich School in Karlovo before moving to Constantinople, where he spent the next two years as a guest in the home of his mentor while studying at the Patriarchal School at Kuruçeşme. Vogoridi also funded Krâstevich's law studies in Paris (1838–44), after which Krâstevich returned to take up senior state office, first as supervisor at Samos and then as judge in the Constantinople trade court.[57]

Following Vogoridi's death in the summer of 1859, Krâstevich emerged as the leader of the Bulgarians' "conservative" faction which sought to avoid a head-on confrontation with the patriarchate on the issue of an independent Bulgarian Church. He gradually earned the Russian Embassy's trust and became involved in all the intermediary efforts between the two sides from 1867, the start of Gregory VI's patriarchal reign, to 1872, when the Bulgarian Exarchate split from the patriarchate. It is quite possible that Krâstevich drafted the firman that established the Bulgarian Exarchate,[58] and most certainly composed the charter of the Bulgarian Exarchate that emerged from the 1871 national clergy–laity assembly in Istanbul.[59]

Krâstevich's conservative views and his fierce clash with the radical Bulgarian nationalists, including Stoyan Chomakov,[60] as well as his subsequent service as general director for Eastern Rumelia, often led

57 For biographical information, see Balabanov, *Krâstevich*; Madzharov, *Iztochna Rumeliya*; Burmov, *Bâlgaro–grâchka tsârkovna raspra*; Stambolski, *Avtobiografiya*; Stambolski, *Protokoli na Bâlgarski naroden sâbor*; Kepov, *Krâstevich*. For the best biographical approach to Krâstevich available today, especially for the period before Bulgarian independence, see Boneva, *Krâstevich*; for the period he was involved in the administration of Eastern Rumelia, see Nazârska, "Iztochnorumeliyskiyat dârzhavnik"; see also her article "Krâstevich," 49–62.

58 Meininger, *Ignatiev*, 137. Meininger's views were shared by Patriarch Cyril of Bulgaria.

59 Temelski, *Tsârkovno-Narodniyat Sâbor.*

60 Bozhinov, "La mission diplomatique bulgare."

representatives of Bulgarian historiography to classify him as either "pro-Russian" or "pro-Turk."[61] Indeed, Krâstevich was politically a "multifaceted" personality—a man trusted by both Ignatiev and the Grand Vizier Âli Pasha and could, thus, simultaneously fit both characterizations.[62]

At the same time, however, Krâstevich never ceased being under the influence of the network through which he assumed important posts in the Ottoman state. After Vogoridi's death, the leadership of this group passed to his son-in-law and Ottoman envoy in London Konstantinos Mousouros and his brother Pavlos, who resided permanently in Istanbul. Both Vogoridi and the Mousouros family could be considered part of the English rather than the Russian sphere of influence, and even at the height of the clash between patriarchate and exarchate, Krâstevich's relationship with the family was not hurt.[63]

Aside from being characterized as "pro-Russian" or "pro-Turk," Krâstevich could also easily lay claim to the "pro-Western" label. In his case, we are not dealing simply with a flexible political personality with great adaptive potential, but mainly with a man who, like his mentor Stefan Vogoridi, appeared to be the herald of the establishment of a new national state, yet operated with the imperial framework in mind with regard to his clientelist connections and chiefly within the hierarchy of cultural values and symbolisms characterizing imperial politics. Perhaps this was the reason that once the Bulgarian Principality was firmly established, Krâstevich abandoned the nascent state for the tranquility of Mega Revma (Büyük Dere), a Constantinopolitan suburb on the Bosporus. He lived there until his death in 1898.

In 1869, the year Krâstevich published his *Bâlgarska Istoriya,* behind-the-scenes activities that lead to the founding of the Bulgarian Exarchate reached a peak. In September of that year, Ignatiev and the Grand Vizier

61 Indeed, there is a series of documents in the Ottoman archives on the Bulgarian nationalists' hostile reception of Krâstevich in Plovdiv when he was appointed deputy governor of Eastern Rumelia. See the State Archives of the Başbakanlık Devlet Arşivleri-Genel Müdürlüğü, Y..PRK.ZB, file 3, subfile 17, 12 Zilhiccee 1302 (Hicrî)-21/9/1885, Y.A. HUS.file 183, subfile 44, 19 Zilhicce 1302 (Hicrî)-28/9/1885, and file 183, subfile 127, 27 Zilhiccee 1302 (Hicrî)-6/10/1885.

62 Especially during periods like the premiership of Mahmud Nedim Pasha, when the foreign policies of the Ottoman and Russian Empires converged. See Abu-Manneh, " Sultan and Bureaucracy," 257–74; Todev, *Chomakov*, 165, 355–56.

63 Stamatopoulos, "Orthodox Millet," 154–70.

Âli Pasha agreed to a clandestine meeting between the latter and Krâstevich, who was tasked with drafting the firman he submitted that November.[64] Thus, publication of his *Bâlgarska Istoriya*'s first volume must be considered a political act: in light of the possible founding of an independent or autonomous Bulgarian ecclesiastical organization that could be preparing the ground for a breakaway state—in Krâstevich's mind perhaps even with Ottoman consent—there was the need to establish an official perception of the Bulgarian past.

Krâstevich's interest in the problem of the historiographical handling of the national timeline did not emerge suddenly in the 1860s. In a letter from Istanbul dated May 2, 1865, Petko Slaveykov informed Spyridon Palauzov of some research he had been conducting into the Bulgarian medieval past.[65] He admitted that he did not wish to compete in the making of generalizations or in offering conclusions, and stated: "If I can, I will speak about this with Krâstevich. He is the best historian among us. He has all the knowledge and facilitations, which is why he occupied himself more with our history as he can access both Byzantine and Turkish sources."[66]

The admiration of his contemporaries did not extend to subsequent generations once Marin Drinov's historiographical structure prevailed in Bulgarian academia. Krâstevich was to be marginalized in relation to this now dominant historiographical paradigm.[67] With Drinov viewed as the principal professional historian who resolved the issue of Bulgarian origin once and for all, Krâstevich could only occupy the position of one of those responsible for a romantic diversion from scientific discourse. As Aleksandâr Burmov notes, "The critical behavior towards the text is replaced with the deliberate intent to emphasize in every way the antiquity and greatness of the Bulgarian people in the past, while the quest for historical truth recedes in the face of a boom in patriotism."[68]

64 Kiril, *N.P. Graf Ignatiev*, 134; Kiril, *Ekzarh Antim*, 334.

65 Spyridon Palauzov was one of the first who was interested in Bulgarian medieval studies. Palauzov's thesis about the slavicization of the Proto-bulgarians was similar to Drinov's. See, for example, Giacomo Brucciani, *La scrittura della nazione*, 121–22.

66 Referenced by Boneva, "Istorikât Krâstevich," 183.

67 It is interesting that at the peak of the clash between Krâstevich and Drinov in 1871, the old neo-Phanariot becomes the first honorary member of the Bulgarian Literary Society (of which Drinov was a founding member), which was still based in Brăila. We do not know, however, whether this was before or after Drinov published his critique of Krâstevich's *History*.

68 Burmov, " Drinov," 107.

Vera Boneva made the last noteworthy effort to highlight Krâstevich's contribution to historiography. A systematic researcher of his work, she nonetheless has an intensely apologetic approach. Her efforts to highlight Krâstevich's "scientific" use of the primary historical sources—she has studied the two unpublished volumes of his *History* at the Historical Archive of the National Library in Sofia—and her emphasis on the achievements of his historical work, conceal its ideological springboard. The need to place Krâstevich in the pantheon of Promethean heroes of the Bulgarian renaissance and overlook the "imperial" prerequisites of his political behavior, which have always concerned Bulgarian historians, underestimate his ideological aims as well as the cultural framework in which he fabricated the Bulgarians' historiographical past. If it was necessary for Krâstevich to be considered a "national" historian, the "romantic" dimension of his work would have been sufficient, as implied by Burmov (for which he is rightly criticized by Boneva), and "scientific" corroboration would not have been necessary to support it.

Perhaps the interpretive key to approaching his work is precisely the content that would label him "romantic." If this suggests a divergence of his work from "scientific truth," then it could be confronted with the terms of nineteenth-century historiographical Positivism. If, on the other hand, the issue was simply the construction of a mythical antiquity for the Bulgarian nation, this could repeat the arguments made by other intellectuals of the Bulgarian renaissance such as Petâr Beron and Georgi Rakovski.

Had Krâstevich sought an antiquity for the Bulgarian nation, he would probably have been content with the Thraco-Illyrians. But as Drinov correctly pointed out in his historiographical treatise, the latter's history was marked by a series of defeats: a shapeless population substrata that received successive blows from Alexander the Great's Macedonians, the Romans, the Goths, and the Slavs. Thus, not only would he have had to solve this problem; he would also have shift to a paradigm more compatible with the imperial framework within which he operated politically. Venelin's work was definitely a solution that could prove useful in this direction—but a solution that had to be amended. Venelin sought to counter the idea that the Bulgarians were enslaved Tatars, yet he also considered the modern Bulgarians to be descendants of the Proto-Bulgarians. The latter's identity remained an open question that had to be addressed.

Krâstevich, however, despite relying on Venelin's structure, did not deny Pavel Šafárik's heritage. And this is precisely because he could not understand the contradictions between these historiographical narratives (just as Gedeon could not understand the contradictions between the Pan-Orthodox and Imperial narratives).

Krâstevich also commenced his *History* with an overview of various writers preoccupied with the size of the Bulgarian population, both within and outside the Ottoman Empire. He criticized those whose estimates were relatively low, like Cyprien Robert[69] and Andreas Papadopoulos-Vrettos, emphasizing the importance of work with estimates greater than four million, like Ami Boué, and especially Šafárik and Ubicini.

Andreas Papadopoulos-Vrettos estimated the Bulgarian population at two million.[70] He even included those who had been Islamized, a fact Krâstevich mocked with the observation that Papadopoulos-Vrettos did not mention "how many Bulgarians are found in other parts of European Turkey, that is, in Thrace, Macedonia, Epirus, and Thessaly—regions in which he recognizes that there were Bulgarians."[71] On the other hand, similar to Boué,[72] Šafárik estimated the Bulgarian population at 4.5 million. Indeed, Krâstevich referenced the following excerpt from Šafárik's book.[73] (The translation is based on Krâstevich's Bulgarian).

> During the peak of the old Bulgarian kingdom through the arrival of the Magyars, Cumans, and Patzinak, one Slavic language was spoken in all the countries that were a part of this kingdom, except for the southern Danubian lands where the Vlachs and Magyars live, and specifically in Wallachia, Transylvania, and present-day Hungary, from the Danube to the Pest . . . From the monuments and translations of the Holy Scriptures and ecclesiastical books, we understand that this language had the same origin and structure as the now very

69 Robert, *Türkei*, 230. However, in a series of articles published in *Revue des Deux Mondes* under the title "Le Monde greco-slave," Robert also took the view that the Bulgarians in the Balkan peninsula numbered 4.5 million.

70 Andreas Papadopoulos-Vrettos, *La Bulgarie ancienne et moderne*, 151.

71 Krâstevich, *Bâlgarska Istoriya*, xiii

72 Boué, *La Turquie d'Europe*, vol. 2, 5.

73 Šafárik , *Slovanský naropodis*, vol 1, ch. 2, n.10

different Bulgarian dialect which is spoken from the Danube delta to Thessaloniki and Kastoria. (Krâstevich, *Bâlgarska Istoriya*, v–vi)

The Cumans were known as Polovci in medieval Russian sources like the *Chronicles of Kiev*. This uniformity of Paleo-Slavic and Paleo-Bulgarian with modern Bulgarian dialects that Šafárik saw was not enough to persuade Krâstevich of the Proto-Bulgarians' slavicization. On the contrary, his view that the latter should be considered Slavs became even firmer. Krâstevich used Ubicini's analysis to support his disagreement with what he ironically dubbed Papadopoulos-Vrettos's "official" data, as the French traveler used statistical data from the 1844 census. Ubicini estimated the Empire's Bulgarian population at four million.[74]

Krâstevich began with an analysis of the population data because the same logical inconsistency also bothered Drinov:

> Since the Bulgarians are so numerous and scattered throughout Turkey, did they always live here, or did they come from somewhere else? If they did not always live here, where were their first known centers? And when and how did they leave there, from where and how did they settle here? And during this period, what military successes did they achieve, and what were their relations with the other peoples and kingdoms? *The History of the Bulgarian People* which we have undertaken to write answers these questions. (Krâstevich, *Bâlgarska Istoriya*, nxvi)

These were the basic aims of Krâstevich's history. But before proceeding to outline events, he had to answer another fundamental question: the chronological starting point for his narrative; a point that would indicate what he considered "antiquity" in the context of the Bulgarian nation's historical evolution. Krâstevich had actually provided an answer a few years earlier in a paper titled *Brief Study on Bulgarian Antiquity* published in 1858–59 in his own journal, *Bâlgarski Knizhitsi*.[75]

This paper was organized into three chapters. The first identified the first Bulgarian centers. The second focused on the issue of the Bulgarians'

---

74 See Ubicini, *Lettres sur la Turquie*.

75 Krâstevich, "Kratko izslidovanie na Bâlgarska Drevnost."

name at the start of their history. The third examined the Bulgarians' race. On all three issues, the ancient writers, contemporaries of the Bulgarians' arrival in the Balkans from the Volga, expressed different or contradictory views on their identity.

Using "important historical data and rational observations," as he described them, Krâstevich tried to prove that the Bulgarians and Huns coexisted during the same period in Asian Sarmatia, that is, the Upper Caucasus between the Don and Volga rivers (an issue he also dealt with in the introduction).[76] He also attempted to prove that based on the previous conclusion, and the fact that contemporary writers often used the term Huns for the Bulgarians, the Huns were nothing more than Bulgarians. Based on this, Krâstevich concluded that Bulgarians and Huns were nothing but Slavs.

As he noted in his introduction, "the Bulgarians and Huns together were neither Tatars nor Mongols, as Dugin and other insolents claim, nor Finns or Chuds (a Finnic-Hungarian people) as Šafárik and others inaccurately believe, but pure Slavs who spoke then as they do now, the Slavic tongue."[77]

This was the reason for Krâstevich starting Bulgarian history with the Huns' appearance in European history in 374–75 B.C., instead of 485 B.C., the earliest Greek and Latin references to the name "Bulgarian."[78] After rejecting Šafárik's views on the Finnic origin of the Proto-Bulgarians as groundless, Krâstevich endorsed Venelin' position although he understood that it stood on the margins of science.[79] His insistence on a "non-scientific" view demands examination.

The correlation between Bulgarians and Huns, and the latter's identification with the Slavs obviously predated Venelin and constitutes a repeated motif in the process of building a definition of "Eastern Europe," as Larry Wolff has adequately shown. For example, Claude-Charles de Peyssonnel referred to the Bulgarians as Oriental Scythians who migrated

76 Krâstevich, *Bâlgarska Istoriya*, xvii.

77 Ibid.

78 On Hun history, see Thompson, *Attila and the Huns*, and Manchen-Helfen, *World of the Huns*.

79 "And because in our opinion—as in Venelin, Savel'ev, and others—the fact that the Huns were Bulgarians is not yet accepted by all writers. To avoid being misunderstood, all we want to say, without altering the folk tradition, is that with the name 'Huns,' we only present the historical foundations [of this people], in other words, that the Bulgarians and not some other people, were called 'Huns.'" Krâstevich, *Bâlgarska Istoriya*, xviii.

from the Volga to "Pontian Scythia" on the Black Sea.[80] The Huns were described as "real Slavs (Scythians) or Sarmatian Scythians" who arrived from European Sarmatia, which he situated along the Don River. Peyssonnel pointed out that the Huns should not be confused with the Hungarians who appeared much later, in the ninth century. He also compared the Huns with the Tatars, especially the Nogais, but concluded that these were two different peoples. "The Huns were Slavs or Sarmatian Scyths, and the Nogai were Tatars and Circassian Scyths."[81] As noted earlier, Krâstevich was educated in France, lived in Paris for several years, and may have been acquainted with Peyssonnel's work. Yet, Peyssonnel was not included in the supposed influences listed by Bulgarian scholars of Krâstevich's work, such as Vera Boneva.[82]

Things become even more interesting if one considers that the semantic confusion between Bulgarians and Huns was reproduced even by Gibbon. According to him, "the savage populations who had settled or roamed the plains of Russia, Lithuania, and Poland in Justinian's time could be reduced to two large ethnic families, the Bulgarians and the Sclavonians."[83] In a footnote to the term "Bulgarian," he noted that he borrowed the term from a series of ancient writers like Ennodius, Jordanès, Theophanes, and the chronicles written by Cassiodorus and Marcellinus, who believed that the Bulgarians were descended from the Huns and are, therefore, related to other "Tatar" tribes like the Kutrigurs and Utigurs. But Gibbon commented that he preferred the term "Bulgarian" as "Hun is so vague" and the "tribes of the Kutrigurs and Utigurs are so unimportant and wild." When he resumed his narrative on the creation of the first Bulgarian state after 680 A.D., he clarified that there was no doubt those Bulgarians spoke Slavic like the Dalmatians, Bosnians, Serbs, Poles, and so on, thus referring to Chalkokondylis. Thus, it is not outside the realm of possibility that Gibbon—whom the Greek-speaking Bulgarian Krâstevich would have read—contributed to the semantic merging of Huns and Bulgarians.[84]

80 Peyssonnel, *Observations historiques et geographique*, 30, 39.

81 Wolff, *Investing Eastern Europe*, 286

82 Boneva, "Istorikât Krâstevich," 185.

83 Gibbon, *Decline and Fall*, vol. 5, 217.

84 Of course, the older correlation of Bulgarians and Huns in European bibliographies must be sought in Leibniz, which suggests the historical depth of this origin theory. My thanks to Yannis Kakridis for this information.

Krâstevich's fundamental position had been formed by 1859 and from several autobiographical notes, it seems that the first volume of his *Bâlgarska Istoriya* had also been completed during this period.[85] The intense political activity of the 1860s and the compilation of material to complete the other two volumes were in all probability the main reasons publication was delayed. But it seems that the international scientific community's gradual consolidation of Šafárik's views were another significant delaying factor. For example, in 1856, Amédée Thierry, an historian for whom Krâstevich had great respect, published a history of Attila and his successors in which he argued for a distinction between the Finnic, Germanic, and Slavic peoples. Thierry saw the Huns as the leaders of a confederation of tribes of Finnic and Mongolian origin.[86] Indeed, he considered the fact that the issue of the Huns' Ural-Altaic identity had been resolved to be an achievement of modern historical science.[87]

Despite Krâstevich's insistence on publishing his work, it was also certain that his positions would not be accepted easily by Bulgarian and international academic communities. For the same reason, Drinov could not believe that an argument that confused Huns and Bulgarians could be accepted by a Bulgarian scholar, although he may have had the 1859 essay in mind. The ideological–political endeavor of publishing, therefore, seems to have been stronger than the scientific one. Indeed, the first volume of his history entitled *Bâlgarska Istoriya i.e., Hunnic* focuses on the period he described in 1858–59 as "Bulgarian antiquity," which spans 374–75 to 468, "when the name Bulgarian began to be heard among the Romans."[88]

---

85 Boneva, "Istorikât Krâstevich," 186.

86 Thierry considers the Hun-led confederation to have been comprised of both Ural Finns (mainly from the West) and Mongols from the Central Asian steppes (in the East). See Thierry, *Histoire d'Attila*, vol 1, 4–9. Earlier, Joseph De Guignes's narrative was based on Greek and Latin sources and did not confuse the Huns with the Bulgarians. The latter did not even appear. He did, however, mention that the peoples of Eastern Sarmatia were dependent on the Huns. Guignes, *Histoire General*, vol. 2., 277–324; 292; 298.

87 Thierry, *Histoire d'Attila*, 13.

88 Krâstevich promised to publish two more volumes of his *Bâlgarska Istoriya*, for which he had collected the material. One would contain the second part of his *History* titled "Bulgarian" spanning from 485 to 668, a period of 183 years; the other, which comprised the third part, covered the period from 668 to 1041, that is, 373 years. For the content of these volumes, which are preserved at the National Library of Sofia, see Boneva, " Krâstevich," 190.

There are two points in this volume that could provide some indication of Krâstevich's political orientation which superseded his scientific reservations. The first is the choice of Attila the Hun's period as the chronological springboard for Bulgarian antiquity. The fact that Krâstevich appeared dissatisfied by the Thracian-Illyrian past must have been precisely for the same reasons Drinov's "scientific" narration precluded these as the ancestors of today's Bulgarians: their successive defeats in history. Krâstevich needed to invent a glorious past that not only corresponded in general to the achievements of Ancient Greek civilization but also balanced what was now its universality. The insistence on its Hunnic origins offered Bulgarian history its own Alexander the Great. The opening paragraph of Krâstevich's *Bulgarian History* was a comparison of the two men:

> The heritage of that great conqueror Attila, who for a few years created a kingdom equal in grandeur to the kingdom of Alexander the Great and who had as his subordinates emperors, kings, and princes and subjects, and who the Greco-Roman[89] emperors themselves feared, had the same fate as the heritage of the Macedonian king—that is, it was decimated and quickly collapsed. (Krâstevich, *Bâlgarska Istoriya*, 411–12)

So not only did the crowning moment of Hellenism's spread find its counterpart in Bulgarian history, but the uninterrupted clash between Bulgars/Huns and Byzantine Emperors was re-certified. But this clash was characterized by two points. First, it was not conducted by an ethnicized state (in which case, the modern Bulgarians' Slavic origin would have sufficed) but from the perspective of the demand for universal space and time. Second, this claim of an imperial past was made with the weapons provided by an adversary, Byzantium.

Just as he had done in his 1858–59 essay, Krâstevich placed these first Bulgarian settlements north of the Caucasus, between the Don and Volga rivers. He linked the ethnonym "Bulgarian" to the name of the biggest

89 It is extremely interesting that Krâstevich used the term "Greco-Roman" to describe the Byzantine emperors, which was also used by Adamantios Korais, one of the leading figures of the Modern Greek Enlightenment some decades earlier.

European river, without knowing whether it was the Bulgarians who gave their name to this or vice versa. The Bulgarian neo-Phanariot—and on this point he is fiercely criticized by his rivals, especially Drinov—based his estimates exclusively on Byzantine sources: the testimonies of chroniclers like Theophanes, Nikephoros, Anastasios, Prokopios, and Jordanès (a Goth). It was common in these testimonies for Bulgarians to be referred to as "Huns."[90]

This Byzantine chroniclers' habit of using old names for new peoples does not bother Krâstevich, even though this was a common criticism of these sources in the historiography on Byzantium of the nineteenth century. Paradoxically, in Krâstevich's narrative, the identity of the Huns/Bulgarians was defined by their great rival, Byzantium and its civilization. The "literal" sense in which he perceived historical truth in the Byzantine sources determined how he understood the meaning of "Bulgarian antiquity."[91] Bulgarian antiquity had to compete against Byzantium, not Ancient Greece, and Attila was the counterpart of Alexander the Great who prepared the way for the First and Second Rome. Krâstevich's narrative created a bizarre medieval antiquity that assumed several ideological roles. Compared to the Greek example, the need to contrive an antiquity appeared more urgent in the Bulgarian case. By choosing to create an Unnic antiquity for the Bulgarian nation, Krâstevich had a dual purpose: to normalize, according to his perspective, the relationship between the Bulgarians and their Slavic origins, and to construct a historiographical example that could compete against the Greek. Both goals had a common denominator: the imperial structure.

Krâstevich perceived the normalization of the Bulgarians' relationship with their Slavic origin as the identification of a chronological moment in which they arrived at the level of constructing a historical universality. This could not be provided by either the Thraco-Illyrian

90 Nonetheless, in the first draft of his *History* in 1859, Krâstevich was already preparing for the identification of the Bulgarians/Huns with the Slavs. Using the testimonies of Prokopios and Jordanès that the Slavs also populated the same Sarmatian lands, he commented: "the Slavic tribes did not only inhabit lands west of the river Don (Tanais) but also to its East in the same lands from where we see the Huns and later the Bulgarians drawing their ancestry." See G Krâstevich, "Kratko izslidovanie na Bâlgarska Drevnost," 100.

91 Conversely, Drinov's "scientific historical discourse" understood the metaphorical nature of the testimonies in Byzantine sources in attempting to decipher them.

past or an acknowledgment that Asparuh's conquerors were culturally weakened to the point that only their name survived. In terms of the comparison with the Ancient Greek past, he could easily have selected another measure to highlight Bulgarian historical achievements: Athens, or even Sparta, instead of Alexander the Great. Krâstevich's choice of Attila as a response to Alexander the Great was not merely a reply to a Droysen-style challenge but the result of an evaluation of the imperial prospect as infinitely more important for the Bulgarian nation's self-esteem. Except that Attila was a retroactive reply to Alexander the Great. As such, the comparison would shift to the dawn of the medieval world. The historiographical paradigm that Krâstevich proposed did not compare two antiquities (Ancient Greek and Illyrian-Thracian) or two medieval periods (Byzantine and Bulgarian), but two imperial potentials at the point of their respective expansions.

With this in mind, it is easier to answer the question as to whether the name "Hun" set as an ideological goal the normalization of relations between the new Bulgarian nation and the Ottoman Empire. Faithfully aligned with Venelin, Krâstevich sought to remove any confusion of his "Huns" with the Tatars or Finns. However, by adopting a position identifying "Huns" with "Slavs," he held the door wide open for a composite of the imperial and the national. If Ottomans and Bulgarians descended from the same population pool as the peoples of Central Asia and the Urals, coexistence within the framework of the Ottoman Empire—indeed, on favorable terms compared to other ethnic groups in the Rum millet— might remain an existing historical potential. Indeed, until Krâstevich published his *History*, the Bulgarians' demands were limited solely to autonomy from the Ecumenical Patriarchate, which (in spite of his occasional patriotic rhetorical flourishes) he also strove to accomplish with as little trauma as possible.[92]

---

92 Here we must observe that his position on the Bulgarians' Thraco-Illyrian past, at least in Rakovski's case (but also in Beron's), resulted in autonomous revolutionary political activity that aimed mainly at mobilizing the Bulgarians settled in the Balkans as well as their cooperation with other "native" peoples like the Serbs and Romanians, whose Daco-Getae past was also linked to the Thraco-Illyrians in various nineteenth-century historiographical structures. See Boia, *History and Myth*, 102–6. Conversely, the insistence on Slavic origin linked the Bulgarians to the great family of Eastern European peoples and, of course, the Russians. This did not imply an absence of autonomous political activity, although it is inconceivable that this would be disconnected from Russian foreign

Although Vera Boneva's line of defense of Krâstevich's work concerns its "scientific" character, she makes the following observation about an unpublished volume of his *History*:

> The Ottoman Empire's early centuries are also partially mentioned in Krâstevich's historiographical heritage. Above, we had presented an extensive new extract from his manuscript on the Bulgarian Middle Ages in which he mentions the Muslim faith. The historian links the reasons for the state legal model with some of Islam's peculiarities. In 1859, the periodical *Bâlgarski Knizhitsi* published an odd article on the creation of the Janissaries unit. In this article, he finds a way to refer to the essence of this "blood tax" through which the [Ottoman] war apparatus was systematically staffed. This article is impressive not only for its topic, but also for the author's calm tone and realistic stance toward the problems of early Ottoman history. A similar approach can be seen in his writings on the Patriarch of Constantinople in which he has the opportunity to present some information regarding the policies of the Turkish Sultans toward Christian civil institutions in the first centuries following their conquest of the Balkans. (Boneva, "Istorikât Krâstevich," 201)

The "strange" article about the "blood tax"—*devşirme*, the forced roundup of children—and Krâstevich's "realistic stance" on the Ottoman past clearly illustrate that this publication's real target was a "scientifically" obsolete Bulgarian history, not merely to normalize the Bulgarians' Slavic past based on imperial needs but to establish some cultural bridges between Bulgarian modernity and the imperial framework that had allowed its emergence. This suggests something more than a simple Turkophile bent. The discourse between Drinov and Krâstevich in the wake of their histories' simultaneous release proves this.

---

policy's strategic needs. In a way, what we have here is a replication of the Greek case, except for the fact that the Greek clash over different policies was in the name of a new nation, while in the Bulgarian case, it was based on origin, with Russia largely filling the role of the West.

5. Drinov's Thesis: The Bulgarians Are Slavs (The Negative Use of Byzantine Chronography)

In 1872, Marin Drinov wrote a harsh review of Gavril Krâstevich's work titled "Hunni li sme?" (Are We Huns?).[93] This was published in the first volume of the Bulgarian Literary Society's periodical review at Brăila and was introduced by Borislav Stoyanov, the journal's editor, who was similarly severe in his critique.

In this short essay, Drinov mocked Krâstevich's certainty that "in ancient times, the Bulgarians were called 'Huns,'" and that the history of the Huns, from the beginning of the Hunnic Empire to its collapse following Attila's death, could be considered the first phase in Bulgarian history. Drinov noted that this claim had been made by writers such as Venelin and Savel'ev-Rostislavich earlier, but without convincing arguments, similarly to Krâstevich's case. "Krâstevich also made use of primary historical sources to prove a theory that has been rejected by rational historical science. He so strongly believed that the Huns were our ancestors that he had no doubt that Hunnic history is our ancient history."[94]

Drinov spoke from the perspective of defending scientific historical work. He accused Krâstevich of being fixated by his irrational idea. Further, he was concerned that the expression of these views by such a "respected" representative of neo-Phanariot thought contributed to the ultimate neglect of the Bulgarian people's real ancestors, the Slavic tribes who settled south of the Danube before it was crossed by Asparuh and his hordes. Drinov did not limit his sarcasm to Krâstevich's work or conclusions, or even to influences on them; his sarcasm was aimed at the broader role Krâstevich had assumed in Bulgarian political affairs. "Nothing new about our history emerges from the Hunno-Bulgarian history, but we have to give it our attention for the following reasons: the respected creator of this Bulgarian history under the Hunnic name has toiled for some time now in this scientific field where his name is known with regard to the scientific studies compiled with historical and ecclesiastical truths."[95]

---

93 Drinov, "Hunni li sme?," 189–217.

94 Ibid., 190.

95 Ibid., 190

Drinov derided Krâstevich's role in secret with the Greek neo-Phanariots and the Patriarchate talks a year earlier,[96] and his scientific criticism became a sort of political intervention against the methods followed by the neo-Phanariot intellectuals in resolving the Bulgarian Question. This attack on Krâstevich's ideas pointed to the weaknesses of the Bulgarian "conservatives'" in their attempt to create a model for coexistence with the Ottoman element as well as with the Ecumenical Patriarchate.

Drinov at least acknowledged Krâstevich's use of primary historical sources and focused his criticism on the first thirty pages of the opening chapter, in which he believed the "misunderstanding" of the identification of Huns and Bulgarians lay. Drinov's critique was organized around three key questions that also comprised the headings of his essay's sections: 1) Is it true that the Huns initially lived in Asian Samartia and were the exclusive sovereigns of this vast area? 2) Is it true that Bulgarian centers have been identified in Asian Samartia and were identical to the Hunnic centers? 3) Do Byzantine writers prove that the Bulgarians and Huns were the same people and how much faith should be placed in their testimonies on this issue?[97]

Of these three questions posed by Drinov and the replies he offered as part of an analysis of Krâstevich's work, the third is obviously of fundamental importance. Whereas it could rationally be suggested that it was not obvious that Huns and Bulgarians were the same people just because they inhabited lands of Asian Samartia, the third question also raised an issue of methodology—the historian-scientist's wariness of his sources. According to Drinov, Krâstevich's lacked this circumspection, and that constituted his basic scientific weakness. Things, however, became worse precisely because his sources were essentially Byzantine: Krâstevich's anti-Byzantine rhetoric notwithstanding, the way in which he determined the identity of the Huns/Bulgarians was based solely on the enemy's perspective.

---

96 We know Krâstevich was severely criticized by Istanbul's Bulgarian community when it became known that along with the proceedings of the first Clergy–Laity Assembly (March–July, 1871), convened to draft the Exarchate charter, he participated in a secret Greek-Bulgarian committee with Ivan Haci Penchovich, Alexander Karatheodoris, and Christakis Zographos which sought a compromise with the patriarchate on a range of issues. See Burmov, *Bâlgaro-grâchka tsârkovna raspra*, 79. This committee was created on the orders of Âli Pasha and discussed issues such patriarchal references by Exarchate Bishops and the patriarch's role in issuing the new berat on the exarch's appointment. The committee failed to reach any conclusion in the shadow of the controversy of the revelation of its clandestine nature.

97 Drinov, "Hunni li sme?," 192; 200, 207.

Indeed, Drinov cited von Stritter, who had expressed the view that the Byzantines' perception of the Huns was so vague that it was obvious that they had little idea of who exactly they were referring to by this name. He continued:

> Just as the Ancient Greeks called "Scythians" all the peoples with whom they were unfamiliar and who lived in the north, the Byzantines gave this name (Huns) to almost all the peoples who lived in the north, above the Lower Danube and the Black Sea. Thus Menander, Theophylactos, Theophanes, Cedrenus, they all called the Avars Huns. Patriarch Nikephoros, Theophanes, and Cedrenus give this name to the Bulgarians; Nikephoros Grigoras to the Cumans. The "Paschal Chronicle" calls the Gepids Huns, Cedrenus calls the Slovenes Huns, Theophanes calls the Turks Huns, Anna Komnene and Cedrenus call the Uzes [by this name]. In short, the Byzantines applied this name to many different peoples: Slovenes, Germans, and Tatar tribes. And it's not hard to understand why. The Huns extended their power far beyond the Roman Empire's borders and into the depths of Asia; many different peoples were subjugated to their authority and brought considerable damage to the Roman Empire's Eastern and Western regions. All these antics impressed the Byzantines, who considered them a great people to whom they attributed the lesser-known tribes under the Huns' jurisdiction or how appeared on lands of the former Hunnic Empire. (Drinov, "Hunni li sme?," 207–208)

Krâstevich's argument that these writers may also have been reproducing the historical testimonies of earlier writers and so their works may also prove useful on this count prompted Drinov's sarcasm:

> Thus, Jordanès relates that the Huns are descended from Gothic witches who lay with demonic spirits, while Prokopios says he has heard that the Cimmerians had lived in Asian Samartia one thousand years ago and, thus, concludes that they too were Huns. Prokopios does not know that the Cimmerians had been chased from those lands in 600 B.C., and I am surprised that Mr. Krâstevich, who knows this well, gives such weight to Prokopios's fairy tales. (208)

In this scientific manner, Drinov stripped Krâstevich's political endeavors bare. The critical approach to sources and their induction into a specific historical framework highlighted his historiographical inadequacy. Furthermore, Drinov noted that if all the identifications of peoples as Huns by Byzantine sources were taken seriously, this would raise another problem: the claim of a common heritage with an uncertain conclusion:

> And the historian who undertakes to speak about the peoples that the Byzantines once called "Huns" must be very careful with Byzantine testimonies. If we trust these, imagine what would happen! The Germans would rise up to prove that the Huns were German because the "Pascal Chronicle" names the German Gepid tribe as "Huns." All Slovenes would say they were Huns because Cedrenus claimed that the Huns are Slovenes. The Turks, the Avars, the Cumans, and the Uzes and all those with the same right would claim the Huns' glory. How would Mr. Krâstevich resist so many rivals? How would he manage to subjugate them? But let us not kid ourselves![98] (Drinov, "Hunni li sme?," 208)

Naturally, with this concluding argument Drinov admitted that the Huns' historical heritage was significant and would be worth claiming. The Bulgarians had little chance of winning such a claim, however, and had to limit themselves to the glorious past of those whom he called their "true ancestors": the Slavs.

> Is it true that the Kutrigurs and Utrigurs are Huns? Can they be identified with the Bulgarians? That is not our job . . . they should not be given a place in our history. . . . Are the ancient Bulgarians Huns? Are they from Tartary or Mongolia? It's the same to us. Our people took their name but is not descended from them. We bear their name, but their blood does not flow in our veins. (208)

98 On the Byzantine writers' naming of barbarian tribes, see Florin Curta's outstanding analysis in *The Making of the Slavs*. Curta notes that the ethnic definition of these tribes is not related to their linguistic or cultural identity but was determined in terms of military and political strength. In this sense, the Byzantine sources, particularly in the case of the Lower Danube Slavs, did not reflect a process of ethnogenesis but rather take part in "contriving" it, attributing names like Adam in the Garden of Eden. (Curta, *Making of the Slavs*, 346–50.)

Drinov, in other words, insisted on Šafárik's views on the Bulgarians' remote past and rejected Venelin's views anew, seeing in Krâstevich's work an inferior imitation. Once again, he updated the work of Paisius which, along similar lines, elevated a Slavic Bulgarian Middle Ages to counter Byzantine civilization's dominant position. In order to achieve this, the last thing one should do is accept Byzantine sources as defining of one's identity.

6. Krâstevich's Response: The Huns Are Slavs

Krâstevich soon learned of Drinov's critique in the pages of the Bulgarian Literary Society's journal.[99] His response was published in May 1873 in Istanbul in the pages of *Chitalishte*, the journal published by his loyal colleague Marko Balabanov and printed on the presses of the newspaper *Makedoniya* published by Petko Slaveykov, the same place where Krâstevich's book had been printed.

A visibly shocked Krâstevich started his article defensively, claiming that when publishing his *History* he "impatiently [awaited] the commentary on any mistakes we have unknowingly or knowingly made so we can correct them . . . to the benefit of our people."[100] But he quickly mounted a counteroffensive, having first observed that Drinov's review and Stoyanov's introductory note focused solely on the controversial first thirty pages: a thirty-five-page review (Drinov's critique ran twenty-nine pages and Stoyanov's introduction ran a further six pages) for just thirty pages of his own work. Even so, Krâstevich would have been satisfied if the criticism had been constructive. Conversely, the article bordered on the malicious as "they claim that nothing of what we wrote is worth anything and, secondly, accuse us of things we have not written, nor sought to prove, claiming that we have said and written them."[101] Given the circumstances and the stakes, the "truth" about an entire nation's history, it may not have been possible for this dialogue to continue. Krâstevich confessed that their two histories, his and Drinov's, were written without one being aware of the other's, and that in December 1871, when he became

99 Krâstevich, *Otgovor*.
100 Ibid., 1
101 Ibid.

aware of Drinov's *Pogled*, he had written about it in *Chitalishte*.[102] Drinov's "'Hunni li sme?,'" was published in November.

According to Krâstevich, this was not a simple scientific critique but an attempt by Drinov to denigrate his ideas and impose the Šafárik line:

> As a scientist and clever man, Mr Drinov, after having read the above text, realized that his opinion, which is based on the so-credible theory of Šafárik and others, will retreat in the face of our precise and strong evidence and arguments. Like a protective father, he took pity on his offspring, that is his theory, and sought ways to defend it from certain death. After much thought, he found a way that seemed right: to strike out at and destroy our arguments, presenting them as false and groundless claims, fighting the foundations of our history on the origins of the Bulgarian people. This is why he wrote his critique in November 1871, wishing in this way to cancel out our opinion so that his would prevail. (Krâstevich, *Otgovor*, 3)

Krâstevich raised the issue in ideological and political terms. In turning Drinov's observations back on him in order to support his own text's scientific validity, it is obvious that the ultimate argument was purely political.

Krâstevich claimed that Drinov distorted his words and argued that the use of Byzantine sources was completely legitimate as they preserved testimonies of earlier writers such as Deuxippus, Priscus, and Olympiodorus, all supposedly contemporaries of the events described.[103] But he continued to insist on the logic of finding the Huns' ancient centers in Asian Samartia, even though he admitted that their origin was difficult to prove and that the problem hovered between historical reality and myth. But he could not accept Drinov's refusal to accept the rationale of the origin interpretation. Commenting on the excerpt we included above—"Our people took their name from the [Proto-Bulgarians] but does not descend from them. We bear their name but their blood does not flow

102 The review was published in issues 5 and 6.

103 "Let me ask Mr Drinov if he wrote something that was based on someone else's written or oral sources, would he say that his study was worthless? Of course not, because in this way, he would deny his love of truth. And he would also reject every history based on oral or written sources." Krâstevich, *Otgovor*, 11.

in our veins"—Krâstevich found it incredible that a scientific historian avoided the question of origin, turning his attention exclusively to the issue of the Proto-Bulgarians' expansion and eventual disappearance/assimilation/dominance. However, he knew full well that the question was not raised to dispute the Bulgarians' Slavic origins—since in his view, the Huns were Slavs—but so they could acquire a more complex identity that was less functional within the imperial framework.

His opponents knew this too: where identity became more complex, there was a concordant loss in the people's "Slavness," which had consequences for both their bloodline but also for the process of recognition by Russia. If Drinov tried to appear careful enough in defending Bulgarians' Slavicness, the same is not true for Stoyanov, who had written the introduction to Drinov's review in 1872:

> Once upon a time there was a barbarian Asian people called "Bulgarians," but we don't know if they were Tatars, Mongols, or Finns simply because we were not interested in knowing. In any case, this people was not Slavic, as proved by Klaproth[104] and Šafárik, and what these two writers claim should be seen as the absolute truth that no one can dispute. This is why we did not wish to research whether this was true or not because it is not our job. All these Bulgarians, after having spread in just six hundred years to the Black Sea and both banks of the Danube—and we are also not interested in what they did there because they were not Slavs, while we are—in the second half of the seventh century, they finally crossed the Danube, conquered Lower Moesia with the seven Slavic tribes already settled there and intermixed with them, slowly losing their national identity so that in the end they were transformed into Slavs without a drop of Bulgarian blood in their veins. How did this happen, when and where, is also not our concern because these Bulgarians who disappeared were not our fathers or even our uncles or our ancestors, nor are we their descendants. And that is the reason we are not interested in anything about them or start our history with them. Really, we inherited their name but that does not mean anything, and it does not give us cause to seek

104 Klaproth, *Archiv fur asiatische Litteratur.*

or research how or what happened because it is not our concern. We must simply accept that our people took their name as the historian Drinov assures us. (Krâstevich, *Otgovor*, 42)

Stoyanov, in a far less elegant (albeit honest) manner, highlighted the power of opinion: "it does not concern us." This view was clumsily and aggressively outlined because he fully understood the danger that any discussion of origin might cast doubt on the question of continuity.

In this fundamental clash between Krâstevich and his opponents, Vera Boneva again tries to excuse his reservations toward their unconditional pro-Slav/pro-Russian understandings by reproducing relevant evaluations by the historian Ivan Duychev.[105]

In the late 1960s, Duychev undertook the task of normalizing the three rival theories of the Bulgarian renaissance in a single ethnogenetic theory: Proto-Bulgarians, Slavs, and Thracians participated, if not in the same way, then at least equally in the process of shaping the Bulgarian ethnos.[106] Duychev was the one who restored the Proto-Bulgarian contribution in the shaping of the Bulgarian nation on scientific terms by criticizing the history Vasil Zlatarski had authored in 1918.[107] In an article published twenty years later, Duychev tried to annul Zlatarski's interpretation of the phrase υπό πάκτον όντας in Theophanes's work.[108] The phrase referred to the seven Slavic tribes' potential dependence on the Proto-Bulgarians. Zlatarski believed the phrase meant that there had been a peace treaty signed between the Proto-Bulgarians and the Slavs aimed at mutual security and that there was a form of equality between the two ethnic groups which may have remained discrete and independent. Duychev interpreted this as proof that the Slavic tribes were tributaries to the Proto-Bulgarians, except perhaps for the Severians with whom he believed they maintained friendly relations. He also claimed that the Proto-Bulgarians kept their ethnic identity discrete (although they did ally with the Severians to subjugate the other Slavic tribes) until the Bulgarians were converted to

105 Boneva, "Istorikât Krâstevich," 189. See also Duychev, "La formation," 215–24.

106 Duychev, "Le problème de la continuité," 138–50.

107 Zlatarski, *Istoriya na Bâlgarskata dârzhava*, especially vol. 1, "Pârvo bâlgarskoto carstvo" [The first Bulgarian kingdom].

108 Duychev, *Protobulgares et Slaves*.

Christianity, the start of their assimilation by the Slavic elements. Commenting on Drinov's position on the Proto-Bulgarians' numbers, Duychev took the opposite position. Yet, he seems to have been attracted to the parallel drawn between the Russian and Bulgarian cases: two Slavic nations that were born from a relationship of dependence on the Proto-Bulgarians-Turks and Russians-Vikings respectively. He cited the instances where the subjugated Slavs abandoned the Proto-Bulgarians to show that there was a submissive relationship. In fact, Zlatarski and Duychev proposed two different models for inducting the Proto-Bulgarian past, Zlatarski through the "peaceful coexistence" model and Duychev through the model of the Proto-Bulgarians' dominance of the other Slavic races. Incredibly, in his 1938 article, Duychev made no mention of Krâstevich.[109]

The defense of Krâstevich's ideas by younger Bulgarian historians like Vera Boneva seems to be a rectification of the weakness of historians at the time to express definitive thoughts about such a difficult problem. But the excerpt from Krâstevich's work that she mentions again vividly points to the political dimension of his endeavor. Mocking himself for being unable at the time to provide incontrovertible proof to support his basic position on the Bulgarians' origin, he states he would continue to "insist on the flattering deceit for every Bulgarian that they were and remain pure Slavs, that is Slavic Bulgarians or Slavophone Bulgarians."[110]

7. The Romantic Reconstruction of Imperial Discourse: Some Conclusions

If we wanted to sum up the discussion on the Greek and Bulgarian cases in terms of the historiographical divergences we have identified, we would say that while there are differences, there are also significant similarities.

The fundamental difference is that in Krâstevich's case, we have a completed historical work with specific targets. In Gedeon's case, there is an apparently fragmented array of historical sources accompanied by a critical commentary. At the same time, in both cases, we have a different—or, to be exact, inverse—approach to the Russian factor.

109 See also Duychev, "La formation," 215–24.
110 Boneva, "Istorikât Krâstevich," 189.

By choosing to emphasize the Proto-Bulgarian component, Krâstevich highlighted the divergence from Drinov's prevalent Slavophile canon; one could also claim that supporting the ideas of Venelin should not necessarily be considered anti-Russian.

Certainly, the clash between Drinov and Krâstevich does not replicate the theoretical clash between Šafárik and Venelin. The dispute of the former was principally political. Of course, in the early 1870s, the consequences of a Russian military invasion were not visible (as they were to become during the period of the Eastern Question). This does not mean that the Krâstevich-Drinov dispute can be interpreted according to the simplistic dipole: anti-Russian and pro-Russian. Chiefly though, the structure that Krâstevich chose—the Bulgarians are Huns, the Huns are Slavs—despite its contradictions, left open the possibility of interpreting Bulgarian history in relation to the history of other Slavic peoples, especially the Russians, as well as in relation to the imperial framework that Ottoman rule provided. What Drinov's theory established as a canon was not the fact that he shattered Krâstevich's ideas at the level of scientific dialogue but that the dominance of radical views on the Bulgarian national movement understood national completion would come with the empire's end. Krâstevich and the other "conservatives" did not consider this a given either with regard to the political dimension (in relation to the Ottoman state) or the cultural dimension (in relation to the Patriarchate).

In the Gedeon-Paparrigopoulos dispute, there was a substantial difference from the Bulgarian case: already by the end of the nineteenth century, Paparrigopoulos had been elevated to the status of a "canon." Disputing him was far more difficult than was the case with Krâstevich's argument over Drinov's expertise. But here, too, there are substantial similarities. In the Greek case, the bipolarity of a "pan-Orthodox" pro-Russian position and a nationalist anti-Russian position was evident. Indeed, from one perspective, Paparrigopoulos related the vision of the Great Idea to Russia's decisive role in the Ottoman Empire's dissolution. But that constituted a significant difference from Gedeon: it was very difficult to assume that the Pan-Orthodox unity that the patriarchate's Grand Chartophylax envisioned hid innermost desires for Russia to dissolve the Ottoman Empire. And that was exactly what emerged through his work: an invincible desire to reconstructed the two then-incompatible strategies: the Pan-Orthodox and the Imperial, the preservation of the unity of the Russian and Ottoman Orthodox East and the defense of the Ottoman imperial model.

In a way, the basic similarity and the common denominator between Gedeon's and Krâstevich's historiographical endeavors, seems to have been the organization of a structure for interpreting the past that merged the influences of the two imperial ideologies, Russian and Ottoman, which we have learned to assume were rival. It is interesting that these two historiographical models appeared at a time when Russia ceased to be a threat to the Ottoman Empire's integrity, the period immediately following the Crimean War in Krâstevich's case and the period after the Eastern Crisis in Gedeon's.[111]

It is particularly interesting that two of these historiographical structures resorted to the ideological/methodological use of Byzantium in order to achieve compatibility between these two types of imperial discourse. Krâstevich did this with the "literal" (one-to-one) use of Byzantine sources through which Bulgaria's "medieval antiquity" (plus Attila) was defined. Gedeon rather followed a metaphorical/metonymic use of Byzantium as a model for Church–state relations applied during the late Ottoman Empire, when Byzantium acquired the role of a pre-modern mold for defining modern empires. Of course, in their political dimension, both arguments could be described as "conservative": in Krâstevich's case, if not preserving the empire, then certainly for denigrating radical modes for the construction of a nation-state; in Gedeon's, by casting doubt on the secularization process, that is the only definite herald of modernity. Byzantium served as the standard against which Gedeon and Krâstevich disputed their respective national historiographical canon (which even in Paparrigopoulos's case also appears to have been rooted in Byzantium). The main similarity between them is that by creating a

111 We might, in fact, claim that in the late nineteenth century, these two great continental Empires were confronted by different versions of modernization processes, and had begun to transform, at the end of the nineteenth century. On the nature of the Hamidian regime and the Ottoman Empire's modern transformations, see Skopetea, *I Dysi tis Anatolis*, 17–26; Deringil, *Well-Protected Domains*. On Russia, see Dominic Lieven's articles "The Russian Empire," and "Dilemmas of Empire," which offers a comparative perspective between the Russian and Ottoman cases, centered on the success of the first and failure of the second to implement military reform (167).

paradigm of ways to understand the nation as empire—Attila as Alexander the Great, ethnos as millet—the political framework which they serve was, in the end, the nation inside the empire.

In Krâstevich's case, the solution to the problem of origin threatened the continuity model, while this did not appear to be an issue in Gedeon's case. But the two factors through which the common denominator emerged—composition of contradictory strategies/merger of imperial discourses and use of Byzantium—suggest a turn toward an examination of other members of Istanbul's broader "conservative" circle, friends of both our historiographers (like Marko Balabanov) and also a guest for whom this issue was a direct concern (Konstantin Leont'ev).

Before analyzing their work, however, a brief discussion of two interventions on the Bulgarian origin issue is in order: the first from Bulgarian historiography, the second from Greek. These interventions were somewhat marginal but serve to highlight the tension between the model of continuity and the model of origins described above.

8. *Povestnost* instead of *Historiya*: Georgi Rakovski's Hyper-Hermeneutic Model

If Marin Drinov constructed a model of continuity for Bulgarian history because he aspired to manage the fundamental problem of discontinuity, especially after the collapse of the Second Bulgarian Kingdom, and if Gavril Krâstevich chose a model of origins whose concealed goal was to avert a rupture with the Ottoman Empire, then Georgi Rakovski outlined a *sui generis* theory of the origins of the Bulgarians' origins that did not merely aim to marginalize the others, but mainly to guarantee that Bulgarian "antiquity" might compete on equal terms with Greco-Roman antiquity.[112] The theory of the "Indo-European" origin of the Bulgarians constituted a reaction to the Pan-Slavic ambitions of the "Russia's deadly-for-the-Bulgarians policy as described by Rakovski, but was also meant to serve the final facilitation of the Bulgarians' recognition by the West. Contrary to Aretov's claim that this theory should be considered to be a "tendency" of early Bulgarian historiography, it should be thought of as

112 For a short biography of Rakovski, see Yonkov, *Rakovski*.

more marginal than Krâstevich's attempt to interpret Bulgarian history by reducing it to a Proto-Bulgarian past. As already mentioned, similar views were adopted by Beron as well as by Rakovski's loyal adherents such as Ivanko Luganov and Tsani Ginchev.

The approach of promoting the Bulgarians as principally Arian was not simply a reworking of the Thraco-Illyrian theory. This latter ranked among the forms that defend autochthony. For someone to claim that the Bulgarians' origin was an issue that pertained to very beginning of Indo-European civilization was an issue of a different order. The nation ceased being a cultural peculiarity and was reduced to the level of a cultural essence. In Balkan historiography, we come across an endeavor like Rakovski's much later, when Turkish historiography identified the Turk's "homeland," the Central Asia steppes, as the cradle of world civilization. There were only few options open for the pursuit of such a solution: either identification with the Arian or with the Altaic family. One precluded the other, so in Rakovski's case, the rivalry with Greek cultural hegemony combined with an intensely anti-Turkish position.

Although Rakovski had expressed his basic positions as early as 1860 in a pamphlet published in Belgrade titled "Brief Thoughts on the Dark and False Beginnings on Which the Ancient History of All Indo-European Peoples Are Based,"[113] he fully outlined his theory in 1865 when it was published in Bucharest as *Bâlgarska Starina* (Bulgarian antiquity).[114] While both texts were written before the Drinov–Krâstevich clash, Rakovski developed his argument with the main positions of the opposing camps in mind.

In *Kratko razsâzhdenie*, Rakovski assumed that India was the cradle of human civilization, he considered the Bulgarians as the purest of the Arians who first left India and brought the cult of Shiva to Europe. In the ancient Hindu faith, he saw a form of perfected religion which he found quite close to Christianity—this being the main reason the Bulgarians were so easily converted by St. Paul.

Although he often expressed his appreciation for Paisius's contribution and the ideas that formed the basis for *Slavo-Bulgarian History*, in

113 Rakovski, *Kratko razsâždenie.*

114 Rakovski, "Bâlgarska Starina," 375. *Bâlgarska Starina* was a periodic publication; the first issue was published in July 1865.

Bulgarian Antiquity (1865), Rakovski rejected the Judeo-centric idea of divine provenance as laid out in the Old Testament.[115]

Rakovski was well-versed in Greek antiquity and ancient civilization and equally well-versed in the intensely "anti-Greek" patriotism-tinged political speech. He studied at the Kuruçeşme School in Istanbul, during which time he had contact with Stefan Vogoridi and his circle. Krâstevich was also a part of this circle, so it is certain Rakovski was familiar with his Hunnic theory.

While Rakovski did not embrace Krâstevich's vindication of the Proto-Bulgarian past, he did "borrow" his method: to counter the glorious ancient Greek antiquity, he had to retroactively vindicate the Barbarians.[116] Through Indian literature, Asia became the cradle of human civilization, especially of the sciences and arts. Rakovski refered to Clarisse Bader, a member of the Asian Society in Paris and a specialist in Sanskrit philosophy, who related a myth on the beginnings of science (which was identified with philosophy) used by Lucian, which appeared in his *Drapetai*. Lucian personified philosophy as a woman conversing with her father, Zeus. "Philosophy, that is Science, initially appeared in India, to the Brahmins, and then in Ethiopia, Egypt, Babylon, and the Chaldeans, and from there in Scythia, then Thrace, where Eumolpus took her to Greece, and she taught the Greeks the meaning of Religion, while Orpheus taught them Music and this is how Science began in Ancient Greece: from the Thracians, who were not Greek but spoke a language related to theirs." [117]

Rakovski drew from the armory of the Orientalist turn in Western science during the nineteenth century whose basic motif was to dispute the Greco-Roman heritage in principle. As Clarisse Bader noted and Rakovski quoted, " . . . Greece and Rome, recognized to date as the sources of Classical perfection, have run dry." [118] The tendency for comparative literature in

115 Aretov, *Bâlgarskoto Vâzrazhdane*, 67.

116 Rakovski often referred to an excerpt from Plato's *Cratylus*, which hints at Ancient Greeks' linguistic loans from the barbarians. See Aretov, *Bâlgarskoto Vâzrazhdane*.

117 Rakovski, "Bâlgarska starina," 377. Clarisse Bader is known for her works *La femme biblique; sa vie morale et sociale, sa participation au developpement de l'idée religieuse* (Paris: Didier et cie, 1866) and *La femme grecque; étude de la vie antique* (Paris: Didier et cie, 1872)

118 Rakovski, "Bâlgarska starina," 378. Even Eden's exact location had been identified through the strict "comparative literary scientific method" with "precise studies of these lands, rivers, mountains, etc." at the Pamir plateau in the Himalayas.

Europe, as Rakovski admitted, was to reveal the true sources of human history and not to blindly follow the Greek, Jewish, and Latin sources.

Taking a cue from Friedrich Max Müller,[119] Rakovski would claim that comparative linguistics could pinpoint a primary period of linguistic formation during which the ancestors of the Indians—Persians, Romans, Slavs, Celts, Germans, and Greeks—lived together "under the same roof." Thus, comparative linguistics became the vehicle for Rakovski to take on rival theories of origin.

> In this direction—comparative literature, that is—we are trying to record the basic beginnings of ancient Bulgarian literature, leaving aside the Scythian and Tatar holes old and new writers mercilessly tossed us into without knowing our folk customs and traditions that have been preserved since antiquity, our old worship, songs, fairy tales, and proverbs, the primeval names and place names we have always had. We also reject the baseless belief that all scientists have held to date that the first migrants of what is known today as the Slavic race supposedly moved from the north toward the south, that is, from the Russian deserts, into which historians tirelessly threw us, and not from southeast toward northwest, as actually happened during the first and oldest migration. (Rakovski, "Bâlgarska starina," 380)

Although Rakovski accepted that there were later migrations to the Balkans from the north, he tried to prove that the Bulgarians were the first and oldest inhabitants of Europe and the purest descendants of the Arians. The Bulgarian-Arians' main movement was from India and the Babylonian lands, where they had remained for a long time, toward Europe in successive waves. These Bulgarians were not Tatar hordes, as historians influenced by the "biased and illiterate" Byzantine writers contended. Some Tatar hordes arrived in the Balkan peninsula, but much later, when the Bulgarian kingdoms had already been founded, and the name Bulgarian was already familiar in Europe. These Tatars remained Tatars forever. According to Rakovski, the older migrations from India to Europe could not have occurred suddenly but required centuries to complete. The

119 Müller, *La science du langage.*

migrants could not have all moved in the same directions or across the same lands because some areas, especially Asia Minor and the Bosporus, were occupied by earlier migrant waves. This was the reason for clashes between them, even though they belonged to the same race.

After describing the Bulgarians' ancient lifestyle, Rakovski developed his own narrative on the Bulgarians' identification with the Arians.[120] While critical of the Biblical roots of the Balkan ethnos's beginnings, he followed a somewhat similar course. The springboard for his narrative was the Flood, as with Paisius. The Indo-European races were, therefore, among those who survived the Flood "because they inhabited the broad and fertile tropical belt and the highest mountains."[121] Rakovski was convinced that he had proved the match between the names *Arians* and *Bulgarians*, and consequently the Bulgarian, and in general the Slavic race, was the first to reach the European mountain ranges. Rakovski also outlined the migration routes they supposedly followed:

> 1. On one of the routes they followed after many years of adventures, they crossed Asia Minor, the Bosporus, and the Dardanelles, settling in all of Thrace, with the broadest meaning, and from there spread as far as the Atlantic Ocean. Many from this small group remain in different parts of Asia, especially Asia Minor, Phrygia, and elsewhere. Greece, which did not yet have that name, was settled by the first wave of the Bulgaro-Slav genus.
>
> This tribe or great race is known in Ancient Greek history by the popular name of "Pelasgians" or Pelasgic nation, a name that is nothing other than "Belgoi"/Belgians="Bulgari"/Bulgarians,[122] corrupted by the Greek writers to "Pelasgians" because of the inadequacies of their language.

120 The contents of this presentation included: 1) the place names the Bulgarians preserved in the land they inhabit today and which have been transferred from their old residences in India; 2) the traces of the old Hindu worship in modern Bulgarian folk celebrations, customs, and rituals, exorcisms and water purifications, songs, fairy tales, and proverbs, cave worship, and the names of gods, etc.; 3) memories of the peoples migration from India; 4) comparison of the Bulgarian language with Sanskrit and living proof of the unique characteristics only the Bulgarian tongue has preserved out of all the European languages; 5) the name Bulgarian; 6) historical memories as safeguarded in folk songs; 7) description of migrations by Asparukh's and Kubrat's military units which were presented as Tatar hordes.

121 Rakovski, "Bâlgarska starina," 397.

122 Rakovski borrowed this from Amédée Thierry.

> The small Greek race had abandoned the primary Indian facilities along with the Bulgaro-Slav race but advanced separately and parallel to the Bulgaro-slovenes in wooded areas, without ever mixing with them. The name Graikos/Greek, which means "people of the woods" (gora=woods) was given to them by the Bulgaro-slovenes.
> 2. Another route taken was from the foothills of the Himalayas where an agricultural people known as Suci (=the one who sows and ploughs) still lives. This race migrated to the northern countries and entered Europe from different directions. A large segment of it arrived in the Moldo-Wallachian areas, crossed the Danube, settled old Thrace, and intermixed with the first wave of migrants which had settled in these areas. This second wave is known in ancient history as the Dacians, Getae, Daco-Getae, names that are nothing but Suci (sowers), Arians, Bulgarians, as we have explained elsewhere.
> 3. The third known wave of migrants were the Cimbri or Cimmerians in Greek,[123] which is nothing more than the name of the Gebroi (Zantes), direct descendants of the Arians. This large wave, as we have said elsewhere, had arrived 700 years before Christ, from the lands of the Caspian Sea, and inhabited different parts of Europe and finally ancient Thrace. One group crossed into Asia Minor. (Rakovski, "Bâlgarska starina," 398–99)

Rakovski's argument of origins did not leave anything uninterpreted: the Indo-European past, to be precise, operated as a hyper-hermeneutic principle that easily incorporated everything from the "Pelasgian" population substrata in the Balkans to the "Thraco-Illyrian" element, from the Dacians and the Getae to the Cimmerians. The form's hyper-hermeneutic character, which was based mainly on false etymologies of ancient ethnonyms (for example correlating the ethnonyms of Belgians and Bulgarians with Pelasgians), was its weakness. Rakovski was unable to realize that the origin structure he was creating appeared strong because it

123 Strabo noted in his *Geography* [2.2]: "For such fables as these, Posidonius justly blames these writers, and not inaptly conjectures that the Cimbri, on account of their wandering life and habits of piracy, might have made an expedition as far as the countries around the Palus Mæotis, and that from them has been derived the name of the Cimmerian Bosphorus, or what we should more correctly denominate the Cimbrian Bosphorus, for the Greeks call the Cimbri Cimmerii."

was stretched to the extremes, but it did not resolve the most important problem faced by the emerging Bulgarian historiography: the expression of a form of continuity that openly recognize the problem of discontinuity without concealing it. This, rather than the scientific collateral with which he framed it, was the advantage of Drinov's approach. On the contrary, the successive waves of Indo-Europeans on the route through the Bosporus, via Asia Minor, to the Balkans not only did not resolve the problem of discontinuity but exacerbated it since Rakovski could not deny that clashes occurred among the Indo-Europeans.

Nonetheless, Rakovski's "Indo-European" theory had one definite opponent: Greek nationalism and its root source, the heritage of Ancient Greece. Precisely because of the structure's hyper-hermeneutic nature, the claim of superiority could not be made at the level of discontinuity in the rival national narrative. (Drinov had the right to cite Fallmerayer, but Rakovski did not.) This was done at a proto-historic level, where the "civilized" Greeks were defined as "woods people" (Graikoi/Greeks, Gora) by the more populous Arian-Bulgarians. To be precise, Rakovski was not content with pinpointing "discontinuity" in rival historical paths, but also sought to challenge their established rights in history and indeed at a fundamental level, the level of historical definition.

Instead of using the word *historiya* in his paper, Rakovski opted for *povestnost.*[124] After "proving" the etymological relationship of the word *Bulgarian* with *Arian*, Rakovski would claim that the term *povestnost* in Bulgarian corresponded to the word *historiya* which all European languages had borrowed from the Ancient Greek *historia*. This term was considered "ancient" because its root was *ist*, which with the addition of the digamma F becomes F+Ist=F-ist and was the equivalent, in his view, of the ancient Bulgarian word *vest* that meant "management, message, knowledge." In Bulgarian, there exists the verb *vedaya, vedayam, vedajam*, *vedam* and the short *vem*, which means "I know, I have knowledge, message, knowledge of something." The word *povestnost* itself means "events, knowledge, news" that man had

124 The correlation of narrative and historical discourse is of course interesting—in contemporary Bulgarian, *povest* means "narrative," "novella."

collected from the time he first appeared in the world and continues to collect.[125] Rakovski concluded:

> For this reason, we preferred to use in the Bulgarian language a purely Bulgarian word, *Povestnost*, in place of one adopted from the Greek, *Istoriya*. Because our language has no need to borrow words from foreign languages, having an abundance of its own, it can borrow from its mother tongue, Sanskrit and Zantskik, and is in a position to create new ones, according to need, and not take its renovated words from the Greek language to which it once gave them. (Rakovski, "Bâlgarska starina," 391)

9. The Balkans as East: Charilaos Dimopoulos's *History of the Bulgarians*

It is as curious as it is interesting that Gavril Krâstevich's *Istoriya Bâlgarska* (Bulgarian history) and Marin Drinov's *Pogled* do not contain bibliographical references to a work that is anything but inconsequential for the Bulgarians' history, or at least deserving of the same attention as the relevant works of Ami Boué and Papadopoulos-Vrettos.[126] One reason this work should not have escaped their attention is the fact that it was published in 1866 in Brăila, the seat of the Bulgarian Literary Society, three years before Krâstevich and Drinov separately published their respective histories. This book was an ambitious project titled *Review of Eastern Nations* by Charilaos Dimopoulos. In reality, this constituted the second, and apparently final, volume of the work; the first had been published in Bucharest in 1863 and was a history of the Turks, outlined rather briefly.[127]

Dimopoulos was a teacher at the Greek Boys School in Brăila and may be the author of the famed *Military Life in Greece*, a novel published anonymously in Brăila in 1870.[128] According to the author, the attempt

125 In Sanskrit, the word *vesta* or *veda* also means "I know something; precise knowledge." In any case, the title of the most ancient Sanskrit book is *Veda*, which is translated as "knowledge."

126 The fact that *History of the Bulgarians* was especially premature for both the Greek and Bulgarian bibliographies is proved by the fact that when writing the second part of the *Review of Eastern Nations*, Dimopoulos knew of the publication of Georgi Rakovski's *Bâlgarska starina* in Bucharest the preceding year, although he admitted he had not managed to read it. Regarding the Greek bibliography, see the sporadic references in Paparrigopoulos, *History of the Greek Nation*, vol. 3.

127 Dimopoulos, *Epitheorisis ton Anatolikon Ethnon*. The book is dedicated to "the fighters at the frontline in the battle for the renaissance of the East, and the future being prepared for the Eastern peoples."

128 Dimopoulos, ed., *I stratiotiki zoi en Elladi*.

to analyze the current conditions of the "Eastern peoples" was made here in the context of the problems arising from the escalation of the Eastern Question. It is noteworthy however that the definition of "Eastern peoples" in reality concerned the Balkan peoples which in one way or another were embroiled in the Ottoman Empire's dissolution. The author, thus, observed in the introduction to the first part:

> Those ignorant of the reasons Turkey cannot be preserved further doubt its replacement by others; they are also ignorant of the moral situation and the means of the Greeks, Slavs, Dacians, and what these peoples have thus far achieved, and they consider a fantasy the prospect of the rebirth of the Greek nation or think the idea of the establishment of a Slavic or Dacian kingdom by Austria and Russia will remain unrealized.[129]

The book aimed to fill the great gaps in knowledge of the Balkans' most important peoples, the perspective being the replacement of the Ottoman Empire with newly formed nation-states. By his own admission, the author found it necessary to resort to works of German and French writers, as the stereotypical approach taken to many of these peoples by the neo-Hellenic consciousness could not contribute to a realistic handling of the region's political problems.[130] Dimopoulos's aim, then, was to offer an analytical presentation of each people's history, including its "moral" and political state. The first part contained all the Turks and Slavs, and seems to have been completed, although the initial plan called for an analysis of the Slavs of Serbia, Bosnia-Herzegovina, and Montenegro and not just the Slavs of Bulgaria. The second part analyzed the Greeks and the Dacians. Especially with regard to the Slavs, the prologue of the first part promised a detailed examination of the origins of the Slavic people and their classification as well as an examination of his main topic, the history of the "equatorial Slavs."[131]

Dimopoulos promised all this in 1863. But three years later, when he published his *History of the Bulgarians*, he confessed that "I wrote the first

129 Dimopoulos, *Epitheorisis ton Anatolikon Ethnon*, vol. 1, folio A, p. 5.

130 Ibid., 6.

131 Dimopoulos's project was indeed ambitious and he was fully aware of the difficulties involved. Ibid., 7.

folio to write, and I wrote the second to say something."[132] This honest admission was accompanied by a self-reflection on the writing of a history book that would be continually exposed to revision by later generations. This observation was not aimed at his peers but rather to internationally distinguished historians such as Gibbon and Hammer.

> I see the works of two distinguished historians: *The History of the Decline and Fall of the Roman Empire* by Gibbon and the *History of the Ottoman Empire* by Hammer, and I recall reading in the first that the Bulgarians occupied 4,600 towns in Europe in the sixth century fighting their enemies by Acheloos river at Thrace (!), and in the second that Varna is ancient Constantia and that the Greeks wrongly translated Boğazkesen as throat-slitter even though it means wave-breaker (or coupeur des flots, fluthen-brecher). . . . I am seeing also Cesare Cantù who called Marko Botzari a Bulgarian in his *Storia Universale*. (Dimopoulos, *Istoria ton Voulgaron*, iv.)

The observation was not coincidental: his aim was not to differentiate his own perspective due to the dramatic changes in political circumstances (from the unification of the Danubian Principalities that required the inclusion of a history of the Dacians to the exacerbation of the Bulgarian Question that limited the topic of the "equatorial Slavs" in a *History of the Bulgarians*). It also constituted an attempt to discuss in a critical manner the now classic bibliography on the history of the Bulgarians: the works of Engel, Papadopoulos-Vrettos, and Venelin. Dimopoulos noted that, "in general, the complete history of the Bulgarians, faithful, unbiased, thoughtful, and in short, corresponding to the needs of the literature, has not yet been written." He believed this was the case because the Bulgarians had not occupied themselves with the writing of their history but that it had been left to foreigners who, when they chose to do so, either faced the problem of limited sources or "did not love the subject."[133]

132 Dimopoulos, *Istoria ton Voulgaron*, iii.

133 Dimopoulos suggested that the following works contributed to an understanding of the Bulgarians' history: Mauro Urbini, *Il Regno degli Slavi*, 1601; the second volume of Johann Gotthelf von Stritter's *Memoriae populorum* (St. Petersburg, 1774); Guiseppe Simone Assemani's *Kalendaria ecclesiae universae* (Rome, 1775); Franjo Ksaver Pejačević's *Historia Serviae* (Coloc. 1799); Venelin's *Histo-*

Dimopoulos provided an extensive introduction on the Slavs' origin in which, in addition to the writers he had already mentioned, he made extensive use of the works of Šafárik, Dobrovsky, Eichhoff, Cantù, and Karamzin.[134] This meant that Dimopoulos checked works in the French and German bibliographies but may have also known Bulgarian (given that he must have been familiar with Venelin's work from the 1853 Bulgarian translation) and Romanian. It is evident that he was aware of virtually the sum total of scholarship on the Bulgarians' origin at the time.

Dimopoulos had one main goal in delving into the Bulgarians' origin (and the Slavs' origin in general): to deconstruct Šafárik's interpretive structure. To this end, his arguments had two basic similarities with Krâstevich's: first, that the common space inhabited by different races was an element for identifying collective/national identity; and, second, that the Bulgarians should not be presumed to be members of the great family of Slavic peoples.

More specifically, taking a position between Karamzin's and Dobrovsky's views that the Slavs' inhabited area had always been Northern Europe and the opposing view that the Slavs' cradle was Sarmatia, this mythical cone between Europe and Asia, the common space of Wends, Scythians, Antes, and Slavs, Dimopoulos commented that some races were generically classified as Slavs while others were given names, but, regardless

ry, which was translated into Bulgarian in 1853, and the *History of the Bulgarians, Croats, and Serbs* which was written in the Bohemian language and translated into German in two editions (Vienna in 1794 and Buda in 1853). Dimopoulos also had in mind the then-referenced manuscripts from the monasteries of Zographou and Rila on Mount Athos and another manuscript written by Polycarp, Bishop of Buzău in Bulgarian and Greek with references to many Slavonic sources. Polycarp's death prevented the publication of the manuscript, which Dimopoulos had seen in Bucharest and had tried to obtain. This may have been one of the many copies of Paisius's *Slavo-Bulgarian History* circulating around this time (see Marin Drinov, *Paisi otec*), although the Greek translation would have rendered it unique. In addition to these references, Dimopoulos also used several other sources like C. Le Beau's *Corpus scriptorum Istoriae Byzantinorum* (Venice, 1729), Segour's *Histoire du bas-Empire* (Paris, 1757–1811), as well as the works of Engel, Ami Boué, and Papadopoulos-Vrettos, Šafárik 's *Slavische alterthümer* (Leipzig, 1842) and *Geschichte der Südslavischen Literatur* (Prague, 1864–65), Dionysios Foteinos's *History of Dacia* (Iasi, 1862, in Vlach translation), Hammer, Gibbon, Karamzin, Aravantinos's *Epirus Chronicle* and Zambelios's *Vyzantinai Meletai*.

134 Pavel Jozef Šafárik, Über die Abkunft der Slawen, Buda, 1828 and *Geschichte der südslawischen Literatur. Aus dessen handschriftlichem Nachlasse hrsg. von Josef Jireček*, 4 vols., Prague: F. Tempsky, 1864–65. Dobrovský, *Untersuchung, woher die Slawen ihren Namen erhalten haben,* 1784; Eichhoff, *Histoire de la langue et de la littérature des Slaves,* Paris, 1839, 395; Cesare Cantù, *Storia universale* (1840–47); Karamzin, *Istoriya gosudarstva Rossiyskogo.*

of whether the races were called Slavs or Sarmatians or Scythians, there do not appear to have been differences between them in language or customs.[135]

Especially on the issue of language, which would make Herodotus's Scythians stand out from the Slavs referenced in Byzantine sources, Dimopoulos again opted to align himself against Karamzin. According to Karamzin's position, the Scythian names recorded in Herodotus were distinctly different from Slavic names. Dimopoulos looked to Eichhoff who "proves," in his view, the Slavic identity in Herodotus's Scythian words.[136]

According to Dimopoulos, "all the peoples came from Asia, there is no doubt about this." Europe was inhabited by three great families of people: the Pelasgians (or Greco-Latin nations), the Germanic (Anglo-Saxons), and the Slavs. In reality, the Slavs' arrival from Asia solved Dimopoulos's problem of "paradoxes" as he described the issues of their origins. Of course, the issue was not identifying the Slavs' original cradle but specifically that of the Balkan Slavs. If the Slavs had not moved from East to West, it would be possible to claim the historical right of autochthony in areas of vital Greek interest. Indeed, historians like Karamzin and Cyprien Robert argued that the Slavs had inhabited Thrace and ancient Illyria from the beginning.[137] Accepting such a position would signify the "Slavicization" of the space amid the process of competitive nationalization during the period of the Ottoman Empire's dissolution. So, the rejection or acceptance of the identification of Herodotus's Scythians with the Slavs proved a vital issue for defining the claimable space. As a result, the solution Dimopoulos chose was agnosticism. The inability to define the origin, initial birthplace, and the later movements of the Slavic populations undermined similar efforts like those of Dobrovsky and Šafárik. One would either have to trace their path from the first referenced source—which meant the first centuries AC— or "we are obligated to jumble the Scythians, Sarmatians, and Slavs into the one and the same history, and consider them having one and the same origin."[138]

135 Dimopoulos, *Istoria ton Voulgaron*, 4.
136 Ibid., 5.
137 Ibid., 11n12.
138 Ibid., 6.

Like Krâstevich, who considered the population mix of Eurasian Sarmatia to be uniform, Dimopoulos tended to identify if not all, then at least some of the Sarmatians[139] with the Altaic peoples. (Remember that Krâstevich's identification of Huns and Bulgarians was rooted in their common places of inhabitance and settlement.) His arguments, however, seem paradoxical as he arrived at his conclusion by negation.[140] Of course the second part of Krâstevich's rationale—that the Huns were Slavs—was absent from Dimopoulos. It was obvious that even though Dimopoulos discussed the problem of the Bulgarians' origin, his arguments resembled the main characteristics of Krâstevich's corresponding arguments when discussing the issue of the Bulgarians' origin. The Slavs crossed Istros (for the purposes of looting) with the Bulgarians (Dimopoulos meant the Proto-Bulgarians) during the rule of Justinian, in the sixth century.[141] Describing their incursions below the Danube in 561, he referred to the Bulgarians and Slavs as "relics of the Huns."[142]

With oversight over the entire bibliography available to Krâstevich and Drinov, Dimopoulos was familiar with both theories on the Bulgarians' origins—schematically in Venelin's clash with Šafárik and their respective supporters.[143] According to Dimopoulos, one theory saw the Bulgarians as "Tatars, that is Mongols, Turks, Huns, Scythians." For Dimopoulos it was obvious that the inclusion of the Bulgarians as Huns would classify them among the Altaic peoples. The second theory saw them as a people of the great European Slavic family. But what was the morphological difference

139 Dimopoulos turns to mythology, and of course Herodotus, for his definition of the Sarmatians, who resulted from the Amazons' union with the ancient Scythians. Ibid., 7–8.

140 Ibid., 6.

141 He generally sided with theories describing the Slavs as merciless and bloodthirsty nomads in contrast to the historians who insisted on the peaceful nature of their lifestyle. Ibid., 17. For a discussion based mainly on the use of the Miracles of Ayios Dimitrios as a source, see Maligoudis, *Slavs in Medieval Greece*. The war-mongering medieval Slav had his counterpart in the Slavic threat to the Southern Balkans in the nineteenth century. Dimopoulos believed that in his day there were two great families of Slavic peoples. The first included the Russians, Bulgarians, and Illyrians (he obviously meant the Slavs of the Western Balkans), and the second included the Moravians, Bohemians, Poles. Dimopoulos, *Istoria ton Voulgaron*, 10.

142 Ibid.

143 Regarding the Bulgarian population of European Turkey, he selected the middle road between Ami Boué (4,500,000) and Papadopoulos-Vrettos (2,000,000): his estimate being 3,000,000 to 3,500,000. He resorted to the means of earlier writers because, as he emphasized, he could not trust the (random) Ottoman statistics on the Balkans' population. Ibid., 26.

between the two theories? The first was rooted in "antiquity," "history," and the "origin" of the Bulgarians (whom it considered the Finns' "brothers"), while the second was based on "language," "religion," and "national desires," that is, on superficial elements. Dimopoulos's opinion is worth noting as it constituted a shift in Greek historiography, from using a cultural criterion for defining a nation, in contrast to a racial criterion or a criterion based on origins (Karolidis would subsequently develop this even further).[144]

The clash between the antiquity rationale and the corresponding different characteristics on which the Romantic definition of nation was founded was nothing but a clash between "being" and "appearing to be" or substance versus surface. The origin of a nation defined its essential subjectivity while elements like language or religion (on which Paparrigopoulos based his reconstruction of the nation after its two collapses) appeared as symptoms of a deeper self. The following assessment made by Dimopoulos regarding the Bulgarians and the intermixing of the Proto-Bulgarians with the Slavs could be considered to be an indirect comment on Fallmerayer and the Greek instance: "intermixing, as important as it may seem, can on the one hand dilute the customs, language, and features of a people but cannot change its character and its origin."[145]

The obvious preference for theories of "antiquity" and origin that led to the revelation of the real subjectivity of peoples was not completely innocent and objective in the Bulgarians' case. And this is because the Greek writer's text had a fundamental political target: Pan-Slavism. The Bulgarians' separation from the Pan-Slavicization program cast their "Slavic" nature into doubt.[146] In a way, Dimopoulos was reversing Fallmerayer: if Fallmerayer questioned the origin of the contemporary Greeks to promote their relationship with Russia (through Slavic intermixing and the Orthodox faith), Dimopoulos would insist on the Hunnic descent of the modern Bulgarians to sever them from the body of modern Slavism. It was obvious that Dimopoulos's endeavor was parallel to Krâstevich's with regard to its political and theoretical aims.

144 Karolidis, *Simeioseis tines*.

145 Dimopoulos, *Istoria ton Voulgaron*, 27.

146 Zannouvios expressed the same opinion a few years later, in January 1872, just before the schism was announced. See Zannouvios, *I Rossia kai to Voulgariko Zitima*.

As for the political aims, a rejection of the Russian influence would be desirable, if nearly impossible, since the view on "Slav-ness" had begun to shape the contemporary national Bulgarian consciousness.

> Most Bulgarians consider themselves Slavs. I do not think this idea predates the nineteenth century and was boosted by the activities of Pan-Slavism. They view as enemies anyone who disputes their Slavic ethnicity. And yet there are many references to the glorious eras of Krum and Symeon and mistrust in the Russian courtesies. The people are flattered by the religious fraternalism and the greatness of their supposed protector; the notables find great moral interest in ethnicity, which is of great importance in Europe. For this reason, there is not a single theory of origin the need of which would mean to abandon the fate of the nation to others. (Dimopoulos, *Istoria ton Voulgaron*, 11n12)

Dimopoulos must have been one of the few Greeks in the 1860s who would admit that a people's "Slav-ness" could be a passport for its recognition in the circle of "developed" European nations. The same went for his assessment of the Bulgarians' removal from the Slavic family, since in this way, the Bulgarians lost the menacing character they had begun to assume in the Greek imaginary. But Dimopoulos's political position was consistent with the deeper theoretical choice that Krâstevich had made for slightly different reasons (to reconcile the Bulgarians with the Ottoman state's framework): the rejection of Šafárik's interpretive form for understanding the character of the Bulgarian people.[147]

Dimopoulos's position was clear. (This was also expressed in his footnotes which constituted an "authentic" part of his treatise.) He considered *Šafárik* "one of the most successful organs of Pan-Slavism."[148]

Šafárik committed a fundamental (methodological) error, according to Dimopoulos, when he "writes Bulgarians, but means Slavs."[149] If, therefore, it was acceptable that the Bulgaro-Slavs had flooded the Balkans

147 It is not implausible that Krâstevich was among the "many" Bulgarians nostalgic for the era of Krum, according to Dimopoulos, as he had expressed such views since the late 1850s.

148 Dimopoulos, *Istoria ton Voulgaron*, 11n13.

149 This was the main reason Dimopoulos offered an extensive introduction to the history of the Slavs in a volume on the history of the Bulgarians.

from the Black Sea to the Adriatic and from the Danube to the Aegean, not only would their supposed assimilation by the Byzantine state pose a problem; it would cast doubt on the identity of the other Balkan peoples such as the Moldo-Wallachians, who were exposed to Slavic influence for many centuries. On the other hand, Šafárik really had distinguished between the Proto-Bulgarians with Finnic origins and the Slavified Bulgarians who settled Moesia with their leader Asparuh in the seventh century. He believed that up until, or because of, their conversion to Christianity in the Boris era (ninth century), their Slavicization had been completed. He blamed Slavicization for the great numeric difference in the subjugated Slavs: just one-fifth of the Bulgarians of Kubrat travelled along the Danube where they intermixed with the more numerous Slavs of the seven tribes.

Dimopoulos disputed this narrative with elements culled from Šafárik himself: the fact that ancient Moesia, which was called Sclavonia under the Slavs, was named "Bulgaria" after the eighth century; the distinction between the Slavonic and Bulgarian languages until the late ninth century; the departure from the Bulgarian kingdom of some 200,000 Slavs in 763 during the incursions of Telles on their way toward Asia; the departure of three other Slavic tribes in 818 which were later united with the Franks of Pannonia; the fact that in 824, the Bulgarian kingdom's Slavs sought King Ludwig's aid and protection "against their oppression."

But while these examples were used in Šafárik's narrative to support the view that the Proto-Bulgarians should not be identified with the Slavs, Dimopoulos used them as examples of their subsequent Slavicization. Dimopoulos believed that the Bulgarians' final Slavicization took place long after the *terminus ante quem* set by Šafárik. "The features, character, customs, traditions, and language of the Bulgarians of Turkey must have first been correlated against the Finns, and when a relationship was not found, it was deemed important to seek out the Slavic element to replace the Bulgarian. I believe that this must have been done in the eleventh or twelfth century. Only then could the Bulgarians, weakened and oppressed, have bowed to the influence of Slavism. . . . "[150]

150 Ibid., 13, 22.

This excerpt appeared to leave open the possibility that if the Bulgarians' Slavicization had not taken place at the time of the founding of the Second Bulgarian Kingdom (which, incidentally, was being claimed using the same exact terms by the descendants of the Dacian Vlachs[151]), the "character" of the Finnic-Bulgarians would have prevailed in subsequent centuries, despite the linguistic Slavicization that Dimopoulos probably would not have disputed.

Dimopoulos solution differed slightly from the one given by Krâstevich, although their common foundations were obvious: the "Turkificiation" of the Bulgarians was the common denominator despite the different political contents. The doubts as to whether the Ottoman Empire's dissolution was desirable did not correspond precisely with the question whether Greek nationalism's greatest rival should retain its connection to the rest of the Slavic world.

Dimopoulos reached his conclusion based on the analysis of the Bulgarian case so that he could express a theory as to what constitutes a nation based on its origins. Of course, he believed that it was necessary to distinguish the modern meaning of nation from its conceptualization in ancient works (Homer, Herodotus). He also insisted on distinguishing the nation from the corresponding meaning of race. Conversely, he seemed attracted by the term *genos*, especially as employed in Korais, not because it contains a direct reference to the single Orthodox community of the Ottoman Empire but because the term immediately conjured up the dimension of origin.

> We abandoned the notion of "Genos" which was highlighted by Korais to the vulgar people, while we accepted the word of "nation," distorting the content of the people's meaning... based on this observation, [Korais] proceeds with a definition of 'Genos'[152] the basic axis of which is origin, the "essence" that is and not the "surface"... (Dimopoulos, *Istoria ton Voulgaron*, 29)

151 Boia, *History and Myth*, 114, 117.

152 It is true that etymologically, if we could translate the word *nation* into Greek, the term *genos*, deriving from *genniemai* (*nascere*), "to be born" would be more appropriate than the word *ethnos*, which eventually dominated.

Neither language (for example, the three Swiss languages), nor a common citizenship (the English extended the United Kingdom as far as India), nor a common civil authority (Ireland under English rule) should be viewed as basic principles for the emergence of a nation. But the question of origins could. Nonetheless, according to Dimopoulos, only the ancient Athenians could brag of "pure and genuine origins," at least until their subjugation by the Macedonians. But at this point, he offered an interesting variation on the development of the model of origins. If there was no nation that could claim "purity" as a result of its origins, especially in modern times, there was necessarily a mixing process. The main parameter for the nation's precise genesis was the "mixing" (of at least?) two different ethnic elements.

Therefore, in contrast with Paparrigopoulos, where the reality of the continuous intermixing of the nation with others turned the theoretical quest for nation into a definition of a cultural type, the Greek scholars of the diaspora seemed to feel more intense pressure from Balkan nationalisms. This offered a response to their opponent's arguments by firing back in kind: the dialectics of culture were replaced by the dialectics of origin.

Chapter IV

Byzantinisms and the Third Rome: Russian Imperial Nationalism

1. Konstantin Leont'ev: On the Edge of Two Epistemological Paradigms

Konstantin Leont'ev and his work were among the most idiomorphic and important pinnacles of Russian intellectualism of the late nineteenth century.[1] Born 1831 in Kudinovo in the Kaluga province's Mestevskoe region, he was the son of Nikolay Borisevich Leont'ev and Theodosia Petrova. Both his parents were from the aristocracy and his mother descended from old nobility, the Karabanov family. This aristocratic background had a profound influence on his ideas, especially in the late nineteenth century as the upper classes saw their privileges eroded by acts like the 1861 emancipation of the Russian serfs by Tsar Alexander II. Leont'ev entered the Moscow School of Medicine in 1849, and two years later he wrote his first comedy, *Zenitba po lyubivi* (Love marriage), which caught Turgenev's attention. After graduating from medical school in 1854, he joined the Crimean War as a volunteer but returned to Moscow in 1857, after the Russians' humiliating defeat at Sevastopol; in 1861, on a trip to the Crimea, he met and married his wife, Elisavet Pavlovna Politov.

The extended period he spent as a consular employee in various Ottoman towns constitutes the most interesting part of Leont'ev's biography.[2] In February 1863, he joined the Ministry of Foreign Affair's Asia Department. His first assignment was as secretary and translator at the Russian

1 His most important political works were collected in *Vostok, Rossiya i Slavyanstvo* (see also an English-language selection of his works: Leontiev, *Against the Current*). See Nelson, *Leontiev*; Lukashevich, *Leontev*; and Berdyaev, *Leontiev*.

2 See Nelson, *Leontiev*, 33–45.

consulate in Heraklion, Crete; he was appointed on October 25, 1863, and held the post for roughly a year.[3] On August 27, 1864, he was reassigned to the Russian consulate in Adrianople, where he served for over two years. After a short stay in Constantinople, in April 1867, he was appointed vice consul to Tulcea, a small town near the Danube, while in 1869 he was appointed Russian consul to Ioannina. Because of the effect of the city's climate on his health, he was transferred to Thessaloniki in April 1871 after Count Nikolay Ignatiev, the interior minister, intervened on his behalf. A brilliant career seemed assured. An assignment to Bohemia was imminent. And he enjoyed the trust of the Asian Department's director Stremuhov, the foreign minister Alexander Gorchakov, and of Ignatiev himself. Leont'ev was, however, contracted cholera in July 1871. The illness ended his career and, after a recovery he attributed to a miracle, also marked his intellectual and spiritual development. That miracle was a prayer before an icon of the Holy Virgin that monks from Mount Athos had brought to Thessaloniki, which he vowed to visit if he was cured. After recovering, Leont'ev did indeed visit Mount Athos, where he stayed until August 1872. This visit completed his spiritual and intellectual transformation. During his stay at Mount Athos, Leont'ev sought to join the Orthodox monastic community but was dissuaded by the monks.[4] His turn toward Orthodoxy was a milestone for his intellectual evolution, which was to be combined with a distinctive approach to political developments in the Ottoman Empire, especially the Greek-Bulgarian dispute.

After his health scare, Leont'ev moved to Constantinople in 1872 and remained there for two years. During this time, he observed—and quite likely also participated in—all the ideological and political processes that shaped intellectuals like Gedeon and Krâstevich. He was definitely acquainted with Krâstevich and may have had contact with Gedeon given that he spent a considerable part of these two years at Halki. As we see below, Leont'ev was also in touch with Marko Balabanov, the link between Gedeon and Krâstevich.

3 Works from this period of his life include his descriptions of Crete, *Ocherki Krita* [Descriptions of Crete], and the novels *Hristo* [Christos] and *Xamid i Manol.* [Hamid and Manoli].

4 For a detailed description of the profound effect of this experience on Leont'ev's spiritual and intellectual development, see Nelson, *Leontiev,* 67. Leont'ev did eventually join the Holy Trinity monastic community in 1890, shortly before his death, on the advice of the elder Amvrosius.

The period during which Leont'ev was in Istanbul was marked by political tensions, which Leont'ev experienced after the schism, with the change in the patriarchal throne from the pro-Western Anthimus VI to the pro-Russian Joachim II (1873). It was also his most productive period. During these two years, Leont'ev wrote *Panslavizm i Greki* (Pan-Slavism and the Greeks), which for self-evident reasons will be examined further here, *Vizantizm i Slavyanstvo* (Byzantism and Slavism), and also completed his most important novel, *Odysseus Polychroniadis.*[5]

The fundamental ideological characteristics of Leont'ev's work began to emerge in these two treatises, albeit in the prism of the political circumstances at the time they were written. In the Greek-Bulgarian dispute, Leont'ev took the Greek side and appeared to defend Orthodox ecumenism against the Western-oriented ethno-racial/nationalist view. This was his first strong stance against Pan-Slavist theorists. Lauding the monarchy and defending aristocracy's privileges and culture, Leont'ev emerged as an anti-Western voice through his condemnation of political liberalism.[6] Leont'ev targeted both liberalism and its opposite, the ideal of social equality around which nineteenth-century sociopolitical movements were revolving. His anti-Asian views were the root cause of his blanket criticism of the West's aesthetic, cultural, and social values.[7] The next logical step in his evident distaste for civil visions of progress was Leont'ev's

5 The text was originally published as *Chteniya v Imperatorskom obshtestve istorii i drevnostey rossiyskih pri Moskovskom universitete* (Moscow: Otdeljnoe izdanie, 1875), no. 3, and was reproduced in Leont'ev's collected works, *Vostok*, 94–155; subsequent citations are from the latter edition.

6 Paradoxically, he took this position differently even vis-à-vis Western liberal intellectuals. From John Stuart Mill, he borrowed views on the power and diversity of individuals; from François Guizot, he drew the idea that the Christian world could contribute to preserving this social and individual diversity within specific boundaries; and from Wilhelm Riehl, he derived the idea that isolating societies and their internal stratification into classes was necessary to preserve the heterogeneity of peoples. See Nelson, *Leontiev*, 48.

7 In a particularly important excerpt that caught both Berdyaev's and later Nelson's attention, Leont'ev observed: "Is it not terrible, is it not shameful for someone to think that Moses scaled Sinai, the Greeks built their own beautiful Acropolis, the Romans conducted the Carthaginian wars, Alexander the Great crossed the Granicus River and fought in Gaugamela wearing a helmet with a feather in it, the Apostles prayed, the martyrs suffered, the poets sang, the painters painted, and the medieval knights shone in jousts only so that the Frenchman, German, or Russian urbanite, dressed in his revolutionary and ridiculous costume, can 'emote' individually or collectively over the ruins of the past?. . . It would be humiliating for humankind if that despicable idea of ecumenical benevolence, that naive and shameful platitude could triumph for ever." See also Berdyaev, *Leontiev*, 74 and Nelson, *Leontiev*, 52.

quest for a reconstruction of historical time modeled on a different value system. Leont'ev found this in Byzantium.[8] The model of the Orthodox Roman Empire could work to repel Western penetration of Russia but also served as a model for the coexistence of the Ottoman Empire's Orthodox peoples. This was sufficient justification in his mind for defending the ideals of Orthodox ecumenism.

Leont'ev's ideological use of Byzantium was not only of pivotal importance for understanding the framework within which historiographical endeavors such as those undertaken by Gedeon and Krâstevich emerged, but also for understanding their relationship with the Russian dimension.

Certain stereotypes of the Russian role—protecting the Orthodox before the Crimean War, the Pan-Slavic orientation afterward—foster a misconception that Russia was single or whole, especially where ideology was concerned. In the mid-nineteenth century, two powerful camps clashed in Russia, the Slavophiles and the Westernizers. According to Elli Skopetea, this clash was unprecedented in any of Balkan national movements but was decisive in shaping Russia's idiomorphic role in European affairs.[9] What remains interesting about Leont'ev's work is that it turned against both camps: he was stridently anti-Western yet, at the same time, he fiercely opposed Pan-Slavism to the degree that it represented a version of nationalism in the East, and all the while, he was time serving Pan-Slavic policy through his various posts in the Russian diplomatic service.

This means his work was not just interesting *sui generis* but also positioned on the epistemological divide where the two dominant paradigms of relations between East and West met: Orientalism and Occidentalism. Leont'ev was just as useful to Maria Todorova's analysis of the Balkan version of Orientalism, with her analysis of his work in the framework of imperial Russia's participation in "discovering" the Balkans (and especially the Bulgarians in the nineteenth century),[10] as he is to defenders of the interpretive model of Occidentalism such as Ian Buruma and

8 Aretov, *Bâlgarskoto Vâzrazhdane*, 53–54.

9 Skopetea, *I Dysi tis Anatolis*, 104.

10 The definition of "Balkanism" tended to support something that did not exist historically in the same way as "Orientalism," that is, institutional awareness of the West regarding anything it viewed as the East. Nonetheless, Todorova's observations on the differentiations of the Balkan from the Saidian normative "Oriental" model are still valuable and useful for understanding the region's history. See Todorova, *Imagining the Balkans*, 85–88.

Avishai Margalit, who both see a Russian Nietzsche in Leont'ev, the archetypal anti-Western Russian supporter of an organic model of historical development.[11]

2. Leont'ev's Byzantism

For Leont'ev, the ideological use of Byzantium was central to his work. There are several reasons for this. Referencing Byzantium legitimized the institution of the monarchy and served as a reminder that the East had produced something extraordinary that could be evaluated in relation to its contribution to world civilization. Mention of the Second Rome would certainly facilitate the historic mission of the Third. Leont'ev's text opened with a definition of what he called *Byzantism* and a comparison to *Slavism*:

> What is Byzantism? First and foremost, it is a special way of education or culture with its own discrete characteristics and comprehensive, clear, strict principles and its own consequences in history. Slavism taken in its entirety is still a Sphinx, a riddle. This remote idea of Byzantism is exceptionally clear and comprehensible. This broad idea is comprised of some other specific ideas: religious, state, moral, philosophical, and aesthetic. We do not see anything similar in Slavism. If we consider Pan-Slavism, we only have an amorphous image, spontaneous, unorganized, something like distant and scattered clouds which create different impressions depending on how far away they are. If you now imagine Byzantism, you will see the clear plan of a spacious and great structure. We know, for example, that Byzantism in the state means absolutism. In religion, it means Christianity with specific traits that separate it from the Western Church as well as from the sects. (Leont'ev, *Vostok*, 94)

According to Leont'ev, Byzantism was a model for humankind that was more grounded than the corresponding model introduced by German feudalism. At the same time, from a moral standpoint, Byzantism

11 Buruma and Margalit, *Occidentalism*, 93. N.B., the authors make a serious error by attributing Danilevsky's *Russia and Europe* to Leont'ev.

was pessimistic with regard to humankind's ability to achieve happiness. But this evaluation was not limited to the weight of the personal choices made by individuals that may or may not lead them to salvation, but also acquired a political content: "Byzantism, like Christianity in general, rejects every hope for the ecumenical prosperity of all peoples." (94.) This meant that ideals like equality and freedom on which civil society was based were rejected as unfeasible due to man's sinful nature.

From that point forward, Leont'ev attempted a brief but comprehensive historiographical interpretation in which he tried to highlight Byzantium's relationship with the West and Russia. Byzantism, according to Leont'ev, followed the Greco-Roman cultural heritage and preceded the Germanic. Constantine the Great's rise to the throne marked its blossoming, while Charlemagne's enthronement as emperor with the Pope's collusion was the first attempt by Germano-Roman Europe to wean itself from the Byzantine cultural heritage. The dissolution of the Holy Roman Empire of the German nation was the springboard for European civilization, and the fifteenth century, when Byzantium fell to the Turks, was the chronological point of emergence of the great autocratic monarchies in Europe as well as, following its disengagement from the Tatar yoke, in Russia.

Leont'ev did not believe this to be coincidental. In reality, the emergence of the Great Powers in Western and Eastern Europe was in large part due to the exploitation of elements from the Byzantine heritage, or Byzantism:

> The remains of Byzantism brought by the Turkish storm to the West and the North scattered over two different soils: in the West, the Germano-Roman was the only one blossoming and tilled, richly developed, and the new approach to Byzantium and through Byzantium with the ancient world immediately brought Europe to this fruitful period that is known as the Renaissance. . . . When Byzantism came in contact with Russia in the fifteenth century and afterward, it found a drabness, simplicity, poverty, and misery. This is why it could not be reborn like in the West. Byzantism came to Russia in its pure form, it entered our lives with its general characteristics, pure and unobstructed. Our Renaissance, our fifteenth century, the origins of our

> complex and organic blossoming, or to express it differently, our unity in diversity, would have to be sought in the seventeenth century, in the era of Peter the Great or, in the final analysis, in the first glimmers of his father's time. (Leont'ev, *Vostok*, 95)

Leont'ev, thus, thought that the West emerged from a blend of German feudalism with Byzantism,[12] while Russia proved Byzantium's heritage in its purest form as it was just exiting an extended period of dependence on the Tatars (from the state of Kiev to the state of Moscow). In the West, it was the political dimension of Byzantium rather than the religious one that was influential: Catholicism did not allow Byzantium's religious side to flourish. This resulted in the emergence of autocratic monarchy. Throughout the West, the monarch's power was reinforced at the expense of the nobility, while the army lost its aristocratic character and became a state corps.

But Russia itself during the seventeenth and eighteenth centuries—that is, after Peter the Great's attempts at reform—was subject to Western influences (Polish, Dutch, Swedish, German, and French) which, in Leont'ev's view, played an equally important, or even more important, role for Byzantium and Ancient Greece in the West during the fifteenth and sixteenth centuries.

It should be noted that regardless of Leont'ev's political aims—confrontation with the fundamental principles of the European Enlightenment—the way in which he legitimized them was not through the twin poles of Westernism and anti-Westernism, or the clash between East and West, but by defending the value system of the Middle Ages versus that of Modernity. The cleft Leont'ev was trying to emphasize was not in space but rather in time: this is why his definition of Byzantium as a type of "education" or "culture" was decisive.

Leont'ev recognized Byzantinist influences in Russian aesthetic creation—architecture, poetry, and so on—as well as on institutions like the family and state. ("What would the Russian family be without Christianity? What would Christianity be in Russia without Byzantine foundations

12 "In Western Europe, the old primordial religious Byzantinism had to be processed by the strong local values of Germanism, that is, chivalry, Romanticism, and Gothism, but not without the participation of Arab influence . . ." (95.)

and its Byzantine forms?" [96]). He believed the influence on the state decreased in the wake of Peter the Great's Westernization of Russian society, although Byzantism had contributed to tsarism since the era of Tartar dependence: "Russian tsarism has further proved stronger than Byzantine caesarism and this is because Byzantine caesarism had a dictatorial origin, a popular electoral nature" (96). This is the way in which he explained the course from Cincinnatus, Fabius Maximus, and Julius Caesar to Augustus Octavianus, Tiberius, and Diocletian and from there to Constantine, Justinian, and John Tzimiskes. The "naturalness" (*estestvennost*) of dictatorial authority in Byzantium allowed this state to exist far longer than pagan Rome. Byzantium's one-thousand-two-hundred-year span signaled an unsurpassed achievement for Leont'ev, who described the Byzantine state as a "bureaucratic state, centralized, autocratic, and democratic." ("Democratic" is used to describe its equality or rather egalitarianism).[13] This state owed its longevity to both the concentration of bureaucratic authority around the emperor as well as to another, far stronger, element that contributed to public discipline, (*obshtestvenaya disciplina*): Church authority and the power of the bishops. Ancient Rome did not have this tool because it never acquired a privileged clergy. "This new and exceptionally salvaging disciplinary tool appeared in Christian Byzantium."[14] Byzantium was history's first combination of autocratic governance (inherited from Rome) and Christian models. The Byzantines may have exiled the Caesars, killed them, or toppled them from their thrones, but they never disputed the organizational foundations of their state, the holy essence of Caesarism.

Leont'ev noted that Russian public opinion was rife with distorted, irrational, and one-sided attitudes toward Byzantium. He attributed this to the fact that "our historical science is immature and lacks authenticity" (97). It was dominated by the views of Western writers who felt obliged to focus on the history of republicanism and feudalism, Catholicism and Protestantism, but were biased against Byzantium which was autocratic and Orthodox. Leont'ev did not ascribe these views to professional historians but to a large segment of Russian society, and it was reproduced through the teaching of history in schools.

---

13 Ibid., 97. For an analysis of the Byzantine state during the early centuries, a time when the emperor's power was stronger, Leont'ev referenced Guizot's *Histoire générale de la civilisation en Europe* (1828).

14 Leont'ev, *Vostok*, 97.

Leont'ev's pro-autocratic/pro-monarchic stance led him to dispute the usual appraisal of a fundamental moment of the rise of Western civilization, the clash between the Greeks and the Persians at Thermopylae. He thus observed that:

> In school, poems, and many articles and novels, we have all been trained, since childhood, with tremors of enthusiasm to read about Marathon, Salamis, Plataea, displaying absolute sympathy toward the Greek republicans while viewing the Persians with distaste. I recall . . . indeed a random text (and, indeed, where? in Herzen!) on how during a storm, the Persian nobles rushed into the sea to help a ship run aground and save Xerxes. . . (98)

This incident which he had read as a child proved that the Persian nobles were at least the equals of Leonidas's Spartans because "without being forced, they chose suicide in order to defend the ideals of the religious-state."[15]

The image of the "dry, boring, Church-ruled Byzantium" embedded in dominant Western culture and the school curricula of the East was hard to overturn. Nonetheless Leont'ev admitted that the reversal had also begun with the Western historiographers, specifically in works of the Thierry brothers, Guizot, Macauley, and Granovski, to name a few.[16] He insisted, however, on the value of works such as Amédée Thierry's and Francois Guizot's because they highlighted Byzantium's significance and linked it to Christianity's dominance and dissemination.[17] As Thierry characteristically noted, "Byzantium extended Christianity, provided it with unity and strength" and "among the citizens of the Byzantine Empire, there were peoples of whom every era and any society could be proud."

---

15 Ibid., 98. Leont'ev believed that the main reason for the Europeans' bias toward the Greeks was that the Persians did not leave a legacy of fine literary works in the way the Greeks did.

16 Timofei Nikolayevich Granovski was among the founding scholars of Medieval Studies in nineteenth-century Russia and was strongly influenced by the works of Leopold von Ranke and Friedrich Carl von Savigny. He was one of the few consistent supporters of the principles of political liberalism during the reign of Nicholas I. See Roosevelt, *Apostle of Russian Liberalism*.

17 Thierry, *Histoire d'Attila*; *Récits*; *Tableau de l'Empire*, and Francois Guizot's *Histoire générale*.

3. The Middle Ages as Canonical Model

Promoting the Middle Ages as a canonical model for the classification of values constituted a means to challenge both modernity and the sources from which modernity drew its legitimacy, that is, Greek antiquity. Here, too, the East seemed retrospectively to have been vindicated against the West, but only because the medieval cultural paradigm supposedly prevailed as the chronological peak of organic development. In other words, if antiquity represented childhood on a timeline, modernity would correspond to the phase of decline.[18]

It is worth comparing Leont'ev's intellectual endeavors to the historiographical efforts made by Gedeon and Krâstevich. Indeed, we might say that Leont'ev's work served to legitimize them. In Gedeon, we saw Byzantium extended into the Ottoman Empire through the Church's dominant role and a proposed uniform extension of Byzantium into the Ottoman Middle Ages. In Krâstevich, the need to construct a fundamental theory of origin for the Bulgarian ethnogenesis led him on a quest for a "medieval antiquity." Leont'ev idealized medieval Byzantium and simultaneously took a positive stance on the values of the corresponding Western Middle Ages, whose basic elements were "German feudalism" and Catholicism.

The references to Byzantium by Leont'ev and the other two Balkan intellectuals were not made to legitimize the process of creating national identity. They should rather be understood as an offset to this process. For this circle of "reactionary" or "conservative" intellectuals, the adulation of the Middle Ages was necessary in relation to the elevation of the Christian world. These designations were made according to the measures of civil construction they refuted—that is, the construction of the national state. It was, however, certain that they could not—or rather, did

18 For the triadic structure of organic development adopted by Leont'ev (who was clearly influenced by corresponding nineteenth-century philosophies such as the theory of Herbert Spencer), see Bohun, "Mikhailovski and Leontiev," 71–86, and Nelson, *Leontiev*, 58–60. As Nelson notes, Leont'ev's structure suggested a process of personalization in the transition from the first phase of "archegonal simplicity" to the second phase of "progressive complexity." By contrast, there was a processes of consolidation in the transition from the second phase to the third (the phase of decline). The second or intermediate phase marked the peak of the amalgamation of natural and cultural organisms as well as their "beauty": the aesthetic dimension of Leont'ev's structure constituted an important part of his argument. See Cloutier, "Leont'ev and Nationalism," 264. This structure was outlined comprehensively for the first time in Leont'ev, *Byzantism and Slavdom*.

not wish to—understand the difference between the national state and empire. With the possible exception of Leont'ev, they historiographically positioned themselves as if they were contributing to the development of a national narrative.

This is an important point because it is vital for understanding that these historiographical endeavors cannot easily be incorporated into Occidentalist structures, even in the case of Leont'ev. Aside from the fact that their admiration of the Middle Ages derived from Western writers, it was also clear that their structures were developed in line with Western-oriented ideological models aimed at garnering the desired recognition as an equal to the West. It was the Eastern Empires who sought a relationship of equality with the West and the ideology of religious ecumenism advanced by these intellectuals appeared as the sole solution not only to the potential problem of national defections but also to their emergence as independent cultural structures.

Leont'ev's proposed structure thus acquired meaning and was indirectly reiterated by the other two writers; Byzantium was worthy of admiration precisely because it contributed substantially to the West's creation. As we have seen in both Gedeon and Krâstevich, the Russian factor was decisive in shaping their structures. Obviously, this was also the case with Leont'ev, albeit in a very specific way.

4. Byzantism as Imperial Discourse: The Parity of Russians and Ottomans

In Chapter Two of his treatise *Byzantism and Russia*, Leont'ev detailed some of the positions outlined in the introduction. He stated that Byzantism yielded fruit for Russian society because it was planted while Russian society was still unformed, a virgin cultural landscape. In Russia, Byzantism did not come up against tribes "exhausted by education" or countries exposed to foreign raiders as was the case along the Mediterranean basin. In Russia, Byzantism found a country that was "wild, young, closed to influences, extensive," populated by a people who were "simple, fresh, with open hearts." The basic consequence of sowing Byzantism in Russia was that it bolstered Tsarism first through the dynasty of the Ruriks and later through the Romanovs. This effect was the result of the strengthening of Russian society's genealogical bias. Whereas in the West, this emotion was linked to the aristocracy, in Russia it was represented by the monarchy which, as a result, was not only stronger than the aristocracy but also than the family.[19] Leont'ev pondered the identity of Greater Russia's (or Russia proper's) population: "What is family without Faith? What is Faith without Christianity? What is Christianity in Russia without its Orthodox character, rules, and institutions, that is, without Byzantism?"[20] The aristocracy, on the other hand, while positioned between the "active influence of tsarism and the passive stance of the citizen-peasant" developed intellectually and politically despite its subjugation to tsarism.[21]

According to Leont'ev, this was the difference between Louis XIV and Peter the Great, who were more or less contemporaries of each other. Louis XIV abolished the nobility, opening the way for democratization in the eighteenth century, while Peter the Great's distinction between two classes of aristocracy (*boyars and pomest'nichi*) allowed the notion of the aristocracy to remain up to the era of Alexander I.[22] The aristocracy's survival was due to a side effect of tsarism and, thus, of Byzantism. Leont'ev identified the following elements as remaining strong in Russia: Byzantine Orthodoxy, patrimonial and unlimited autocracy, and perhaps the peasant world. Tsarism, of course, was strengthened under the influence of Orthodoxy, Byzantine ideals, and even Byzantine culture. Indeed, Leont'ev believed that even the great peasant uprisings—perhaps with the exception of the Pugachev-led insurrection that was directed specifically against Catherine the Great—never disputed the monarchy's authority, but targeted extensive landownership.

In discussing the power of tsarist absolutism against the uprisings, Leont'ev made an interesting reference to the Ottoman Empire that is worth noting, given the corresponding analyses by Krâstevich and Gedeon:

---

19 Leont'ev, *Vostok*, 99–100. He argued this by comparing the image of the family described by British novelists like Walter Scott and Charles Dickens to that in the works of Tolstoy. The comparison, of course, favored the former.

20 Ibid., 101. Leont'ev believed that the ideal of family among the Germans, Ukrainians, Southern Slavs, Greeks, and even Turks (even though the Christian family ideal was stronger than the Muslim one) was stronger than among Russians.

21 Ibid., 102.

22 Obviously he meant the distinction between the inherited aristocracy and the noble titles awarded for service to the state.

> Let us pause briefly to look at the Muslims. It is interesting that after the Muslims in Turkey were familiarized with the West and with us, the Russians, that despite so many wars and our old rivalry with the Turks, we have satisfied many Turks privately, at the personal level, but also because of the nature of our state, far more than the Western Europeans. Our empire's ecclesiastical nature suggests respect toward them; and they themselves find in this characteristic a great similarity with the religious nature of their national character ["narodnost"]. Our discipline, our respect, and our conciliatory approach have obligated them; these traits show that this is our strength, they envy us, and we hold each other up as a good example. If the Turkish government was forced out of the Bosphorus and the Turks abandoned the Balkans, then, naturally, they would turn their hopes toward us as their defenders against those inevitable oppressions and insults to which they will be subjected by their heretofore slaves—the Southern Slavs, the Greeks, and generally the merciless and brutal. Even now, the Turks prefer us over the Bulgarians, the Serbs, and the Greeks. (Leontiev, *Vostok*, 106n)

Indeed, Leont'ev cited personal discussions with a pasha cognizant of Russian reality—for example, he mentioned liking Gogol's characters. The pasha liked the Russians because they were concerned only with their faith, in contrast to the Greeks and Bulgarians who were concerned with politics, constitutions, and other such "nonsense", and even concluded that "Russia will remain strong until it acquires a constitution."

Leont'ev's work clearly illustrated that imperial discourse only recognized equality at the level of its counterpart.[23] It became even clearer to Leont'ev and the pasha, as communicators of this imperial discourse, that they were confronted by common enemies that would dissolve imperial structures in the near future: nationalism and republicanism.[24] The

23 In an equally important article written in January 1873, during the early part of his stay in Constantinople, Leont'ev claimed that preserving the Ottoman Empire was also the aim of Bulgarian extremists because its political and cultural weakness would foster a further strengthening of their movement, while Greek extremists would want to ally with the Turks in the Bosporus against the common enemy, Pan-Slavism. This article, titled "Panslavizm i Greki" was included in Leont'ev, *Vostok*, 38–55.

24 On this point, Leont'ev cited Thomas Carlyle and a passage in a letter to Herzen in which he stated that he prefered tsarism or Great Turkism to the anarchy represented by "parliamentary expressiveness" and "freedom of the press." Leontiev, *Vostok*, 107.

insistence on religion's role in the defense of imperial absolutism seemed to bring the former eternal rivals closer to each other than to their respective citizens (in the Ottoman case) or protégés (in the Russian).

Oddly, the "merging" of the values that Leont'ev saw as the final phase of decline of Western civilization (and every society considered an "organic whole") took place in the production of imperial discourse, as expressed by representatives of history's dinosaurs. The sympathy Gedeon and Krâstevich exhibited toward the Ottoman Empire was in the end followed by Leont'ev too.

In the case of all three intellectuals, we are not looking at the use of religion as a tool in the hands of crypto-nationalist historiographers. In fact, we find the opposite. Faith led to the rejection of civil modernity (chiefly in Gedeon and Leont'ev) and nostalgia for the Middle Ages as the idealized moment in history which constituted more than just a link in the continuity of the nation. As Leont'ev noted, in all great religions, "aside from the immense poetry, aside from their exceptional organizational power, there is also something real, something tangible."[25] Conversely, none of the modern state's basic characteristics seem to have inspired Leont'ev: neither blood ("all great nations have mixed blood"), nor language ("language itself? The language of the street is mainly the expression of ideas and emotions of those closest to us"); nor the principles of liberal democracy that Napoleon introduced to Europe:

> Equality of persons, equality of classes, equality (and monotony as well) of the provinces, equality of nations—are all part of the same process. In essence, complete universal equality, universal freedom, universal gain, the common good, universal anarchy, or universal global boredom. The idea of nationalities in the form of racial purity as presented in the nineteenth century is an idea that in reality is completely cosmopolitan, anti-state, anti-religious, and which has its own destructive power. . . . Individualism destroys the individuality of the people, of the provinces, of the nations. (Leont'ev, *Vostok*, 108)

25 Ibid., 107.

And he continued in an intensely prophetic tone: "France destroyed itself with this principle [of nationalities]. Let's wait to see what unfolds in Germany."

Recall that Leont'ev was writing shortly after the Prussian victory in the 1871 war and the unification of German. But for someone faithful to the idea of religious ecumenism, the ending to this story was preordained.[26]

5. Leont'ev's Slavism: Greeks/Bulgarians, Germans/Czechs

"There is no answer to that question!" was Leont'ev's reply to the rhetorical query of what he considered Slavism to be. It was futile to look for characteristics common to all Slavs. Slavism, outside of an abstract ethnographic racial designation and linguistic similarities, did not suggest

26 Is it possible that in Leont'ev's case we are faced with a composite of Christian ecumenism and Romantic nationalism similar to the one we encounter later in Vladimir Solov'ev? See, among others, Gaut, "A Christian Nationalist?," 79, where Solov'ev's solution is discussed. Solov'ev was an intellectual who outlined his theoretical framework in the period following Alexander II's assassination in 1881. He turned against the most conservative nationalists, arguing a position in favor of a "Christian policy" according to which all Christians, from the tsar to the lowliest peasant, would have to uphold Christian principles in order to bring about the Kingdom of God on earth. It is interesting to see how he resolved the contradictions between Christian ecumenism and its splintering into denominations (80). Solov'ev wrote a series of articles for Ivan Aksakov's journal on the removal of the Schism between Orthodoxy and Catholicism. These triggered a clash between himself and the publisher as well as other Russian Pan-Slavists. This clash resulted in his political shift toward the liberals. As Gaut notes, "Vladimir Solov'ev's critique of nationalism began as a defense of the ecumenical model. However, Solov'ev soon began to believe that the chauvinism displayed by the conservative intellectuals and the government was, in reality, a denial of Christianity itself." (81) He launched systematic attacks against Nikolay Danilevsky ("Russia and Europe"), Dostoevsky, and other Pan-Slavists. Gaut summarizes Solov'ev's views on this issue in six points that comprise the subsections of his article: a) Nations have a positive but transitional role in history (82); b) Nationality and national differences are positive elements that are enriched in history (83n); c) Nationalism violates the principles of "Christian policy"; it is viewed as a discounted nationalism marked by patriotism as national states follow a realpolitik in defense of the national interest and, thus, betray Christianity, with England offered as a negative example; d) Christianity demands denial from nations; e) Nations have the right to self-determination (although this does not lead him to support national self-determination for non-Russian states within the Russian Empire like Poland, despite his admiration of the poet Adam Mickiewicz, 86); f) Christians must be more patriots than nationalists (87n). For Solov'ev, nationalism teaches us to love our own nation over all others and indifference to other nations, unless we are involved in a clash with them. Patriotism, on the other hand, is based on the principle that the ecumenical Christian ideal of Divinity is supreme and that by serving this idea, the nation participates in creating heaven on earth. According to Gaut, Solov'ev saw nations through the prism of "philosophical Romanticism" just like the Pan-slavists, except that he extended the idea of the "live organism" from nations to humanity, the latter being a unified organism whose nations corresponded to the body's extremities. See also Poulin, "Solov'ev's *Rossia*."

some specific cultural entity as did, say, Sinoism (Chinese civilization) or Europeanism (European civilization). The latter, with its underpinnings of Germano-Roman culture and Catholicism, was easily distinguishable from other cultural forms like the Sino-Japanese, Islamic, Ancient Egyptian, Ancient Greek, Roman, or Byzantine. But what was a cultural difference for Leont'ev? A single literature, a shared state structure at the peak of the cultural entity's development, a common religion, and consequently common elements in painting, architecture, and so on? All these elements painted in broad brushstrokes could conjure up a meaning like Europeanism, but not Slavism. Slavic states existed, indeed as early as the Middle Ages, but they never created a single cultural entity. Leont'ev specifically referenced the Balkan Slavs, the Serbs, and the Bulgarians. He considered the history of their medieval kingdoms "bland" and saw them as easily succumbing to Byzantine influences. On the other hand, the Czechs participated in Western European culture through their Germanization: "The Czechs were a tool of German policy, which the Slavs are now turning against Germanism."[27]

But what did Leont'ev think about the Bulgarians whom he had firsthand experience of during the crucial years of their Church struggles around which the interest of Moscow's Pan-Slavists revolved in the 1860s?[28] "The Bulgarians were trained by the Greeks in the same way that the Czechs were trained by the Germans." And just like the Czechs who turned against those who had nurtured them into European culture, the Bulgarians turned against modern Hellenism.[29]

Leont'ev saw an important similarity between the Czechs and the Bulgarians with regard to their handling of the religious element. The

27 Leont'ev, *Vostok*, 111.

28 Leont'ev's descriptions of the Bulgarians also interests Todorova, for obvious reasons. See Todorva, *Imagining*, 200–202.

29 Stefan Launer's *The Character of Slavdom* (1847) outlined the Czechs' cultural dependence on the Germans. According to Launer, the Slavs' fragmentation corresponded to different cultural influences from Western European nations. More precisely, Croats, Poles, Russians, and Czechs (including Moravians, Silesians, and Slovaks,), must be considered the cultural progeny, respectively, of the Italians, French, English, and Germans. Launer tried to establish his position based on political principles and religious analogies. Although comparing the English and Russians seemed exaggerated (especially based on their respective influences on Western and Eastern Europe), comparing Czechs and Germans seems to have been common ground for such analyses during the nineteenth century. See also Gbúrová, *Slavdom in Europe*.

Czechs, while not as staunchly Catholic as the Poles, concluded their medieval existence by experimenting with Protestantism (in the form of the Hussites).[30] Similarly, the Bulgarians, although Orthodox, inaugurated their reappearance in history by clashing with the Patriarchate of Constantinople. Leont'ev implied that the Czechs' clash with official Catholicism and the Bulgarians' distancing themselves from the institutional expression of Orthodox Christianity were steps in a process of secularization: "In the new Bulgarians as with the modern Czechs, the religion of personal conscience does not completely coincide with the religion of national interest."[31]

This was the reason Leont'ev effectively adopted the Ecumenical Patriarchate's argument against the Bulgarian Exarchate almost in its entirety. The similarities between Bulgarians and Czechs also suggested a reverse movement: for the Czechs, idealizing Hussitism led closer to the principles of Byzantism (that is, to Russia), while for the Bulgarians, the clash with the patriarchate meant their distancing from these principles and the Russians who represent them in history.

This observation deserves comment because its historical context may be related precisely to how the "canon" of Bulgarian historiography managed its relationship with the West and Russia. Remember that the Russophile Marin Drinov drew on the work of a Czech, Pavel Josef Šafařík,[32] and not the work of a Ukrainian (or "Little Russian"), Yuriy Venelin, to defend his form of continuity. Throughout his career he also maintained close relations with the Czech historian Konstantin Jireček.[33]

Leont'ev saw few differences between Bulgarians and Greeks in their customs, traditions, agrarian lifestyle, architecture, and so on. He observed that the differences between the Greek of Crete, Epirus, or Kefalonia and the Greek of Thrace or Macedonia were greater than the

30 It is widely acknowledged that the teachings of Jan Hus (1369–1415) heralded the Protestant Reformation in the sixteenth century.

31 Leont'ev, *Vostok*, 112.

32 See also Danova, "Bibliothèque," 111–20.

33 See also Danova, "Dobrovski à Vienne"; Danova, "Dobrovski v New York"; and Danova, "Arhivât na Dobrovski." On Drinov's relationship with Jireček, see Nikolaj Radnev, *Drinov i Jireček*. Konstantin Jireček was the son of Josef Jireček and taught at the University of Prague. In 1879, he entered the civil service of the newly-formed Bulgarian state and in 1881 was appointed Minister of Education. In 1884, he became Professor of World History at Prague and in 1876 wrote a *History of the Bulgarians*, which was published simultaneously in Czech and German.

differences between the latter two and the Bulgarians. This applied to agrarian populations, but urban Bulgarians and Greeks were also seen as having similarities: both were susceptible to demagoguery and constitutionalism; they were also preoccupied with the notion of progress concerning affairs of state and were fiercely protective of the institution of the family. The Greeks, specifically, were closer to the French with regard to the spirit of debate and closer to the Germans with regard to their idealization of the family. Nonetheless, both Bulgarians and Greeks definitely lacked harmony with the Russians, whose approach to affairs of state was rooted in the value of discipline.[34] Broadly speaking, Leont'ev's argument focused on the points where the Bulgarian diverged from the Russian, silently targeting the rival arguments of the Russian Pan-Slavists. In his view, the Bulgarians forced the Russians to cross their own Rubicon.

Leont'ev criticized the Bulgarian extremists in Constantinople led by Stoyan Chomakov who encouraged bishops like Hilarion of Makariopolis and Panaretos of Plovdiv to break with the patriarchate.[35] The extremists were fully aware that the Greeks would blame the movement on the Russians ("the Greeks would furiously accuse the Russians and the Russians would answer in kind"), while this would be welcomed by the Ottomans. On the other hand, Russian public opinion could not be shaped by the few Greek monks traveling the Russian countryside but could be shaped by the Bulgarian professor, student, or journalist who had access to the

34 Leont'ev, *Vostok*, 112. In reality, historiographical efforts like those of Gedeon and Krâstevich aimed precisely at correcting this "disharmony."

35 The rise of the moderate Anthimus VI to the patriarchal throne was followed by the events of the holiday of the Epiphany of 1872 which thwarted the Russian embassy's efforts to achieve reconciliation. It is very interesting to note how Leont'ev interpreted the path toward the schism. In a significant text from that period (1873) titled "Ešte o greko-bolgarskoi raspre" [On the Greek–Bulgarian dispute] (Leont'ev, *Vostok*, 82–93), Leont'ev emphasized that "after the Schism's announcement, the Greeks succumbed to much nonsense. In their thirst to declare the schism, they fell into two contradictory camps, two powerful driving forces of their nationality [*narodnost*]: on one hand, their dedication to the old clergy, the strictness of Orthodoxy, the Church's spirit and its discipline against sects, the Pope, and so on, which the Church defends to this day; and, on the other, their desire to distinguish their nationality from the Slavs and Russia, to save it from the Pan-Slavic current disguised as austere Orthodoxy, to slowly create a new religion. The old Greek priest and the young lawyer, journalist, or professor with a European education who believes in nothing else except the progress and ingenuity of the modern Greek are joined in their mutual desire to benefit from the [Holy] Canon and declare the Schism. The old clerics' anger at the Bulgarian daring and the joy of the young dreamers at the thought of separation from the Slavs are joined in a single aim but with different motives."

media. That was exactly what people like Zhinzifov and Drinov had in mind, despite Leont'ev's dim view of the quality of their writing. Unable to directly influence Russian diplomacy or the Russian Holy Synod, the Bulgarians decided to take their case straight to the Russian public.[36]

The Bulgarian position, therefore, could not be described from the perspective of the dissolution of the Orthodox millet (that is, the Ottoman Empire's dissolution) but rather from the perspective of the dissolution of the bonds between Orthodox peoples as heirs of Byzantism's principles. Leont'ev's perspective did not dispute the existence of differences in national identity between the Orthodox, as would have been the case had he adopted the millet's traditional ecumenicity. Byzantism's dissolution was not identified with the millet's dissolution, yet the two perspectives tended toward a shared rationale: the rationale of the hierarchization of nations within the millet in the former case, and the hierarchization of the nations within the Orthodox world in the latter case.

On the other hand, the Greeks rebelled for "Christ's holy faith and the homeland's freedom" because Byzantism was their historical creation (in spite of the Modern Greek's republican beliefs). For them, Christianity was synonymous with Orthodoxy and its holy rules and ceremonies, in other words, with Byzantism. Although Italians, Spaniards, and even Egyptians, Syrians, and Africans also participated in shaping the Orthodox doctrine, the fact that its sacred texts were written in Greek rendered the Greek cultural heritage indelible. Thus, the grandeur of Greek history in its entirety, the Greeks' fall, their tribulations, and their revival, were inextricably linked to Byzantism. This was in stark contrast to the Bulgarians, whose medieval phase and national awakening stem from a merciless war against Byzantism's basic principles.[37]

---

36 Typically, he noted that it was easier for a clueless Russian to comprehend a lead like "the long-lasting troubles of our friends the Slavs under the Phanariot yoke" rather than a position that would attribute to the Bulgarian Exarchists the desire for a break from the Mother Church, as some of them hoped to obey to a Bulgarian bishop in violation of the Holy Canons that prohibited the coexistence of two bishops of the same Orthodox doctrine in the same city. See Leont'ev, *Vostok*, ibid. Leont'ev offered a fine description of the mutual suspicion fostered among all parties by the Exarchate's founding. On the contrary, Greek historiography reflected the view that Ignatiev's back channel activities were behind the firman of 1870, while Bulgarians were convinced that this functioned as a protective shield for the Patriarchate of Constantinople.

37 Leont'ev, *Vostok*, 114–15.

Of all the nations of Eastern and Southeastern Europe—Czechs, Poles, Serbs, Greeks, and Magyars—none was a greater threat to the Russian Empire than the "innocent and humble Bulgarians." Although Slavs, their contestation of Byzantism's essence in effect turned them against it. By disputing the Orthodox Church's ecumenism, Holy Canon, and spirit, the Bulgarians effectively attacked the foundations on which Russian society was built. Naturally, Leont'ev did not blame this on all Bulgarians but on the radical elite that swayed the masses, these latter not understanding what a violent rupture from the Eastern Orthodox Church this entailed.

There are two points to note: a) based on his understanding of the meaning of Byzantism, Leont'ev constructed a conceptualization of a binary continuity/discontinuity model to which the Greek and Bulgarian national movements corresponded; and, b) Byzantism in the Balkans seemed, to Leont'ev, to suggest its true face as a form of hegemonic imperial policy. Leont'ev offered an imperial discourse that was nonetheless lined up against the defense of the imperial structure of the Ottoman state itself before Pan-Islamism took shape as the prevalent Ottoman state ideology, and it placed the issue of religion's unifying role at the center of Ottoman Modernity.

6. The Three Romes

But how did Leont'ev establish the Russian Empire's leadership role? Its hegemony was not simply based on Byzantism, but also provided greater sense to the vacant meaning of Slavism. "Russian power is vital for Slavism's existence. Byzantism is vital for Russian power."[38] Thus anyone who turned against Byzantism, indirectly and unknowingly, undermined the unity of the Slav world.[39]

To position Leont'ev's choices in the framework of dialogue between the Russian intelligentsia's Westernizer and Slavophile camps in the nineteenth century, one needs to remember his criticism of Danilevsky for not including Byzantium in his proposed classification of

38 Ibid., 116.

39 See Stamatopoulos, "Vyzantism," 330–32. For a detailed analysis of the internal differentiations of the nineteenth-century Russian intelligentsia, see Schelting, *Russland und der Westen*, 66–68, 79–182.

historio-politico types in *Russia and Europe*,[40] as well as Leont'ev's polemic against Solov'ev proposal for reconciling the Orthodox-Catholic Schism. In the interchange among the three scholars, all possible solutions for Russia's relationship with the West were proposed based on the model of the three Romes.

Through Christianity's unifying nature, Solov'ev proposed the reconstruction of the First Rome as a solution, as the East–West Schism would be removed and healed through a united Christianity. Leont'ev opted for the revival of the Second Rome; he fiercely disputed the arguments and aims of Pan-Slavism in the belief that it severed Russia from the Byzantine heritage. Danilevsky was loyal to the theory of the Third Rome which would not only be the seat of a vast Orthodox Empire but the epicenter of a new culture, a Slavic civilization that would supplant the dominant neo-German (European) one. Danilevsky considered Russia to be the ideal fusion of Orient and Occident (the idea of Russia as a cultural crossroads), possessing an advantage when confronting the West. Danilevsky's hostility to the evolutionary type supposedly represented by the West throughout its historic development stemmed from his adoption of a cyclical view of history, combined with an evolutionary teleology (i.e., an organic understanding of the "evolution" of civilizations).

Of course, Danilievski and Leont'ev were not to change their respective positions: the former as a defender of the Third Rome and the latter as a defender of the Second Rome, provided they represent variations of a shared imperial nationalism. In all three cases, religion's role was decisive in the expression of each argument. Yet, in Solov'ev, the East–West Schism was experienced traumatically, while in Danilevsky's and Leont'ev's cases it constituted the springboard for a process of self-determination.

Leont'ev therefore did not use religion to sanctify the regime, as would be the case in Russia during the reigns of Alexander III and Nicholas II, but as a means of imperial policy. He did this by citing the foundations of what Dimitri Obolensky would later call the "Byzantine Commonwealth." Orthodoxy's cultural tradition was the only one that could

40 Danilevsky's ten basic politico-historic types were: 1) the Egyptian, 2) the Chinese, 3) the Chaldaean (Assyro-Babylonian, Phoenician), 4) the Indian, 5) the Persian, 6) the Hebrew, 7) the Hellenic, 8) the Roman, 9) the Neosemitic (i.e., Arab and Muslim civilization), and finally 10) the Neo-Germanic (i.e., European civilization).

transform the amorphous racial underpinnings of Eastern Europe's Slav world into a single cultural unit and provide meaning to the vacuum dubbed "Slavism."[41]

7. A Romantic Reconstruction of History: The Vindication of the Persians

Leont'ev attempted a Romantic reconstruction of the two incompatible, at the time, "ontological" categories: Orthodox Christianity and Slavism, that is, faith and race or ethnicity. While they appeared to conflict at the level of shaping individual and collective identities, they could coexist or rather fuse in Byzantism's cultural form. In reality, Leont'ev completed an endeavor undertaken by Gedeon, at the level of historiography, by resolving the incompatibility between the imperial and Pan-Orthodox, as well as by Krâstevich, at the political level, by resolving the incompatibility of imperial and national. Leont'ev provided a far more comprehensive response, politically and historiographically, in the late nineteenth century, to the modernization process sweeping across Eastern Europe: preservation of the imperial structure and preservation of the prevalence of the religious element as completing its ethnically and linguistically decimated populations.

But in order to reconstruct history so that it could be used as a measure for comparison against its medieval rather than its modern version, the meaning of progress on which the modern was built had to be disputed. Leont'ev proposed a triadic form for understanding progress: the first phase of development was marked by primary simplicity (*pervonachal'naya prostota*); the second by perpetually increasing complexity (*slozhnost*); and the third by secondary combined simplification (*vtorichnoe smeshitel'noe uproshtenie*).[42] He applied this structure of organic evolution to living and still nature—from mammals and germs to the movements of the stars, art and architectural styles—but to two extremely interesting fields, history and the state.

41 This does not mean that Leont'ev did not take nineteenth-century reality into account. In his contemporary Christian East he saw religion becoming "a convenient tool for insurrection and racial fanaticism. . . . This is the truth and I do not know whether we Russians, primary representatives of Orthodoxy in the world, have the right to conceal this truth from each other or contrive to forget it." Leont'ev, *Vostok*, 124.

42 Leont'ev, *Vostok*, 129.

On history, the structure was applied incrementally to the history of poetry, literature, technology, and philosophy. But what represented the final stage, the re-simplification or decline, in Leont'ev's view? Decline was seen as the amalgam of "classical" elements, the eclecticism that paved the way for realism's dominance. The latter was not a "system" but a method for examining the collapse of systems prevalent at the peak of the evolutionary process. He saw the accompanying materialism as a "system," albeit the simplest of all. Realism was the rejection of every system and all metaphysics. The origins of a new start in the evolutionary process could be sought in metaphysics and especially in religion. For Leont'ev, this turn toward metaphysics and religion typified antiquity as well as the nineteenth century, his century, which responded to the eighteenth century's materialism. Metaphysics and religion remained "real forces" and "unworn necessities of humankind."

Introducing a model for interpreting politics based on the relationship between form and content ("form is the dominance of an internal idea"), Leont'ev would once again turn against progress and the liberal-equalizing process which he believed ran counter to the meaning of "development" (*razvitie*). In reality, progress corresponded to the third phase of the evolutionary process he described.[43]

By adopting an organic model (a Herderian concept) of the state, Leont'ev compared it to a tree covered by aristocratic bodies in its first phase of growth ("Athenian patricians, Persian feudal lords, Roman senators, French marquises, English lords, Egyptian soldiers, Laconia's Spartans, Russian boyars, Polish nobility, Turkish beys" [131]). Its second phase, its peak, was marked by the dominance of dictators, emperors, kings, or even populist tyrants (as in the case of Ancient Greece). Its third phase, decline, was characterized by the fall to "democracy."[44] There were

43 "But progress ... which was fought by every despotism ... is nothing but the process of dissolution or the process of this secondary simplification in toto and the mixture of its composite parts ... the process of blunting the form's outlines, the process of destroying the special features that are organic characteristics of the public body. The phenomena of the liberal-egalitarian process are similar to razing, erosion, the melting of the ice ... for example, they are like cholera symptoms that gradually change very different people into monotonous carcasses (equality) and then into identical skeletons, and finally into free elements: nitrogen, hydrogen, oxygen ..." (130). It is worth noting in Leont'ev's necrophiliac simile for liberal ideas and the abiding influence of his earlier health-scare on his thinking.

44 It is interesting to note the upending of the Aristotelian approach to regime decline, from monarchy/tyranny to aristocracy/oligarchy to democracy/ochlocracy. In the philosophy of history which

many steps on this ladder between Pericles, a real dictator, and an emperor who based his authority on inherited succession and religion, albeit steps in the same upward direction. This was the phase that corresponded to the "tree expressing in a comprehensive way its internal morphological notion." On this form, he tried to interpret history's course from ancient Athens (where the demand for egalitarianism was reignited with the Peloponnese War) through to German unification by Bismarck in 1871. Reinforcing the demands of nineteenth-century liberalism and egalitarianism had the effect of strengthening the various members of the single state-organism ("the organism's cells, nerves, clothing, and limbs") against the internal idea that contained it as a form.[45]

Since he adopted an organic concept of the interpretation of the state, it was only logical that he viewed longevity as the most important criterion for assessing it. To prove the power of his argument that monarchies and centralized regimes were the highest form of state structure, he attempted a historical review prioritizing longevity from Ancient Egypt and the Chaldaeans to Rome and Byzantium. The argument that Rome spanned 1,229 years, from 753 B.C. to A.D. 476, and Byzantium spanned 1,128 more years, from 325 to 1453, seemed incontrovertible in terms of his conclusion.[46]

The principles on which the enduring Byzantine Empire was founded survived through the Ottoman Empire, and this in spite of European cosmopolitanism. In the Greek-Bulgarian dispute, the Greeks were those

Leont'ev proposed, aristocracy preceded monarchy and was the Promethean starting point for creating a cultural totality. This may be the reason his philosophy of history could not consistently serve the nation's case, as Zambelios's philosophy of history could. And if democracy was viewed as an "ideal" (Zambelios) or as a "decadent degeneration" (Leont'ev), it was not as dependent on the management of the historical role of monarchy but rather that of aristocracy.

45 Although it seems that Leont'ev's attempt to counter the liberalization process of European societies in the nineteenth century was based on a Herderian-inspired Romantic theoretical review of the late eighteenth century, one can discern certain early characteristics of a "systemic" approach in the method of analysis. It is not just the triadic structure that concluded in "deconstruction" rather than "construction," i.e., was dialectic. It is also his very interesting observation that the demand for equality and freedom were a common denominator of "simplification" of the increasing complexity of the fields of European culture, see Leont'ev, *Vostok*, 141: "... the complexity of machines, the complexity of administration and legal rulings, the complexity of large cities' needs, the complexity of activities, the effect of newspapers and books, the complexity of scientific method ... all that are nothing but the tools of this mixture."

46 Leont'ev, *Vostok*, 137.

defending them—that is, the necessity of the people's subordination to the clergy—while the Bulgarians were defending the new European values of collective and individual rights. The Greeks represented the defense of honest subordination to organized religion; the Bulgarians represented the start of national self-determination. At stake in their dispute was not just the establishment of a church organization independent of the patriarchate but the survival of the principles of an empire that had already broken every record of longevity. Of course, it is interesting to note here that Leont'ev seemed to immediately accept that the continuity between Byzantium and Ottomans must be perceived as "smooth," otherwise he would not be defending Byzantium's seminal values.

Commenting on the future of various European monarchies in the event of their adoption of a constitution and their undergoing liberalization—and he was, of course, pessimistic about the outcome—he also focused on the Ottoman Empire. He predicted the argument that was in reality to become the early legitimization of the Hamidian regime: the empire's end was assured if it attempted to adopt some type of constitutional restrictions on the Sultan's autocracy. He observed:

> If we give it another parliament, as the English desire so that the influence of Russia and Count Ignatiev on the autocratic Sultan become asphyxiating, once we add liberal confusion to the equalizing weakness, Turkey could not last for more than a few years. (Leont'ev, *Vostok*, 143–44)

It is impressive to note how Leont'ev, at the apogee of the Tanzimat (in the wake of the Bulgarians' attainment of the "national" goal of recognition of an autonomous church and just before Midhad Pasha's constitution), provided a unifying paradigm for the ideological-political convergence of the two autocracies. It was precisely based on this paradigm that both Krâstevich and Gedeon built their historiographical models.

As already noted, the legitimization in principle of Byzantium and its heritage by Leont'ev was paralleled by his position on the basic component of European culture even though he may have thought that its basic principles survived in a more pure form in Russia. Mindful of Guizot's *Histoire des Civilizations* as well as Pichler's discussion of the Church's role in Byzantium alongside a centralizing emperor who did not allow for the rise of an aristocracy, Leont'ev attempted to offer an interpretation of what he considered to be European culture.

European culture was a composite of Byzantine Christianity, German feudalism, Greek aesthetics and philosophy, and the Roman civil tradition. But between the two, in Leont'ev's contemporary West, a merciless battle that the Roman republicanism eventually won was fought. Civil society prevailed over Christianity,[47] German individualism, Roman (Byzantine) caesarism, and the aesthetic and philosophical principles of Ancient Greek civilization. Favoritism and the practical spirit replaced Christian love, hedonism replaced the principles of Greek aesthetics and philosophy, and democratization limited the authority of absolutist monarchies in the countries of the West. According to Leont'ev, the substantive difference between the ancient states and the modern European states of the West was the manner in which they made the transition to the final stage of entropy, that is, the "secondary simplification": in the former, the ancient states, this process was "random" and "empirical while in the latter it was organized and "rational."[48]

In drawing this historical parallel, Leont'ev was not inspired only by Guizot's work but also by Georg Gottfried Gervinus's *History of the 19th Century*.[49] Indeed, Gervinus's work began with his claim of similarity between the period of Ancient Greece's decline and the triumphal Europe of his day. Based on these similarities, he developed an evolutionary structure that, in contrast to Leont'ev's, was based on the ideas of freedom and democracy. He believed the secure progression of political and spiritual freedom that was initially the prerogative of the few would expand from this circle to include the majority. But this process also followed a reverse course: when the state reached its peak, then freedom and consequently power, would slowly shrink back into the hands of the few. Gervinus implied—and wrote in the first edition in 1855—that in Ancient Greece, this process took place shortly before the collapse of tyranny, while in

47 Implicit here is the notion common among Orthodox intellectuals that Papism was Christianity's subordination to the Roman political spirit. For a discussion, see Stamatopoulos, " "I Ekklisia os politeia," 183–220.

48 Leont'ev, *Vostok*, 148.

49 Gervinus, *Geschichte*.

Europe, it took place with absolutism. Gervinus, thus, followed an anti-dialectical form and reversed Aristotle's political theory.

As expected, Leont'ev differentiated his position from Gervinus, with an interesting twist. After accusing Gervinus of remaining bound to the ideas of 1789, he implied that he did not view absolutist monarchy as the ultimate remedy for "entropy" when it was not accompanied by the restructuring of society's values system. He too drew on antiquity as an example:

> The two main representatives of Hellenism, Athens and Sparta, followed a democratic form. But if we consider the period of the Macedonian monarchy as a continuation of the Greek state structure (although it is quite vague), we will conclude that absolutism . . . is not of itself an anchor of salvation. [Absolutism's] reality is not as solid if it is not accompanied by an influx of disciplined diversity. The Greek–Macedonian monarchies did not last very long. Like Napoleon III's France, so too the future [longevity of] a united . . . Germany, by analogy, can be considered doubtful.

In other words, according to Leont'ev, the Macedonian monarchy served to slow the decline down, without achieving its goal of preventing decline, precisely because it did not entail some dramatic change to the systems of values of its time.

The three phases also applied to Rome. The first phase corresponded to the period of *res publica,* the rivalry between plebeians and patricians. The second phase corresponded to the imperial period, with Julius Caesar and Augustus Octavianus as its emblematic figures. The third and final phase of the "secondary simplification of democratization" corresponded to Caracalla's famous decree. This was the point in time where something significant happened: a new Rome was born from the collapse of the old. Here Leont'ev's structural interpretation of Byzantium's evolution remains relevant:

> The old Greek-Roman civil tradition, the old Roman caesarism, the new Christianity, and the new political elite in the Asian model are already present as Byzantium enters its first millennium. However, as a state, Byzantium did not act defensively throughout its duration. As

> a civilization, as a religious culture, it was dominant everywhere and conquered whole new worlds—Russia and the other Slavs. As a state, Byzantium was already old. It got a second lease on life—Rome's life. It remained new and vital thanks to religion. (Leont'ev, *Vostok*, 149)

If there was something particularly interesting about Byzantium in relation to Leont'ev's model of historical evolution, it was not simply that it was an autonomous and otherwise great civilization that passed through the three inevitable phases of historical evolution; rather, it was that by adopting Christianity it renewed the life of an old and powerful empire, while simultaneously introducing something new to history. It was not just a return of an autocratic monarchic institution but a new value system, a new entity characterized by intense internal diversity.

Leont'ev considered Byzantium's decline to have begun after the eleventh century—after it managed to remove the West from the Church, exercised a decisive influence in the shaping of Russian culture, and managed the threat from the Bulgarians, finally conceding that "Symeon's Orthodox Bulgarians proved more dangerous than Krum's Bulgarian Idolaters."

In Leont'ev's theoretical structure, the relationship between the flourishing of diversity and the period of decline is clear. The decline did not derive from the denial of diversity, but conversely was the result of the most vital elements of cultural composition that the former represented. Orthodoxy and its spread through the Balkans served as an equalizing process that in the end was to turn against its source.

Leont'ev's used Byzantium to construct a model of continuity in a history of empires—Roman, Byzantine, Russian—and not as with Paparrigopoulos, for example, who used Byzantium as a model for the continuity of the nation. This was because religion was vital to its structure. Nonetheless, in his arguments, he did not settle for idealizing Byzantine culture but returned to the root of evil: the defeat of his beloved Persians by the Ancient Greeks.

Discussion of Cyrus's rule and the Sassanid dynasty was not, of course, as easy as making references to his Greek, Roman, or Byzantine counterparts. Despite continuous archaeological discoveries, the dominance of Greco-Roman sources created a skewed image of Persian civilization.

According to Leont'ev, Persian civilization's period of "primary simplicity" was expressed through the pyrolatric cult of Zoroastrianism as well as the feudal leaders. At its apex, this empire managed the differences within it: the conquest of the Medes and Chaldaeans, the coexistence of the empires of Greeks, Lydians, Egyptians, and so on, suggested a colorful panorama of civilizations within a strong imperial structure.

> It was easy for one to imagine, without too much exertion and without mistake, how great the diversity of lifestyles, religions, languages, rights and privileges must have been in such a vast empire from the time of Cambyses to the time of Darius. . . . Everything was united under the great king who personified God on earth. (Leont'ev, *Vostok*, 150)

The provincial satraps may have been Persians in their majority, but the Chaldaeans, Greeks, and Jews had penetrated the Achaemenids' court. And while one would expect to define the third and final phase of "democratic disorder" as the period of Darius and Alexander, Leont'ev observes that despite Persia's conquest by the "Greco-Macedonians," the states that emerged after Alexander's death collapsed rather quickly, not just under the pressure of Rome but also because the population of the old empire did not consent to Macedonian dominance. In the wake of Alexander's death, the Hellenistic states' territory had been limited to the Persian Empire's northern and eastern edges, while in the east, the Persian cultural heritage was being renewed through the founding of the Parthian kingdom (third century BC–third century AD). This race, according to Leont'ev, was directly linked to the ancient Iranians. Within the Parthian kingdom, which the Romans never completely subjugated, the old Zoroastrian cult survived as late as the eleventh century and the arrival of Arab Islam. Leont'ev was less certain with respect to the Sassanid dynasty's (third–seventh century) preservation of the old spirit of empire perhaps because their rule was combined with the abolition of slavery. Here, too, help is found in Gobineau's *Histoire des Perses*, which confirmed that the Sassanids renewed the Parthians' military feudal system and, of course, Zoroastrianism as well.[50]

50 Gobineau, *Histoire des Perses*. For the clash between Paparrigopoulos and Gobineau, see Asimakopoulou, " Gobino kai Falmeraier," 331–48, which also discusses the *History of the Persians* at length. Note that Hegel similarly admired Persian antiquity in his *The Philosophy of History*. "The Persian

Leont'ev's treatise concluded by indulging in his favorite, and occasionally successful, pastime of making predictions:

> . . . in any case, France, Germany, Italy, and Spain will collapse at some point in the future. They will become provinces of a new state, just like Italy originated from the union of regions like Piedmont, Tuscany, Rome, and like Germany originated from the union of Hesse, Hanover, and Prussia itself. . . . (Leont'ev, *Vostok*, 150)

This prescient comment can only be compared to his prediction that Russia would transform into an extreme egalitarian regime that would herald the collapse of tsarism as well as the very principles of Byzantism.

Far more important was the juxtaposition he attempted among the three empires on which he focuses his analysis: the British Empire, the Russian Empire, and the Ottoman Empire. The criterion used for comparison was the relationship between state-building and nation-building.[51] In England, the conqueror Saxons and Normans intermingled with the conquered Celts to form a new nation. The demarcation between conquerors and conquered was reproduced as a class difference but within a new single state entity. The successful national unification corresponded to an equally successful construction of a state. In the Ottoman Empire, the conquering Ottomans did not intermix with the conquered Christians (although some segments of the latter acquired an Ottoman mentality); as a result, the state's unity did not correlate to a national homogenization. In Russia, the intermingling of the Varangians and Slavs appears to have resolved the problem of ethnogenesis (Russia proper) but not that of the state structure.

For Leont'ev, the Bulgarians were a thorny issue: not only did they threaten the Ottoman Empire's integrity, but, for the first time, Russian support of a Slavic people cast doubt on the unity of Slavism and Byzantism, that is, the two principles which provided the Russian Empire's foundations and which he had tried to reconcile.

Empire was an Empire in the modern sense of the word, like the one that existed in Germany and Napoleon's great imperial" (206).

51 Hosking, *Russia*, xxiv.

8. Leont'ev and Marko Balabanov: Byzantism as a Bridge

We can extrapolate from Leont'ev's discussion and examine how certain Bulgarians, not so much the Pan-Slavist radicals against whom Leont'ev launched his attacks, but the Pan-Orthodox ecumenists who shared his ideas, were to discuss the role of Bulgarians in the Ottoman Empire.

In the Historical Archive of the Saints Cyril and Methodius National Library in Sofia, there is a letter from Konstantin Leont'ev to Marko Balabanov dated December 27, 1874.[52] It was sent from the Monastery of St. Nicholas the Miracle-Worker at Ugresha (present-day Dzerzhinsk) where Leont'ev journeyed after leaving Constantinople. The letter's tone was especially cordial, suggesting the two men had been in contact during Leont'ev's stay in Istanbul and Halki. Gedeon's testimony that he collaborated with Balabanov on the consequences of the Schism acquires even greater significance if we consider that this politico-ideological convergence occurred under the "discreet oversight" of the "Byzantinist" Leont'ev. But who was Balabanov, the Bulgarian in this fascinating relationship?

Marko Balabanov was born into a merchant family in Plovdiv's Kleisoura area in 1837.[53] He attended the local school but showed an early interest in a Greek education. He followed his father to Constantinople and later to Proussa (Bursa) and Triglia (Tirilye). It was around this time that he became the protégé of Metropolitan Constantios of Proussa (Bursa), who introduced him to the Halki Theological School (1855). It was there that he first made contact with members of Istanbul's Bulgarian community like Georgi Rakovski, Gavril Krâstevich, and Vasil Aprilov. He learned about Greek antiquity, which became a life-long enthusiasm, as well as modern Greek literature. The library's holdings included books by Greek writers of the Enlightenment such as Korais, Koumas, and Pharmakides, as well as the more politically conservative works of Romantic nationalism by Oikonomos, Paparrigopoulos, and Renieris.

52 NBKM-BIA. 386, document 77: Konstantin Leont'ev, Ugresha Monastery, to Marko Balabanov, Constantinople, December 27, 1874.

53 Stefan Bobchev set his birth year at 1837, although in Balabanov's application to the University of Athens, the date was 1840, which may have been due to age restrictions on applicants. See Bobchev, *Balabanov,* 86–130.

After completing his studies at Halki (1855), Balabanov attended the Sorbonne's School of Law in Paris (1864),[54] before continuing his studies at Heidelberg; during the interim, 1862–1864, he studied at the University of Athens.[55] This period had a decisive influence on his intellectual development as it coincided with sweeping political changes in the Kingdom of Greece.

Returning to Istanbul, he published the *Chitalishte* with Petko Slaveykov and Dragan Chankov from 1870 to 1874. Despite the Ottomans' harsh censorship, the journal promoted education for the Bulgarians in contrast to those devising revolutionary plans for breaking away from the empire. From 1874 to 1876, when it was banned, Balabanov published the weekly review *Vek*. After the 1876 uprising was put down, he and Chankov traveled to Europe's capitals to spread the news of the cruel Ottoman reprisals against the Bulgarian rebels.

During Bulgaria's occupation by the Russian army in the war of 1877–1878, Balabanov was appointed by the Russians as deputy governor of the Târnovo province (specifically, for the towns of Svishtov and Ruse), and in 1879 he took part in the Bulgarian Constituent Assembly in Veliko Târnovo. In the clash between conservatives (Stoilov, Nachevich, Grekov) and liberals (Karavelov, Chankov, Slaveykov), he usually voted with the conservatives. In other words, he served as the representative of moderate conservatives, retaining his strongly pro-Russian orientation. Nonetheless, the proposal for a constitutional article rendering "titles of nobility

54 Significantly, during his stay in Paris, Balabanov decided to translate the French abbot Vladimir (René-François) Guettée's *Exposition de La Doctrine* into Greek. Guettée had converted from the Roman Catholic to the Orthodox faith in 1862, around the time when considerable segments of the Ottoman Empire's Bulgarian-speaking provincial populations who had joined the Uniate Church were returning to the Orthodox Christianity. This may have influenced Balabanov's decision to translate this work. In the introduction, he emphasized that while the Papal state was collapsing and criticism of it was testing the Christian faith in the West, the Christians in the East were seeking new life in Orthodoxy.

55 Balabanov's diploma is held at the National Library in Sofia (File 386, document 1:3) and bears the signatures of all the professors at the University of Athens whose classes he took. These include Paparrigopoulos, Nikolaos Saripolos, I. Kokkinos, and D. N. Vernardakis. A list of the books in Balabanov's personal library at Halki is contained in File 386, document 1:1; the list is dated April 25, 1862, and was obviously made shortly before he left for Athens. Books marked with a cross were left in his roommate, Christos Goussis's care. The list was organized by language: Latin, 12; French, 7; Greek, 54; and Slavo-Russian, 19. French titles included Charles Rollin's *Roman History,* Oikonomos's *Tetrabiblos*, Suavius's history of the Jewish people, an anonymous Byzantine history, and the first volume of Paparrigopoulos's *Istoria*.

and other privileges . . . unacceptable" was his. He contributed to the formation of Alexander I Battenberg's first cabinet in which he served as minister for foreign relations and religious affairs.

In 1880, he became the envoy to Istanbul. This was a period during which the issue of the exarchate remained unresolved, and Joachim III, with whom Balabanov was especially friendly, had risen to the patriarchal throne. In the wake of the royal coup and the establishment of the Proxy Regime, Balabanov joined Dragan Chankov's Liberal Party and served as foreign minister from 1883 to 1884. He was later elected Professor of Roman Law at the School of Law and, in 1911, inducted into the newly formed Bulgarian Academy of Sciences.[56]

But the defining moment of his political and academic career was participation in the clerical–lay National Assembly in Istanbul in 1871.[57] As the assembly's secretary, Balabanov kept records of all the proceedings. While initially aligning with the radical nationalist faction led by Stoyan Chomakov, over the course of the conference, he moved into the Krâstevich camp.[58] He was, thus, considered an "evolutionist" politically.[59] Balabanov's alignment with Krâstevich contributed to the moderates' dominance and the imposition of Bishop Anthim of Vidin as exarch in the place of Chomakov's ally Bishop Hilarion of Lovech, who had been elected to the post in February 1872. The pro-Russian/pro-Ottoman block managed to prevail.[60]

A shift in Balabanov's position is evident both before and after the Bulgarian rupture with the Ottoman Empire, although this is shift hard to trace in a provincial intellectual who usually took a comparative view to ideological models imported from Europe.

---

56 Balabanov also translated several works by Molière and George Sand. For his brief biography, see Balabanov, *Filosofski i sotsiologicheski sâchinenia*, 8–13; Danova, "Balabanov," 58–71, esp. 60–61; and Yordan Ivanov, *Balabanov*.

57 For an extensive analysis of the proceedings and a comparison to the assembly at the patriarchate almost a decade earlier (1858–1860), see Stamatopoulos, "Orthodox Millet," 243–70.

58 Balabanov remained close with Krâstevich until the latter's death in 1891. See, for example, Krâstevich's October 1887 letter to Balabanov in Paris. BAN F 26, no. 1 a.e. 31, Gavril Krâstevich, Constantinople, to Marko Balabanox, Paris, 13/25 October 1887.

59 According to Nadya Danova, Balabanov's profession as a journalist was key to his adoption of the fundamental ideas of the European Enlightenment. See Danova, "Balabanov," 60.

60 Stamatopoulos, "Orthodox Millet," 249–51.

Plamen Bozhinov, one of the most important scholars studying Balabanov's work, also classifies him politically with the "evolutionists," that is, the category of Bulgarian writers who did not desire an open break with the empire.[61] Bozhinov says Greek literature (both Enlightenment and Romantic) guided Balabanov toward the French Enlightenment and German Romanticism as well as toward Positivism, Liberalism, and Conservatism. Balabanov's encounter with these ideas did not necessarily mean he adopted them. Aside from the awkwardness of inducting Balabanov (unlike Krâstevich) into the national mythology of scholars of the Bulgarian renaissance, it is also hard to pigeonhole his ideological leanings after his visits to the capitals of Europe in 1870.

The contradictions in Balabanov's case may be easier to interpret if one considers that his political radicalization took place in post-Othonian Greece. Bozhinov insists that this process began with the events of the Easter of 1860, when Bulgarian students of the Theological School at Halki, including Balabanov, joined with the radical nationalists in demanding separation from the patriarchate. Despite their ban in the school's charter, Bulgarian newspapers like *Dunafski Lebed*, *Knizhitsi*, and *Tsarigradski Vestnik* circulated among the students. According to Bozhinov, this fostered the transformation of the "theologians" into "patriots."

Bozhinov notes that both Balabanov's correspondence with Rakovski and Gregory of Hilandar and his meetings with prominent Bulgarians in Istanbul influenced his decision against a monastic life, a path that he appeared to have chosen in the 1850s. It is worth noting Balabanov's parallel yet inverse direction from Leont'ev during the crucial decade of the 1860s: Leont'ev, who had followed a diplomat's secular career gradually turned into a defender of Orthodox monasticism, while Balabanov, who early in life had appeared ready to follow a career in the priesthood, turned toward a secular life, albeit one that approximated monasticism. Balabanov's political radicalization, of course, was especially limited when it came to any head-on collision with religion and all that it symbolized, but if we want to identify the major point of difference between him and Leont'ev, it would be that Balabanov never showed the same decisiveness in turning his back on the allure of the West. Both men, however,

61 Bozhinov, "Balabanov."

could be categorized as "secular monks," and their obvious similarities to Gedeon should come as no surprise.

Balabanov's transformation from "theologian" to "patriot" during his stay at Halki notwithstanding,[62] his experiences at the University of Athens School of Law were also quite contradictory. On the one hand, he shows signs of having been influenced by Greek Romantic historiography, as represented by the works of Paparrigopoulos and Markos Renieris. Their lessons and writing introduced him to the ideas espoused by Vico, Herder, Schelling, and the Schleger brothers on continuous progress, cyclical development, and the role of Divine Providence in history. But at the same time, it was obvious that during his stay in Athens, he also realized the aggressive nature of Greek irredentism and what the dream of the Great Idea might mean for the other Balkan peoples, especially the Bulgarians, were it ever realized. His meeting with Georgi Rakovski in Athens played a decisive role in Balabanov's radicalization.[63]

After 1870, Balabanov did not openly reject political liberalism or radical nationalism. But his political views were completely aligned with the neo-Phanariot ideological framework represented by Krâstevich, although he did not sever his relations with radical nationalists like Chankov, something evident from their joint tour of European capitals in 1876. His positions were expressed through his journalism, where he made an effort to overlook contradictions and recompose rival strategies.

Balabanov became widely known after 1870 for his articles in the newspapers *Pravo* and *Makedoniya*, where his views on the national Church struggle and the Exarchate's organization emerged. Many of these articles were polemics against Oikonomov and Slaveykov, who represented the most radical perspective on the exarchate's role in Bulgarian society. Balabanov was quite insistent on strict adherence to the doctrines and

62 This "transformation" that Bozhinov implies took place in the framework of normalizing a "peculiar" personality in terms of national ideology harbored several surprises. This obsession with a monastic lifestyle and worldview can be seen in two letters to a fellow student and close friend at Halki, Constantinos Pliziotis. The first, dated November 6, 1862 (BAN, File 26:1, document 46:1–2) was a reply to Balabanov's letter from the Greek capital informing him that he had been accepted to the University of Athens. The second, dated January 2, 1873 (BAN, File 26:1, document 46:3), is also a reply and perhaps even clearer on the two friends' ideological leanings.

63 His political radicalization is also evident after 1864, when financial assistance from Zolotovich allowed him to go the Sorbonne. In Paris, he joined anti-Bonapartist circles as a reaction to the autocracy exercised by Napoleon III.

the Holy Canons of the Orthodox Church, and categorically refused any reform in this area. Even after an independent Bulgarian state was founded, he remained conservative on issues concerning the Church.

Bozhinov quite rightly pays attention to *Vek*'s publication, which Balabanov managed to launch in early 1874 amidst clashes in Constantinople as to how the exarchate should be organized, clashes that pitted moderates against Ivan Naydenov. These disputes highlighted the need for a new paper that expressed this circle's views. Through *Vek*'s launch, Balabanov emerged as a leader of the "old" group, that is, that of the conservatives. Bozhinov also oversaw two phases in the newspaper's existence: the first ended in 1875, with the emergence of the Eastern Question, while the second was marked by the Herzegovina uprising.[64]

In *Vek*'s first phase, Balabanov was concerned chiefly with issues related to the exarchate's organization and its relations with the patriarchate. In actual fact, he adopted Russian views on Orthodox unity and adhered to the Sublime Porte's rules of censorship. This conciliatory line forced him to depart from his personal beliefs; the paper's quality suffered, and it also came under criticism from the radical Bulgarian press. Balabanov's conservatism on Church matters alienated some of his readers. At the same time, he supported all the reforms of the Tanzimat's final years, claiming that these provided opportunities for educating the Bulgarian people, and thus created the prerequisites for its independence. Despite his veiled criticisms of the Ottoman Empire, Balabanov's sympathies for a constitutional monarchy were evident.

The Herzegovina uprising injected a more radical tone into *Vek*, which focused on winning the Great Powers' favor for Bulgarian nationalist ambitions. The consequence of this switch was the paper's ban in 1867, which forced it to change its name to *19th Century*, although it maintained the same editorial policies.[65]

However, it seems that *Vek*'s editorial line during the first phase was the reason Leont'ev recognized its contribution to defending the "Byzantine ethos." A letter by Leont'ev held in the National Library's Historical Archive[66] is thus significant and worth examining more carefully.

64 Bozhinov, "Balabanov," 18–19.

65 Ibid., 20–21. Bozhinov believes this was a sign of Balabanov's patriotism and courage.

66 NBKM-BIA, File. 386, document 77.

From the outset Leont'ev indicated to Balabanov, the letter's recipient, that he agreed with him on a fundamental issue, the condemnation of Pan-Slavic ideals. Ironically, he recalled that they were communicating in a foreign language, French, and not a common Slavic language, as the preachers of Pan-Slavism would have preferred.[67] Leont'ev expressed his approbation for *Vek*'s political line and content ("*Votre* Vek *m'interesse beaucoup*") and praised Balabanov's objectivity. He expressed particular admiration for Balabanov's efforts to restore Byzantium's contribution to world civilization,[68] and also for his providing readers with translations of important Western literary works like George Sand's *La Mare au Diable*. Leont'ev believed Western science was late in recognizing Byzantium's value because "it was not feudal or Catholic or Protestant or liberal or democratic . . . it was original."[69] He also believed that Western literature highlighted the West's decline, his anti-Westernism defined by Western cultural output. His insistence on the contribution to Western science was a result of his recollection of the value of Byzantine civilization. This civilization was unrelated to events in the West, whether on the economic (feudalism), religious (Catholic–Protestant clash) or political ("democracy") level, superficially at least, but it nonetheless contributed decisively to the West's genesis.

Leont'ev's letter concluded: "I'm almost an enemy of the Bulgarians from 1872 onwards . . . yet there are Bulgarians and Bulgarians! If people like you led this nation, it would be my pleasure to quickly change my feelings about them."[70] Leont'ev's honest confirmation of his animosity toward the Bulgarians—aside from exceptions such as Balabanov—and

67 "Mon très bien et très - estimé Monsieur Balabanov, avant tout je vous prie d'observer que le Pan-Slavisme a fait (grâce à Dieu!) encore si peu du progrès que nous sommes obligés de recouvrir à la langue française pour correspondre entre nous. Je crois que c' est plutôt...que malheureux pour les Slaves, il fait que chain garde son Turc – autant que possible et une langue Slave commune nous ferait peut-être plus de doute qu'une langue totalement étrangère..." See NBKM-BIA, File 386, document 77.

68 "Vous faites très bien de prêter tant soit peu en faveur de cette malheureux Byzance, pour laquelle (jusqu'à Amedée Thierry) l'histoire européenne fut très injuste...." See NBKM-BIA, File 386, document 77.

69 "La civilisation Byzantine...n' était ni feodale, ni Catholique, ni Protestant, ni libérale et démocratique...elle était originale." See NBKM-BIA, File 386, document 77.

70 "Je suis presque ennemi des Bulgares depuis 1872..., mais il y a Bulgare et Bulgare! Si des hommes comme vous se trouveraient à la tête de la nation – se serait un plaisir de changer vite le sentiment à son égard." See Bulgarian Archive, File 386, document 77.

his opposition to Bulgarians' decision to emerge as a nation by splitting the Orthodox world, rendered his theoretical intervention even more interesting.

As is evident from this letter, Leont'ev and Balabanov converged intellectually on two points: their belief in Byzantine civilization's seminal contribution to the emergence of the modern West (and its tendency to downplay this) and their wariness of Pan-Slavism and its effect on the Bulgarian national movement. These two basic elements in the intellectual development of Leont'ev's work were discernible in the articles Balabanov published in the early 1870s and may have been decisive in shaping the Russian scholar's views. Still, it could be argued that the rejection of Western civilization could only be expressed comprehensively by an intellectual from a country like Russia, which was undergoing the consequences of a dramatic resurgence of tensions in relations between East and West but not necessarily by a an intellectual of the Balkan periphery.

9. The Meaning of Progress and the Possibility of an Ottoman Nation

Returning to the intellectual of the "periphery" and his comparative perspective, it is worth examining the ways in which Balabanov handled similar ideological issues in Istanbul during this period, especially as a journalist and publisher. As Bozhinov notes, in most *Chitalishte* articles—that is, circa 1870 and before his shift to the camp of conservative "evolutionists"—Balabanov focused on issues of social equality, understandably given that the events in France in 1871 had pushed issues of private ownership into the spotlight.[71] Balabanov also wrote on issues related to theology as well as Church and international rights. His worldview, which Bozhinov describes as "objective idealism" is evident along with his "moderate liberalism" and especially his "evolutionism" on issues of Bulgarian national liberation.

During this period, there was an evident preoccupation with progress, which was also pivotal to Leont'ev's world view.

71 Balabanov criticized the Paris Commune's socialist ideas. He believed creating social equality through violence was catastrophic, as destroying private property struck at society's foundations. Balabanov believed equality could only be achieved in a moral or religious framework, as well as within a legal framework that saw all citizens as equal in the eyes of the Law. See Bozhinov, "Balabanov."

In one editorial, Balabanov examined how progress was defined by different European ideological traditions. He identified three main schools of thought.[72] Before analyzing them, however, he offered this observation:

> There always existed many and varied causes obstructing the progress of human societies for centuries. The people's own mentality, their religion, their mythological and social customs, their political situation, social morals, accepted laws or better traditions according to which daily relations are conducted, the organization and activities of neighboring societies, the battles, the conquests, the migrations, the laziness or productivity, the good and bad habits, and finally, geographic location and the surrounding natural environment as well as natural phenomena and events, all these noticeably and essentially affect the fate of a people, and affect their progress in society. But for those peoples who for various reasons remain stagnant for a long time, for whatever reasons or as the result of historical laws and events, there comes a time that determines their fate for an indefinite period. Blessed are the peoples who under these circumstances are led to a better, more fortuitous condition. (Balabanov, "Trite shkoli i napredâkât," 86)

Obviously, Balabanov's proposed definition of progress did not initially fall within the framework of organic theory as was the case in Leont'ev's case. This was a multifaceted phenomenon whose evolution depended on the effects of multiple variables. Although Balabanov was not writing history, his management of the issue sought to resolve the same issue as Krâstevich and Drinov during roughly the same period, the problem of "discontinuity" in the evolution of the Bulgarian ethnos.

The Bulgarians' stagnation, their low education and agricultural rather than civil activity, the lack of collective (national) self-awareness, and their dependence on the Ottoman state's complex processes had to be interpreted form a different perspective. An exit from the quagmire constituted "progress" and would be the result of the interaction of many and different, mainly external, factors. The greater the importance of the external factors, the less urgent the mass civil mobilization of the "nation"

---

72 Balabanov, "Trite shkoli i napredâkât," 86.

would be. When the problem of discontinuity was outlined so emphatically, it was hard to develop a definition of progress with an organic nature as an irreversible passage from one phase of cultural decline before the final phase of the "second simplification." A nation's history did not have the privilege accorded a culture or civilization. This distinction of the nation as a specific historical unit of culture and civilization must be understood as decisive for the different understandings of progress in Leont'ev and Balabanov's writings. From this perspective, it is not coincidental that Balabanov opted to translate Ernest Renan's *Qu'est-ce qu'une nation?* (What is a Nation?) into Bulgarian almost immediately after its publication in France.

Balabanov believed that the first school of thought to tackle this issue was the *philosophical school*, by which he meant the great ideological movement of the eighteenth-century European Enlightenment. The issue of progress was not discussed separately but in the context of the system of social organization that would lead to collective and individual happiness. Faith in God's Word was its cornerstone. This is where the Enlightenment found its solution, but for Balabanov this turn toward God's word was merely a return to the old Platonic question on the ways in which politics and philosophy were identical.

> This is the source of the so-called philosophical school according to which peoples should not be led to their social organization by anything other than the teachings of the human mind, taking into account neither past nor present. According to this school, peoples should abandon the (old) establishment in their political or religious or social lives and adapt their society to the philosophers' advice. (Balabanov, "Trite shkoli i napredâkât," 87)

Balabanov saw the philosophical school's theoretical nature as its greatest weakness. He thought it impossible that entire societies, with their social inertia, could pass so easily from a phase of stagnation to a phase of progress simply by implementing plans for social organization devised by the "philosophes," plans which were often not viable. Overlooking history as a factor, that is, the specific elements that define a people based on its course through history, constituted a huge theoretical and political error.

This was an important enough point for Balabanov to make him adopt an organic theory of the nation at the very moment he decoupled it from the definition of progress and thus civilization.

> Those holding an erroneous view of their origin also neglect that the peoples comprise an organic body through which everything is organized and linked, and which moves in such a peculiar atmosphere that it is hard for it to remain unspoiled and undiluted when, instead of its gradual, unfettered evolution, someone decides to organize it according to some foreign and often unsupported system. A people's life is deeply rooted in its past and no matter what its impatient reformers say, it is not easy to sever this with the axe of one or another theory in order to set it off on a new course. (Balabanov, "Trite shkoli i napredâkât," 88)

The nation's "gradual, unfettered evolution" was precisely that which dictated against its inclusion in the Enlightenment definition of "progress." The turn toward Herder was necessary in order to establish a structure of national awakening in step with its reality, that is, in step with the Ottoman political and social framework.

The general tone of Balabanov's work was to bring need to the fore in the face of freedom, boundaries in the face of free choice, the "natural" and "moral" laws on which social development was based in the face of those grand plans aimed at society's restructuring. This worship of necessity ultimately culminated in the recognition of divine intervention and providence as an indissoluble principle in human society's historical course. Its place, however, was not enough to make it accept the basic principles of what he calls the *theological school*.

According to Balabanov, this school attributed all progress made by human society to God's will, which became known either through revelation or faith and traditions. This school of thought was founded in the early nineteenth century by Joseph de Maistre but its principles were spread through the West by Catholic intellectuals enlisted in the cause, such as Cardinal Louis Jacques Maurice de Bonald and Heinrich Adam Müller. In the mid-nineteenth century, these ideas were renewed through representatives of Protestantism and established as philosophical and historical principles in the work of F. J. Stahl. If the theological school was content with identifying the role of divine providence in history, this would have been acceptable for Balabanov "because truly, no progress, real and stable, can be achieved outside the great and comforting religious ideas."[73] But the theological school did not understand the importance of divine providence in development; on the contrary, it sought to ground human society in an immutable idea and constrain the concept of progress within a narrow circle. It therefore blurred this definition with that of religion, given that progress and religion were indeed two different things.[74]

Clearly at odds with his subsequent arguments for the need for strict adherence to the Holy Canons which hardline nationalists considered nothing but a hangnail, Balabanov claimed that religion in the pre-modern era was "the only high source of social rules." Nonetheless, this role could not have been and should not have been preserved into the modern era.

> But as long as humanity evolves, as long as religion begins to become distinct from other social norms, its mission is recognized." But if religion's representatives persisted in their desire to maintain their dominant position in society, they obstructed its evolution; religion then "exercises a despotic authority and tries to keep people on ancient roads instead of contributing to their continuous progress. (Balabanov, "Trite shkoli i napredâkât," 91)

The "historical" school positioned itself between the philosophical and theological schools and, as a result, was able to create a composite from these two different examples. In fact, this "historical" school that Balabanov mentioned was the only true school of thought in the Historical School of Jurisprudence prevalent among European intellectuals throughout most of the nineteenth century.[75] To describe its stance, Balabanov referenced the names of its founders such as the French expert in sixteenth-century Roman Law, Jacques Cujas, Charles-Louis de Secondat Montesquieu, whose work Balabanov had presented in translation in

73 Balabanov, "Trite shkoli," 90.

74 Ibid., 90–91.

75 Discernible opponents in the disagreements referenced by Balabanov include Thibaut, a law Professor at Heidelberg University. See Balabanov, "Trite shkoli," 93.

Chitalishte,[76] and Edmund Burke.[77] According to Balabanov, the Historical School of Jurisprudence was founded on the intellectual traditions of England and Germany. This was why Burke was a vital link as his work had a decisive influence on corresponding collaborations with Gustav Hugo and above all Freidrich Carl von Savigny, this school's most significant representative in Germany.[78] If Hugo was the one who laid the foundations of the School, then Savigny was the one who gave it a systematic character in terms of case law.

It is well-known that the emergence of Romantic nationalism in the nineteenth century was rooted largely in the historical/comparative nature of the Historical School of Jurisprudence. The school translated the organic theory of state to the level of jurisprudence, placing great emphasis on its historical path. This was why normalizing jurisprudence lent gravitas to the question of respect for local peculiarities and especially customs.[79] Balabanov was aware of the connection between the Romantic ideal and the work of the representatives of the Historical School of Jurisprudence, and although he seems to have maintained an equal distance from the three "schools,"[80] the fact that he placed the Historical School of Jurisprudence "between" the other two (in the role of "composer") is indicative of

76 "Montesquieu does not seek the causes and origins of human evolution and social structures in random or hypothetical causes but in the effects of religious, historical, and, as we have seen, natural events on human life." Balabanov, "Trite shkoli," 92.

77 The reference to Burke was deliberate "as at the start of our century, he is fighting vigorously and not in vain against the silly theories and works of the French revolution; he predicted, also like a prophet, the mistakes that the French people would be led to by these theories and unequivocally rejected the thought of reforming social rules in accordance with some abstract principles. According to Burke, human society is a mysterious creature, whose limbs are all connected with a tight and invisible bond. The art of creating and improving a people cannot be based on hypothetical principles." (92)

78 He was greatly influenced by Hugo's work on the History of Roman Law. See Hugo, *Lehrbuch*. Savigny, *Geschichte des Römanischen Rechts*. Savigny's work influenced a generation of Greek legal scholars, including Pavlos Kalligas and Markos Renieris. See Pantazopoulos, *Church and Law* in the Balkan.

79 "National customs and traditions are the true expression of every people's needs and are more valuable than the foreign or improvised theories that can never be a source of life for the properly perceived progress of a people." Balabanov, "Trite shkoli," 93. See also Pantazopoulos, "Gustav Geib," 1377–89.

80 We should not forget that Balabanov studied Law and was a Professor of Roman Law. He noted: "Not religion on its own nor philosophy with its absolute theories or history with its numerous events can singly make a substantial and effective contribution to the improvement of a people's circumstances. Human progress is gradual and its path illuminated by the teachings of all three guardians of the human species." Balabanov, "Trite shkoli," 92.

his inclination to adapt the meaning of progress to a "Romantic" framework for understanding the state rather than to adopt an optimistic ecumenical perspective that would reduce this to the world view of the old Enlightenment.

We might concede that the comparative perspective Balabanov adopted on several issues, which has been noted by scholars like Danova and Bozhinov, actually fostered a Romantic way of conceiving the world, especially the history of the Bulgarian ethnos. To be precise, the Romantic perspective in Balabanov did not seem to stem from an initial predisposition toward the establishment of the nation and the adoption of schismatic policies; on the contrary, it stemmed from a theoretical weakness in offering a resolution to existing contradictions. Romanticism would as a result be invested not only with the perception of a nation as an organic unit but also would posit the nation's inextricable relationship with the Church. Splitting the political and the religious was inconceivable for Balabanov, at least with regard to the Bulgarian nation. But what could be done about the possibility of the on-going existence of an Ottoman state?

In 1875, in the midst of the crisis over the Eastern Question which would mark the end of Ottomanism, Balabanov declared the end of the era of empires in an article published in *Vek* titled "The Origins of Nation."[81] The new era that dawned, the late nineteenth century, is the period that nations would come to dominate. Balabanov claimed that recent events radically changed the European political landscape, proving that the start of nation-building was the force that would mark European peoples' modern history.

Balabanov noted that there were, however, many who were attracted by the possibility of the creation of an Ottoman nation. "This tempting idea, no matter how removed from reality, is not one of those that would pass without attracting devotees as have many other ideas that have yet to be implemented . . ."[82] The Slavs' revolt in the Balkans ended Ottoman hopes of creating a single national conscience among the empire's populations, and this was fully understood by Balabanov:

81 Balabanov, "Nachaloto na Narodnostta."
82 Balabanov, "Nachaloto na Narodnostta," 135.

> The notion of an Ottoman nation involves a population of 35 million souls scattered over a geographic area that has great, global significance yet has not seen an organic structure operate over it throughout its history. Conversely, throughout history, this land was the theater of battles between different elements already established there and those seeking to establish themselves there. Here, the historical struggle spanned millennia during which no element managed to assimilate, to swallow and digest, the rest and we see it awakening again, with new strength that it draws from the spirit of the times. Can these living elements that were forged during many years of battle to keep their independence, can they, I ask, be used like a potter's head in shaping a single organic body and become a whole nation? To this question, history replies with a triumphal "No." (Balabanov, "Nachaloto na Narodnostta," 135)

Balabanov's cry of "No!" marked the end of an era for the Empire. Recognition of the nation's role was a given even if it was impossible to predict that the last refuge for the empire's unity would be the element that he, too, had been unable to abandon: religion.

10. Byzantium and the "Groundless Accusation of Ethno-Phyletism"

Despite ascertaining the end of imperial nationalism, Balabanov insisted on defending the unity of the Orthodox world in a way that often conflicted with the more radical segments of Constantinople's Bulgarian community. In the midst of the crisis triggered by the Eastern Question, he wrote to the Grand Vizier Midhad Pasha to ask him to help reduce the negative effects of the 1870 firman. He identified these as the unrelenting clash between the Orthodox Romioi/Greeks and the pro-Exarchate Bulgarians. Like Leont'ev and Gedeon, he argued against the schism, albeit along slightly different lines. Balabanov could not take a paternalistic stance toward his compatriots and admonish them over the ills of "ethnoracism" as Gedeon had, much less challenge the nineteenth century's most widespread disease, "constitutionalism," as had Leont'ev. Nevertheless, he too turned to Byzantium for the ideological foundations of his clash with radical nationalism, although he did not appear to have shared the others' optimism for the Ottoman Empire's survival.

Balabanov did something that only Greek historiographers had done, enthusiastically, in the Balkans: he defended Byzantium from Western historiography's attacks, especially those launched by Gibbon.[83] It was worth noting here that Balabanov had been Paparrigopoulos's student. For him, Byzantium reignited the ideas and civilization of the Ancient Greco-Roman world. Accepting a continuity form of national historiography that had stood in opposition to the Bulgarians did not seem to bother him in the least:

> The Byzantine Empire may not have developed in a special manner, but it at least preserved the loan it had accepted from the ancient world when it died in Christianity's brilliant lights yet in the face of the vibrant flood of new unknown tribes it preserved that heritage so that it could hand it over in the last moments of its life to other tribes and peoples. It happens often in history that beneath the ruins and in the desert of one city or one state appears new life full of vibrant and fruitful forces. (Balabanov, "Istoricheska lâzha," 171)

This was the prism from which Balabanov would relate the well-known story of Tsar Symeon's arrival at the walls of Constantinople somewhat differently from Gedeon's telling a few years later (in which Gedeon emphasized the role of Patriarch Tarasios and the peaceful part played by the Orthodox Church). Balabanov argued that Symeon desired to be the Byzantine Empire's successor and Roman Emperor. At a critical juncture in time, where Byzantium was shaken by internal strife and conspiracies, Symeon appeared on the scene as a possible reviver of the Orthodox East, a potential that was never fulfilled. ". . . if Symeon had succeeded in his ambitions, these would have revived the era of Constantine the Great,

83 "Whatever the Byzantines who remained in Orthodoxy are, no historian, not even the famous Gibbon with his multifaceted science and all his clever wit, or some biased Western writers can erase the justified glory of the Orthodox Byzantines who despite being described as rife with faults and sins, endured over thousands of years and sieges and were at the pinnacle of contemporary civilization when, during this long chronological period, the West did nothing before or after the schism with the Eastern Church but behave with servitude toward a Bishop who could rule with mind and conscience and who had unlimited secular authority." See Balabanov, "Izoblichenie na edna istoricheska lâzha," 171. Of course the "historical lie" that Balabanov revealed was Western historiography's negative assessment of Byzantium.

the entire East would have been reborn, and glory would rain down on the Greeks and Bulgarians together. Greek wisdom and Slavic optimism would, hand-in-hand, benefit culture and humanity."[84]

From the moment that this historical possibility was eliminated, the work of the East's renaissance was assigned to another dynamic people: the Turks. Divine providence imbued the Turkish people with dominance over Greeks and Bulgarians. Mehmed II the Conqueror did nothing more than complete the process of revival that Symeon's Bulgarians had abandoned mid-stream.

But the problem with citing Pan-Orthodox ecumenism and the historiographical forms that provided it with support was that they placed the blame on the Bulgarians for giving in to the siren calls of "ethno-phyletism." It was obvious that Balabanov could not reach such a conclusion, so he attempted an interesting maneuver: he reduced Orthodoxy to the same characteristics as the Bulgarians. In actual fact, he transformed the Byzantine heritage into a peculiarity of the Bulgarian nation in much the same way Greek nationalism during the period. This maneuver sought to persuade the Great Church to change its stance toward the Bulgarians. The Patriarchate had to contribute to the development of the Bulgarians' intellectual life, just as it had done for the Greeks. He believed this would lead to an effective reconciliation between the two elements as Bulgarians sought to learn Greek rather than consider this a policy of Hellenization forced on them by the patriarchate. By the same token, the Greeks would open themselves to Bulgarian literature and to the Bulgarian language.

> Some will say this is impossible because the Bulgarians do not wish to know the Great Church (Patriarchate) because they avoid it, because they are racists, because . . . because . . . But these "becauses" have no place here. Just as the Bulgarians were faithful to and respected the primacy within the Orthodox Church, they will soon be enthused by such sentiments when they see that their language, their national identity, becomes an object of recognition and respect. Is it necessary to prove the charges of ethno-phyletism against the Bulgarians are completely groundless? (Balabanov, "Borbata mezhdu Gârtsi i Bâlgari," 264)

84 Balabanov, "Borbata mezhdu Gârtsi i Bâlgari," 261–62. The article appeared in *Vek* on February 22, 1875.

But how could Balabanov distance himself from the dominant example that modern Greek national historiography had constructed? Precisely by distancing himself from whatever could be considered an Orthodox compromise with Western religion and especially Protestantism. In other words, he followed in the exact footsteps of his teacher Paparrigopoulos.

While Balabanov believed criticism of Protestantism was exaggerated, he could not overlook the fact that the emergence of Lutheranism was synonymous with what was known as "Modernity." But he believed this was due Ancient Greek philosophy's decisive influence on Protestantism. His central argument outlined in "Izoblichenie na edna istoricheska lâzha" was that progress was a far more complex phenomenon, and it could not be reduced to the Protestant Reformation. The Byzantine endeavor constituted a part of this. Balabanov noted that France, for example, while not Protestant, participated nonetheless in this progress and was included among the countries at the pinnacle of Western culture alongside Europe's Catholic countries such as Belgium and Italy.

Balabanov claimed that some "foreigners and practitioners of other religions" engaged in propaganda, taking advantage of the naïveté and even "the purest emotions" of the Bulgarian people, spreading the lie "that our Faith is the supposed obstacle to progress for the cultures of the peoples of the East in general and ours specifically." Unfortunately, many Bulgarians had embraced this notion. For Balabanov, however, faith and social or economic progress were not oppposites. The Jews' religious superiority in antiquity due to their monotheism did not mean that Jews were unable to overtake the intellectual progress made by the Greeks during that same period.[85]

Consequently, Byzantium's defense was through the prism of the defense of Orthodox civilization. How, then, could Balabanov handle the clashes between his Bulgarians' ancestors and the Eastern Roman Empire?

> Because our ancestors' relations were more hostile than friendly toward the Byzantine Empire, which did nothing more than defend itself as is natural for every state to defend against all types of sieges.

---

85 "...The Jews' progress compared to that of other peoples, mainly the Greeks and Romans, were like a dry and rocky hill in front of a verdant mountain." Balabanov, "Istoricheska lâzha," 170.

> The foreign propagandists were able to use this to foment among the weakest of us a hatred toward everything Byzantine and toward Orthodoxy, which they seek to present as reactionary, just as they seek to present the Byzantines, as if Orthodoxy were not the fruit of some historical truth but conversely the work of some reactionary people. But national feeling is different from the unbiased quest for truth in the pages of world history. (Balabanov "Istoricheska lâzha," 170–71)

This interesting distinction between "national sentiment" and "historical truth" would cause great personal expense to Balabanov in his relations with the Bulgarian patriots, albeit an expense which he bore willingly: the true is not the national.

11. Balabanov and Renan: "The Balkans Will Turn into a Volcano"

Roughly a decade later, as mentioned above, Balabanov translated Ernest Renan's famed lecture "*Que'est-ce qu'une nation?*" into Bulgarian.[86] The translation was framed by an extensive introduction, and Balabanov's commentary on various points create a continuous text.

The issue which Renan raised was outlined in the introduction to the 1887 French edition and it made Balabanov uneasy from the outset.

> The part of my collection which I value most and on which I want to focus readers' attention is my lecture 'What is nation?' I have weighed every word carefully. . . . Man doesn't belong to either his language or his race. He belongs exclusively to himself because he is a free being, he is a moral being. (Renan, *Discours et Conferences*, 2–3)

Balabanov attempted to overcome the depth of this provocative statement that sought to restore the Enlightenment ideal of the definition of the state versus the prevalent Romantic readings of the late nineteenth century.

Balabanov recalled the force of internal clashes in the Balkans. He did not do this to refute the potential for creating a single Ottoman nation,

86 Balabanov, *Shto e Narodnost?* The translation was based on the lecture as published in Renan, *Discours et Conferences*. The lecture itself was delivered at the Sorbonne on March 11, 1882.

a vision which, in any case, had already become an intellectual artifact by the 1880s, but to undermine, or even mock, the model of progress and the wave of unchecked nationalisms flooding the Balkans.

According to Balabanov, the nineteenth century, the century of nationalisms, brought to the fore three types of nation. The first were nations that were constructed during the era of modernity and their origins were in the nineteenth century, although he did not offer specific examples of these. The second were nations that were "forgotten and almost dead" but which rose from the ashes to acquire a contemporary political life, as in the cases of the Serbs, Greeks, Romanians, and the Bulgarians themselves. This was the group of "awakened" nations. The third were nations that survived through the centuries splintered into multiple state entities, like Germany and Italy, and which in the nineteenth century were offered the opportunity for unification. This classification positioned Balabanov quite close to the thoughts of contemporary theoreticians of the state (including Renan), as he also approached the question of the phenomenon's political and cultural nature:

> Unfortunately, not for everyone and not always, a vague response is usually offered about the nation, about the significance, broader or narrower, [of its meaning]. In other words, is the content of the meaning only political, as in the case when a people build a state, or does it have broader importance, as in the case where a people is not comprised solely within a state but is scattered in different lands and living under different regimes despite common origins, language, etc., precisely as, for example, the Bulgarians, Serbs, or Greeks today, to save us from seeking other more remote examples. (Balabanov, *Shto e Narodnost?*, 3)

Implicitly, the "cultural" dimension of the nation corresponded to examples of "ethnic nationalism" even for an internal observer of the phenomenon, and even more so given that the Balkan peninsula had constituted a "battle ground" for various ethnic groups through the centuries.

For Balabanov, of course, the diverse origins of races and ethnic groups that inhabited or crossed the Balkans served as an indicator of the area's "vitality":

> And if listing these peoples in the past resulted in a long list of different races, then the present has nothing to envy from the past. The Balkan peninsula remains, in terms of the above criteria, a fertile and rich land, not only in terms of its nature but also its ethnic groups, each of which always sought to live according to its own special, distinct way, and in permanent conflict with the others. The ancient Krobyzi, Celts, Triballi, Moesians, Odrysians from the Thracian group; the Istrians, Illyrians, Paionians, Dardans, etc., from the Illyrian group; the Dolopes, Lyngistes, etc., from the Epiro-Macedonian group were all victims of continuous killing and clashes and, thus, are already extinct from the face of the earth. Only a few very patient ethnologists seek to find to what degree traces of them have been preserved in the vast ruins of this devastated world. (Balabanov, *Shto e Narodnost?*, 4)

This excerpt from Balabanov's introduction was significant as it conveyed his understanding of progress and also as his discussion of the ancient tribes of the Balkans referenced in Drinov's widely known history.[87]

The excerpt's sarcastic tone notwithstanding, Krâstevich's devout follower during the schism and fiery supporter of the equivalence, if not superiority, of Church doctrine over secular law in the mid-1880s, accepted the basic outlines of the prevalent model for understanding Bulgarian history, as outlined by Drinov in the early 1870s:

> The peoples who emerged later, from the Roman period onwards . . . numerous and with different names and different racial origins, from those who simply passed through the Balkans leaving nothing in their wake but incredible devastation, some intermixed with other groups and some settled permanently. The Bulgarians are among the first who established Slavic dominance beyond the Danube inside the Byzantine Empire.[88] (Balabanov, *Shto e Narodnost?*, 5)

87 The reference is to Marin Drinov's thesis, " Zaselenie Balkanskago Poluostrova Slavyanam" [Slavic settlements in the Balkan peninsula] which he submitted, in Russian, in 1872.

88 Indeed, it seems he accepted the theory of the Bulgarians' Thracian origins in Rakovski. Mindful of Herodotus's saying that the Thracian population was big and that "after the Indians, it is the most numerous but lives scattered and divided into tribes hostile among each other", he added that this people were known "by the name of Slav." See Balabanov, "Borbata mezhdu Gârtsi i Bâlgari," 261–62. He was also certain about the distinction between Greeks and Macedonians, who were none-

Thus, the Bulgarians established a "Slavic dominance" (*slovyansko gospodarstvo)* within the Byzantine Empire's territory while other peoples did not do anything other than cause "incredible devastation" or "intermingle" with other peoples. Obviously, the ghost of the Huns haunted even those who had sided politically against the Ottoman Empire.[89] Just as Balabanov abandoned the prospect of constructing an "Ottoman nation," it was only natural that the only thing that remained in terms of reorganizing historical time within the framework of the now-established national state was to admit to the Bulgarian past's "Slavicization." But the point of "ethnicizing" or recognizing the "Slavicization" of the Bulgarian past by a friend of Leont'ev who was wary of Pan-Slavist ideals was also the moment when the definition of progress as constructed through the interaction between the Enlightenment and Romantic examples was brought into question.

Balabanov's work erred in its nostalgia or rather melancholy with respect to the failed potential for the Balkans to acquire political homogeneity that would prevent future clashes among the ethnic groups populating the peninsula.

> Century upon century passes, but the character of this place does not change with regard to the peoples who inhabit it. Regimes change, and rulers occasionally change, but the conditions in the Balkan peninsula as far as a permanent and stable state structure for the free but guaranteed development of its people has not undergone any change nor does it seem that the past has yielded any lessons for the present and future....

---

theless unified by Alexander the Great's military genius and their shared enmity to the Asians of the Persian Empire. Balabanov, "Borbata mezhdu Gârtsi i Bâlgari," 260.

89 In his biography of Gavril Krâstevich, Balabanov was especially critical of his mentor's views on the Bulgarians' Hun origin and of their favorable treatment of Attila. He was incredulous that the appellation "Great" was used for someone viewed by history as the "Plague of God" when his greatness was raised on "a pile of destruction and ruins." Balabanov believed his mentor's judgment was swept away in a tide of "Bulgaro-Hun patriotism." See Balabanov, *Krâstevich*, 387. Indeed, he noted that Krâstevich had translated into modern Bulgarian an ode that the Huns supposedly chanted at Attila's burial, ibid. 388. His purpose in translating this was so that it could be sung by contemporary Bulgarians as a folk song in honor of their great "forefather." The text had been preserved in Latin by the Goth historian Jordanès.

> . . . The principle of "divide and conquer" usually supported there with or without the knowledge of the Balkan peoples by foreign guests or uninvited friends: for example, in ancient times set the Romans against one another and became the cause for not creating a stable state structure after the dissolution of the Byzantine Empire. This principle gave the Turks a pretext for invading their territories and subjugating them for centuries. Throughout all this, they [the Balkan peoples] have not had sufficient time to think nor were they even too concerned about it. They have not learned or unlearned anything with regard to the theory of these issues, even though it has been taught to the young since their own years [the years of the Roman Empire]. (Balabanov, *Shto e Narodnost?*, 6)

According to Balabanov, the reality of the nineteenth-century Balkans was nothing but a revival of the corresponding historical conditions of the fourteenth and fifteenth centuries, augmented by the increase in international interventions as a result of the complexity of the Eastern Question: "The Phoenix is born and again becomes a Phoenix after a long, eternal slumber. . . . "

The Ottoman conquest did nothing more than conceal the severe conflicts between the various ethnicities vying for dominance:

> The various peoples had been silenced, they had been calmed during the four to five centuries of Turkish dominance, but that seems to have been the ash that covered, warmed, and protected these peoples not only with their peculiarities, traditions, and customs but also with their civil hostilities defined by hatred and envy. Whatever emotional or friendly intentions had fallen remained on the field of battle beneath the Ottoman saber, and they awoke and rose again in the present century. (Balabanov, *Shto e Narodnost?*, 6)

The nineteenth century pulled the lid off the Pandora's box of the old medieval clashes. The Balkan peoples did not appear to have learned their lesson and opened new cycles of bloody confrontations. No one could foresee where they might lead.

Written in the aftermath of the Bulgarian-Serbian war of 1885, the first bloody war between Slavic "brothers" in the Balkans, Balabanov's text acquired a didactic dimension as it anticipated history's inability to provide lessons: not only do peoples not learn from their past,[90] they actually "worship the past," thus renewing the enmities between them.[91] This process was merely "preparation for a future similar to the past, [a future] filled with uncertainty and constant threat of new political catastrophes. . . . "[92] Even though the Ottoman Empire was understood as a "conquest" and, perhaps with a negative symbolism, as a "freezing of time," the new era of uninterrupted national and ethnic clashes seemed to frighten the Bulgarian scholar. Nostalgia for the imperial past was not permissible but the splintering of the "universalism" it represented was experienced in a particularly frightening way. The problems of the Balkan peoples were precisely their long memories, and not the opposite.

In these circumstances, adopting an early critical stance toward the phenomenon of nationalism led Balabanov to train his fire on the meaning of progress, to the degree that in the late 19th century this had become identified with the Hegelian form of successive "embodiment" by the respective peoples toward the "Absolutist spirit" of History. If then every people was destined at some point to become its vehicle, then the sheer volume of ethnicities inhabiting the Balkan peninsula should be some type of divine blessing. But this was not the case at all:

> If it is true that peoples, instead of obstructing human progress, are actually useful in helping it as special and independent instruments of humankind, then according to the number of peoples inhabiting it, the Balkan peninsula would have to be a very developed and privileged place. . . . Such a colorful and ancient ethnic mosaic is rarely encountered in such circumstances. Given its numerous ethnicities, the Balkan peninsula should have continuously been a functional

90 "On the other hand, the louder the noise between [ethnic groups] about the often baseless liberation and independence, which in most cases is due solely to coincidental events, the more they are exposed to dangers, the more they are decimated and exhaust the vital popular forces, opening roads in the downward course of national destiny. This is unfortunately why the past remains without benefit for the present." Balabanov, *Shto e Narodnost?*, 8.

91 This was the reason Balabanov agreed with Renan's observation that unconsciousness was the general prerequisite for the existence and construction of a nation. Forgetting that some great catastrophes condemned "in the mind and in history" was more valuable than any organized systematization of its collective memory.

92 Balabanov, *Shto e Narodnost?*, 7–8.

> instrument for human progress, taking into account that one wonderful corner of its southern territory and specifically Ancient Greece was a sun-drenched hearth of human education on the one hand and that Byzantium, on the other, no matter what is said, was a cradle and epicenter of a [spiritual] current of a different sort and form. (Balabanov, *Shto e Narodnost?*, 8–9)

The reference to Byzantium, and, of course, to the "sun-drenched" Ancient Greek past, as well as his citing of an imperial structure that had attempted to politically unify the Balkan peninsula, was no accident. While this was how things should have been for this troubled corner of Europe, with its ethnic diversity guaranteeing everyone's participation in human "progress," the exact opposite occurred: "There is no doubt that the situation on this peninsula does not correspond to theory."

The fact that there was such semantic confusion on what constitutes a people (*narod*) and a nation (*narodnost*) among the Balkan peoples and nations, points to the contribution of the translation of a text like Renan's. The case of the Balkans, according to Balabanov, required a "supplementary interpretation" of these meanings, precisely because they were difficult to induct into the models of understanding that emerged in Europe.

Like Leont'ev, Balabanov was sensitive to the situation in the region and would make similarly accurate predictions. He wrote of:

> . . . the chaos in this area of Southeastern Europe, where aside from internal discontinuities and endless misunderstandings and decimations, there is an intersection of external interests so great and so contradictory that there is continuous fear that the Balkans will turn into a volcano whose eruption will shape Europe deeply, sweeping away in its lava the people who inhabit it, along with their dreams and expectations. (Balabanov, *Shto e Narodnost?*, 8–9)

This prognostication of the Balkans as Europe's tinderbox was made by a man from the Balkans, and, indeed, a Bulgarian, who, in the aftermath of the failed vision of a Great Bulgaria, had witnessed the Bulgarians' triumphal victory over the Serbs in 1885 and the final annexation of Eastern Rumelia into the new state. For someone to choose to translate

Renan in the wake of the Bulgarian state's most important military victory and to embellish the translation with pessimistic notations about violent ethnic clashes in the Balkans should not be considered coincidental. The spirit of Pan-Orthodox ecumenism and the imperial tradition appear to have survived, even indirectly, in this organic intellectual of the contemporary Bulgarian state.

Nonetheless, Balabanov's continued his former "schizophrenic" handling of the problem of identity and belonging that characterized his writing in the 1870s. While in the introduction, he lamented the "worship of the past" that led the Balkan populations into perpetual conflicts, when he approached the issue of the Bulgarian nation's survival in the modern era, his sole solution was to idealize its history. To achieve this, he sought to turn some of Renan's minor observations against Renan's own overall model. While it was widely known that Renan sought to correlate "objective" characteristics like race, language, and religion, on which the traditional Romantic definition of nation was based, so that he could position the meaning of will at the epicenter of the process of constructing national identity,[93] Balabanov chose to emphasize those aspects of Renan's text that focused on the influence of historical circumstances in shaping nations' characteristics. At the same time, Balabanov used a number of the places where Renan referred to a nation's "spiritual" characteristics.

To undermine Renan's arguments, Balabanov developed a rationale for exceptions:

> As we have already referred to at the start, for the moment there is nothing supporting Renan's work, at least as he presents it and assuming he has viewed it from all sides. However, with regard to the degree to which these principles and views can be adapted everywhere without conditions, without exception, and under all circumstances for each people, that is another issue.

This, of course, did not initially concern the Bulgarian nation alone, but all Balkan peoples:

93 Renan, *Discourses et Conférences*, 298–99; 301–302.

> It is sufficient here to note just this: that if according to Renan's theory, history is always the primary and main creator of nations, states, and that their condition, no matter how honorable and respected, is the principle of the will of the people who comprise these nations and states, then certainly the fact must be recognized that history, with its diversity, does not unfold at the same pace everywhere, it does not yield the same results, and does not create the same circumstances, despite the existence of the same ambitions, heroisms, or battles. History has created very special and singular conditions in Europe's southeast. (Balabanov, *Shto e Narodnost?*, 38)

Balabanov, however, would not rest on the rationale of the exception, but would dispute the usefulness of prioritizing the principle of will in defining the nation in the Balkans. "And the question one might ask is: if the important and lofty principle of seeking the national (*narodna)* will of different ethnic groups (*narodni grupi*) was applied here, would it create once and for all, under the current conditions, a new and stable situation?" According to Balabanov, the model of defining the nation as a political community was not prevalent in its pure form anywhere, not even in France.

History's weight in the Balkans rendered it unfeasible to base the definition of ethnic identity on the principle of will. Again, freedom had to bow to historical necessity and the possibility of exercising irredentist policies, no doubt supported on the basis of "ethnic bonds," was reduced to its historical limitations. "History has its current. And this current is difficult, or rather impossible, to reverse." Attempts to "reverse" might prove fatal for the peoples and races that would become the object of such efforts."[94]

Balabanov's analysis of the interpretation of two different models of conceptualizing the nation, the "political" and the "cultural," corresponded to two different terms in the Bulgarian language: he used the term *narod* (nation, people) to describe the "cultural" or rather the "ethnic" dimension of the phenomenon and the term *narodnost* (nation, ethnicity) as nation-state achievement. The Bulgarian people, who were his

94 Balabanov, *Shto e Narodnost?*, 39.

primary interest, could not be defined solely on the basis of their "free will." History's weight was more than just powerful:

> Among the Balkan peoples, the Bulgarian people do not occupy the last position, either through its geographical location or population size or history, no matter how this is interpreted. As a people (*narod*) in the broader sense of the word, it is a significant community whose numerous parts are linked by the same spirit, emotions, origins, culture, language, memories, and customs regardless of political structure. As a nation (*narodnost*) in the political sense of the word, a large segment [of the Bulgarian people] today comprise a nation, it lives under the same law, participates in its government, in other words, according to science today, it is a public legal entity that it previously was not.
>
> But being a people (*narod*) in the broader sense of the word or a nation (*narodnost*) in the political sense of the word, the Bulgarian people have the necessary prerequisites not only for a perpetual existence but also for a fruitful evolution independent of any difficulties and complicated circumstances linked to the fate of the peoples inhabiting the Balkan peninsula. (Balabanov, *Shto e Narodnost?*, 40)

Accepting the analysis that Renan attempted, and at the same time disputing the model for understanding the nation as a result of political volition, not only served circumstantial needs but also legitimized a number of positions outlined by Balabanov in an article published many years earlier, in 1870, in *Periodichesko Spisanie*: "While one could say that Bulgarians and the Bulgarian people (*narod*) existed before there was a Bulgarian nation *(narodnost)* in the term's political sense, there was not yet a Bulgarian state for which Russia fought." Titled "*Zhivotopisanie*" (Biography), the article was published in the first three issues of the journal's first period. In it, Balabanov outlined the view that there were three preconditions for a people's perpetual existence: a) territory and a unified/homogenized population; b) a self-sufficient intellectual and moral life; and c) recognition of this people's importance by other peoples. The article concluded that the three prerequisites existed in the case of the Bulgarian people, so the moment of political and state completion could not have been far away. While Balabanov believed that the second and third prerequisites were elements that the nascent Bulgarian state should strive to achieve, it is worth noting the value of identifying the third, that is, the nation's recognition by other nations. Recognition, especially by the West, was the real point where Balabanov transcended both models of origin as indirectly described by Renan. Balabanov, of course, indirectly meant that a nation's value depended upon the way it was viewed by its rivals. The weight of history was the only route a nation could follow toward recognition:

> And if a people are a soul, a spirit, a spiritual principle according to Mr. Renan, then the Bulgarian people have a soul, a spirit that was created during the centuries of adventure that haunt its body and maintain it. . . . What is this soul? What is this spirit? Is it how it was created by history, by conquests and endeavors, the same torments and victims throughout the centuries in the sphere of Eastern politics, in the circle of the so-called Greco-Slavic East . . . and cannot be otherwise. . . . This soul, this spirit, pervade such a people in its past, revive it in the future, and preserve it so it can fulfill its destiny. . . . If it is extinguished, if this soul and this spirit disappear, then the people is extinguished and the people's life and fate is killed. . . . The Bulgarian people can be saved and survive for a better destiny under the condition that it does not deviate from the path laid by history, that it does not deny its national beliefs, that it does not sever its ties with the past that are an inextricable part of the national culture, that it does not kill the soul and spirit at its core, that it does not rip up the history book, thereby preparing the way for its disappearance from the face of the earth. This is the basic prerequisite for it to be able to survive the troubles of the Balkan peninsula and for its future development. (Balabanov, *Shto e Narodnost?*, 42–43)

Balabanov's translation of Renan's work, thus, began by condemning "the cult of the past" that paved the way for turning the Balkans into Europe's tinderbox and ended with the recognition of the importance of the past, or rather of history, for the self-determination and especially the determination by others of the Bulgarian nation. The weight of history became a fate that had led the nation into the circle of Europe's civilized nations. The problem of the past redefined Balabanov's position on the question of progress. While this seems to have been rejected for as long as the Balkan nations constituted the axis of analysis, it proved its importance once more in the nation's movement from its cultural to its state foundations, that is from *narod* to *narodnost*.

The contradictions in Marko Balabanov's position did not correspond to those of Gavril Krâstevich's. As long as the tangible possibility of preserving the Empire led Krâstevich to a real policy, his ideological horizon remained imperial precisely through his defense of the religious element's superiority over the political. In Balabanov's case, the commitment that he had to play the role of the organic intellectual in the nascent national Bulgarian state, at least after the 1880s, rendered his ideological and scientific choices seemingly incongruous, or at least that would have been the case had someone possessed the criteria to make this observation. As an individual who was well-versed in events in the West, it remained hard to raise the issue of his ability to be eclectic in his use of Western ideological currents. In any case, the problem in Balabanov was not identifying his tendency toward eclecticism regarding rival Western currents, something typical of all intellectuals in the Balkan periphery, but understanding why, despite the lack of serious reasons, he insisted on being a political defender of religion's role notwithstanding its political and theoretical implications for his position.

12. Byzantium and the Great Idea: The Serbian Perspective

Stojan Novaković was definitely never a defender of some variation of religious universality in Serbian historiography. On the contrary, he was in all probability a representative of Greater Serbian nationalism, especially in the eyes of the nineteenth-century Bulgarians who, along with Jovan Cvijič, contrived Macedonism, the Slav-Macedonian national identity, as distinct from the Bulgarian.[95] Strangely, some of his theories on Balkan nationalism were quite close to elements in Balabanov.

95 It is extremely interesting that both of the forefathers of the Slav-Macedonian nationalism, Georgi Pulevski and Krste Misirkov were strongly influenced by Belgrade in their efforts to distance themselves from the Bulgarian ethnic identity. See Pulevski, *Rechnik od tri yezika*, and especially *Slavyansko-Makedonska Opshta Historiya*; Misirkov, *Makedonski Raboti*. Macedonism could be consid-

Novaković was a distinguished member of the Serbian Academy and served as the minister of education and of the interior; he sat on the Council of State and was twice prime minister. But for five years, from 1886 to 1891, Novaković lived in Istanbul as the Serbian envoy, a post to which he returned in 1897. Novaković was the author of some very important works of Serbian literature. He also translated Leopold von Ranke's *Serbische Revolution* from the German. But his most significant work on the Serbs' relations with the Turks was published in 1893, after his first posting in Istanbul.[96] This was a very productive period for the Serbian intellectual as he penned a series of essays published as a collection in 1906.[97] These include an essay on the Ecumenical Patriarchate's history, the tone of which approximated Drinov's essay, which had been written some twenty-five years earlier.[98]

Perhaps the most important essay in the collection was "The Balkan Peninsula and Ethnographical Discord: Serbs, Greeks, and Bulgarians."[99] In it, he discusses, among other things, the issue of the Greeks' Great Idea and its relationship to the Byzantine heritage, a commentary mainly on the works of Konstantinos Paparrigopoulos and Alfred Rambaud, a noted French Byzantinologist who, a few years earlier in his *Constantin Porphyrognete*, had described the Byzantine Empire as "Greek."[100] (We examine Rambaud's influence on Romanian historiography below, in chapter X.)

In his essay, Novaković argued that the Greeks' understanding of nation differed radically from the Serbs' and Bulgarians' perceptions. The Greeks approached it based on geography, social status, and especially history, while the Serbs and Bulgarians saw it in terms of ethnic

---

ered as a vanishing point of three national arrows in the Central Balkans area: the Greek where it was conceived as metonymy and prerequisite of the imperial past's incorporation in the dominant national narrative, the Bulgarian, where it was perceived as local version of Bulgarian ethnic identity, and the Serbian, where it was promoted as a national differentiation from the Bulgarian nationalism. From this point of view, it would be hasty to use Pulevski's *Historiya* to identify the Slav-Macedonians with the ancient as primitive repetition of Rakovski's revelation of the Ancient Thracians. The adoption of the Ancient Macedonians would be also an ecumenical imperial moment of the new nation exactly as it was proposed by Gabrovski's ritual succession of Alexander the Great or Gavril Krâstevich's perception of Attila as the ancestor of the Bulgarians.

96 Novaković , *Srbi i Turci*.

97 Novaković , *Balkanska pitanja*.

98 Novaković , "Carigradska," 409–56.

99 Novaković , "Balkansko Poluostrvo," 305–408.

100 Rambaud, *L'Empire grec*.

ties. The Greeks did not draw "ethnographic" borders on the map like the Serbs and Bulgarians, but "ethnocratic" ones based on the existence of a state tradition in the past and based on the definition of statehood (*dârzhavnost*).[101] Given that the Ancient Greek states predated the Slavs in the Balkans, the Greeks drew their boundaries of the modern Greek state according to the ancient idea of statehood which they renewed in the Middle Ages (Byzantium) as well as during Turkish rule (church and patriarchal administration).

Novaković saw Constantinople as Hellenism's historic center based on Rambaud's claim that the Byzantine Empire could easily be called a "Greek Empire." According to Rambaud, seeking out Byzantium's "Hellenic identity" in its uniform ethnography was not necessary, but rather in the "unity" (*edinstvo*) of its administration, religion, and grammatology, a position that the Serb scholar adopted.

On the other hand, Novaković completely embraced Fallmerayer's theory although this was not sufficient. He referenced Rambaud precisely because it was through his work and its emphasis on the Byzantine Empire's Greek character that he sought contradictions that could verify Fallmerayer's structure. Rambaud accepted the Slavs' existence in the Balkans but believed some had been Hellenized and others had been Latinized following from their incorporation into Constantinopolitan rule. He claimed that during the tenth century, the area of Thrace all the way to the Evros River was populated by pure Greeks and that if there had been some Slavs there, they had been Hellenized. Regarding Macedonia, however, he wrote that even in the tenth century, this was inhabited by Slavs, at least in the area between the Strymon and Nestos rivers to Rentina.[102] He believed the same to have been true of the Thessaloniki area, as well as the Peloponnese, particularly during the tenth century. According to him, there were many Slavs among the contemporary Greeks, but that the Slavs assimilated very quickly and easily "forget their gods, language, and customs," retaining only their patronyms. A similar development could be observed among in Germanic tribes in France, the Scandinavians in Russia, and the Normands in England.

---

101 Novaković , "Balkansko Poluostrvo," 314.

102 Novaković recalled the existence of an village near Thessaloniki called "Servia" and figured it was thus named because it was populated by Serbs (255).

This indirect proof in Rambaud's work effectively confirmed Fallmerayer's positions. As expected, he used these positions to counter Paparrigopoulos, who sought to push the Slavs' ethnographic borders as far north as possible.[103] But the transformation of Novaković's arguments was unexpected. While one might assume he would have employed aggressive arguments against the claims of Greek nationalism, he used Byzantium's "Greekness" to establish his view on the federation of Christian peoples in the Balkans and, ultimately, on a Greek-Serb alliance.

In Novaković's opinion, Balkan history functioned in accordance with three fundamental laws. First, a "pure" historical ethnicity, or corresponding "pure" political entity or state, could not exist in the Balkans. Second, given that every authority centered on Constantinople, a clean, independent state could not exist without including it. Third, no people could consolidate its presence in the Balkans without claiming Constantinople.[104]

The Serb historian's conclusions based on these laws was that the Balkan peoples should unify on their road toward liberation, they should transcend their rivalries and unite into a federation. No one should be above the other, but no one should transcend themselves either. The federation would have to be based on the equality of all Balkan states. Serbia, Bulgaria, Greece—Romania had not expressed a willingness to ally with the peoples south of the Danube—had to overcome their differences, but Serbia had to secure its rights in Macedonia and Montenegro.

Paradoxically, Novaković needed the Greek Byzantium in order to establish his views regarding a federation while simultaneously attacking anything that represented the Great Idea. For this, he used the arguments of those Greek writers seeking to "de-Byzantify" Greek foreign

103 Indeed, Novaković referred to the fifth volume of Paparrigopoulos's *Istoria* that had prompted Gedeon's reaction. Novaković noted the Greek historian's confirmation that the Greeks had failed to place the Balkan Slavs and Asia Minor Muslims under their control via the patriarchate, and that Western Europe had committed an injustice by not helping Byzantium. Novaković disputed the fact that the Slavs or Illyrians had been Hellenized because they learned Greek. He also employed Paparrigopoulos's argument that under Turkish rule, everyone under the Ecumenical Patriarchate's authority was known as Roman. Paparrigopoulos, in any case, admitted that all the Orthodox were lumped under this classification without denying the rivalry between Greeks and Slavs. Novaković , "Balkansko Poluostrvo," 325–33. Thus, Paparrigopoulos's position proved particularly useful for Novaković 's argument for the existence of a discrete Serbian identity in the Ottoman-enslaved Balkans.

104 Novaković , "Balkansko Poluostrvo," 316.

policy.[105] What existed as a modern Greek state was a small territory near the Aegean coast which, according to Novaković, did not in any way correspond to Byzantium in history; there was no reason for it to expand beyond the area it now occupied, and what is known as the Great Idea was effectively a delusion refuted by history:

> While igniting flames in the Greeks' souls and leading them as an idea, the Greek kingdom's Great Idea has long since aged and no longer guides the Greek people; it expresses Greek policy but not Greek popular policy. The Greek people are ready to become a whole, a soul, only so that Constantinople may return to Greek hands. But it is estranged from the idea of what the Greek state's northern borders might be, whether they will reach above Kerkyra or if the Aegean borders will include Chalkidiki or if Macedonia will be included within its borders. The only thing certain is that this state's southern border is Crete. Here we [Serbia] have a problem with both Albania and Montenegro. Greater Serbia must reach the Greek border. (Novaković, "Balkansko Poluostrvo," 404)

Thus, accepting Byzantium's Greekness once more resulted in support for an attempt at an alliance with the Greek factor at a transnational level in much the same way Balabanov had expressed an attempt at a Greek–Bulgarian alliance at a communal level within the framework of the Ottoman Empire. And perhaps the result was the same because Novaković's attempt to reveal the "singularity" of Macedonia's Slavophones was similarly marginal in terms of the rest of Serbian historiography. Defending the Empire was not the same as defense of the nation-state. Novaković's case, however, illustrated that Byzantium could not easily be manipulated, even by a consistently Balkan nationalist.

105 Specifically, he referred to Dimitrios Vikelas's lecture in Paris titled "The Greek Position on the Eastern Question." Vikelas criticized the "Byzantinism" of Greek foreign policy, noting that Byzantium and the Greek people were not identical. Vikelas believed that Byzantium was the heritage of the Roman Empire. The 1821 revolt essentially breached that line, and the modern Greek state became the embodiment of the Greek popular idea and not Byzantinism. From 1821 forward, these two ideas, Byzantine and Greek, were in constant tension. Athens was chosen as the capital as a symbol of antiquity and the Greek popular idea, while Constantinople expressed the older Byzantine idea. Novaković , "Balkansko Poluostrvo," 401–2.

13. Ivan I. Sokolov's Byzantinism

Many years later, early in the twentieth century, a young intellectual named Ivan Ivanovich Sokolov, at the time Professor at the Chair of History of the Greek Eastern Church at the University of St Petersburg, revisited the definition of the Byzantine past. In his inaugural lecture for the 1903 academic year titled "Byzantinism in Ecclesiastical-Historical Relations," he raised the issue from a different perspective.

In contrast to Leont'ev, who had outlined an anti-Western argument on Byzantium, Sokolov followed the broader Western scientific-historiographical currents, albeit with similar aims.[106] Byzantium was promoted on a scientific rather than a theoretical basis. In Sokolov, Byzantinism was largely a "scientific term" pinpointing the special relationship between Church and state as established in the Eastern Roman Empire. Sokolov's definition, in other words, was remote from the historico-political theory attempted by Leont'ev. There is a shift from an ideologized perspective, toward the objectivity of a scientific analysis. Sokolov viewed Byzantinism as concerning Byzantium as history; Leont'ev viewed Byzantism as a vital cultural heritage.

Sokolov's claim that his definition of Byzantinism had scientific credibility does not mean that he was not taking part in an Orientalist construction of the East; quite the contrary.[107] Instead, in referring to the defense of the institution of monarchy, his reference aimed at defending a special model of relations between Church and state, the model of "mutuality," the equality of civil and religious, albeit a model that could only be claimed within the imperial milieu. Oddly, in the early twentieth century,

---

106 Sokolov, *O vizantinizme.*

107 This shift from a cultural to a "scientific" criterion had another interesting consequence at the theoretical level: the ways in which the two intellectuals understood continuity. Following the Russian Empire's collapse, Sokolov managed to survive the 1920s as a professor at the Leningrad Institute of History. Much of his work during this period was devoted to studying the Ottoman Empire. Aligned with a long tradition of European Byzantine scholars such as Alfred Rambaud and Herbert Adams Gibbons, he argued that the Ottoman Empire was in fact a continuation of the Byzantine Empire at the institutional level. Sokolov accepted the timar's Byzantine origin, espoused by Scala and Deny, and argued that the Ottoman tax system had Byzantine roots. In the chapter on Turkish historiography, we see how important Sokolov's contribution was to the organization of a neo-Orientalist approach. For how the adoption of the national "scientific" historiography was related with the colonialism and imperialism in European history, see Berger, *Writing the Nation*, 2–3, 140–97.

attempts were made to implement this model in Russia as well as in the Ottoman Empire.

> Byzantinism, in other words, is a composite of Byzantium's most important characteristics as a specific, independent polity of the prevalent spirit and nature of the ecclesiastical-religious system, the principles of civil life, the basic directions and mark of local culture, the ideals of the dominant population . . . as a phenomenon of historical order, Byzantinism grew gradually. (source?)

There were, however, some other points in Sokolov's treatise that deserve attention. The transfer of the Russian capital from Rome to Constantinople was the first expression of Hellenism's superiority over the Roman, the East's superiority over the West. Christianized Eastern Hellenism formed the foundations of Byzantine culture. What had begun during the era of Constantine the Great was completed during Justinian's rule, mainly at the level of the law.

According to Sokolov, Slavic influences also played an important role in shaping Byzantium. Unlike Leont'ev, who saw the relationship between the Byzantine and Russian worlds as one of cultural heritage, Sokolov believed that the Slavs contributed to shaping what is known as Byzantinism. The Slavic element exerted an influence on the empire, although the latter managed to gradually absorb it into its administration and military. The long interaction between Greeks and Slavs resulted in the assimilation of elements of Slavic culture into Byzantinism, with Leon III's (717–741) Agricultural Law an example of this process. The Slavic (as well as the Vlach) influence remained important during the Macedonian dynasty, when Byzantinism flourished. Here Sokolov adopted a theoretical approach similar to Leont'ev's in order to understand the phenomenon of Byzantinism as an organic collectivity, a type of live organism whose members comprised a single whole. The various ethnic elements—Greeks, Romans, Slavs, Armenians, Georgians, Illyrians, and even traces of the old Thracian tribes—contributed, through their subordination to the state's Roman or Byzantine nature, to the creation of a cultural whole. This did not mean there was no strife between them. According to Sokolov, this was the only way to explain the frequent dynastic changes.

There was, however, a unifying authority to which they all submitted: the defense of Orthodox doctrine. What distinguished the West from the East was the East's strict devotion to the Orthodox Church tradition.

But while Leont'ev saw the decline of the organic whole as a result of an internal process of "simplification," Sokolov saw it as the consequence of external intervention. Byzantinism, which peaked during the Macedonian dynasty, began to decline with the Latin conquest of Constantinople. The process of decline which began in 1204 was completed in 1453, yet it only affected Byzantinism's cultural aspects. The religious aspect remained vigorous and creative. The Church emerged as the heir to Byzantinism's culture and managed to reproduce itself at the level where the organic whole had reached its peak. The Church transferred some of Byzantinism's fundamental principles, political and ecclesiastical, to modern Hellenism.

To counter the views of his contemporary Western writers who ranked Byzantium under caesaropapism as far as Church–state relations are concerned, Sokolov claims this constituted an erroneous theoretical approach. The dominant model of relations between political and religious authority was expressed in the text of *Epanagogi* which dates from the era of the Macedonian dynasty's founder, Basil I, and Patriarch Photios I. *Epanagogi* established a model of diarchy in a single civil-clerical organization where the patriarch was equal to the emperor. If the Iconoclasts had won, then the caesaropapism of which Byzantium was accused by the West, would have prevailed, and the emperor would have also become the head of the Church, as Leo III Isaurian had hoped.

By shifting the interpretive approach to Byzantinism from Leont'ev's cultural influences to the level of Church–state relations, Sokolov became directly involved in the dispute on the Church's role vis-à-vis the state then taking place in Russia. At the time, Russia was divided between the model of secularization and Church subordination to state control introduced by Peter the Great and a tendency toward Church autonomy we now recognize as have intensely anti-systemic characteristics. Thus, the model of an "ecclesiastic" state (*tserkovlennogo dârzhava*) like that defended by Sokolov became part of this dispute. Yet, in spite of its "anti-state" characteristics, Sokolov's criticism was more useful for its shaping the image of the Russian Empire abroad as the defender of the values of Eastern Romanity.

14. Pan-Orthodox Ecumenism and Byzantinisms: Gedeon's Two Moments

By the early twentieth century, the two empires, the Russian and the Ottoman, had become more differentiated. Leont'ev had the ability to predict the convergence of two imperial discourses in a period, the mid-1870s, when the Pan-Islamic characteristics of the Hamidian regime had not yet been shaped.

But Sokolov contributed to the deconstruction of this convergence with his work from the early 1900s. His treatise was published in 1903, and he followed this a year later with publication of an important study—his doctoral dissertation—on the history of the Ecumenical Patriarchate in the nineteenth century.[108] Here he condemned the Tanzimat reforms that introduced the lay element into the patriarchal administration, and considered it a result of a "Protestant–Muslim" conspiracy. Several years later, in 1915, he predicted that after the Great War, Constantinople would fall to the Russian army.[109] For Leont'ev, whether the ruler of the Second Rome was Ottoman or Russian was of secondary concern. The main thing is that he should withstand the Western onslaught. Sokolov aligned himself with the conquest of the Second Rome by the Third.

The two writers shared an ideological preoccupation with what constituted the Byzantine past. But both were also somewhat linked to events taking place in the Patriarchate of Constantinople. Leont'ev, as we have seen, was in Istanbul during a period of great unrest—the two years following the schism of the Bulgarian Exarchate—and seems to have played a role in creating bridges between those in both camps who were opposed to the disagreement, an example being the Bulgarian intellectual Marko Balabanov. In fact, Leont'ev offered the theoretical foundations for a political convergence: supporters of Pan-Orthodox ecumenism saw their arguments delineated clearly for the first time in his work. In the two years Leont'ev spent at Halki, he saw a change on the patriarchal throne: Anthimus VI, who was the pro-British patriarch of the schism, was replaced by Joachim II, a protégé of banker Georgios Zarifis, who was characterized by a strongly Pan-Orthodox, that is, pro-Russian,

108 Sokolov, *Konstantinopolskaya tserkov.*

109 Sokolov, "Konstantinopol," 143–219.

orientation.[110] Sokolov's theoretical intervention regarding Byzantinism would coincide with the second rise to the patriarchal throne of Joachim III, spiritual son of Joachim II, and also a protégé of the Zarifis family.[111] Could it be considered a coincidence that the two most critical interventions in the ideological use of the Byzantine past by the Russian intelligentsia coincided chronologically with the two moments when the clerical–lay group most devoted to the ideals of Pan-Orthodox ecumenism controlled the patriarchate's inner circle? Probably not. The hermeneutic approach of the historicity of the latter would not have been possible only with reference to the Pan-Islamic framework; the transformations of the Russian imperial ideology as represented by these intellectuals required additional dissection.[112] Despite the shift between Leont'ev and Sokolov from a "cultural" to a "scientific" focus as to what constituted the Byzantine past, and in spite of the theoretical differences this shift produced in their respective works, they shared a political-ideological foundation: the reference to Byzantium established an ideological discourse on the "Orthodox East," and contributed to a conceptual re-invention of Russian imperial ideology that defined Russia's interventionist capability in the broader region of Eastern and Southeastern Europe. And the crucial difference with similar elaborations of the "Greek Project" [Grecheskiy proyekt] of Catherine the Great or the "Orthodox Enlightenment" proposed by intellectuals like Alexander Sturdza in the 1810s and 1820s was that precisely these old versions of the Russian imperial nationalism set up the Ottoman Empire and the Islam as main enemies. After the Crimean War, the Pan-Orthodox Ecumenism of the Russian intelligentsia considered the West to be the main enemy.

Actually, the two phases of Gedeon's intellectual development in Constantinople corresponded to two phases in the development of Russian

110 Leont'ev described Joachim II as a "distinguished, prescient, and honest" and deemed his stance on the Saint Panteleimon Monastery favorable to Russian interests. See Konstantin Leont'ev, "Eshte o greko-bolgarskoj raspre" in Leont'ev, *Vostok*, 89–91.

111 In 1901, the year that Joachim III returned to the patriarchal throne, Sokolov published a laudatory monograph on his first patriarchy. See Sokolov, *Svyatiyshiy Ioakim*. A copy of this pamphlet with "Ioannis Sokolov," written as a personal dedication to Patriarch Joachim III and dated June 25, 1902, is held in the Ecumenical Patriarchate's library.

112 Selim Deringil, author of the most thorough study of the Hamidian regime's ideological orientation, recognized how the Russian model influenced its development from the era of Nicholas I (1825–55) on. See Deringil, *Well-Protected Domains*, 17.

imperial discourse as represented in the worlds of these two Russian scholars, from the condemnation of "ethno-phyletism" to the defense of a specific model of "concordance" in relations between Church and State.

This correlation was, in fact, the result of an internal rift between the intelligentsia of Russia and Constantinople on the question of nationalism. The two camps that defended the unity of the Orthodox world made their respective arguments. The Russian's invention of the "Orthodox East" obviously reflected Orientalist models.[113] Likewise, the patriarchate's Russophile intellectuals, like Gedeon, defended a Pan-Orthodox ecumenism which sought to eliminate the schism's negative consequences.

Here we must note the following: there was a substantive difference between the "Orthodox East" of Russian imperial ideology and the "East" of Western Orientalism. The latter structured the image of its East as remote, its irrationality and mysticism suggesting it was inferior to the scientific-technological paradigm of the West. Russian imperial ideology invented the Orthodox East as something familiar, something to which it belonged. The image of the Orthodox East had Orientalist components precisely because it reversed the West's negative connotations, while accepting the West's basic argument: that the core cultural difference was religion. Nevertheless, Russia's place in the Orthodox East did not blunt its desire for dominance. Just as the image of the secretive, fatalistic, irrational East contributed to the West's ideological hegemony, reversing these traits as positive indicators when invoking an idealized Byzantine Orthodoxy, were decisive in allowing Russia to do the same during a period when the guns fell silent in the Balkans: that spanned the period from Leont'ev, as prophet of the Eastern Crisis, up until the time of Sokolov as the possible conqueror of Constantinople in the First World War. It would also be a mistake to assume that the construction of such an argument regarding the Orthodox East permitted a revival of the ideology of a Third Rome, or even of the spirit of Küçük Kainarca. As seen in the description of the discussion between Leont'ev and Sokolov, Russia experienced a dramatic end to the nineteenth century, with internal rifts over the question of whether

113 In addition to Leont'ev and Sokolov, we should not overlook the substantial role of the Russian Archaeological Institute of Constantinople under the Byzantinologist Fyodor I. Uspenski as well as representatives of the Russian Embassy like Georgios Vegleris. For the circle of all these "ecumenist" Russians, see Gerd, "Russian Imperial Policy," 93–100.

it belonged to Europe or was a crossroads between East and West. All the arguments sprang from the West, whether from the armory of the positivists (of science) or of the neo-Romantics (of organic theory). But, most importantly, Russian imperial ideology at the level of intervention in the East was fed by theoretical elaborations that were most definitely not predominant within Russia itself.

Chapter V

The "Roman Byzantium" of the Albanian Historiography

1. Namık Kemal and Renan

It is well known that the emergence of Pan-Islamism as a sovereign imperial ideology in the years of Abdul Hamid II was conditioned by the theoretical elaborations of the Young Ottomans and, above all, Namık Kemal.

The group of Ottoman intellectuals known as *Yeni Osmanlılar*, or Young Ottomans, were the vanguard of the Muslim intelligentsia in the last decade and a half of the Tanzimat. Central to the concerns of such thinkers as Namık Kemal (1840–1888), İbrahim Şinasi (1826–1871), and Abdül Ziya (1825–1880) was the effort to link Islamic tradition with liberalism and constitutionalism. The image of "true" Islam they presented as part of this effort was not bereft of contradictions. They saw Islam as compatible with the demands of the Enlightenment and liberalism, political freedom, equality, a constitutional and parliamentary structure, and the perception of society as an indivisible corps of citizens. Promoting this selective construction of "true" Islam, Ottoman intellectuals emphasized the ambitions of cultural divergence (and indirectly of political autonomy) in relation to Europe while simultaneously emphasizing that this ambition did not contradict the need for modernization.[1]

As we saw earlier, Marko Balabanov attempted to rescue the principles of Pan-Orthodox ecumenism in the era of nationalism by turning to Ernest Renan's treatment of the nation. Paradoxically, Balabanov did not adopt Renan's identification of the nation as a political community but

---

1 For more on the ideological quests of the Young Ottomans, see, among others, Mardin, *Young Ottoman Thought*, and Hanioğlu, *Brief History*, 103–104.

rather sought to recall "the weight of History" in the shaping of cultural identities in the Balkans. Namık Kemal followed a similar approach to determine the horizons of Pan-Islamic ecumenism.

In contrast to Balabanov, however, Namık Kemal was more interested in another lecture given by Renan the following year, 1883, entitled "Islam and Science." This lecture was criticized by Namık Kemal as well as by Jamal al-Dîn al-Afghânî, the rapporteur of a Pan-Islamic ideology. In his text, Namık Kemal criticized Renan as well as other well-known orientalists such as Hammer and Barthélemy d'Herbelot (1623–1695), who, due to their lack of knowledge of the Ottoman language and Ottoman culture had been led to many false conclusions. He found Renan's fundamentalist attack particularly disturbing with respect to two points. First, the supposed arrogance of Muslims toward science and education, since wealth, power, and especially happiness are guaranteed by God:

> From the beginning of his religious initiation, at the age of ten or twelve years, the Muslim child, until then [hitherto] still quite aware, suddenly becomes fanatical, full of a foolish pride in possessing what he believes is the absolute truth, happy with what determines his inferiority, as if it were a privilege. This senseless pride is the radical vice of the Muslim. The apparent simplicity of his worship inspires him with a contempt for other religions that has little justification. Convinced that God determines wealth and power to whomever He sees fit, regardless of education or personal merit, the Muslim has the deepest contempt for education, for science, for all that constitutes the European spirit. (Renan, "Islam and Science," 2)

Namık Kemal was well aware of the characteristics of this French scholar: he knew that he was faced here not with the traditional rejective Orientalism of a Western Christian (he knew, for instance, that Renan, the author of the famous work "The Life of Christ," had left the seminary in which his family had enrolled him as a result of his attempt to avoid studying "Christian beliefs"), but a "modern type" of Orientalism that invoked a new god, science. In fact, an atheist Orientalism was far more dangerous than the old one of Christianism, which Islam had in any case "canceled" (as Kemal pointed out). The critique, therefore, on the subject of a superiority complex that supposedly distinguished the Muslims and led to a devaluation of the scientific achievements of the West, was the main point on which Renan insisted. But further criticism was to follow from this, posing an even greater problem related to Renan's lecture:

> This bent instilled by the Muslim faith is so strong that all differences of race and nationality disappear by the act of converting to Islam. The Berber, the Sudanese, the Circassian, the Afghani, the Malaysian, the Egyptian, the Nubian: once they become Muslim are no longer Berbers, Sudanese, Egyptians, etc. These are Muslims. Persia alone is an exception. It has kept its genius, because Persia was able to assume a separate place in Islam; it is basically more Shiite than Muslim. (Renan, "Islam and Science," 2–3)

Renan, wishing to clarify terms such as "Arabic" and "Islamic" civilization, made an appraisal that would lead Namık Kemal into difficulties in his analysis of the relationship between Islam and nation: for Renan, Islam eliminates national differences and ethnic peculiarities.[2] The creation of the global Islamic community (Ummah) runs through the dissolution of the national groups that compose it. Namık Kemal insisting on this point in Renan's lecture actually serves to connect it to Renan's lecture of 1882 on the nation: if the latter was a classification of a national phenomenon, mainly on the basis of European realities, the former opened the perspective out of Europe, but only to reproduce a dominant colonial and Orientalist approach.

However, Namık Kemal's response to such an "accusation" is of great interest, especially if one considers that he was one of the proponents of the reconciliation of Islam and modernity according to the al-Afghānī line. He thought that Renan's assessment was related to an erroneous judgment of the arrogance of the Islamic religion setting itself against science. Precisely because Islam neglects science and religion, it opposes, for Renan, the coming of modernity. But that, according to Namık Kemal, is not the case. This is why national differences have been maintained within Islam. Namık Kemal notes:

2Kemal, *Renan Müdafaanamesi*, 19.

> It is a historical fact that, regarding some disputes that arise among the Islamic states, almost all the tribes included in Islam have been able to maintain their tribalism. Only if asked about his Islamic faith, for example if he uses it before his name as a Turk or Afghan, but this is also valid according to other religions. (Kemal, *Renan Müdafaanamesi*, 25)

His last sentence certainly indicates an embarrassment regarding how to resolve the problem: in favor of maintaining "racial" differences, or in favor of a transcendent legitimation principle that would be religion.

And negotiating the exception, the case of Iran, makes things even more difficult for the Ottoman intellectual. On the one hand, he reminded Renan that Iran should not be considered an exception because the Shiites are Muslims, while on the other hand, faithful to the Ottoman Sunni, Namık Kemal would recall that the Persians became Shiites through violence during the last three centuries of the Safavid Dynasty.[3]

The difficulty, however, is essential, and was not just related to the opponents of the Ottomans. Kemal, the pioneer of Pan-Islamic ecumenism, was to face exactly the same dilemmas as an Albanian-born intellectual in Ottoman Constantinople during the same years: is it possible for nation and Islam to be compatible? And this is a problem that has always been identified with the degree of Arabization of the Islamic religion.

2. The Rupture of Pan-Islamic Ecumenism: Şemseddin Sami vs. Sami Frashëri

Sami Frashëri was one of the most important figures of the Albanian renaissance, or *Rilindja* (which corresponds to the Bulgarian *Vâzrazhdane*). An active participant in the Albanian nationalist movement, he wrote its charter, *Shqipëria ç'ka qenë, ç'është e ç'do të bëhetë?* (Albania, what was it, what is it, and what will become of it?). The text was published in 1899 in Bucharest and can be read as his political and ideological manifesto, the first text that outlined Albanian demands for a national state independent of the Ottoman Empire.

3 Kemal, *Renan Müdafaanamesi*, 26.

But Sami Frashëri was equally important for Ottoman cultural life. Known as Şemseddin Sami—*Şemseddin* is Arabic for "sun of the faith"—he wrote a series of vital literary, lexicographic, and historical works that were published mostly in Istanbul and infused with the spirit of Hamidian Pan-Islamism.[4]

So, the same individual hovered between two different political models and, mainly, between two different value systems. It is logical that the transition from one to the other would be mediated by the same individual through a confrontation with the dilemma of empire or nation-state. Nonetheless, it remains important for us to look at Sami's analysis, which presented a somewhat different organization of both the national and the imperial/Pan-Islamic ideal.

Born 1850 in the Southern Albanian village of Frashër in the Berat-province, Sami adopted the name of his birthplace as his surname, as did his equally famous brothers, the poet and writer Naim and the League of Prizren leader Abdyl.[5] In Frashër, the three siblings received their early education in the Bektashi tekke. The family seems to have belonged to the Bektashi Order of Dervishes.[6] In 1865, a few years after the death of his parents—Halit Frashëri died in 1859 and his mother in 1861—Sami and his seven siblings moved to Ioannina where the oldest brother, Abdyl, had been appointed as an officer of the now-Ottoman administration. Abdyl looked after his younger brothers and ensured they were accepted into the Greek-language Zosimas School. His education there

4 On Sami Frashëri's "split identity," see Bilmez, "Sami Frashëri or Şemseddin Sami?," 7–29, Bilmez, "Shemseddin Sami Frashëri," 341–71.

5 See, among others, Bilmez, "Shemseddin Sami Frashëri," Kristo Frashëri, "Şemseddin Sami Frashëri"; Gawrych, "Tolerant Dimensions," 519–36; Clayer, *Nationalisme albanais*, 272–84, which contains the reference to Sami's dispute with the Constantinople-based newspaper *Neologos* (1878–80). Sami accused Greek nationalism of expanding its leagues throughout the empire in support of its irredentist aims rather than contributing to the education process. He also charged that the use of the term "Rumeli" was a deliberate attempt to confuse the words "Rum" and "Greek", with the latter's secessionist visions. This criticism in the late 1870s against all the unstated goals of Greek nationalism lay the ground for Sami's complete his about-face on the ideas of an emerging Albanian nationalism in the framework of the Hamidian Pan-Islamic policy. But the issue of abandoning the principles of the Islamic Ummah was even more complicated for a Bektashi nationalist.

6 On the significance of Bektashi influence on the work of Naim Frashëri, see Duijzings, "Politics of Albanianism." Citing Naim's Bektashism was actually a process of disengaging from the Ottoman imperial model which was dominated by Sunni Islam. On this issue, see Clayer, *Nationalisme albanais*, 477–80.

had a decisive effect on his intellectual development. Along with Greek, he learned Latin, Italian, and French, and his attendance at a Muslim school, *medrese*, improved his knowledge of Ottoman Turkish, Persian, and Arabic. In 1871, he too received an appointment to an administrative post in the Ioannina vilayet.

One year later, Sami and his brother Naim left for Istanbul where he worked in the imperial government's press service, in other words, as a censor for the Porte. He also worked as a translator for newspapers and magazines. During this same period, Leont'ev arrived in the Ottoman capital (it is also possible that their paths had crossed during his stay in Ioannina), Gedeon emerged as the patriarchate's "organic intellectual," and Krâstevich confronted Drinov's ideas on the mythologizing power of Hunnic origins. Sami, of course, did not defend the imperial model from the perspective of Pan-Orthodoxy, but certainly from the viewpoint of Pan-Islamic ecumenism.[7]

In the capital, Sami was exposed for the first time to the Young Ottomans' ideas on reforming the Ottoman state and transforming it into a modern, constitutional entity that nonetheless preserved its Islamic character.[8]

In 1880, on orders from Abdul Hamid, Sami was transferred to the Military Audit Committee's secretariat. Despite later Albanian historians' contrary claims of persecution by the Hamidian regime, it was from this position, which he held until his death in 1904, that Sami wrote his most important works.[9]

---

7 On Pan-Islamism as the Ottoman state's dominant ideology during the reign of Abdul Hamid, see Özcan, *Pan-Islamizm*; Eraslan, *Abdülhamid ve Islam Birligi*; Landau, *Politics of Pan-Islam*; Deringil, *Well-Protected Domains*; Karpat, *The Politicization of Islam*; Türköne, *Siyasi Ideoloji*. On the positive way in which the Hamidian state handled the "Albanian nation" (*Arnavut milleti*) as a fundamental part of imperial policy in the Balkans, see Safvet Pasha's 1880s memorandum as presented in Clayer, *Nationalisme albanais*, 262–63.

8 Yazici, *Osmanlilik Fikri*.

9 Sami published *Kamus-ı Fransevi*, the six-volume historical and geographical encyclopedia *Kamus'ul Alami* (1888–89), the *Kamus-ı Arabi*, and the *Kamus-ı Turki* (1899–1901), thus inaugurating a new period in Ottoman and Turkish linguistics and lexicography. On Sami's work as the herald of language reforms of 1928, see Trix, "Stamboul Alphabet." As early as 1879, Sami had proposed the adoption of the Latin alphabet to the members of the Albanian Society of Science (Cemiyet-i İlmiye-i Arnavudiye), which should be considered as the correspondent of the Greek Literary Association of Constantinople. Both associations were established on the model of the *Cemiyet-i İlmiye-i Osmaniye*, a fact that to date has not been addressed in related research.

One year earlier, Sami founded the *Cep Kütüphanesi* (Little library) with Mihran Efendi, publisher of the newspaper *Tercümân-i Şark*.[10] The book series featured titles in all the epistemological fields like linguistics, mythology, anthropology, and geology in which Ottoman scientific thought was lagging behind the West.[11]

3. Between Ancient Greeks and Modern Europeans: Islamic Civilization as a Mediator

One of the first books published in the series was Sami Frashëri's *Medeniyyet-i Islamiyye* (Islamic civilization), one of the first cultural histories written by an Ottoman, yet simultaneously closely aligned with the Hamidian regime's ideals. Along with his İslamiyetin *Yayılması* İçin *Yapılan* Çalışmalar (Studies for the accomplishment of the spread of Islam, 1885),[12] Sami joined the broader discourse on creating a uniform Pan-Islamic foundation for the Ottoman Empire's survival, even though at the time, like his brothers, he was also a member of the League of Prizren (1878–81).[13] Since the early 1880s, he was also the president of the Albanian National Committee in Constantinople (*Komiteri Kombetar i Stambollit*)[14] and made an important contribution to the creation of the

10 Sami contributed to both the newspapers *Tercümân-i Şark* (Translator of the East, 1878) and *Sabah* (Morning, 1876). See Bilmez, "Shemseddin Sami Frashëri." *Sabah* was financed by a wealthy Greek merchant named Papadopoulos and enjoyed the longest publication of a daily newspaper in the history of the Ottoman Empire (1876–1914); see Gawrych, "Tolerant Dimensions," 523.

11 Written in modern Turkish, these slim volumes aimed to disseminate information in order to acquaint Ottoman society with Western culture. Sami wrote 15 volumes of 11 works out of the 32-volume series. The writers Ebuzziya Tevfik (1849–1913), Beşir Fuad (1852–1887), and Ahmed Rasim (1865–1932) also contributed to the series. These small works were: *Medeniyyet-I Islâmiyye* (Islamic civilization, 1879), *Esatir* (Myth, 1879), *Kadinlar* (The women, 1879), *Gok* (The sky, 1879), *Yer* (The Earth, 1879), *Insan* (Man, 1879), *Emsal* (The partner, 4 vols, 1879–1880), *Letaif* (Anecdotes, 2 vols, 1883), *Yine Insan* (Human again, 1886), *Lisan* (The language, 1886), *Usul-I Tenkid ve Tertib* (Criticism and construction, 1886).

12 This was first published in 1885 in Arabic and at the same time translated into modern Turkish by Renzi Demir. See Şemseddin Sami, İslamiyetin *Yayılması*. All references henceforth are to the 1997 edition.

13 On the League's founding, see Skendi, " Autonomous Trends," 221. On the League's contributions to the formation of a definition of national unity in Albanian nationalism, see Prifti, "Lidhjes së Prizrenit," 43–59.

14 The Committee was founded by a circle of intellectuals including Pashko Vasa, Jani Vreto, Ymer Prizreni, Zija Prishtina, Sami Frashëri, Ahmet Koronica, Mihal Harito, Iljaz Dibra, Mehmet Ali Vrioni, Seid Toptani, Mustafa Nuri Vlora, Mane Tahiri. See Korkuti, et al., *Historia e Popullit*

Society for the Dissemination of the Albanian Language.[15] Turkish historiography viewed his occupation with issues relating to Albanian national identity and the embrace of Albanian nationalist ideals as limited to the three years of his involvement in the League of Prizren. Conversely, Albanian historians have claimed that the national liberation struggle occupied him up until the time of his death.[16] The publication of *Shqipëria* (Albania) cannot contribute to either side of this argument: although the charter for Albanian nationalism, the fact that this was published anonymously offers many opportunities for disputing its origin.

This division, however, occurred not only in retrospective readings of Sami's work. It reflected the contradictions in his disengagement from the (Ottoman) Islamic world, and the strategy of alliance that the nascent Albanian nationalist movement was forced to follow.[17]

Through *Medeniyyet-i Islamiyye* (which was published twice during his lifetime, in 1879 and 1885), Sami hoped to promote the Muslim contribution to world civilization by presenting the broad outlines of medieval Islam in astronomy, mathematics, geography, the natural sciences, medicine, philosophy, literature, industry, and history. This work was considered a big step as Sami's orientation toward a type of cultural

Shqiptar, vol. 1, 433. Abdyl Frashëri was elected president. The Committee proceeded to found local committees in Ioannina and Shkodër. Their aim was promoting Albanian independence by organizing an anti-Ottoman, revolutionary, national liberation movement and presenting international diplomacy with a fait accompli.

15 The Society's title in Albanian is *Shoqëria e të Shtypuri Shkronja Shqip*. It could be described as a counterpart to the Greek Literary Association of Constantinople or the Bulgarian Literary Society in Brăila.

16 Frashëri, "Şemseddin Sami Frashëri," 79–94.

17 The division is very interesting from the viewpoint of confrontation between Drita (1881) and Dituria (1887), two societies in Bucharest. The leader of latter, Nikolla Naço (1843–1913) believed that the group of Albanian patriots and wealthy benefactors could resist neighboring peoples' annexation plans as Serbs, Bulgarians, and especially Greeks, who were motivated by Pan-Slavist or Great Idea ambitions if cooperation between Albanians and the Vlachs in Albania, Macedonia, Pindus, and eventually Romania was forged early enough. But not everyone in the Albanian diaspora was in agreement. Conversely, Albanian intellectuals around Drita attempted to bolster cooperation with other Balkan peoples and with the Russians, aiming to create a more resilient front against the Ottomans. Drita and Dituria each engaged in independent activity, but their rivalry marked both for quite some time. Drita expanded, forming branches in Brăila, Focşani, Constanţa, Ploieşti, and elsewhere where it found support among Albanian migrants. Most Albanians in Bucharest joined Dituria, whose President was Kostaq Duro. It did not expand to other cities at first but instead published several of Sami's and Naim's works, starting with *Dheshkronj* (Geography) and *Dituritë* (Physiography), respectively, in 1888. See Korkuti, *Historia e Popullit Shqiptar*, vol. 1, 481–93.

historiography transcended the established traditions of a narrowly defined political and military narrative of Ottoman historiography.[18]

Certainly, however, it was a premature work—not just in terms of its early publication, but it was also Sami's first politico-ideological work—and it was characterized by a number of weaknesses. Numerous excerpts contained lists or names, while there was little evaluation of the contents of referenced works and personalities. Despite the wealth of information, Sami did not include a bibliography of his sources. However, his work is extremely interesting from the perspective of "imperial memory" and religion's role in the modern era, especially the introduction, and it deserves closer attention.

First, Sami tried to define civilization in terms of race as well as development and progress. Going against the tide (and the historical development of Albanian and Turkish nationalism that directly linked race to national identity), Frashëri attempted to define civilization as a human conquest, regardless of racial differences:

> This land, which is a small piece of countless creations by God's hand, and its importance is equal in importance to the entire universe or perhaps even more because we are on it, even though it may be the residence and homeland of many, countless, animals, because of the human mind and perception . . . it is appropriate for it to be considered as residence and homeland of the human species. Let us look at the humans who are on earth, examine the species and the race of the peoples inhabiting the five continents. . . . Observing such great difference among them, we would hesitate to include them in a species of the animal kingdom. The so-called difference is not in the color, the face, or clothes. The difference between a black man and a white man are the same as the difference between a blond and a brunette. It does not create distance between them, this so-called difference . . . People's difference is in the strength of their minds; he who differs from the other animals has a strong mind, and he who is close to them has a weak mind. (Sami, *Medeniyyet-i Islamiyye*, 11–12)

18 See Renzi Demir's introduction to Sami, *Medeniyyet-i Islamiyye*, 7–8.

Racial differences—and these were due to the divine origin of the human species—were neither a sufficient nor requisite condition for producing cultural differences. Differences existed among people, but their cultural differences cannot be interpreted by their dispersion around the globe. Since the criterion of space, which, as shall be discussed further on, was important to him, had been set from the outset, Sami would attempt an approach to the problem by introducing the problem of time. Again, he distanced himself from the perception of civilizations' linear progression, which was predominant in the nineteenth century. This he did not completely reject, but rather noted that:

> the difference we can see among people based on the space we can also verify based on time, that is, by directing our gaze towards human history. We thus see, when taking geography into account, modern people in France, while in Borneo we see savages; as we look at history, we see some savages in France two thousand years ago, while now they are modern and in the Tigris valley then they were modern, now they are Bedouins. (Sami, *Medeniyyet-i Islamiyye*, 12)

Thus, if, as Frashëri claimed, space determined cultural difference, France would always have to have been inhabited by modern people and the Tigris Valley continuously inhabited by Bedouins. But things did not happen in that way, and a historical perspective can prove this:

> We know that a modern race inhabited the Tigris Valley two thousand years ago . . . while today the same area is inhabited by the Bedouin people, and that France was inhabited by some savages . . . while today it is inhabited by moderns. If this difference was something related to time . . . two thousand years ago the people should have been in one state and now in another, but we seem the opposite happening. (12)

Linear evolution and the theory of progress are both cast into doubt, but not necessarily so that Sami can adopt a corresponding theory on "decline" as in Konstantin Leont'ev's case. According to Sami, all people have the same capacity for civilization (" . . . the causes of becoming civilized were prepared by God"), yet civilization, or rather its peak, was and is always a temporary state. Civilization has always been related to the cognitive development of the human being.[19] This was the only weapon this earthly creature, "naked and devoid of any arms," had to survive in competition with the rest of the animal kingdom. The human mind, thus, initiated the process of civilization, leaving behind wildness and creating a way of life commensurate to its ability to create, removing the human race from savagery and advancing human intellect step by step.

Nonetheless, this evolution was always dependent on the fact that peaceful coexistence between human tribes and societies was not the norm, but rather the exception:

> If every member of the human race was gathered in a single space and spoke a single language, and there was an alliance and a harmonization among them and were removed from hostility, hatred, and fighting, they would suddenly walk together on the road of civilization and would reach their destination with greater speed and ease. . . . But often a tribe that reached civilization was destroyed or assimilated by other tribes or its neighbors. (Sami, *Medeniyyet-i Islamiyye*, 12–13)

Sami seems to have adopted the civilization model of uneven development between tribes and societies. This uneven development was the result of a process of clashing: the destruction of a civilization could become the prerequisite for the emergence of another. But in proposing the model of uneven development, Sami's aim was not to make the civilizing process dependent on a process of clashes, but rather to set up a continuity in the evolution of civilizations. If space could not be a determining factor in this continuity and in the rise of a civilization—in the Tigris Valley, the civilization of earlier millennia was replaced by that of the Bedouins—civilizations did evolve over time, through shifts in space, encapsulating the material and intellectual successes of their predecessors.

19 This evolution is seen as a continual accumulation of knowledge and invention by "outstanding" representatives of the species. "Yet, some people emerged who discovered great truths and useful things for people. At first, they pondered by accidence, and most of this was not or could not be used by the human race, thus, leaving unprocessed a great natural asset like thought and perception. As soon as someone discovered something small from the treasure of things, another came along who could invent a truth, pushing natural thinking after learning this truth as he built something useful for humankind; others who followed were able to improve it or discovered something else." Ibid., 13.

But what preceded European civilization if European civilization was the absolute measure of the material and intellectual growth of the world's cultures? Sami questioned European culture's relationship to the Greek (implying its Byzantine version) world, and he suggested that for the unity of the historical evolution of civilizations to be restored, it was important not to overlook the importance of Islamic civilization. Islamic culture acquired the value of an intermediate link that salvaged the structure of humankind's cultural continuity:

> It is beyond our scope to refer to the Chaldaeans, Assyrians, Medes, Indians, Egyptians, Greeks, and the new European nations that served the human race by conquering civilizations from the ancient times. Nonetheless, we will prove that contrary to what most believe, these eight or nine intervening centuries between Greek civilization (*Yunan medeniyyet-i*), which was the last of those ancient civilizations, were not far from contemporary European civilization.
>
> The Europeans believed, to a certain point, that modern civilization was born directly from Ancient Greek civilization and that civilization in Europe was awakened by the Ancient Greek texts that some Rum teachers brought. The latter migrated to Italy after the fall of Constantinople. Even today, most peoples and writers hold the same view.
>
> We are not among those who deny the power and importance of Ancient Greek civilization, but we cannot accept that these Greek texts were those which, through the Rum scholars (ö*ğretmenler*) who left Istanbul for Italy, served Europe's awakening. Also, we cannot say that all of the Earth was buried in the darkness of ignorance and wildness, that it strayed from civilization from the day that Ancient Greek civilization disappeared until the day it was born European, and that the new European civilization resulted solely from the study of the Rum who left Istanbul (Sami, *Medeniyyet-i Islamiyye*, 16–17)

Sami seems to have adopted a Hegelian approach to history, whose spirit was sometimes embodied by the culturally dominant civilization or society. There could be no gaps in this process. For Sami, history's absolute spirit was synonymous with culture, which was not conceived as an historical idiosyncrasy, nor as the particular conquest of a people as they followed their historical path, but as an absolute value, a target that peoples sometimes approached and from which they were sometimes distanced. Since it was impossible to eradicate civilization from the face of the earth, someone had to attain it.

> When we examine these eras, we will see that civilization hardly disappeared from the earth. It appeared in one or more tribes from the first day it emerged until the destruction of Greek civilization. Civilization thus could not arrive directly from the Greeks to the Europeans as several centuries intervened. (Sami, *Medeniyyet-i Islamiyye*, 18)

So, the intermediate centuries—not identified precisely—were not a gap in the history of civilization. On the contrary, they were represented by a civilization clearly superior to the Greek: Islam. Between Greek civilization's decline and Europe's awakening, Islamic civilization played the role of intermediary.

> This civilization is Islamic civilization. A race, although in savage condition and living nomadically, can adopt and assume the cultural works of a civilized people. The subsequent civilization is always more perfect than its predecessor because it can mature its achievements, adding the fruits of its own powers of understanding [and this happens] when a civilized people receives the completed cultural achievements of another civilized people. There is no doubt that Islamic civilization is more perfect than Greek civilization just as there is no doubt that Greek civilization was more perfect than the civilizations of the Egyptians, Phoenicians, and other Asian peoples, and that contemporary European civilization is more perfect than Islamic civilization. . . . Today the European researchers do not deny this civilization because these Islamic achievements did not disappear and still exist, and even today the Europeans have these works in their hands and this proves that European civilization comes directly from Islamic civilization. Faith in European civilization's birth from the Greek and overlooking Islamic civilization is a mistake that derives from the prevalence of the Ancient Greek language and ethics

> among the Europeans and the invisibility of the Islamic languages and respective ethics. (Sami, *Medeniyyet-i Islamiyye*, 18–19)

Thus, if Europe, as a result of its prejudices, was incapable of recognizing the value of the intermediary role played by Islamic civilization, the same was not true of the scientists at the European academies, especially the medievalists. According to Sami, they were the ones who highlighted the importance of the Latin translations of the great scientific and philosophical works of Arab Islam (and, of course, all of the great works of Ancient Greek literature) while Europeans languished in ignorance and remained hostages to their prejudices against Islamic civilization. For Sami, scientific objectivity was a sort of refuge from the danger of Orientalist prejudice. He simultaneously offered an interpretation of the question raised in the above excerpt: why was the Tigris Valley inhabited by Bedouins now rather than the worthy descendants of the ancient Eastern civilizations? This was because the History of Civilization had moved West, a Hegelian idea that was useful to the Ottoman scholar. Islamic civilization's great works, which raised the seeds of the older Greek civilization to a higher level, were lost to "the contemporary cultures of Old Asia" at the very same time they were becoming known to the West.

Sami did not believe that Islamic culture should be identified with Arab culture. Nonetheless, the Arab language played a pivotal role in the spread of Islamic culture. According to him, Arabic was the "scientific language of all Islamic countries." Like Persian culture, Ottoman civilization was inextricably bound to the use of Arabic.[20] Arabic was the language of science and literature, while Turkish and Persian were used almost exclusively in demotic poetry. Thus, the Arab language effectively had the same status as Latin in the Western world.

Through this reference to Arabic, Sami tried to build an ecumenical model similar to those of Gedeon and Leont'ev. Religious ecumenism that corresponds to the sanctity of a language did not disappear in the great melting pot of nations, yet it was precisely the prerequisite for cultural expression. Reminders of the ethnic origin of a culture's

20 "Even the Ottoman scientists in Istanbul a century ago wrote their scientific and literary works in the Arabic language. The works of scientists like Kemâlpaşazâde, Ebusuud, Molla Gürânî, Kâtip Çelebi, and Râgib Pasha attest to this." Sami, *Medeniyyet-i Islamiyye*, 21.

protagonists were vital exactly because the nation could not (yet) be conceived as a producer of culture.

> If those who want to call Islamic culture Arabic knew that most of the scientists whom they considered to be Arabs actually came from Persian and Turkish tribes, not Arabic ones, that Avicenna (Ibn-Sina), one of the greatest Muslim scientists was Persian, that the philosopher al-Fârâbî was Turkish,[21] and that Salâhüddin Eyyûbî, who highlighted this culture, was Kurdish, they would have no doubts and abandoning their claims would agree with us that this civilization was Islamic and that all Islamic nations (millet) shared in this civilization.[22]

According to Sami, at the peak of its conquests from the borders of India, China, and Siberia to the Atlantic coast and from Sumatra ("lapping the ocean waves") to Sudan ("crossing the African desert"), the Islamic world carried the illumination of knowledge and civilization to millions of people. A single civilization to which "the Cordoba philosophers could refer in the works of Avicenna, who came from the distant West, and the scientists of Baghdad at their conferences could refer to the ideas of Averroës (Ibn Rushd), raised in the distant East." And this at a time when the other sides of the world were "tumbled into the darkness of ignorance and fanaticism."

This vision of Pan-Islamic civilizing expansions would become even more intense a few years later in his *Islâmiyetin yayimasi için yapilan* çalismalar, which was published in 1885 by the Mihran printing house under the title *Himmetu'l Humam fi Nesri'l- Islam.* The book was released with permission from the Ministry of Education and was written in Arabic. It is quite interesting that *Himmetu'l Humam* was published in Hania, translated into Turkish by the Cretan Mustafa Nuri Efendi in 1888 only a short time after it was written. This brief essay had two parts. In the first section, Sami described the spread of Islam (13–15), while in the second he provided information about the nations that had adopted it. (The Albanians were only briefly mentioned and probably in passing.)

21 Of course, al-Fârâbî is usually considered to be a Persian from the Khorasan province. See the chapter on al-Fârâbî in King, *One Hundred Philosophers.*

22 Sami, *Medeniyyet-i Islamiyye,* 21–22

In the first part, Sami again compared Islam's fundamentally peaceful proselytizing which civilized the Asian and African races to the violent and aggressive ways of the European Christian colonists. According to Sami, Islam was a faith that civilized savages and herein lay its difference to Christianity. The savage tribes were enriched with "positive values" as soon as they accepted Islam, whereas in the past "they were cannibals, lived in caves and forests, prostituted themselves and pillaged." Conversely, the aim of the Christian colonists was not to civilize the savages but to destroy their culture and plunder their societies as they had done in America and the Pacific Ocean. Finally, he pinpointed two basic causes for the Islamic civilization's decline: the Muslims' fatigue and the destruction of their most important achievements as a result of their countries' conquest by the Christians and the Mongols. Indeed, in his epilogue to *Medeniyyet-i Islamiyye*, he stated that two more works would follow as part of the Cep Kütüphanesi series. In these, he would try to explain the reasons the Islamic nations receded into ignorance and nomadism. The first book would be Ümem-i *Islâmiyyenin Mâzi ve Hal ve Istikbâli* or *Islâm Milletlerinin Geçmisi, Bugünüve Geleceğ*i (The past, the present, and the future of the Islamic peoples) and the second was *Avrupa Medeniyyeti* (European civilization) and dealt with the issue of contemporary European civilization's origins in Islamic civilization

Sami's insinuation was clear: not only should Islam be considered the intermediate link between Ancient Greek and modern Western civilization (the continuity scheme thus acquired a real foundation in relation to Ottoman imperial "nationalism"), but this intermediate link also brushed away the stigma of medieval obscurantism since this was linked solely to Western feudalism. The impressive similarity between the arguments made by Sami and those made by Leont'ev should not allow us to forget that the latter built his evolutionary form in relation to the organic model. By contrast, Sami seems to have remained faithful to the dialectical model. On the other hand, the Islamic Ummah for Sami seems to have had several parallels to Manuel Gedeon's conception of the Orthodox ecumene. However, Gedeon, rather smugly, as was the case with most nineteenth-century Greek scholars, insisted on the Orthodox world's Greek character, while the Albanian scholar promoted a de-Arabification of the Islamic Ummah.

4. The "De-Arabification" of Islam

According to Sami, Islamic civilization was the first global civilization unrelated to the historical dominance of a single race. Earlier civilizations remained identified with a race or a people. This was essentially the case with Ancient Greek civilization which, despite its enormous influence, failed to homogenize neighboring peoples and tribes. This position had direct implications for the issue of managing the Thracians' past, especially in the case of the Illyrians:

> For example, even during the glorious periods of Greek civilization, other tribes, races, which were just 40 to 50 hours away from Athens, the capital of Greek civilization, were wild. Even if the Greeks could take their own civilization as far as Italy and Africa or the shores of Asia Minor and the Black Sea, in these lands, their civilization belonged only to themselves and did not assimilate the other races under their influence. (Sami, *Medeniyyet-i Islamiyye*, 23)

Conversely, Islamic civilization did not belong to a race or people. It was based on the spread of the Islamic faith and, according to Sami, was not linked to the dominance of any race within its boundaries despite Arabic's importance, simply because Islamic civilization was the heir of all great ancient civilizations: Chaldaean, Assyrian, Phoenician, Mede, Egyptian, and, of course, Greek.[23] The Arab tribes, as either merchants or warriors, naturally had a decisive role in spreading Islam until it gained autonomy as part of this process. "This civilization shone and spread like a fire that suddenly erupts. Islam's spread trigged the expansion and evolution of Islamic civilization and the expansion and evolution of Islamic civilization triggered the spread of Islam." Sami's narrative shifted the

23 It is not coincidental that Sami wrote his second most significant work on Pan-Islamism, *Islâmiyetin yayilmasi için yapilan* çalismalar, in Arabic, which, in his view, was the common scientific language in the Muslim world. It is also likely he would take a positive stance on the use of Arabic as a *lingua franca*, although he realized this was not feasible. Consequently, his solution was to preserve the "national" tongues—Arabic, Persian, Urdu, Turkish, Kurdish, and so on—but with the use of a single script, Arabic. Writing his book in Arabic constituted precisely such a gesture. See Sami, *Medeniyyet-i Islamiyye*, 42–43.

subject from the Arabs to the Muslims. Furthermore, Islamic civilization not only transcended its Arab origins but contributed to the rise of a New Europe precisely because it provided the intellectual weapons—that is, the translations of Ancient Greek works— to manage the barbarian flood tides from the north:

> After the birth of Islam, civilization belonged to the Muslims for a period of eight or nine centuries. There was no other civilized people or race on earth other than Islam. The Muslims saved Asia and Europe from the destruction of the Roman wars that continued unabated; they were the ones who revived a new culture and saved Europe from the savagery and inhumanity of the barbarian tribes descending from the north and those who offered a civilizing example to the nations of this continent. In the beginning, the Europeans did not know anything about Greek civilization. They learned the names of the Greek philosophers while training at Andalusia's madrasahs; they learned of them from the Arabic translations because the original texts had been lost. (Sami, *Medeniyyet-i Islamiyye*, 29)

The difference between Islam's dissemination and that, for example, of Western civilization was that the first was peaceful. Contrary to the West's image of a war-mongering Islam that conquers parts of the Middle East and Northern Africa through fire and iron, Sami claimed that Islam's expansion—either by the Ummah Caliphs toward the West or the Abbasid Caliphs toward the East—was the result of its civilizing dynamic, and this was why it was based chiefly on the promotion of philosophy, the sciences, and invention. Consequently, Islamic civilization's emergence and its quick expansion and evolution was due primarily to the fact that it had internalized the heritage of all the region's earlier civilizations, especially in terms of peaceful coexistence based on the Islamic faith as promoted by the Caliphates.

During the same period the Young Ottomans were attempting to prove Islam's compatibility with the basic principles of the state's transformation in the West (liberty, equality, fraternity), Sami was trying to establish Islam's compatibility with science, and indeed with the Western science that was at the core of Western civilization. Sami, in any case, endorsed what the Prophet had expressed: "Seek science, from the cradle to the grave" and "seek science even if it is found in China."[24]

However, for Sami it was not enough to prove that the Islamic civilization was an authentic heir of the ancient world but also to de-Arabize Islam, highlighting its supranational character:

> While the ruins of the Greeks and others were useful as a base for the structure of Islamic civilization, the character and foundations of this new building are in the wisdom and justice of Islam. The Muslims did not just take the ethics and laws of the Greeks, receiving the knowledge, capability, and their intellectual and scientific achievements. They utilized Greek and other civilizations, but did not imitate them; they took their works and after study and evaluation and their rendering in Islamic knowledge, Islamic civilization arrived whole in another form and manner at a higher level than Greek civilization, dissimilar to it because it was more perfect than the Greek. We cannot say that Islamic civilization was a fruit of the Arab people, their intellect and effort, because then all Arabs would have had to have been civilized before Islam and the other Islamic countries would not have been civilized alongside the Arabs. We can only say that Islamic civilization was the result and fruit of Islam since this civilization emerged with Islam's emergence and spread with Islam's spread. Islamic civilization reached where Islam reached. This civilization was the result of Islam because most rules and laws are rooted in the Qur'an (Koran) and the prophet's words. (27)

5. The Management of Time and Space in Islam

To prove how Islam promoted the sciences, Sami would take his reader on a tour of Islamic civilization's great achievements in astronomy, mathematics, the natural sciences, philosophy, justice, and literature. Aside from his obsession with highlighting achievements in astronomy, he also showed a special interest in geography and history. Advances in geography, which he saw as evolving over three periods, were but an expression of a united and geographic continuity that Islam's expansion imposed over

24 "Ilmi, besikten mezara kadar arayin!" and "Ilmi, ta Cin'de bile olsa, arayin." Ibid., 27–28.

a large area of the world, internal differences notwithstanding.[25] Historians' descriptions of events and notable Islamic kingdoms, however, were merely the consequence of a scientific rationalism imposed, in a strange way, by the faith. Thus, the development of geography and history as sciences were nothing but the expression of Islam's spatial and chronological mold, a mold that Islam, as a "nation" or *ümmet* (nation, faith), in reality established in its own "domain."

With regard to geography especially, it was evident that Sami believed Islam's expansion over a wide area led to an internal homogenization:

> Since Muslims held the larger part of then-known world, they did not face any difficulty in developing geography according to their own knowledge, observations, and new discoveries. They used the great commercial routes that extended from China's borders to the Atlantic coast and crossed through Islamic countries. . . . The main routes extended in four directions. The first as far as Balkh, Kabul, and Kasmir through Turkestan, starting from Tanta and Andalusia in Europe, crossing through France, Germany and Islamic countries. The second again starting from Andalusia's north and reaching the Maghreb, crossing the Ceuta strait, through Algeria, Tunisia, Tripoli, Benghazi, and the northern part of Africa and through Egypt and Damascus and the Euphrates Valley to Baghdad, Basra, and a section of it reached as far as China and India, passing through Persia and Kirman and Balochistan. The third extended from the Mediterranean coast and islands as far as the Syrian coast by sea and from there overland to Basra and then again by sea from the Indian coast and Indian Ocean. The fourth set off from the Mediterranean, passing through Gibraltar and reaching the Oman Sea through the Red Sea, where it

25 According to Sami, the first period was marked by the publication of *Resmül–Ard*, [Earth's description], a work based on the translation of Ptolemy's *Geography* while it was reedited over subsequent centuries by many later geographers. Probably Sami had mentioned as such regarding *Kitāb Ṣūrat al-Arḍ* [Book of the description of the earth] written by Al-Khwārizmī' in 833. The second period was marked by Al Beyrûnî's work and the third by the work of the great geographer İbn Zerkâle, who lived in Andalusia and discovered that the Mediterranean was situated at 42 degrees longitude, as well as by the work of Ebû'l -Hassan Ali, who was raised in Morocco. The works of Al Beyrûnî and İbn Zerkâle provided Europeans with quite a bit of useful information about the Islamic East, while the work of Ebû'l -Hassan Ali provided considerable information about the Islamic West. Ibid., 69–74.

> met with the third route in the Indian Ocean. Thus, Muslim traders and travelers who never strayed from these routes secured the continuity of their commercial and scientific links, taking Islamic civilization to faraway lands and helping with the development of (science) of geography. (Sami, *Medeniyyet-i Islamiyye*, 69–70)

Describing achievements in the discipline of geography, with several references to the West's debt to Muslims for this field's advancement, Sami was also describing Islam's unification of space.[26] He also saw history's development as equally typical of the Muslims' religion: "The Muslims showed more courage than any other nation (*ummet*) in the field of history."[27]

Although the topics studied by the most notable Muslim historians covered a broad spectrum from the history of the Islamic peoples and the Byzantine Empire (Ebû'l-Fidâ), Mongol history and Genghis Khan's conquests (Ebû'l-Ferec), and the history of Arabs and Berbers (Burhânüddîn) to the philosophy of history (Ibn Haldûn's famed three-volume *Muqaddimah*), Fatimid and Mamluk Egypt (Makrîzî, Eyyûbî), and Andalusia (Ibnü'l-Kûtiye, Ahmed ibn Muhammed Ibn-Hatîb), Sami arranged references to areas of the Islamic world as though they were part of the same common denominator.[28]

In reality, these disparate histories reconstructed the Muslims' dispersion within a single chronological unit. History as a rational management of the past could only be a complementary process to the process of homogenization conducted by Islam throughout its dominions. Of course, the

26 "Additionally, Muslim scientists even created nautical maps and these remained an Islamic invention, something the Greeks never achieved. A nautical map in Arab script created by a Muslim was quite useful to the famed Portuguese explorer Vasco da Gama, who discovered many of the Atlantic Ocean's islands in 1497, who took the map with him on his boat" (75). As noted earlier, Sami considered *Resmü'l–Ard*, which renewed cartography, as the seminal Islamic geographic work as it was based on the translation of Ptolemy. In Sami's view, the Christian cartographers before believed the earth was square or round, they considered that its center was Jerusalem. By contrast, Muslim cartographers tried to correct the mistakes and omissions of Ptolemaic geography from the very moment it was translated. This "correcting" spanned three centuries, and Sami implied that all the great discoveries made in the fifteenth and sixteenth centuries were the result of these corrections.

27 In his *Kesfü'z-Zünûn fi Esâmîi'l-Kütüb ve'l-Fünûn*, Kâtip Çelebi referred to the existence of some 1,300 historians in the Islamic world. See Sami, *Medeniyyet-i Islamiyye*, 96.

28 Sami, *Medeniyyet-i Islamiyye*, 96–103.

fact that Sami skirted the problem of conflicts within the Islamic world allowed him to view Islamic civilization as a single unit. This intention was served by the simple listing of various historians' work: a more gradual analysis of the history of Timur's conquests, the collapse of the Fatimid Caliphate, and the expansion of the Ottoman Empire would logically have necessitated greater attention to the contradictions within the Islamic world, contradictions that remained unresolved in the nineteenth century.

Sami was compelled to silence these contradictions in order to advance his efforts to establish the compatibility of Islamic civilization with scientific and technological advancement.[29] He did not make this direct link in *Medeniyyet-i Islamiyye*, but he would clearly do this later, in his *Islamiyetin Yayilmas Için Yapian Calismalar* in 1885. Here, in his discussion of the issue of communication within the Islamic world, he realized that faith on its own (given that a religion's various denominations did not always coexist peacefully) was as inadequate. So too, was the use of a common "sacred" language (for Sami, this meant the preservation of the common Arabic script). The only solution for attaining "internal communication" was political unity ensured by preserving the Caliphate and obviously the Ottoman Sultan's dominant position within it.

In the same way Byzantium's invocation constituted a "continuity," although it served the construction of linear national narratives, trying to avoid a rupture with the imperial past by citing the "modern" character of medieval Caliphates also worked as a factor of "continuity" that tried to preserve and not dissolve the empire. Thus, reference to "continuity" had a dual and contradictory role: it was not always certain that "continuity" in historiographical discourses produced within Empire contributed to the construction of a form of linear national development. The reference to the notional Middle Ages, Christian or Islamic, was made precisely to

29 Sami had no doubt that the discovery of paper, gunpowder, and the compass, which historians attribute to the Chinese, were Islamic discoveries. He claimed that by the end of the first century after Hijra (7th century AD), paper was being made from silk in Samarkand and Bukhara. Writers in Constantinople meanwhile referred to paper being made in Damascus from flax in the early eighth century. Paper was first made from cotton and fabric scraps in Andalusia, and the technique was then transferred to France, Italy, England, and Germany. Gunpowder was also supposedly being used by Muslims as early as the first century of Hijra in the siege of Mecca and the wars in Egypt, Tunisia, Granada, and elsewhere. The compass was also used to find Mecca's direction. Sami, *Medeniyyet-i Islamiyye*, 108.

obstruct the development of "national variations" that resorted to secessionist solutions (and which were always prepared to develop forms of origin in order to establish their rights to the contested space). This is the reason why in Sami Frashëri's case too, a comparison of his early and later works remains very important for evaluating this phenomenon.

6. From the Islamic Ummah to the Albanian Nation: The Return of the Pelasgians

During Sami Frashëri's time in Constantinople, he aligned himself ideologically with the basic elements of the Hamidian regime's Pan-Islamic policy while politically supporting the main aims of the Albanian nationalist movement. Nonetheless it seems that through the mid-1890s, the prospect of an Albanian national affirmation did not necessarily suggest a break from the empire. One could claim that Sami's stance could be linked to the corresponding ideological and political positions of Gedeon and Krâstevich; that is, the imperial dimension of their historiographical approach was directly connected to the prospect of a strategic alliance of the ethnic element they represented with Ottoman power.

However, even as late as 1899, *Shqipëria ç'ka qenë, ç'është e ç'do të bëhetë?* was published in Bucharest anonymously.[30] The reasons are obvious: such an open declaration of the death of the Pan-Islamic dream could have placed the Albanian scholar in Constantinople in even greater jeopardy.

The continuity scheme is inherent in *Shqipëria*'s title: the past, present, and future of the Albanian people were the object of Sami's attention.[31] Here it is the first part, Sami's study of Albania's past, that will be examined. This is the section in which he first established an origin

30 References are to the Greek translation by Athanasios Sinas published in Sofia in 1907. I thank Thomas Kolios for reading this against the original edition reprinted by Mesonjetoria (Tirana, 1999).

31 For a brief overview of the work, see Clayer's *Nationalisme albanais*, 449ff. Clayer dealt with it through the perspective of the construction of the Albanian as European identity among non-Turkish Muslims in the Balkans. See also Bilmez, who focuses on Sami's textual loans from European historiography on Illyrians and Pelasgians as well as on the similarities of the 1899 text with the entries Sami wrote in his *Kamus-ul Alam*: Bilmez, "Sami Frashëri or Şemseddin Sami?" 9–26. Certainly, Sami followed the line of Pashko Vasa (see below) on the topic of the Pelasgian origins of the Albanian nation, and this should be explained: why did he do it in spite of the fact that the Pelasgian theory had already been dismissed in the late nineteenth century?

scheme. Sami would not be content with expressing the Albanians' link to the Illyrians, which was common ground in such discussions during the nineteenth century. On the contrary, he sought to "occupy" a vacuum left by Greek historiography: the Albanians' relationship of origin with the Pelasgians.

Sami strove to win the battle of "antiquity" from the outset:

> The land inhabited by Albanians is called Albania.[32] The Albanians are the oldest of the European nations. It seems that they arrived from Central Asia to Europe before everyone else, bringing with them the knowledge of building a home, sowing, and harvesting as those people then inhabiting Europe were savages and lived in caves and forests eating wild berries and hunting for meat. (Sami, *Shqipëria*, 1)

Just as Sami had previously reserved for Islam the role of civilizing vast regions of the world, he now verified the Albanian nation's importance in the same way, reserving for it the role of Europe's civilizing force. But such a huge role required the identification of the Albanians with Southeastern Europe's entire Indo-European underpinnings. The Pelasgians solved this problem.

In any case, Sami was not the only representative of the Albanian national renaissance in the nineteenth century who staunchly supported this position. Perhaps the most typical case of connection of ancient

32 Frashëri's etymological summary of the "Albanian" ethnonyms is especially interesting: "This is why our ancestors were called *Arbënë*, which we, Tosks, as was our habit, reverted to *Arbërë*, as we use it today. In other words, this most ancient nation since called *Arbënë* or *Arban* were people working the land, sowing and harvesting. [Here, the translator inserts the following note: The Albanian word *are*, which is related to the Greek *aroura*, means *agro* (field) and thus *Arbënë* means "cultivating the fields."] The Romans converted this word to *Alban*, and they called the country *Albania*, as the Europeans have been called it to the present day. The later Greeks called us *Arvanites*, transforming the *l* to *r*, and by this the word of the Greeks the Turks formed the word *Arnaut*, which has been used by them till today to describe us. However we, with the word Arbërë, mention only to one tribe of our nation, which we also call *Lap*; the whole nation has been called *Shqipëtar* and our homeland *Shqipëria*, words formed by the word *shqipe* which means the eagle, the sacred bird of Zeus, who was worshiped by our ancestors, and whose shape had been used in our flags. But this word seems not to be not so ancient or generall speaking, the Albanians who live in Italy, Greece, and other places ignore it and they call themselves *Arbërë*." Sami, *Shqipëria*, 3–4. The review of the ethnonyms, in fact, includes all the possible perceptions of the Albanian nation: Roman, Greek, Ottoman, and finally different perceptions of national self-determination.

Pelasgians with modern Albanians can be found in Pashko Vasa's work, "La vérité sur l'Albanie et les Albanais," published in 1879.[33] However, the crucial difference with Sami's work was that Vasa was still writing at a time when the theory of Pelasgic origin of the Albanians had been scientifically legitimized by the work of a great German linguist, August Schleicher.[34] On the contrary, by the end of the nineteenth century, the Pelasgian theory had faced many attacks, mainly through the scholarship of the Austrian linguist Gustav Meyer who supported the identification of the modern Albanian language with an Illyrian dialectic branch.[35] So the question is, why did Sami insist on claiming the Pelasgians? A question similar to what occupied Bulgarian historiography forty years ago: as we have seen, although the problem of Slavic descent of the Bulgarians had already been resolved through Venelin's conflict with Šafárik, Gavril Krâstevich restored the question of a "Volgic theory" within a framework of new political balances with the Ottoman factor, provoking Drinov's response.

Likewise, although the theory of the Albanians' Illyrian origin had been firmly established, Sami, realizing that the greatest threat to the latter was the contentions of the Greek nationalism on a common origins background between Greeks and Albanians, would attempt to renew Schleicher's arguments. But Sami did not just try to Albanianize the Pelasgians because they had been subject to expropriation by Greek nationalists, but quite the opposite: because, as we shall see, the main organizer of Greek national historiography, Konstantinos Paparrigopoulos, had rejected them.

Sami's Pelasgians had at one time flooded all of Eastern and Southeastern Europe: the entire Balkan peninsula including Hungary and from the Greek mainland to the Adriatic and to Asia Minor were areas inhabited by

---

33 See, for example, the solution which has been given by Pashko Vasa, in Vasa Pashko, *La vérité*, 7–10. Vasa identified Epirotes and Macedonians with the Pelasgians like Sami (as supposed descendants of the son of Pelasgus I, Phaedon), using a scheme of a supposed expulsion of the Pelasgians by Greeks from the coastline to the hinterland. See also the comments of Bayraktar "Mythifying the Albanians," especially, fn 76.

34 Schleicher, *Compendium*.

35 See mainly among others, Meyer, "Die stellung." See also Skendi, *Albanian National Awakening*, 114–15.

the Pelasgians, Sami's "ancient Albanians."[36] According to him, some Pelasgians crossed the Adriatic to reach Italy, and the Etruscans, Latins, and other peoples inhabiting Italian areas were also descended from them. In reality, this massive Pelasgian diaspora accorded to the Albanians the position of originator and, thus, privileged their role in relation to other peoples, especially those whom the Albanians considered their favored allies.

But for Sami, it was not enough for the Pelasgians to be considered the underlying population of the Balkan and Italian peninsulas. This did not secure their inclusion in the great family of Indo-Europeans and the possibility of being excluded from this group had potential consequences for the European academies' perception of Albanian identity. Thus, their point of origin had to be identified; as they also came from the East (as well as the Caucasus, according to Paschides), their links to the other Indo-Europeans could be verified, especially their close relationship with the Latins of Western Europe:

> But in the places claimed by Greeks,[37] they were of the same race as the Pelasgians, like the Slavs, Germans, Celts, Gauls, and other ethnicities arriving from Asia and which were all called Arians and which comprised a large family that included the Persians, Indians, and other ethnicities of Asia. But those closest to us are the Latins, and this is because our language resembles Latin very closely, and this was the language from which Italian, French, and other languages sprung. (Sami, *Shqipëria*, 5–6)

Having insisted on the Albanians' Pelasgian origin and having secured their place in earliest antiquity (just as Rakovski had done with the Indo-European Thracians), Sami proceeded to broaden the intermediate link, that with the Illyrians.

> The Pelasgians, in the countries they inhabited, were divided into many races and genuses according to their land of residence and were divided into many tribes and clans of which the largest and most widely-known

36 Sami's etymologically cites "Pelasgian" as deriving from the Albanian *plak* (elder) and *pleq* (elders).

37 "Later, there was a small ethnos called Hellenes or Graikoi that settled in Greece, the islands of the Aegean Sea, and the coasts, forcing the Pelasgians out of these places or living alongside them."

> were the Illyrians (*te-lirete* or *te-Dliretë*, "the free"), the Macedonians, the Thracians (*te-trashetë*, "the coarse"), the Phrygians, and others. The Illyrians inhabited Albanian and land to its north, which is today called Bosnia, Herzegovina, Montenegro, Croatia, Dalmatia, and so on to the Adriatic inlet and beyond Sava; the Macedonians and Thracians inhabited Macedonia and Thrace; the Phrygians lived in Asia from the coast to the Halys River, which today is called Këzëll-Irmak (Kızılırmak). It is said that the Illyrians were related to the Macedonians, the Thracians, and the Phrygians. All were one nation and knew each other's language. (Sami, *Shqipëria*, 6–7)

The Illyrians were unique among the Pelasgian tribes, according to Sami, because they managed to survive the Roman conquest and also the Slavic invasion. The Macedonians and the kingdoms that emerged from Alexander the Great's conquests were subjugated by the Romans. The Thracians and Phrygians "were lost fighting or intermixing with races that mingled with them." When the Bulgarians, "a Tartar nation," invaded the Balkans in the sixth century, and the Serbs and Croats, "Scythian nations," occupied the largest part of the Balkan peninsula, they displaced the Pelasgians or bred into them. Macedonians, Phrygians, and Thracians were lost in history. The Illyrians were the only Pelasgian tribe that managed to survive.

Sami believed that ancient Illyria did not cover all of Albania because it extended south of the Vijosa River. To the north, it extended as far as the Sava River and the northern Adriatic shore, encircling Bosnia and other lands. If there were many reasons for Albanian nationalism not to aim its irredentist ambitions north, a solution had to be found for territories further south, "from the Aoos river to the Ambracian gulf, that is the south of what is today Tosks' land and is called Epirus (*Ipere, Hipere, a Sipere*: upper), which is an Albanian word." The Illyrians were, thus, reexamined alongside the "Epirotes" who, in a way, were considered the other "Pelasgian branch" (or rather, Illyrian variant) that contributed to the creation of the Albanian nation even though Greek influences upon it were recognized.[38]

38 The Illyrian dialect is little known today and very few names of people, places, or tribes have survived. Its relationship to Albanian is not disputed by the majority of Albanian scholars, although most believe that the Illyrians never spoke the language spoken by the Albanians.

The Illyrians and Epirotes may have been defeated by the Romans, but they were not subjugated to the Roman yolk. The Illyrians' and the Epirotes' leadership may have been seized by representatives of the Roman authorities, yet the Albanians retained their autonomy. The same occurred under the Byzantine Empire when Rome's control was supplanted by Constantinople's. In this same period, the Albanians converted en masse to Christianity although the degree of their independence from the central authority increased.

7. The Problem of Discontinuity in Albanian History

Nonetheless, the huge problem for Albanian history was a fundamental discontinuity which was not easily interpreted. From the Illyrians' disappearance from the stage of History (roughly around the time of their defeat in the wars with Alexander's Macedonians) until the Albanians' appearance, there was a huge large gap reflected in linguistic and historical sources.[39]

Sami would attempt to resolve this. With the arrival of the Byzantine Middle Ages, the flood of Slavs in the Balkans during the sixth and seventh centuries changed the landscape. The Serbs occupied tracts in northern areas of Illyria, that is, Bosnia, Herzegovina, Dalmatia, Montenegro, and present-day Serbia, while the Bulgarians, intermingling with the Slavs, dominated in Macedonia. Macedonia's Albanians withdrew to the northern and western heights where they also mixed with the numerous Slavs; as a result, their language was lost as over time they adopted Serbian. But instead of accepting the discontinuity of the Albanian nation in medieval times, the gap between the Illyrians' disappearance and the Albanians' emergence in the eleventh and twentieth centuries, Sami argued for the opposite. He claimed continuity and indeed continuity in bloodlines.

> With regards to this, we can say that the Bosnians, Herzegovinians, Dalmatians, and Montenegrins are more Albanian rather than Slav;

39 For the importance of the origin relationship of Albanians and Illyrians and the arguments of contemporary Albanian nationalism, see Hoxhaj, "Mythen und Erinnerungen."

> they have lots of Albanian blood in their veins; their height, features, traditions, songs, and dances are closer to those of the Albanians than the other Slavs, who do not have the same height or features. But because today they speak Serbian, they are called Slavs and not Albanians because language is the first distinguishing factor of nations (Sami, *Shqipëria*, 11–12)

In contrast to Paparrigopoulos, who managed Hellenism's two fundamental discontinuities with "cultural" tools—language (Rome) and faith (Ottoman)—and, as shall be seen, also in contrast to the Romanian case—where the Romanian language's Slavicization nonetheless had been counteracted by the Romanian people's incorporation into a "Latin" identity—Sami resorted to a completely racial solution. Continuity was verifiable at the racial level of facial features. So, adopting the structure of the Albanian nation's continual linear development and continuity over time led him to abandon the "cultural" solution to bridge the gap, as he had done in 1879 with *Islamic Civilization*.

Sami, of course, did not accept a gap between Illyrians and Albanians, yet he recognized that as a consequence of this Slavic flood, the Albanians' geographical space became limited: half of Illyria and half of Macedonia were detached from Albania and became areas of Slavic expansion, while Albanian remained a small region occupying half of Southern Illyria, half of the Northern and Western parts of Macedonia, and all of Epirus.

> During the Roman and Byzantine eras, the following names were lost and forgotten: Illyria, Macedonia, and Epirus, and the remaining Shqipëria, as we said, started being called Albania by most, from the Albanian word Arbëni. Since then, Albania has not changed boundaries and today is the same, except for a few areas ceded to Serbia and Montenegro under the Berlin Treaty, like Vranja Leskovaçi, Ulqini, and so on. For the most part of the above areas, the Albanians committed a sin by leaving and abandoning their homeland to the Slavs. (Sami, *Shqipëria*, 12)

It is obvious that Sami was trying to settle the boundaries of Albanian irredentism even before the establishment of an Albanian state. The "racial" and "irredentist" or territorial potential combined in an explosive but effect mix. But the (direct) proof of continuity that contributes to the citing of racial resilience could not answer the problem of the lack of sources. This is why Sami was forced to also discuss the issue of language.

In his view, the Albanians did not simply speak one of the most ancient tongues but also one that unlike related languages—Greek, Latin, Sanskrit, the languages of ancient India and Persia, Celtic, Teutonic, and so on—remained alive and was spoken even today in the same way as in the Pelasgians' day:

> Undoubtedly, the Pelasgians are the most ancient of the Arian nations. We have many signs and much proof that those Pelasgians in the myths of distant antiquity spoke the language that we speak today. The names of the gods the Pelasgians worshipped, which Greek and Roman mythology has borrowed, and many other words preserved by history, and place names, etc., appear to be purely Albanian words and demonstrate that the Pelasgians who spoke so many thousands of years ago spoke the same language as us today, almost unchanged with such few transformations that we can say that it if the Pelasgians were around today then we could communicate with them just as the Tosks communicate today with the Ghegs, the *Çams*, and the Gorars. (Sami, *Shqipëria*, 21)

For Sami's theoretical approach, language and national identity were intertwined. For him, every ethnicity survived through language. Over time, those who forgot their language or neglected it for another became the people of the nation whose language they now spoke. This had not occurred with the Albanians as it had with other Pelasgian tribes, and this was offered as proof of their unbreakable continuity from the Pelasgians:

> The Macedonians, Thracians, Phrygians, and upper Illyrians, and so many other peoples who were Pelasgians like us do not exist today because they lost or forgot their language, exchanging it for another. But the Albanians of the lands today called Albania safeguarded their language and the ancient language of the Pelasgians of mythology is spoken today in these lands. (Sami, *Shqipëria*, 22)

But even so, Sami wondered why the Philip II's and Alexander's Macedonians or Pyrrhus's Epirotes did not record their language and let themselves come under the influence of Greek culture. Naturally, this argument actually suggested the other pillar of Sami's endeavor (aside from the disengagement from the Pan-Slavic ideal): that Pelasgian antiquity was only claimed to dispute Greece's cultural penetration of the Balkans. In other words, Pelasgian antiquity was set up as a counter to Ancient Greece. According to Sami, the Greeks claimed Pyrrhus and Alexander and named them Greeks because even though they conquered the world in just a short period of time "they did not bring anything as a gift for Albania." In all the lands they conquered, the Macedonians spread the Greek language and culture and not their own, that is, Albanian. The Ptolemies, who were secretly Albanians from Çameria, and all the Macedonians abandoned their language, Albanian, and instead used Greek, the language of Demosthenes, detractor of the Macedonians. But since they had not recorded their language, they had been forced to employ and compose in the Greek, Latin, Slavic, Turkish, or Arabic languages and this constituted a selfless assimilation into the history of the other nations:

> ...the greatest of the Ancient Greek philosophers, Aristotle, was a Macedonian, thus an Albanian and not a Greek. Indeed, in Stageira, where he was born, there were Greeks but Aristotle's features, as we can see from the statue of him, and his forced Greek language, which is not completely correct, as well as his friendship with Philip, the Greeks' foe, and much more suggest that this great philosopher was not born in Stageira to Greek sojourners but to a local Stageiran who was Macedonian, that is pure Albanian. (Sami, *Shqipëria*, 28–29)

This line of Albanian sons claimed by rival nationalisms, primarily Greek nationalism, is long. It started with Philip II and Aristotle and extended to the Greek revolutionary war heroes Markos Botsaris, Kitsos Tzavellas, and Andreas Miaoulis. It also included Sinan Pasha, the Köprülü family of great viziers, Mehmet Ali of Egypt, and the poet Yahya bey from the Ottomans. As a consequence of their selflessness when serving one or another, the Albanians neglected their language and with it their national consciousness.

Sami, of course, did not seem to realize the enormity of the problem posed by the lack of written sources and added another: his certainty about the language spoken by the Pelasgian-Albanians. But what is more important than the problem was its solution: the answer to the reason why the Pelasgian-Albanians did not disappear or assimilate was that they remained isolated and self-governed. Neither the Slavic raids nor the imperial multicultural environment touched them. Once again, in order to establish Pelasgian-Albanian continuity at the linguistic level, Sami approached the question at the level of racial purity. The real continuity was at the racial level, and only then at the linguistic level, since the language one chose to speak was a matter of conscious choice.

> The response to these questions is very easy: the Albanians did not preserve their language or ethnicity through literature or education or culture but only with freedom, having remained isolated and independent and not mingling with other ethnicities and not welcoming foreigners into their land. Standing far from the world, from education, and from culture, their way of living wild in the mountains saved the Albanian language and ethnicity. (Sami, *Shqipëria*, 23)

Thus, in Frashëri, continuity did not need either faith (as in the case of Pan-Islamism) or language: both, despite the latter's favorable treatment in relation to ethnic identity, belonged to an indivisible linear racial evolution, although the same people appeared with different faces at various points in history.

The Albanians were able to safeguard their national and linguistic peculiarity in the face of so many misfortunes. Despite their shifts in religious faith as a result of the changing times, on the threshold of the twentieth century, the Albanians constituted the same entity as they had thousands of years earlier: "the Albanians were the Pelasgians of mythology, the Illyrians and Macedonians of antiquity, the Epirotes of Skënderbeu's time. An ancient nation, which remained the same today as from the beginning."[40]

40 Sami, *Shqipëria*, 37.

There was no "medieval antiquity" in the Albanians' case as in Krâstevich, nor a "cultural" antiquity as with the Greeks, but a "mythical antiquity" in which the mythological dimension of the origins provided an enormous boost to the Albanian people's historical course that allowed it to survive in different guises.

The Ottomans' and Albanians' common stance on the issue of preserving the empire was emerged against the backdrop of a strategic collation of their interests. This ended with the Tanzimat era and the stalemates of Pan-Islamism. The "realistic" line of national completion that Sami chose was obviously a far cry from the "idealism" of Pan-Islamic unity that he had attempted two decades earlier.

8. Konstantinos Paparrigopoulos and the Pelasgians

Sami's solution to the Albanian nation's origin model was broadly similar to that used by Rakovski in the Bulgarian case. In both instances, the Pelasgian theory worked as a hyper-hermeneutic principle for identifying the nation with the body of history from the moment that the nation discovered its essence in its furthest origins. And in both cases, this origin theory was marginalized by more refined versions of assembling the origins: the Pelasgians were progressively sidelined by the Illyrians on one hand, and by the Slavs on the other. Also, in both cases, the model of origins was compiled on the basis of an important political attempt at rejection. In Sami's case, citing the Pelasgians/Illyrians aimed at creating distance from the Ottoman Empire; in Rakovski's case, citing the Arian/Bulgarians aimed at creating distance from the Russian Empire. In some ways, the racial factor, and resorting to a scheme based on origins, acted as another fundamental rejection of the imperial discourses whose convergence Leont'ev's had pinpointed in the 1860s.

But there was another important similarity: both theories turned against Greek nationalism and aimed at legitimizing an antiquity that was equal to that of Ancient Greece.

The use of Pelasgians in the Greek historiographical discourses could serve two different national narrations: on one hand, the convergence of the Greeks and Albanians based on a common Pelasgian past. This was, for example, the case of the works of Thymi Mitko, who in 1859 published an article in *Pandora* magazine in which he attempted to prove the relationship of Albanian and Greek based on their common Pelasgian vocabulary or the editor of the bilingual *Pelasgus* journal Anastas Byku who supported the idea of the Greek origins of the modern Albanians[41]. On the other hand, and especially after the years of Eastern Crisis, many Albanians used the Pelasgian motif to prove their national differentiation from the Greeks. But the new in Sami's elaboration was not only the transitional character of his thought from Pan-Islamic ideas to nationalized visions but also the clear distinction of Pelasgians (as ancestors of a wider category of tribes) from the Illyrians (the most important of their descendants), and at the same time of the "Pelasgianization" of the Macedonians, a thesis very useful, as we will see, against Paparrigopoulos's perception of the Greek continuity.

The canon of Greek national historiography, as embodied in Paparrigopoulos' work, permitted such an endeavor. If we assume that Albanian or Bulgarian nationalism's claim to the Pelasgians was the result of a "generous" stance by the Greek national historiographical canon, the question of the differences in the definition of the cultural in an imperial context versus a national context still had to be faced.

Dedicated to a methodology defined by using sources objectively, Paparrigopoulos refuted any possible link between the pre-Hellenic "Pelasgians" and the Greek tribes as they emerged at the start of the second millennium B.C. Although he describes as "Pelasgian" the branch of the Indo-European family comprising the Greek tribes "linguistically" related to the tribes of Middle and Southern Italy, when called to manage the problem of the pre-Hellenic populations, he was particularly cautious in his discussion of the Pelasgians, Leleges, Curetes, and a number of other tribes named in later historical sources. Referring again to George Grote's views, Paparrigopoulos questioned the supposed relationship between Pelasgians and Greeks, citing a lack of sources proving a continual Pelasgian presence in Greek lands. In Paparrigopoulos's view, seeking out such a relationship would only make sense if it could resolve some of the problems of the emergence of Ancient Greek civilization: "Whoever wishes to call the period preceding the Greeks as Pelasgian is free to do so.

41 Clayer, *Nationalisme albanais*, 198.

That name, however, does not imply a real meaning and above all doesn't by itself clarify the important issue of how and when the Greeks received the origins of their first civilization."[42]

Consequently, the Pelasgians are not especially useful for Paparrigopoulos's scheme precisely because he could not, under any circumstances, accept their contribution to the formation of Ancient Greek civilization. Were the Pelasgians not simply irrelevant but perhaps potentially dangerous? Allowing the possibility that pre-Hellenic races like the Pelasgians helped shape Ancient Greek civilization—especially when there were no sources confirming this—would blunt arguments for disputing the influence of peoples from the East, like the Phoenicians and the Egyptians. In other words, any concessions to a model of autochthony with regard to the relations between Pelasgians and Greeks could boomerang since they promoted the East's defining effect on the shaping of Ancient Greece. Black Athena lay in wait, and it was not at all certain whether the Pelasgians could be detached from the barbarians of the Ancient World.[43]

This is the reason for Paparrigopoulos' frequent references to Grote's work, both in relation to the orgiastic nature of the Eleusinian mysteries and also in the case of the underlying Pelasgian population, and finally in the careful refuting of arguments that might have supported Ancient Greek civilization's Egyptian origins. Grote's dispassionate and objective approach provided a consistent rejection of the East. It was, therefore, impossible, in Grote's view "to accept that the Greek language, the most noble of human languages in its internal symmetries and harmonies resulted from the contribution of two external barbarian languages, the Phoenician and the Egyptian, and two or more native barbarian tongues, the Pelasgian, Leleges, and other such."[44]

When Paparrigopoulos adopted the cultural criterion as the baseline for determining the succession process of three (or five) Hellenisms, he clearly did so in an Orientalist framework. Rejecting pre-Hellenic and Eastern influences on Ancient Greek civilization worked in the same way, just as Iconoclasm had during the medieval period by distancing Byzantium from the East.

---

42 Paparrigopoulos, *Istoria tou Ellinikou Ethnous*, vol. I, 61.

43 For a short biography, see Vaio, "George Grote."

44 Paparrigopoulos, *Istoria tou Ellinikou Ethnous*, vol. I, 63.

Antiquity and the Middle Ages were not defined according to the cultural criterion as a result of a conscious rejection of racial or ethnic nationalism but rather because the historiographical narrative had to be enshrined in the prevalent manner by which the West understood the East, even if such an approach created the prerequisites for a counteroffensive by the Illyrians and Thracians.[45]

In our opinion, the use of the cultural criterion was linked to the influence of the imperial scheme, while its seeking to reaffirm the racial origin was usually linked to a "national" perception of the past. Rakovski, Drinov and later Sami were typical examples of the second model; Gedeon, Leont'ev, and Paparrigopoulos were typical of the first. However, in Paparrigopoulos's case, the cultural criterion was not defined within the framework of a pre-modern empire but according to an Orientalist conception of his contemporary Western colonial empires.

It is interesting that Krâstevich's "imperial" narrative allowed him to avoid self-definition through the "barbarian space" he was given by Paparrigopoulos (via Grote). Conversely, both Frashëri and Rakovski did not choose the Illyrians (Pelasgians) and the Thracians solely to reaffirm their dominance over space. Any perception of Illyrian or Thracian antiquity would have to be built as a rival to Ancient Greece. We are, of course, referring to a period when Greek nationalism had also adopted racial theories to support its claims on Macedonia and Thrace. The Pelasgians and Thracians were now in contention and would not be abandoned easily to the imaginary management of rival nationalisms.[46]

45 Paparrigopoulos believed the Illyrians' and Thracians' relationship with Ancient Greece was one of "familiarity" or even a process of civilizing osmosis, at least as far as the Greek tribes with which they had contact like the Epirots and the Thessalians. With regard to the Macedonians, he recognized that the issue of origin was still open: "it is disputed if the Macedonian tribes north of Thessaly belonged to the Illyrian or the Greek race", ibid.59.

46 Writing in the Constantinople daily *Neologos*, a columnist commented: "From the ancient times, the Pelasgian race, the once-inhabited and civilizing East, is divided and each of its branches enjoys the same thought that it is descended from the same national existence when in fact this division weakens these to the benefit of the other races' dominance. The division was sometimes the result of faith; the Mirditans, the fearless Tosks, forgot that they are the scions of the same mother as the other Pelasgians before they changed faiths. The Vryones neglected that from their roots a Byzantine imperial dynasty came from, and the Beys of Tirana that Kastrioti blood of flows in their veins. . . . Our split (into Albanians and Greeks) facilitated the dominance of others, but awakening one day we will suddenly see what we lost while thinking we were being reborn." Cited by Paschides, *Alvanoi kai Ellinismo*, 6.

It stands to reason that an effort would eventually be made to deliberately cover the gap that Paparrigopoulos had consciously left. For example, writing about the Albanians immediately after the Eastern crisis, Paschides claimed Greeks and Albanians shared a common origin in the Pelasgians, and aimed precisely at persuading the Albanians that they were nothing but a branch of the Greek race. Yet, in one way, it was impossible not to recognize the Pelasgians' "Albanization" as this was common ground in nineteenth-century statements on antiquity. He introduced his lecture as follows:

> Pelasgians! The first inhabitants of Greece were descended from Japheth (the Jewish version) or Japetus (the Greek version), known alternately as Pelasgians or the Japetian tribe according to Pindar, Hesiod, and the immortal Homer. They arrived from various parts of Asia, but mainly the Caucasus, where there is a land already and widely known as the first Albania and through the Albanian Gates, the Albion or Alps, the White mountains, hence the name Albanians, Alb, and Alp in the Goth, Celt, and Dacian dialect but also in the Greek means white mountain from the snow.[47] (Paschides, Alvanoi kai Ellinismo, 5)

9. The De-Islamification of Albanian History

Sami described the Ottoman period Albania entered with the death of Skënderbeu (whose mythology he also supported, for obvious reasons) as "Turkish occupation."[48]

This was why his approach to Islam as the link between the majority of Albanians and Ottomans is important. The Albanians, as great warriors, often fought alongside the Ottomans. But according to Sami, the

47 Conversely, Sami cited the etymology of *Arbënë* the words "arë bën," or kneading gold, according to the renaissance practice of explaining Pelasgian and Illyrian words using Albanian roots, thereby certifying Albanian–Illyrian–Pelasgian continuity in the unrecorded distant past.

48 Skënderbeu's fascination with Alexander the Great is worth noting here. See Biçoku, "Aleksandri i Madh në kujtesën historike të Skënderbeut e të shqiptarëve," 7–29. Of course, Albanian nationalism needed the identification of Skënderbeu with Alexander the Great more than Skënderbeu did.

Albanians had begun to adopt Islam long before the Ottomans arrived on the Balkan peninsula's western shore. Of course, as soon as the Ottomans seized Albania, the Albanian's turn to Islam became more widespread or, as the Albanian proverb says, "religion follows the sword."

According to Sami, the Albanian temperament was not set solely by a faith as Albanians were prone to changing religions. He implied that the Albanians did not hesitate to adopt Islam so they could benefit from the Ottomans' favorable stance towards them, even though as Christians, they were not enslaved as *râya* (*rayah*) ("flock" subjects) like other populations but were allowed to maintain both their dignity and their weapons. In the Albanians, the Turks found a loyal and capable fighter, while the Albanians found in the Turks a master to open the doors of social mobility, as the Ottoman Empire's twenty-five grand viziers of Albanian descent attest.

In reality, faith should be subjugated to the needs of creating an ethnic identity, and this, according to Sami, can be seen in the fact that the Albanians' religious diversity—Muslims, Catholics, Orthodox—did not dilute this identity.

> But these divisions created no distinction or separation among the Albanians. Religious hatred and discord, did not exist only in the East but also in Europe and in the civilized-enlightened countries and have often become the cause of great and horrifying massacres and murders which are unknown in Albania as in this country nothing heinous has ever happened between Muslims and Christians, between Catholics and Orthodox, or between Sunni and Bektash. The Albanian is an Albanian before he is a Muslim or a Christian. This is because he has his religion, the religion of the Pelasgians, which he has even though he became Christian or even though he embraced Muhammad's faith. Religion has not changed this ever or at all because he always places nationality above faith. (Frashëri, *Shqipëria*, 36–37)

Sami was effectively trying to disengage Albanian nationalism from the dominant framework set by the Ottoman Empire: collective self-determination based on faith. Contrary to what one would expect based on his Pan-Islamic writings—that is, subordinating religion, especially Islam to the needs of shaping an ethnic ideology—he completely disconnected Albanian national identity from religious choice. His position cannot be explained solely by the Albanians' religious diversity. Adopting Islam as the nation's dominant faith would lead to a rationale of exclusions as well as to the need for Albania to be distanced from the East where national identity was, in his view, still determined by faith.

> In the Eastern lands, people everywhere set religion higher than ethnicity. The Greek, for example, when changing his faith, also leaves his ethnicity; if I become a Catholic, he says I am a Frank, if he becomes a Muslim, he says I am a Turk. Only the Albanian puts faith in a lesser position and sets ethnicity in a higher position. The Albanian, whether Muslim or Orthodox or Catholic, is always an Albanian.[49] (Sami Frashëri, *Shqipëria*, 46–47)

It seems that Sami had forged the opinion that the Albanians' religious diversity could be used by representatives of rival nationalisms in the aftermath of the Eastern crisis. On February 20, 1881, he sent a letter to Jeronim de Rada (1814–1903), an Albanian patriot and representative of the Albanian Renaissance. The letter was published by Xholli, along with other correspondence between members of the Albanian nationalist movement such as Naum Vequilharxhi and Abdyl Frashëri.[50] This letter could be considered a preview of the views Sami was to outline in the 1899 essay. He distanced himself from the need to maintain the Ottoman Empire's unity while seeming to adopt the solution of secession, something that even the League of the Prizren shied away from. Secession from the empire had to be the logical conclusion of any plan or attempt. In the letter, he explained to his friend how the union had

49 Sami thought that the Albanian case needed to be distinguished from what happened in the West, comparing the Albanians' religious tolerance with the fierce clashes of the religious wars during that period, just as he had once compared Islamic civilization's tolerance with the bigotry of Western colonialism. "Faith never caused separation or division. This is why discord and hatred between faiths even in this enlightened Europe, half of these are not known in Albania and have never taken place among Albanians." Nonetheless, this observation was a repetition of the arguments of those aware of the Ottoman Empire's tolerance on the issue in relation to Western religious bigotry. Thus, his attempt to approach the issue of religious intolerance sprang from the Ottoman East he rejected and not the European West whose recognition he sought.

50 Xholli, *Sami Frashëri*, 28–38.

achieved in three years what the Porte had been unable to complete: to assemble armed units and expel the beys from Kosovo, thus actively supporting their demands. He implied this was a historical starting point and that nothing had been finalized, that the Great Powers were involved and that, as with other issues, so with regard to the Albanian national issue also, power played the key role. He also envisaged Albania without a king but as a republic of demo-gerontes, an idea he reiterated in 1899: "Albania must be unified and undivided" [Shqiperia duhet te jete nje dhe e pandare]. Sami signed the latter with his name, omitting Şemseddin. He was addressing an Albanian intellectual as an Albanian. He ended with a reference to a poem by Pashko Vasa, most likely his "O moj shqipni e mjera shqipni" (Oh my Albanian, poor Albanian) which was written in 1870 and popularized as a song.

Sami took this position precisely because he understood that religion had become a powerful weapon for national irredentism in the Balkans, rather than the opposite. What made him abandon the ship of Pan-Islamism and by extension that of the Ottoman Empire was the fact that it persisted in defining the populations within its borders according to *millet*. So, for example, the Ottomans' insistence on assimilating the Orthodox Albanians into the *Rum millet* aimed at separating them from their brother Albanian Muslims. In his view, this policy only benefitted the empire's enemies, Greek and Slav, who refused to acknowledge the existence of a discrete Albanian national identity in an attempt to define their co-religionist (obviously Orthodox Christian) Albanians. Albania, or rather Albanians, surrounded by the irredentist ambitions of Greece, Montenegro, Serbia, and Bulgaria could not turn their back on reality. They had to take into serious consideration the view that their "innocent" internal religious diversity could be used by their rivals. The world of nations was generally a harsh world: "There is no friendship in ethnicity, just as there is none in gambling. Nations are like fish; one eats the other. Alas for the nation that is weak."[51]

51 Sami Frashëri, *Shqipëria*, 49.

10. Pan-Islamic Ecumenism and Roman Byzantium: The Immanence of Empire

In contrast to their neighbors who were conspiring against them—here Sami again borrows the argument used by Bulgarian and Romanian nationalists against the Greeks and the Patriarchate—the Albanian nation had powerful friends: all the European powers, without exception, and including Russia. It is especially interesting that Sami called these "empires."

This, however, was not a description he uses for the nation's "enemies," especially the Greeks who, along with the Ottomans, would be the ones who might claim the term not only for their current ambitions, but historically also. Having tried through the Pelasgian theory to excise the Macedonian era from Greek history by relocating the Macedonians into the Pelasgian-Albanian race, he attempted to do the same with Byzantium. To offset Greek antiquity, he had to drastically curtail its limits. Greek nationalism's validity rested on the Macedonian and Byzantine periods.

> The Greeks gained the freedom and kingdom they have today with the blood of the Albanians Botsaris, Tzavellas, Miaoulis, and other Albanian heroes; the Greeks did and today do preserve the dress, the fustanella, socks, tsarouchia, dances, and songs of the Albanians; they are, I say, the bitterest enemies of Albania. Everyone knows the Great Idea of the Greeks; while in the age of Pericles when they reached their highest glory and peak, they had less land than what they do today and have no right to demand more, yet they demand to be given all the lands conquered under Alexander the Great or to revive the state of the Byzantines without considering that Alexander was a Macedonian and the Byzantines were Romans, nations that are both enemies of the Greeks and which destroyed Greece. In this "Great idea." the Greeks want to conquer and bring under Greece the entire Balkan Peninsula and Romania and Bulgaria. But despite all their constant shouts and cries, they have lost these lands and now have limited their hopes and demands to Albania and Macedonia. As a general rule, they use religion to support this, seeking to attract the Orthodox Albanians as co-ethnics and separate them from their Muslim and Catholic brothers,

> attempting to make them forget their beautiful language and learn to speak and write in Greek... (Sami bey Frashëri, *Shqipëria*, 52)

This joint attack on Greek foreign policy and the Patriarchate's role required the ideological delegitimization of the "historical" rights that Greek nationalism sought in Alexander the Great's Macedonia and Byzantium. Nevertheless, Frashërit followed a different road from that taken by the Bulgarian and Romanian nationalists. Their attack on the patriarchate's role was combined with an attack on Phanariotism as both were indisputably part of the Greeks' Byzantine heritage. But Sami disconnected the Phanar from Byzantium, believing that Greek nationalism arbitrarily appropriated the Byzantine Middle Ages.

This is an interesting point that deserves further explanation. In the Bulgarian case (and certainly in Leont'ev's), the Byzantine Empire was implicitly or explicitly accepted as a "Greek" empire. The old clashes between Byzantium and the Slavs were revived in the clashes between Greeks and Bulgarians over Ottoman Macedonia. But in the Albanian case, there were no such clashes as Skënderbeu resisted the Turks, not the Byzantines. Furthermore, there is no mention of Fallmerayer anywhere in Frashëri's essay. Although he did refer to the Albanian "diaspora" and the Arvanites who populated Hydra, Spetses, Attica, and other areas, unlike Drinov, he did not insist on the "Slavicization" of the Greeks, despite having numerous reasons to do so.

What is most likely is that Sami experienced the end of the Ottoman Empire in a traumatic manner, and this is evident throughout his essay. "Traumatic" because it was an empire whose end he did not wish to see. It was as if he was trying to first persuade himself of this—splitting from the imperial model was hard—and only then could he persuade his compatriots. This was the reason the Empire continued to captivate him despite his shift in perspective (from the subject-*ummah* to the object-nation), even though he fully applied the linear scheme of continuity based on the construction of a "mythological antiquity." He could acknowledge this imperial past in the Ottomans but did not want to bestow it upon specifically the Greeks (although he accused the former of working with the latter to destroy Albanian national identity). This was the only explanation for his obsessive denial of the Macedonians' relationship to the Ancient Greeks and, primarily, his denial of Byzantium's Greek character. For Sami, the meaning of empire was (he emphasized) of great importance, even while he was setting in motion the process for the emergence of the nation-state.

The solution given by Sami Fracheri was to "de-Hellenize," Romanizing Byzantium and weakening the strength of Greek nationalism in the Balkan region resembles what Namık Kemal provides in his *Ottoman history.*[52] There, Kemal adduced an extensive introduction to Roman history: the history of the Roman Empire was transformed into a prelude to the arrival of the Ottomans, who only in Asia Minor had to come into conflict with their Byzantine (Eastern Roman) inheritance. The claim of the Romanism of Byzantium seemed to be a precondition for the survival of Ottoman imperial nationalism.

52 Kemal, *Osmanlı Tarihi*, vol. I, 37–81.

Chapter VI

Byzantium as Second Rome: Orientalism and Nationalism in the Balkans

In the early twentieth century, especially during the 1930s, Byzantium reentered the mainstream discourse of Romanian and Turkish historiographies, both tasked with resolving the issue of continuity. To be precise, this was not merely a general reference to medieval Byzantium but to the continuity of the Byzantine and Ottoman Empires. This was a lofty endeavor undertaken by representatives of Balkan Orthodoxy in the late nineteenth century, as we saw in the first chapter, but had also been adopted by a significant segment of Western European academics in the late nineteenth century. Two historians engaged in this effort, Nicolae Iorga and Mehmed Fuad Köprülü, who one way or another were connected to the reconstruction of Greek national ideology of the interwar period. In Iorga's case, this occurred during a 1931 trip that appears to have had an influence on his *Byzantium after Byzantium*; in Köprülü's, this occurred in 1937, when the University of Athens conferred the title of honorary professor on him.[1]

Of course, the two historiographies were in different phases of development at the time. In the 1930s, Romania had enjoyed independence for seven decades, and Transylvania had been incorporated into its territory some years earlier, although the trauma of losing Bessarabia to Russia was still alive. By contrast, Turkey's Kemalist republic was taking its first steps. Romanian historiography had adopted the continuity model in the nineteenth century, with the Daco-Getae providing an ancient ancestry just as the Albanians and Bulgarians drew their lineage from

1 Iorga, *Eikones*. For Köprülü, see Papageorgiou, "Introduction."

the Illyrians-Pelasgians and the Thracians, respectively. Turkish historiography followed the course set by the First Turkish Historical Congress in 1932.

Nonetheless it seems that adopting the model of origins did not yield the same results in terms of understanding the model of continuity. Specifically, the problem re-emerged in the management of "medieval" discontinuity. This discontinuity was problematic for the Romanians, given the gap between the Daco-Getae and the appearance of the Moldo-Wallachian kingdoms of the Late Middle Ages, but chiefly because of the Romanians' cultural "Slavicization." For the Turkish nationalists, however, discontinuity was welcome as it provided a break from the Ottoman imperial legacy. Byzantium's use in relation to the Ottoman Empire took on opposing meanings, but with both of their relationships with the East as the common ground. Iorga, the architect of "post-Byzantine" continuity, supported the view that Romania was part of Southeastern Europe rather than the Balkans.[2] Thus, the question arises whether the ideological use of Byzantium helped Romanian historiography achieve one common goal: detachment from the Balkan East. Conversely, Turkish historiography's rejection of continuity with Byzantium (and the Ottoman Empire) supported the East's legitimization, despite disagreements over whether this legitimization should be "cultural"—for Köprülu, the Turk is defined by language—or whether it should be "racial," as argued by Afet İnan. The latter did not require a "radical" detachment from the East, while earlier approaches to Ottoman imperial ideology dating back to the Young Ottoman thought (see the influence of al-Afghānī) played a decisive role.

But it is worth examining these two cases more closely by juxtaposing the work of four writers, A. D. Xenopol and Nicolae Iorga in the Romanian case and Afet İnan and Fuad Köprülu in the Turkish.

---

2 According to Iorga, defending the use of the designation "Southeastern Europe" was not an exclusively Romanian issue. He argued the Bulgarians were the only people who could "claim" the "Balkan" designation; the Serbs (who inhabited the peninsula's west, at Europe's edge), the Greeks (whom he defined as "Mediterranean"), and the Romanians (who shared in central European culture) could not be described as "Balkan peoples." This problem was further exacerbated by the inclusion of the Hungarians and especially the Turks under the Balkan classification. "And thus, a Balkan peninsula, that extends as far as Pannonia, a Balkan peninsula that reaches Asia Minor, is something I cannot comprehend." In his first lecture on Greece, Iorga set out the reasons why he declined an invitation to participate in an "Inter-Balkan" conference, while accepting an invitation to a congress on Byzantine studies, both of which took place in Athens in 1931. See Iorga, *Eikones*, 124–27.

1. From the Daco-Getae to the Romanians: In the Shadow of the First Rome

Throughout the nineteenth century, Moldo-Wallachian intellectual life had been decisively influenced by "Latinism," the dominant approach to history that had entered the culture through Transylvania. This ideological current ran through historiographical analyses of the Școala *Ardeleană*'s Latinists who, in the late eighteenth century, expressed the view that the inhabitants of Moldavia and Wallachia descended from the Roman conquerors, just like Transylvania's Romanian-speaking populations.[3] These scholars espoused the Romanians' continuity with Roman antiquity, a position naturally supported by the obvious etymological similarities between "Roman" and "Romanian."[4] The need to disengage from the Ottoman past and the Orthodox religious identity as a determining factor—it should be noted that the a large segment of Habsburg Transylvania's population had joined the Protestant faith—led these historians to seek a genealogical link to the ancient Roman world. Rome, thus, supplanted both the dark Ottoman past and the Byzantine cultural heritage. But the distancing from what Dimitri Obolensky dubbed the "Byzantine Commonwealth"[5] also stemmed from the Romanians' attempt to shake off the influences of their long coexistence with the Slavs. The medieval rulers of Moldavia and Wallachia were consequently transformed into "islands of Latinism" within a Slavic flood.[6]

Of course, proponents of this position, even when it migrated east of the Carpathian Mountains and was adopted by Moldavian and Wallachian intellectuals, faced a serious problem: how to establish a Roman presence

---

3 Obviously, this required expunging the Dacians from Romanian genealogy. According to this view, the Roman–Dacian wars in the 1st century resulted in either the Dacian population's destruction or expulsion. See Drace-Francis, *Modern Romanian Culture*, 60.

4 Most notably, Samuil Micu (1745–1806), Georghe Sincai (1754–1816), and Petru Maior (1761–1821). The latter went as far as to claim the absence of any interracial mixing between Romans and Dacians because of the Dacian women's "barbarism." See Maior, *Istoria pentru începutul românilor*. August Treboniu Laurian, whose *History of the Romanians* was published in 1853, was a prime example of these authors and their indisputable leader. The springboard for his work is 753 BC, that is, the founding of Rome. Thus the history of the Romanians is perceived as the unbroken continuation of Roman history. See Boia, *History and Myth*, 46.

5 Obolensky, *Byzantine Commonwealth*.

6 Hitchins, *Romanians*, 140.

north of the Danube given that these were the empire's very furthest reaches. The problem actually increased with acceptance of the migration of the Latinized Daco-Getae south of the Danube after being abandoned by the Romans.[7] This position was first expressed in the late eighteenth century by Franz Joseph Sulzer and Johann Christian Engel.[8] But this slight deceit, which was papered over by some historians' persistence in describing the life of the Roman legions south of the Danube, was not important enough to deter the attempt to create a Romanian connection to ancient Rome. In terms of the West's recognition of the Romanians as the sole Latin people of the Balkans, the benefits were obvious and powerful.

Nonetheless, Latinism, a product of the eighteenth century, did not seem sufficient to become a strong factor for legitimization in the nineteenth, at least not on its own. In developing Romanian nationalism, the problem of recognition by the West, especially Napoleon III's "Latin" Second Empire, has already been resolved. But the intra-Balkan conflicts urgently required Romanian historiography to adapt to the new conditions: that is, to ratify ancient rights to the space and establish a unity in time. This meant adopting a version of autochthonous discourse along the lines of its rival nationalisms, especially Bulgarian nationalism. Of course, this did not mean rejecting Romaism as the core of the Romanian national identity and its implicit cultural superiority but rather accepting a hybrid of racial indigeneity and Western-style national ideology. The combination could be more functional for the ambitions of Romanian nationalism. The Dacians returned as Daceo-Romans, despite these difficulties inherent to this position.[9]

References to the Dacians emerged in the early 1860s. Their return was marked by an article by Bogdan Petriceicu Hasdeu (1838–1907) in

---

7 Boia, *History and Myth*, 47.

8 Sulzer, *Geschichte des transalpinischen Daciens*. Engel, *Commentatio de expeditionibus* and Engel, *Geschichte der Moldau und Walachei*. The second book of Engel reiterated the first one's position that because Aurelian could not defend it against the Goths, he was forced to withdraw the Roman legions from Dacia to Moesia. This was where he then founded two new Dacias, Dacia Ripensis on the banks of the Danube River and Dacia Mediterranea in the Balkan interior. According to Engel's theory, the Romanians settled the Danube's left bank where they were subjected to Slavic raids and cultural influence. They were then subjugated by the Bulgarians, who supposedly imposed the name Vulgar and Valaques, also derivatives of Volga, which gave the Bulgarians and Vlachs (Woloch = Wolga) their names.

9 Boia, *History and Myth*, 90–96.

the journal *Foţta de istorie* şi *literatura* titled "The Dacians are lost?" (1860). Hasdeu argued that the Transylvanian school, which imposed the Latinist cult, was bound by an erroneous interpretation of ancient, mainly Latin, sources.[10] Eutropius's reference to a decline in the male population was read as a complete annihilation of the Romanian native element. Nonetheless, Hasdeu claimed that the Latin colonization of the Romanian space should not be seen only as Roman expansion but as a Latinization of the native population, that is, the Dacians. This questioning of the ancient sources is again central to the Romanian autochthony model, just as in the dispute between Krâstevich and Drinov in Bulgarian historiography. Hasdeu picked up the Dacian issue again a few years later in the introduction to *Etymologicum Magnum Romaniae*, claiming that the peoples of the Balkan peninsula resulted from successive waves of population layers, from the Pelasgians and Thracians to the Roman conquerors and finally the Slavs. Linguistic traces could be found in the continuity of each of these peoples, moving from the ancient Thracians to the modern Bulgarians, and from the ancient Dacians to the Romanians, and so forth.[11]

2. A. D. Xenopol: The Slavic Middle Ages and Phanariot Modernity

The work of Alexandru Dimitrie Xenopol might be considered the epitome of this historiographical form.[12] A Professor at the University of Iaşi since 1883 and a member of the Romanian Academy since 1893, Xenopol started from the definition of Romanian national identity as being "trapped" between other ethnic groups. In the introduction to his first work, in which he attempted to answer the question of the Romanian nation's survival during medieval times, he cited the difficulty of preserving Romanian national identity between the clashing rocks of the Ottoman Turks (given that most of Romania's territory was under Ottoman control), the Greeks, (given that the fate of the Danubian Principalities had been in the hands of the Phanariots for a considerable period), and

10 Cited by Boia, *History and Myth*, 90–91.

11 Ibid., 91.

12 For a description of Xenopol's work as a characteristic example of compositional historiography, see Zub, *L'historiographie roumaine*.

the Slavs (given that they were identified with the Orthodox faith, according to Xenopol).[13]

In his *Une énigme historique*, he did not restrict himself to dealing with Romanian historiography's main concern—that is, whether Dacia was or was not evacuated in the wake of the Roman withdrawal in 270,[14] which was more of an issue in the conflict between Romanian and Hungarian historiography—but devoted a large part of the work to the issue of Slavic influences on the emergence of the Romanian nation. In reality, *Une énigme historique* had been written as a response to Robert Roesler, who in his 1871 *Romänische Studien* supported the Danubian origins of the Balkan peninsula's Vlach populations, a theory that presumed the evacuation of Roman troops from Dacia and the Latinization of the Daco-Getae. Roesler argued for a link between the Daco-Romanian and the Macedo-Romanian (Aromanian), as he called it, dialects. He claimed both were variants of the same language, although the second had been subject to strong Slavic influence precisely as a result of the populations' early migration south of the Danube[15]. Seeking to counter this argument, Xenopol would claim that while the split into the Daco-Romanians and the Macedo-Romanians had occurred at a very early stage, the Slavic influence occurred north of the Danube and not in Moesia, where the Romanian presence was limited. (Xenopol also introduced a third class, the Istro-Romanians).[16] As Lucian Boia astutely notes, "in order to distance the Romanians even further from the Balkan sphere, [Xenopol] removed them from the Danube and pushed them towards the mountains."[17]

However Xenopol undertook a task much more important than proving the Romanian character of Transylvania: the threat represented by the

13 Xenopol, *Une énigme historique*, I.

14 Ibid., 15–37.

15 Roesler, *Romänische Studien*. For an extensive review of Roesler's position, see Vryonis, "Prior tempore," 200–202.

16 The Romanian version of Xenopol's *Une énigme historique* appeared one year earlier, as *Teoria lui Roesler: Studii asupra stflruintei românilor* în *Dacia Traianfl* (Iasi, 1884). A year later, Dimitre Onciul tried to modify slightly the main argument of the latter: the thesis for a Romanian continual habitation of the areas north of the Danube does not exclude the possibility one part of the Latinized Daco-Getae they have passed from Dacia and Moesia south of the river. This modification could interpret the relation between the different Vlach dialects which allows Roesler to doubt the continual presence of Romanians in the areas of modern Western Romania. See Onciul, *Teoria lui Roesler*.

17 Boia, *History and Myth*, 116. See also Cioroianu, "Impossible Escape," 212–13.

work of Roesler activated him to produce a scheme of national continuity in Romanian historiography exactly as Paparrigopoulos used the threat represented by Fallmerayer's theories to construct a scheme of national continuity in Greek historiography some decades earlier. The threats (as Skopetea proposed in her *Fallmerayer*) should be invented even if they did not exist.

According to Xenopol, Slavic influence occurred during the first Bulgarian kingdom, which also extended north of the Danube into the area of present-day Romania. Thus, in an odd way, the Romanian need to prove that the continual habitation of Romania, and especially Transylvania,[18] led to highlighting, or rather an acceptance of the position that Slavic influence had occurred north of the Danube; the further "West" the Romanian nation moved, the more "vulnerable" it was to Slavic cultural intrusion. Here, Xenopol's arguments came up against the contradiction between unity of space and temporal continuity. Responding to Hungarian arguments on Transylvania's ethnological character, and more generally suzerainty in the broader Romanian space, meant accepting the arguments made by Slavist writers about the Romanian nation's "Slavicization."

Xenopol was not satisfied with the argument for selective links between Romanians and Slavs during the "Roman-Dacian" antiquity, but he insisted also on the influence of the Bulgarian "Patriarchate" of Ohrid in Romanian cultural life during the Middle Ages.[19]

Considering the Romanian nation as "une fraction de la grande famille latine perdue sur les confins de l'Orient,"[20] this should be seen as a contribution to corresponding efforts by European scholars to counter rival views expressed by Slavic writers. Oddly, this occurred through an acceptance of the latter's basic arguments. In the efforts of Romanian historiographers to develop their argument against the counterpoints of rival nationalisms, they fell into a substantive contradiction: the model of (ethnological)

---

18 As early as the 19th century, Bogdan Petriceicu Hasdeu sought to correct the impression that Transylvania was the sole cradle of Romanian ethnogenesis by arguing for an expansion of the space in which this took place to Oltenia, Banat, and Transylvania's Western region (see Boia, *History and Myth*). It is worth noting here that Hasdeu was a professor at the University of Bucharest. One could also argue that Iași (Xenopol) and Bucharest (Hasdeu) offer different possible interpretations in the discussion of the Romanians origins.

19 Xenopol, *Une énigme historique*, 56.

20 Ibid., 1.

continuity could not be used simultaneously against Hungarian and Bulgarian nationalism, while the autochthony model of Romanians as indigenous latinized Daco-Getae was aimed at Western recognition and incorporation into European Latin culture rather than supporting the continuity model. Instead of shifting the definition of a nation from a cultural to a racial basis, invoking the Romanian nation as indigenous was Romanian historiography's most substantive move "away from the Balkans."[21]

In *Une énigme historique*, Xenopol argued that "the Romanians are descended from the colonists settled in Dacia by Emperor Trajan after conquering the province."[22] Their fate in successive centuries of barbarian raids was hard to ascertain, according to Xenopol, due to a lack of sources for a period spanning almost ten centuries (270–1200). The problem of Slavic influences on language and Romanians' religious life was directly linked to the continuity of the Romanian nation: had the relationship between Latin-speakers, who appeared as Vlacho-Romanians in the twelfth and thirteenth centuries, and Trajan's Roman colonists been severed or not?

This question can only be answered by accepting the Latinization of the Dacians and the Getae.[23] Xenopol's *History of the Romanians of Trajan's Dacia*[24] constituted a major contribution to this, as in it he set the start of Romanian history in 513 B.C., Herodotus's first reference to them.

---

21 Of course, this applies to Romanian historiography in the late nineteenth century but not the early twentieth century, when it sought disengagement from the European (mainly French) cultural heritage. See Boia, *History and Myth*, 59–63.

22 Xenopol, *Une énigme historique*. 2.

23 According to Xenopol, the Romanians, that is, the Latinized Daco-Getae, survived by withdrawing to Transylvania and a part of Hungary despite the advantageous position of other peoples subjugated there, Hungarians, Germans, and Szeklers. In reality, Xenopol was adopting Johann Thunmann's position that the Romanians who had settled north of the Danube "were the brothers of those in Macedonia, descendants of the Thracians, who played an important role as Dacians and Getae.... During the raids by the Vandals, Goths, Huns, Gepids, Slavs, Avars, and Bulgarians, they fled to the mountains for shelter.... The Hungarian raids found them in Transylvania and in a section of Hungary that lies on the Danube side. But the Vlachs also seized and held for a long time Wallachia and Moldavia and did not settle there for the first time during the thirteenth and fourteenth centuries, during the reigns of Rudolph the Black and Bogdan." (Thunmann, *Unterschungen*, cited by Xenopol, *Une énigme historique*, 6). Xenopol saw Thunmann's work as opening a new era in history for the Romanians and drew from his work the arguments he used against the Hungarian writers disputing Transylvania's control by the Romanians. An opposing view to Thunmann's was expressed by Gibbon in *Decline and Fall* and by Thierry in *Attila*.

24 Xénopol, *Histoire des Roumains*. The first volume had been published eight years earlier in Romanian (Xénopol, *Istoria românilor din Dacia*). Five more volumes followed by 1893. It should be noted that Xenopol was writing during the reign of Carol I Hohenzollern-Siegmaringen. In "The Im-

But this work was particularly important because it outlined the continuity of form in the Romanian nation's history based on the three phases known from other historiographies: antiquity, the Middle Ages, and modernity. The problem of Slavism resurfaces, albeit not in relation to the ethnogenetic procedures of the late-Roman years[25] but as the prevalent cultural influence which, along with the Ottoman conquest, would determine what constituted the Romanian "Middle Ages."

Thus, in Xenopol's view, Romanian *ancient history* (l'histoire ancienne) was the period during which their nationality was shaped, and this began with the reference to the Daco-Getae in historical sources (Herodotus) through the Romanian exodus from Transylvania as a result of the oppression suffered at the hands of the Hungarians and the founding of the states of Wallachia and Moldavia.[26] Romanian antiquity, thus, extended from 513 B.C. to A.D. 1290. The process of Romanian ethnogenesis was understood through a composite of the Daco-Getaean racial origins with Roman cultural influences. "The natural foundation of

possible Escape," Adrian Cioroianu observes that the reference to Trajan prompted associations and parallels between the Roman Emperor and Romania's first king: both hailed from the West and had traveled on the Danube. Both were also born in their respective Empire's provinces, Trajan in Spain and Carol in the Rhine, which allowed them to understand the "border" Latinness of the Daces and the Romanians. And, in the end, both were also forced to leave Dacia when conditions became unbearable for them.

25 The initial influences in his narrative, at the level of either place names or language as a result of the Slav and Romanian coexistence—that is, before the Slavs traveled down the Danube to settle in the lands of ancient Moesia—or on level of faith, with the subordination of the Romanian Orthodox to the Ohrid "Patriarchate" are incorporated in the period of Romanian "antiquity." See Xenopol, *Histoire des Roumains*, vol. I, 123–30; 144–47.

26 The national identity of the Dacians and Getae was the subject of intellectual clashes throughout the nineteenth century. German writers such as Jacob Grimm claimed they were of Germanic origin, citing the Getae's identification with the Goths by their chronicler Jornandès. Nineteenth-century Slavists similarly "claimed" the Dace based on toponyms. A third theory claimed Celtic origin for the Dace-Getae as an Arian (Indo-European) race. This was initially argued by Jean Maiorescou and subsequently adopted by Obèdénar and M. de Rosny. Although such a solution would have been useful on multiple levels as it linked the Daco-Getae with the Gauls long before the Latinist link between Romanians and French, Xenopol chose instead to present the Daco-Getae as a Thracian tribe of the Indo-Europeans. For this, he cited a reference in Herodotus in a passage of Menander mentioned by Strabo—"All Thracians and especially the Getae abstain from marriage"—as well as to Strabo, who considered the Dacians and Getae to be branches of the same race with a similar dialect to the Thracians. See Xenopol, *Histoire des Roumains*, vol. I, 20–24. The Thracian origin of the Daco-Getae offered a good springboard for claiming the national identity of the underlying population in the Eastern Balkan interior at a time when Balkan nationalism appeared to be abandoning its claim to "Thracian origins" in favor of joining the great Slavic family.

Romanian nationality was Thracian (as seen in Xenopol, the Daco-Getae were considered a Thracian branch of the Indo-European race); the intellectual foundation was offered by Rome."[27] Slavic influence interfered with this configuration's early phase, but this was not enough to cause Xenopol to doubt the Roman's decisive contribution to it. "Thus, ethnicity is the combined result of these three fundamental elements: the Thracian, the Latin, and the Slav. The Latin is dominant and, thus, gives the Romanian people the characteristic of a Latin nationality."[28]

According to Xenopol, Romania's medieval history (*l'histoire moyenne*) was a period when it was dominated by Slavism. This extended from the founding of both principalities in the thirteenth century to Matei Basarab's rule in Wallachia (1632) and Vasile Lupu's in Moldavia (1634). Their reigns mark the start of the replacement of *Slavism*'s cultural influence with the *Graecism* (Grécisme), a process that reached its apex during the Phanariot period.[29] It is worth noting, however, that Slavic influences reached their height at the beginning of the Ottoman conquest: cultural subjugation to the Ottomans and the simultaneous establishment of serfdom in the Danubian Principalities acted to suppress the onset of Romanians' national self-determination and created conditions for cultural subordination to Slavism.

During modern history (*l'histoire moderne*), Greek cultural influence grew and expanded until the Greek War of Independence that brought the Phanariots' hegemony to an end (1633–1821). This period would be replaced by contemporary history (*l'histoire contemporaine*), during which a new cultural and political dynamic dominated: Romanianism. Its dominance from 1821 to 1859 led to the principalities' unification and the founding of the modern Romanian state.[30]

In Xenopol's structure, therefore, antiquity's extension through to the foundation of the Moldavian and Wallachian principalities shifted the Romanian Middle Ages into a large part of the early modern era, exactly as Bulgarian "medieval antiquity" had been identified with the largest segment of the Byzantine Middle Ages. The Romanian Middle Ages also had

27 Xenopol, *Histoire des Roumains*, vol. II, 381.

28 Xenopol, *Histoire des Roumains*, vol. II, 382.

29 Ibid., vol. II, 171–77.

30 Ibid., vol. I, 4.

a dark period: the influence of Slavism. In the Romanian historian's narrative, Slavism assumed the same role as Phanariotism/Ottomanism in Drinov's structure—that is, a confirmed discontinuity in the history of the nation that did not relate to its racial (as in the case of the Greeks and Fallmerayer) but to its cultural alienation. This did not mean a lack of resistance—resistance is always necessary in a structure of confirmed discontinuity, as was the case with the resistance to Phanariotism by the subjugated Bulgarians. For example, the Slavic language was established as the official language for church services, liturgical texts, and official administrative documents in the principalities, yet it could not replace the Romanian language in daily life.[31]

The Graecism that succeeded Slavism in "alienating" the Romanian nation constituted a fundamental danger as an "external threat." Slavism was "an unbearable and unconscionable oppression" of the Romanian people by "a foreign mentality." It was, thus, a mode of thought, albeit without any investment in political aims. By contrast, Graecism served not merely as a cultural influence but was also a "means" for imposing foreign domination. It constituted a conscious attempt to destroy the Romanian nation.[32]

Despite his rejection of Graecism's influence and its political expression in Phanariotism, it remains interesting that Xenopol included both as inextricable elements in Romanian history's entry into the modern period (although, unlike Iorga, he did not contribute to the latter's legitimization). While Drinov's Bulgarian medieval times included Phanariotism, extending through Paisius's promethean discovery of the Bulgarian nation, Xenopol set the start of modern Romanian history to the arrival of the Phanariots in Moldo-Wallachia.[33]

Defining the Romanian Middle Ages using the twin poles of Slavism-Ottoman rule and the attack against Phanariotism/Graecism seemed to

31 Xenopol, *Histoire*, vol. I, 459.

32 Even if it favored the introduction the use of the Romanian language instead of Slavic in church services. See Xenopol, *Histoire*, vol. II, 172.

33 To be precise, Xenopol believed Phanariotism marked the peak rather than the effect of Greek cultural influence that began before the Phanariots' emergence. He therefore distinguished the Greeks who had arrived earlier in the Danubian Principalities and had become assimilated from those who came later and retained their Greek identity (as was the case with the Cantacuzène, Doukas, and Ghikas families). See Xenopol, *Histoire*, vol. II, 181–82.

complete the Romanian disengagement from the hostile surroundings of rival nationalisms.

Xenopol attempted to turn Thunmann against Engel and Sulzer—that is, the position that held that the Latinization of the Daco-Getae[34] ensured continuity on the racial level versus the position that asserted their complete obliteration and the subsequent withdrawal of Roman legions from Dacia. But, in reality, he accepted one of his opponents' basic positions: the Romanian people's subjection to Slavic influences on two levels, linguistic and religious. Both Engel and Sulzer believed that the Slavic influence was not limited to the area along the Danube but could be seen in Transylvania itself. According to Xenopol, the issue of Slavicization in nineteenth-century Romanian history became a consistent point of reference in the works of all the great nineteenth-century Slavist scholars such as Šafárik (who argued insistently for the Slavic etymology of toponyms) and Jernej Kopitar.[35] Xenopol, thus, attempted to manage a tangible problem.

The problem persisted precisely because of the insistence on the First Rome's definitive influence on Romanian ethnogenesis. Latinization could not invalidate the tangible issue of Slavicization. Antiquity's extension at the expense of the Middle Ages and the advancement of the origin model to resolve the continuity problem did not seem as effective in the early twentieth century as it had seemed in the nineteenth. On the contrary, attention should have been paid to the meaning of the Romanian Middle Ages. And this was the basic reason why it was now necessary to confront the challenges posed by the Second Rome.

3. Nicolae Iorga's *Byzance après Byzance*: Invoking the Second Rome

Nicolae Iorga was a historian introduced into the Romanian historiographical community by Xenopol[36] himself. He was Xenopol's student at

34 If, as Lucian Boia observes, Xenopol appeared to view the Roman element as superior in the Daco-Roman composite, he took pains to limit the extent of Roman colonization of the Romanian space. See Xenopol, *Histoire*, vol. I, 63–64. The Roman element existed as a racial element but primarily as a cultural presence.

35 This is a position shared by many Romanian scholars, including Ioan Bogdan; see his *Istoriografia Română*.

36 According to Zub, Iorga displays the same "obsession" for the great historiographical compositions as his teacher Xenopol. See Zub, "En quête d'une synthèse."

the University of Iași and owed his induction into the Romanian Academy to his teacher. However, the basic pillars on which Iorga rested his historiographical efforts led him to distance himself from Xenopol's solution to the problem of continuity in Romanian history and also from Xenopol's understanding of Romanian legitimization as a part of the broader history of Europe.

Iorga's historiographical pillars could be summarized as follows: consistent reference to a type of "agrarian nationalism" (Romania's agrarian culture as a source of national pride but mainly as proof of national continuity; the road from the Daco-Getae to modern Romanians was rooted in the relationship with the land and not a question of the Romanians' autochthony);[37] the attempt to curtail elements of Slavic influence (for example, Iorga refuted Xenopol's views on the First Bulgarian Kingdom's suzerainty north of the Danube);[38] and, finally, the promotion of the Romanian nation as the heir to the great cultural tradition of "Eastern Romanity." This last point was shaped mainly in the early 1930s, with the publication of *Byzantium after Byzantium*.[39] Not coincidentally, this was accompanied by Iorga's direct involvement in nationalist political activity

37 Iorga takes a critical stance on racial perceptions of national identity. From this perspective, he adopts a position on the modern Romanians' Dacian (more racially "modest" than Roman) origin. But he has the same views with regard to the other "non-Balkan peoples": "I reiterate that I do not believe there has not been any interracial mixing and whenever someone mentions the Slavic Serbian race, I observe the square heads of some. And whenever someone mentions the Bulgarians' turanic character, I discover Thracian traits in them. Only the Serbian ethnologist Cvijić had a collection of Bulgarian heads of a particular shape with large bones and a different structure than that of the Serbs. When he wanted to show that the Serbs are right to be against the Bulgarians, he displayed these terrifying skulls. . . ." He had the same views on racial intermixing with regard to the Hungarians and the Greeks. But while Iorga accepts a nation's "cultural" prospects as the result of intermixing, he counters Fallmerayer's views. Therefore, while he observes the influence of the pro-Greek, Illyrian and Thracian elements in shaping Ancient Greek civilization, he adopts an almost "Hellenocentric" interpretation on the issue of coexistence with the Slavs in the Middle Ages. "The Greeks, people of the urban centers or the low mountains; the Slavs, people of the (open) countryside . . . the Slavs, who were farmers, arriving with their ploughs needed land. What would they have done on Parnassus or Helicon?" It was obvious that accepting a position on the Greeks' "Slavicization" during the Middle Ages would not leave much room for rejecting the Romanians' "Slavicization" during the same period. "But since all Slavs seemingly comprise a secret society, it is enough for a Bulgarian or a Serb to introduce an idea for the entire Slavic world to accept it." See Iorga, *Eikones*, 157–59.

38 We must emphasize that the Second Bulgarian Kingdom did not enjoy the same treatment as Xenopol considered it a "Vlacho-Bulgarian Empire," with the Vlach element prevalent within the state entity. See Xenopol, *Histoire des Roumains*, vol. I, 172–86.

39 Iorga, *Bizanț după Bizanț*.

that ended violently with his murder by the Iron Guard in November 1940. This activity, academic and not, dated from the early twentieth century and the publication of the nationalist review *Sămănătorul* (1902–1906) and later the newspaper *Neamul românesc* (1906).

But what made this dedicated Latinist seek out the glory of Byzantium in the sixteenth- and seventeenth-century Moldo-Wallachian Hospodars, who he cast as heirs of the Byzantine emperors and protectors of Eastern Orthodoxy (chiefly through their donations to the monasteries of Mount Athos)? The need to supplant the First Rome with the Second should be viewed as a foundational component of Iorga's work.[40]

Iorga replaced Xenopol's older paradox with another: if Xenopol's insistence on the continuity of the Latinized Daco-Getae led to the unreserved acceptance of Slavic influences in the Romanian Middle Ages, for Iorga the shift from the First to the Second Rome resulted precisely in the rejection of the latter. The real function of the historiographical reference to Byzantium was not so much to shift the center of the Romanian ethnological reference from the West to the East, from Transylvania to Moldo-Wallachia and the Balkans, but to eliminate the dangers of a probable Romanian Slavicization in the cultural melting pot of the Eastern Roman Empire and its successor, the Ottoman Empire.

The issue of Byzantium, and more specifically its differentiation from the West (the Second Rome's relationship with the First), had preoccupied Iorga in the mid-1920s. In 1927, he made an announcement before the Second Congress on Byzantine Studies in Belgrade in which he examined the pivotal issue of the very existence of a Byzantine Middle Ages.[41] He posed this question: had Byzantium, during the course of its history, lost its ancient, Roman character and experienced a new "medieval" era like that of feudal Europe?

The definition of medieval by which he compared the West with Byzantium was surprising. "The Western Middle Ages existed through the unchanged structures of Empire and Church." Iorga appeared to mentally equate the Middle Ages with the Carolingian Empire and its successors, and

40 The reference to the agrarian population's revitalizing influence was the result of his broader ideological orientation aimed at distancing itself from the Western European model and, thus, from its Latin roots

41 Iorga, *Y a-t-il eu un moyen-âge byzantin?*

not some fragmented politically feudal Europe. In any case, it was against this backdrop that he made his comparison, expressing the view from the outset that "Byzantium carefully protected the former (that means the Empire)."[42] The strong state centralization contributed to the establishment of a Church that rarely indicated any inclination to break from the state. The Church affirmed and legalized secular authorities[43] without suggesting that it was not powerful itself. Of course, its power grew more after the collapse of the Byzantine Empire and its subjugation by the Ottomans, when it tried to bring under its spiritual control regions like Moldavia, Ukraine, and Russia which were outside the borders of the Ottoman domain.

Iorga supported his position on the existence of a "Byzantine Middle Ages" through the assertion of the strong state (for example, he referred to Justinian's "Asian kingdom"), observing that this model was attractive to many of Byzantium's enemies. Despite the existence of a strong network of urban centers in Byzantium, he did not dispute the strangulation of the "native" urban class through the privileges accorded to the Venetians and the Genoans. He further noticed that the Empire's two most important regions, the Italian and the Balkan peninsulas, did not follow a different historical course to the Empire's center.[44]

Iorga attempted his comparison on multiple levels: state structure, the Church's role, urban networks, the role of commerce, and the emerging urban class. This seemed to legalize the view that Byzantium, especially the populations of the two Mediterranean peninsulas, did not follow a different path from that followed by the West. He would return to the comparison of West and Byzantium with an even greater emphasis on the value of Byzantine culture a few years later.

> In the Middle Ages, the West did a lot in terms of the daily life, a free life, I would say, from the local and urban perspective. These are the grand eras of the Church and the Empire. But power, wealth, brilliance, millennia of tradition, glory, and all that belong to Byzantium, and when you write about medieval history, you must have before you

---

42 Iorga, *Moyen-âge byzantin?*, 1.

43 Iorga considers the reign of Michael I Cerularius the exception and implies that the Schism of 1054 was the result of his overweening policies. See Iorga, *Moyen-âge byzantin?*, 2–3.

44 Iorga, *Eikones*, 173.

> all of Byzantine history. The West is linked to everything innovative, Byzantium to what is "conservative." Byzantium represents stability for all periods: its ageing is only superficial. It is a concept that can embrace all nations; it is Roman idea, Orthodox Church, Classical Greek education, and aside from all these elements, it also represents the potential for cooperation of all nations. Thus, it can never grow old, it cannot be exhausted, but it continues to serve the Roman idea in the East. (Iorga, *Eikones*, 174)

It is very interesting that Iorga "de-Hellenizes" Byzantium using motifs employed by the religious ecumenism of the late nineteenth century (it is strongly reminiscent of Leont'ev's writings), aside from the political ramifications of endorsing a position on Byzantium resulting from the cooperation of the nations that comprise it. To remove any such doubts, on the pretext of the clashes during the Byzantine Studies Conference in Athens, he added:

> But the Byzantine Empire is first and foremost Roman; from a political perspective it is so Roman that those who are politically subjugated to it are "Romans" or "Romioi." We are Romanians, they are Romioi, they speak Romaic (Greek), so far as the Roman spirit penetrated Byzantium. (174)

Equating Byzantium with the West was a good way to see the Balkans not as an exception to European history but as an inextricable part of it. "As far as the Balkan peoples are concerned, their development followed the absolute same path with that of Western societies, but with a completely fertile process of transformation during this wonderful era of continuous renewal, a creativity that was not interrupted by what is unfairly dubbed 'Middle Ages.'"[45] And this did not only apply to the peoples within its boundaries but also to those invaders who created new states on its former lands. Indeed, for Iorga, the period of establishing these commonwealths contributed to the idea of the national state, especially in societies with primitive financial and political structures.

45 Iorga, *Moyen-âge byzantin?*, 6.

Iorga's views on the similarities between the Byzantine and Western Middle Ages would not be so significant without his position on the continuity of Byzantium and the Ottoman Empire. According to Iorga and the school of thought he represented, most of the Ottoman Empire's institutions had been established under Byzantine influence. This view, which later evolved into *Byzantium after Byzantium* centered on the Danubian Principalities, constituted a common theoretical approach among Byzantinists at the time, especially French historians like Alfred Nicolas Rambaud.[46] Rambaud played a decisive role in shaping the theory of Byzantine-Ottoman continuity which Iorga eventually adopted. It should be noted that Rambaud wrote the introduction to the French translation of Xenopol's *History of the Romanians* published in 1896.

Iorga called the Ottomans "Neo-Byzantines of Islam" and concluded the statement referenced earlier with the following observation:

> Before and after [the Ottoman conquest], there is a centralized state which is relentless in the face of every type of liberty and spontaneity, a government machine [driven by] an inclusive presence that knows [and claims]: at the beginning, Rome of the Orient (Rome Orientale), and at the end Rome of Turan (Rome Touranienne). (Iorga, *Moyen-âge byzantin?*, 8)

Iorga's citing of the Second Rome softened the Slavic influence in the process of establishing a Romanian ethnic identity. As Xenopol demonstrated, this continuity in Romanian Slavicization was not interrupted by the "Middle Ages" and was actually bolstered after the Ottoman conquest, making it necessary for Byzantium to continue to exist after its fall. The Ottomans, as "Neo-Byzantines of Islam," and the privileged Moldo-Wallachian hospodars could function as redefining factors for this effort

46 See, among others, Rambaud, *L'Empire grec* and Rambaud, *Le monde byzantin*. These two works formed the basis of his doctoral thesis. His work on Byzantine history was posthumously published in the volume Études sur *l'histoire byzantine*. Rambaud is also known for authoring a history of Russia, *Histoire de la Russie*. He lived in Russia for a short period, learning the language as well as Russian history and culture. Rambaud served the Méline government as minister of education from 1896 to 1898. During this time, he coauthored a history text with Erneste Lavisse; Rambaud's contribution included the chapters on the history of the East. For an assessment of his work after his death in 1905, see Pingaud, *Notice sur Rambaud*.

to effectively disengage from the Balkans. Paradoxically, *Byzantium After Byzantium*'s stance that the Second Rome did not come to an end at the cultural level after the Ottoman conquest, indeed, distanced the Romanians from the Slav-held Balkans and incorporated them into Southeastern Europe.

4. Mehmed Ziya Gökalp's "Canon": The Rupture with the Imperial Middle Ages

Contrary to the Romanian case, where the main concern was the appropriation of the Byzantine and "post-Byzantine" Middle Ages, the historiographical venture that took place in Turkey during the interwar period seemed a late adoption of the model of autochthony with far less flexible characteristics. Nevertheless, the famed *Turkish History Thesis* (Türk Tarih Tezi) presented at the First National History Congress in 1932 was the result of several processes during the 1920s, from the clarification of the Kemalist position on Islam after the 1925 Kurdish uprising to the first Turkological Congress held at Baku[47] under the newly established Soviet regime in 1926, which aimed to control the Turkish populations of the Caucasus and Central Asia.[48] The insistence on constructing a Turkish antiquity on the Central Asian steppes (inspired by views expressed earlier by Leon Calhoun), the rejection of the Ottoman past, and the corresponding delegimitization of Islam as determining contemporary Turkish identity would become decisive for the construction of the Kemalist historiographical canon.

Rejecting the Ottoman Middle Ages and idealizing an ancient origin introduced into Turkish historiography the problem of continuity between the Byzantine and Ottoman Empires, viewed either as a negative (as had been the case with Drinov) or as a positive (as with Gedeon and Iorga). The rejection of the Ottoman Middle Ages also laid the foundation for an approach closer to the former. But for Turkish historians, the span of history looked rather different in contrast to the historiographical narratives of Balkan thinkers. Turkish historians did not

47 Gasimov, "Transfer and Asymmetry," 3.

48 See Copeaux, *Espaces et temps*; and "I efevresi tis Istorias," 199–214.

reject Byzantium because it had contributed in some way to their cultural and political enslavement. On the contrary, the Ottomans were the only ones to have emerged victorious from their clash with Byzantine Empire. But Byzantium was rejected precisely because it was a representative and metonymy of the imperial model the Ottomans had subsequently reproduced. For Turkish historians, the arrow of history did not run in the direction of a "past future" (Byzantium's rejection was necessary since its Hellenization had been accepted) but toward a "past past" (as the Ottoman Empire could not have existed without Byzantium).

One of the first scholars to deal with the issue was Mehmed Ziya Gökalp, an intellectual who wrote one of the charters of Turkish nationalism. In *Principles of Turkism*, a work published shortly before his death in 1923, he expressed the view that the Ottoman Empire's dissolution had been assured for two reasons.[49] The first was that the imperial model was outdated. The simultaneous collapse of the Ottoman, Russian, and Austro-Hungarian Empires following World War I was proof thereof. The second was the process of exterminating "Eastern civilization" set in motion by the West. Western civilization had replaced the Eastern in Russia and the Balkans, and it was destined to do the same in the Ottoman Empire. This extract outlines the ways in which Gökalp defined "Eastern civilization": "Eastern civilization was not really Islamic as some believe. Its source was Eastern Roman civilization, just as Western civilization was not Christian by the continuation of Western Roman civilization."[50]

According to Gökalp, the Ottomans did not receive Eastern civilization directly from Byzantium but through intermediaries: the Islamic civilizations of the Arabs and Iranians. It was to this that he attributed the confusion of "Eastern" with "Islamic." Nonetheless, the main point of his thesis remained that the Ottoman Empire was no more than a part of the Byzantine heritage, and as such, it was condemned to collapse under the dominance of Western civilization. This rejectionist stance toward Empire (Byzantine and Ottoman) recalled the Westernization ideological venture represented by Korais's circle in the Modern Greek Enlightenment. In Gökalp's case, however, citing Turkism opened the way for a

49 Gökalp, *Türkçülüğün Esasları*. For biographical information, see Heyd, *Foundations* and, especially, Parla, *Social and Political Thought*.

50 Gökalp, *Türkçülüğün Esasları*, 41.

racial reading of Turkish national identity even though he did everything he could to avert emphasizing that the latter should be related to the concept of "culture."[51]

But while Gökalp rejected the imperial past as medieval, he also adopted a tripartite model for understanding Turkish history. This was not exactly a linear progression within the Turkish nation itself, but its inclusion in three different types of civilizations. (Gökalp saw culture as having a national character, while civilization was hypernational.) Thus, when the Turks were organized as a racial state, they were part of the Far Eastern civilization. When they managed to organize an imperial state, they were included in what he calls "Eastern civilization." Finally, the era of the nation-state marked the transition to Western civilization.[52] He outlined a similar structure in his *History of Turkish Civilization*, which was published two years after his death, but used Islam as the basic criterion for periodization.

> The periods of the history of Turkish civilization: the Turkish people experienced different lives under three civilizations. For this reason, the history of Turkish civilization is distinguished by three periods:
> 1. The ancient period: from the appearance of the Turkish race to the adoption of Islam.
> 2. The middle period: from the adoption of Islam to the adoption of Western civilization.
> 3. The modern period: from the adoption of Western civilization to the present. (Gökalp, *Türk medeniyeti tarihi*, 8.)

Narrating the Turkish nation's history, Gökalp adopted a three-phase model of ascending development of a *substantialized* collective subject and its incorporation into three different cultural paradigms.[53] In a way, this hermeneutical scheme included a linear progression, but it simulta-

51 Inspired by the German conceptual dichotomy between a techonologically defined *Zivilisation* and a spiritually perceived *Kultur*. Gökalp, *Türkçülüğün Esasları*, 26–42.

52 Gökalp, *Türkçülüğün Esasları*, 38–39.

53 Gökalp argued that a society (or a "nation") could change cultural camps during the course of its history, that is, it might be incorporated into a different cultural environment from the one in which it originally emerged. See Gökalp, *Türk medeniyeti tarihi*, 8.

neously required discontinuities and ruptures between the phases; in any case, this was the only way to legitimize the revolt against the empire.[54]

5. M. Fuad Köprülü's "Opposition": The Reappropriation of the Ottoman Middle Ages

The adoption of a triadic scheme and the connection of the Ottoman medieval period to Islam was not aimed at the legitimization of the latter. Quite the contrary. The arrival of modernity would result from the rejection of the medieval "intermediate" link and, thus, its Byzantine origins. While Gökalp's cultural interpretative approach was not taken into serious consideration by the protagonists of the First Congress, the core of his argumentation for the rejection of the imperial medieval times was adopted as the dominant reading of the Turkish past during the interwar period. This did not, however, mean that there were no critical reviews of the initial structure which, much later of course, would emerge as dominant and contribute to the *Turkish-Islamic synthesis* (Türk-Islam Sentezi) in the 1970s, or in other words, the reappropriation of the Ottoman past.

Mehmed Fuad Köprülü,[55] published his seminal work, *Les Origins de l'Empire Ottoman*, a series of lectures delivered in Paris in 1935, exactly the same year that Iorga's *Byzance après Byzance* was also published in French. And just as the ideological and scientific research for Iorga's *Byzantium* had preoccupied him throughout the 1920s, *Les Origins* had its roots in Köprülü's earlier work, specifically "Some Observations on the Influence of Byzantine Institutions on Ottoman Institutions," which was first published in Istanbul in 1931.[56]

---

54 From this perspective, Gökalp's scheme was additional proof of how Turkish nationalism balanced between the model of "territorial nationalism" and "ethnic nationalism." See Poulton, *Top Hat*; and Poulton, "Turkish State and Democracy." For the differences between "territorial" and "ethnic" nationalism, see Smith, *Nationalism and Modernism.*

55 In this work, Köprülü emphasized the Ottoman dynasties in an attempt to interpret their rise to power based on political and social factors rather than nationalist ones. On this critical issue, see Ersanlı-Behar, "Ottoman Empire," 132.

56 Köprülü's research was originally published under the title "Bizans müesseselerinin Osmanlı müesseselerine tesiri hakkında bâzı mülâhazalar" in *Türk Hukuk ve İktisat Tarihi mecmuası*. In 1981, his son Orhan F. Köprülü republished the work as an independent volume with some additional notes and appendices. The work became known to Western academics through its Ital-

In this paper, Köprülü tried to reverse an idea widely held in Turkological scientific circles: that Ottoman institutions were nothing but an imitation of the corresponding Byzantine institutions. Naturally this view was based on the implicit assumption that the Turks had not offered anything to world civilization. Soldiers and marauders were not capable of entering the circle of nations that at one point or another expressed the "Absolute Spirit" of History.

Köprülü would gradually negotiate the positions of most historians expressing similar views: from sixteenth-century authors such as Leunclavius (*Leonclavii Pandectes historiae Turcicae*) to seventeenth-century authors such as Du Cange (*Glossarium ad scriptores mediae et infimae graecitatis, Lugdum*, 1688), Busbecq, and Pietro Della Valle who expressed, among other things, the view that the Ottoman habit of applauding was copied from the Byzantines in the fifteenth century. The Turkish historian critiqued their work but focused especially on nineteenth- and early twentieth-century writers who supported the continuity of the Byzantine and Ottoman Empires. Among them was Rambaud—whose views, as we have seen, had been effectively adopted by Nicolae Iorga—Herbert A. Gibbons, and Charles Diehl.[57]

In reality, Köprülü would take the exact opposite standpoint from Iorga's scheme of post-Byzantine continuity. His criticism commenced from the Romanian historian's point of theoretical reference: Rambaud's work. Rambaud offered a one-to-one correlation between the officials of the Byzantine and the Ottoman courts (the Grand Domestic to the Grand Vizier, the Domestic of the Schools to the Beylerbey, and so on), administrative institutions (Byzantine themes to Ottoman sancaks), and ranks of military officers.[58] Rambaud's views were further promoted by

ian edition published in 1953. An English translation by Gary Leiser was published by Türk Tarih Kurumu Basımevi in Ankara in 1999. References in this book are to the third Turkish edition published in 2002.

57 For Iorga, see, especially, Iorga's *Geschichte des Osmanischen Reiches*; For Gibbons, see Gibbons, *Foundation*. For Diehl, see, among others, Diehl, *Byzance*; and *Histoire de l'Empire Byzantin*.

58 In *Histoire générale du IVe siècle jusqu'à nos jours*, which he coauthored with Ernest Lavisse, Rambaud outlined four phases in the Ottoman Empire's evolution. These were marked by the three most important reigns: those of Orhan, Mehmed II, and Süleyman the Magnificent. The first period was the Ottomans' nomadic life. The second started with their intersection with Islam (via Alâeddin Pasha and during the reign of Sultan Orhan). The third commenced with the first conquests, especially of the lands of the former Byzantine Empire (Mehmed II), and the last was the period of the

historians like Gibbons, who claimed that the Byzantine influences on the Ottoman institutions dated from before the Fall of Constantinople; Diehl, who claimed that Ottoman institutions were no more than an imitation of Byzantine institutions; Rudolf von Scala, who suggested Ottoman institutions like the timar had been influenced by the Persian Sassanids;[59] and, Ivan I. Sokolov, who sought Byzantine influences on the Ottoman tax system.

Köprülü, however, placed special emphasis on Iorga's views as the basic representative of this school of thought.

> Prof. N. Iorga is the one who has recently done the most work. But recently Professor N. Iorga occupied himself with this very important issue. Professor Iorga, who believes that the Ottoman Empire was founded by Mehmed II in Constantinople as the continuation of Byzantium and who mentions him as half-Serb . . . and even more Byzantine than Constantine Dragases (Palaiologos), has referred to these issues in many of his articles and books, along with the publication of a special study on the issue of the Byzantine institutions' influence on Ottoman institutions. The well-known Romanian historian, who explains the Ottoman Empire's influence on the history of Southeastern Europe objectively, and quite differently from many Western historians, also claims that this tradition stems from Byzantium. . . . But these fragmented observations clearly indicate N. Iorga's concept. N. Iorga has summarized it quite clearly in his broadest work [Geschichte des Osmanischen Reiches]. According to him, Mehmed II founded the Ottoman state after the Fall of Constantinople, imitating Byzantium. . . . All the functions and

---

Empire's transition to Europe's most powerful state during the reign of Suleiman. (See Köprülü, *Bizans müesseselerinin*, 11.) Thus, even though Rambaud used the dynastic criterion, the periodization he outlined was not that different from the one used by Ziya Gökalp.

59 Conversely, in his entry on *timar* in the *Encyclopédie de l'Islam*, Jean Deny attempts to prove that the timar was an imitation of the Byzantine *pronoia*. Leunclavius had suggested that the word "timar" derived from the Greek "timarion" in the late sixteenth century, a theory adopted by Baudier and Du Cange. A 1598 reference to a similar Persian word by the Venetian Lazzaro Soranzo led Hammer and other writers to suggest "timar" was Persian. According to Köprülü, the word "timar" was never used in Persian in the same way as it was used by the Ottomans. Hammer and Vorms, Belin, and Tischendorf associated the institution of the timar with the existence of an Islamic feudal system. See Köprülü, *Bizans müesseselerinin*, 16.

> elements of the Byzantine palace continued in Mehmed's palace while even the Sultan's orders came to be known as *kanun*, a term inspired by the Greek word *kanonas*. Understandably, N. Iorga's ideas are in perfect accord with those of Rambaud and Diehl, and particularly with the views that Byzantine institutions were an object of imitation by the Ottoman Empire after the Fall of Constantinople. (Köprülü, *Bizans müesseselerinin*, 18–19)

Köprülü accused Rambaud and the school he created of manufacturing a "continuity" between Ottoman and Byzantine institutions based on evident but superficial similarities, without these being examined on the basis of historical proof and methodology.

> Rambaud had the obligation to show with satisfactory evidence the modernization that took place after the Fall and the institutions that may have been inherited only from Byzantium . . . before the Fall of Constantinople. Thus, N. Iorga supports his theory solely with his own imagination when he claims that the Ottoman state was an Asian state when its capital was in Proussa (Bursa) and Adrianople (Edirne) before the Fall of Constantinople and the acceptance of Byzantine institutions. Rambaud's views on the influence of the palaces of Baghdad, Peking, or Karakorum on the Ottoman institutions, Gibbons's ideas on a strong Byzantine and correspondingly strong Persian influence on Mehmed's state, Grousset's hypothesis about an Ottoman Empire that is half Byzantine and half Mongolian are but fantasies that these historians have adopted without any practical proof and cannot be accorded the status of historical hypotheses. (Köprülü, *Bizans müesseselerinin*, 20)

Köprülü undertook the task of reviewing and criticizing these historical sources. Indeed, his paper looked at the range of state, social, and financial institutions in the Ottoman state, from offices such as the Grand Vizier and Beylerbey to the Kapudan Pasha and Chief Eunuch and from the timar system's origins to whether the half-crescent symbol was borrowed from the Persians, as Scala claimed, in order to debunk the arguments made by opposing scholars. Köprülü believed these distortions of

Ottoman and Seljuk history resulted from Western scientists' prejudices against Turkish culture.[60]

Of course Köprülü would pay considerable attention to the role of the state of the Eastern Seljuks, as in his view, they played a decisive role in the composite process of shaping institutions taken from the Persian, Arabic, and, naturally, Byzantine traditions.[61] The Ottomans were their natural successors: the palace traditions, the tax system, and the timar were not borrowed from the Byzantines but had been formed by the region's Turkish-Islamic states (Seljuks) and, thus, inherited by the Ottoman state. Implementing a "genetic and comparative" method, he concluded that "the Ottoman state became the heir of the administrative traditions of the Eastern Seljuks and in part was a Turkish-Islamic hegemony that was influenced by the Mamluks and the state of the Ilkhanids (a subordinate hegemony)."[62]

Nonetheless, Köprülü would not respond to the attempt to "Byzantify" Ottoman history with a corresponding, comprehensive "de-Byzantification," but instead tried to describe the complexity of the the Ottoman institutions' process of formation. He did not approach this with a method based on "origin" (the Byzantine, Arab, or Persian roots of the Ottoman institutions) but through a scientific method focused on interaction. Even when disputing the direct Byzantine influence on an institution, Köprülü recognized Byzantium's intermediate effect on its final formation. To be precise, his purpose was not to doubt Byzantium's role *per se* but to impose an equal approach to the evaluation of the two empires.

Köprülü himself opposed the view expressed by Iorga, among others, that the Ottoman Empire must be seen as an "Islamic continuation of Byzantium" ("Bizans'ın İslamlaşmış devamı"). Nonetheless, he recalled that the Ottoman state had occupied the same space as its predecessor and influenced strongly the formation European politics, not only in medieval but in modern times as well. The Ottomans' arrival in the Balkans

60 Here Köprülü had in mind the work of the German Orientalist Theodor Nöldeke, who referred to the appearance of the Seljuks as a disaster for world history. See Nöldeke, "Dernschwam's Tagebuch," 156–58. For Nöldeke's "contribution" to the compilation of basic Orientalist structures, see Said, *Orientalism*, 26.

61 See also Köprülü, *Seljucks of Anatolia*.

62 Köprülü, *Bizans müesseselerinin,* 152.

marked the end of an extended period of anarchy triggered by the Byzantine state's decline. The Christian populations in the Balkans no longer enjoyed the same "peace" and "prosperity" as they had during Byzantium. Just as Byzantine culture managed to express itself through the Orthodox Christian doctrine and Greek language, Ottoman culture expressed itself through Sunni Islam and the Turkish language. Köprülü also found it noteworthy that the Ottoman conquest marked the Eastern Orthodox Church's salvation from Latin dominance.[63]

6. Nationalism, the Other Face of Orientalism: The Persians' Return

Although Köprülü disagreed with Iorga and his school on the issue of Byzantium and the Ottoman Empire, he strenuously defended the view that all Southeastern Europe was under Ottoman influence, a view verified by the intrinsic value of the Ottoman culture. For him, the fact that the Albanians (Muslims) and Bosnians adopted Islam was a tangible testament to the Ottoman presence in the Balkans. The influence of the Turkish language and Ottoman writing on many peoples within the empire were self-evident.

Paradoxically Köprülü's clash with the Rambaud school—that is, with the legitimization of Byzantine cultural power through its continuity in the Ottoman Empire's institutions—also implied conflict with Gökalp, in other words, with the rejection of the Ottoman and Byzantine Middle Ages. Rambaud and Gökalp set off from different theoretical positions: Rambaud's was the legitimization of French imperial discourses in the Near East; Gökalp's was the establishment of Turkish national identity through a confrontation with the Ottoman imperial past. They converged, however, due to their common theoretical starting point: the use of the continuity of the Byzantine and Ottoman Empires to downgrade the Ottoman. Rambaud and his school based their arguments on an Orientalist understanding of the Ottoman Empire, which was regarded as incapable of producing an autonomous culture. Gökalp attributed the negativity to the Byzantine heritage. The result was nonetheless the same.

---

63 Köprülü, *Bizans müesseselerinin*, 153–54.

In building his case, Köprülü made use of Gökalp's contention of Byzantium's indirect influence on the Ottoman Empire (although he followed a different course from Gökalp). This is because Köprülü's argument about the Eastern Seljuks' state's decisive role in the formation of Ottoman institutions was open to additions: the Seljuks, and the Abbasids before them, had also, it could easily be claimed, assimilated Byzantine influences into their institutions. Consequently, the problem of Byzantine influence persisted, albeit through the Byzantified peoples of the Middle East. Gökalp's solution was, thus, inadequate in Köprülü's opinion. Acknowledgement of earlier cases of cultural interaction with Byzantium rather than with the Islamic peoples of the Middle East would render a reconstruction of a relationship of "parity" between the Byzantines and the Ottomans. Köprülü found a solution to this problem in the Persian Sassanids.

Just as Leont'ev looked to the Persian Achaemenid dynasty as an early example of an enemy, albeit discredited, of the Ancient Greek "democratic" heritage, Köprülü used the Sassanids to establish their decisive influence on the Late Roman and Proto-Byzantine period, making them responsible for the process of institution formation, a process that could not be attributed solely to Byzantium. As such, the scheme of "direct Byzantine influence" was set along a course that differed from Gökalp's: instead of the linkage that connected Byzantium with the Seljuks-Ottomans through the Abbasids supported by Gökalp, Köprülü proposed a new genealogy according to which the relationship between Byzantium and the Seljuks-Ottomans should be traced not just to Rome but to the Sassanids.

According to Köprülü, Rome had already been influenced by the Achaemenids organizational structure, and this influence was further reinforced by the rise of the Sassanid dynasty (A.D. 228). Thus, a waning Rome saw in the Sassanids an example for transcending its own crisis:

> Rome noted the Sassanids rise and began to see Persia as an example (for imitation) for avoiding its own decline and weakness. The palace of Diocletian replicated the Sassanid palace with the cult tradition of its emperors who were elevated to the level of God, with employees and officers controlled by systematic rules described by chroniclers of

> that period. The Emperor Galerius makes clear reference to the introduction of the model of Persian rule in the Roman Empire. . . . The Sassanid influence also remained strong in Eastern Rome for a considerable period of time. (Köprülü, *Bizans müesseselerinin*, 156–58)

Once more, the Persians served as a deus ex machina, not to save the relationship between Russia and Europe as was the case in Leont'ev but to save the relationship between Byzantium and the Ottomans.

7. Kemalist Nationalism: The Prevalence of Origin over Continuity

Kemalist nationalism was reluctant to adopt Köprülü's solution. In its first decade, it was vital for the Turkish Republic to be recognized by the West according to the definition of "Turk" as this was shaped by the latter during earlier centuries, that is, on racial terms.

In 1932, a year after Köprülü's paper on the Byzantine influence on Ottoman institutions was published as part of the effort to legitimize the Ottoman Middle Ages as an inextricable part of the new Turkish national identity, the First Congress on Turkish History was convened in Ankara.[64]

The proceedings' tone was set by Kemal's daughter, Ayşe Afet İnan, who gave the keynote presentation at the opening. A leading figure of the Congress, she perceived her work as that of a "missionary," as Büşra Ersanlı-Behar correctly observes, in light of Kemal's order to reconstruct Turkish history.[65] This led her to adopt the model of origins in its most extreme form.[66]

In her keynote speech at the congress,[67] Afet İnan outlined the theory that Central Asia was not only the original cradle of Turkish, but of all of the world's civilizations. She observed that by shrouding the East in

64 For the best analysis of its proceedings, see Ersanlı-Behar, *İktidar ve Tarih*, 119–60. See also Ersanlı-Behar, "Ottoman Empire," 115–54. The congress proceedings were published in *Birinci Türk Tarih Kongresi*.

65 See Ersanlı-Behar, *İktidar ve Tarih*, 126. This incident is widely known: Afet İnan addressed Kemal and asked if there was truth in the findings of the racist European anthropologists on the Turkish race's inferiority vis-à-vis the Aryans.

66 Afet İnan had written a book on Turkish history, and also taken the initiative of founding the Turkish Historical Society (Türk Tarih Kurumu) in 1930.

67 Ersanlı-Behar, *İktidar ve Tarih*, 405–44.

mysticism and Orientalism, the Europeans had not paid sufficient attention to the internal crises that created successive waves of Turkish arrivals to the edges of Europe, which was, in any case, merely an outgrowth of Asia. She described these waves, beginning with the Huns, whose nomadic social structure she disputed (populations settled in urban and rural areas with strong central powers), while she constructed a direct link between the Turko-Huns and Turko-Bulgarians, just as Gavril Krâstevich had done, albeit for different reasons. Interestingly, the model of origins supported the preservation of the imperial structure in one case, and was employed as part of the construction of a national identity in the other.[68]

During the proceedings, Afet İnan faced a serious challenge from Fuad Köprülü.[69] Indeed, her arguments outlined above aimed at countering his objections to her keynote speech. In his first interjection,[70] Köprülü observed that all of Afet İnan's information about the Turks' prehistory and protohistory was drawn from literary sources and was not based on archaeological research. Like the nineteenth-century Balkan historiographers who clashed over the validity of the Byzantine texts, Afet İnan and Köprülü also argued over the value of their respective sources, with the question of empirical verification based on archaeological findings at the center of their dispute.[71]

In his intervention, Köprülü argued that the word "Turk" appeared in Chinese sources in the sixth century, but this did not mean that Turkish states had not existed prior to this. ("A Turkish word that the Chinese wrote as *Tukyu* was given to the name of a Turkish tribe in the sixth century and later as the name of the Turkish state."[72]) Köprülü noted that while museums in Berlin, Paris, London, St. Petersburg, and Beijing had numerous archaeological finds and written sources, both Turkish and Chinese, in their collections, there had been scant research aimed at broadening Turkish history and scant research on the origins of the Turkish language. This observation was important as it cast doubt on the confidence

68 Afet İnan also attacked the Chinese Emperors for their ill treatment of the Turkish people, despite the fact that many of them were of Mongol—that is, of Turkish—origin.

69 For their confrontation during the congress, see also Daldal, "Afet İnan," 234–48.

70 Ersanlı-Behar, *İktidar ve Tarih*, 42–47.

71 Ibid., 129.

72 Ibid., 42.

with which Afet İnan reached her conclusions on the Turks' origins. Furthermore, Köprülü cited various European linguists who had disputed the unity of the Ural-Altaic linguistic branch (a position adopted by Gökalp in *Türkçülüğün Esasları*), in other words, the view that the Finnish and Hungarian languages (Uralic) should be related to the corresponding language of the Turkic peoples of Central Asia (Altaic).[73] This position ran directly counter to both the ideological movement of Pan-Turanism, a splinter of Pan-Turkism that had been substantially weakened in the early years of the Turkish Republic, and the Sun Language Theory (Güneş Dil Teorisi) expressed a few years later (1937), which extend the model of the origin from the race to the language level. Köprülü did not appear to believe that the Indo-European and Semitic languages could be linked to a common origin in an ancient Turkish language.

But the most important aspect of Köprülü's intervention was his direct challenge to the racial definition of "Turk." While he may appear to have been in agreement with Afet İnan here, taking advantage of an ambiguity in her definition of race,[74] he disputed the entire argument of the Turkish nation's theory of origins and saw it as a reaction to blind European racism:

> For the most part, race is an anthropological concept. . . . Language is completely different. Because we know of the existence of races which lost their identities by adopting other languages. Thus, the term "Indo-European" expresses a linguistic category but not a race. It is not anthropological, it is linguistic. But today in most work, a race is understood according to this term, and Indo-European fanaticism has prevailed among European thinkers . . . that this race that includes all European nations is the strongest and the cultural creator of all other [races]. It is a privilege of this race to lead and rule

73 These scholars include the Polish linguist Władysław Kotwicz whose *Contributions aux études altaiques* (1929–30) concluded that Tungusic, one of the Altaic languages, was not related to other tongues in the same family. Conversely, the French linguist Aurélien Sauvageot, in his *Recherches sur le vocabulaire des langues ouralo-altaiques* (1930), supported the existence of a large Ural-Altaic linguistic family even though according to Köprülü he did not adequately develop this argument. See *Birinci Türk Tarih Kongresi*, 43–44.

74 Büşra Ersanlı-Behar correctly noted that this "ambiguity" owes a lot to the influence of the theories of Eugene Pittard on Afet İnan's work. See Ersanlı-Behar, *İktidar ve Tarih*, 129.

humanity. The racial principle that was born with the emergence of European imperialism in the nineteenth century was defended first by French officials, such as de Gobineau,[75] and found many supporters, especially in Germany, where historical works were written based on this theory. But today such a theory of race is not justified. The true and scientific importance of race was determined thanks to the development of either anthropology or social studies. (*Birinci Türk Tarih Kongresi*, 45)

Köprülü, thus, reminded the Congress members that this play had been staged before: the elevation of the Turkish race as the natural and cultural ancestor of humanity was no more than a repetition of the argument of Indo-European origins as fundamental pillar of European (scientific and political) racism.[76] To hammer home his point, Köprülü offered two examples. The first was Mahmud Gaznevi (962–1183), an Anatolian ruler whom Köprülü viewed as indisputably Turkish, but whom Europeans classified as Indo-European. ("Mahmud Gaznevi's work states that he is Turkish, yet, they claim this was the fruit of Arianism; that Mahmud Gaznevi was a ruler with a Persian mentality who tried to express Arianism during a period of Islamic occupation and Turkish thinking!")[77]

The second example involved the character of the Persian Safavid dynasty. European historians considered the founding of the Safavid state as the revival of the Sassanids' ancient empire, a reconstruction of the Persian nation and Indo-European identity. This victory of the spirit of Arianism managed to prevail over the Turkish mentality as expressed by the Seljuks. For Köprülü, a racial approach to Safavid rule as Indo-European

75 It is odd that while challenging the nineteenth-century racist theory, which had found its best advocate in Gobineau, Köprülü neglected to note that this French intellectual made a decisive contribution (*Histoire des Perses*) to re-legitimizing the Persians as the people at the center of the Indo-European branch.

76 In *Aryans and British India*, Thomas R. Trautmann shows how in India's case, the rival schools of Orientalism and racial theory converged in the late nineteenth century, classifying the dark Indians in the sphere of civilized people once they had accepted the fact that they belonged to the large Indo-European linguistic family. An Aryan origin was, thus, cited through racial upgrading. From the moment the relationship between Sanskrit and European languages was discovered, Indians and Britons belonged to the same cultural group. The redefinition of Aryan from a racial to a linguistic framework allowed the blurring of the line between colonizer and colonized.

77 *Birinci Türk Tarih Kongresi*, 45.

was also the result of similar prejudices. On the contrary, Köprülü considered the Safavid Empire "a work of the Turks who use the Turkish language as their mother tongue," exactly like Shah Ismail, who co-founded the state with the Turkmeni Kızılbaş tribes.[78]

For Köprülü, the appropriation of Mahmud Gaznevi or the Safavids by the ideologues of Aryan superiority was scandalous. His argument against appropriations as well as his censuring of Orientalist views like those of Theodor Nöldekecast, the Turkish historian and a defender of the Turkish historical heritage.[79] But while this argumentation legitimized his views at the congress, it was not enough for Köprülü to reverse the direction in which "official" Turkish historiography was moving.

Büşra Ersanlı-Behar described Köprülü's appearance at the First Turkish History Congress as "opposition" (*muhalefet*) to the dominant narrative of Turkish national history.[80] This opposition, however, was not limited to a dispute over the proper methodology for evaluating sources relating to the Turkish past. At stake was whether the Turkish past had its own Middle Ages and whether the Turkish present was familiar with and proud of that medieval period. The model of origins proposed by Afet Inan endangered the continuity model. Köprülü's constant references to Noldeke-type views were meant as a reminder of this: if the link to the Ottoman past was lost, it would be hard for someone to claim it for the Seljuks who constituted the Turks' link to Central Asia.[81]

78 *Birinci Türk Tarih Kongresi*, 45–46. By using the term *Kızılbaş*, Köprülü (like any Turk using this expression) makes a derogatory reference to the Alevi who allied with the Shiite Safavids against the Sunni Ottomans.

79 Aside from his claim that the Seljuk state had been disastrous for history as it marked the decline of classical Islamic civilization, Nöldeke also argued that the Turkish presence in the Middle East was the basic reason for the Crusades.

80 Ersanlı-Behar, *İktidar ve Tarih*, 130.

81 This underscores Ersanlı-Behar's reminder that the publication of Köprülü's *Origins* in Turkish was delayed for forty years.

Chapter VII

Iconoclasts against Iconolaters: Conclusions

1. Imperial Iconolaters and Nationalist Iconoclasts

Concluding his article on Vladimir Solov'ev's critique of Nikolay Danilevsky, Konstantin Leont'ev expressed his awkwardness at being summoned to define Russian views on the global arena of the time, that is, the mid-1880s.[1] Russia was entering the twentieth century with an air of superiority recognized even by its rivals. For Leont'ev, this superiority was fragile. He posed the question: what was Russia in the late nineteenth century, or better yet, what should it become: a new Athens, a new Rome, or a new Macedonia? The glory of Athens lasted just fifty years, from the Battle of Plataea to the death of Pericles (579–529 B.C.). Napoleon III's France and Germany after Bismarck's death seemed to be following this same example. Athens (in Sicily) and France (in Alsace) collapsed because of their failed expansionist policies. Germany also appeared to be moving in the same direction. Russia should not become Athens. It should become Rome. But it should not follow the route set by Alcibiades; it should follow the route of the modern British Empire. On the other hand, Europe viewed Russia more as a new Macedonia than as a new (Third) Rome: an aggressive and slightly primitive power that was ready to embrace and unite under its scepter the Slavic populations of Eastern Europe, just as the Macedonians had once done with the city-states of Southern Greece.

Leont'ev recognized that the truth lay somewhere in the middle. Russia preserved the certain institutions and Orthodox Christianity, which had

1 Solov'ev's believed the schism should be repealed, criticizing Danilevsky's view that Russia should stem the tide of Westernization. See Leont'ev, "Solov'ev protiv Danilevskogo," 510–11.

made the Second Rome one of history's more resilient states. But Pan-Slavism appeared to dispute the element that provided for Russia's continuity with Rome: Orthodoxy's primacy in the structure of imperial ideology.[2]

Leont'ev stated that in all honesty, he could not predict the course of future events. Conditions were reminiscent of Iconoclasm: no one knew who would prevail, Leo III the Isaurian or Theodore the Studite?[3] But Leont'ev hoped the latter would prevail. Like Gedeon, who had realized that Paparrigopoulos's interpretation of Byzantium with a positive approach to Iconoclasm risked the empire's Christian character, Leont'ev also understood that only an "Iconolatric" approach would revive and save Byzantium's spirit.

Calvin's condemnation of the Seventh Ecumenical Council as the work of Satan and his association of the ban on "Idololatric" practices in organizing the ideal Christian (albeit deeply civil) state[4] had created a long tradition in the West where Iconoclasm was not only a metonymy for the (religious) Reformation (Gibbon) but also a prerequisite for the emergence of the modern state (Hegel). In short, the end of the worship of icons (and the empire) marked the start of the worship of the state.

Following the same path as Paparrigopoulos in lauding Iconoclasm would have been difficult for Marin Drinov given the historiographical canon on which he based his rejection of medieval Byzantium. Nonetheless, his attack on Phanariotism was inextricably bound to the rejection of the clergy's leadership role in the Orthodox "Iconolatric" tradition, a position that had been defended by Krâstevich-Balabanov. But the same did not occur with the two historiographers who played what was, as we have seen above, a vital role in reconstructing the Romanian and Turkish historiographical canon of the twentieth century: Köprülü and Iorga.

2. M. Fuad Köprülü: The Iconoclasts as Muslims

Köprülü composed *Bizans müesseselerinin Osmanlı müesseselerine tesiri* in 1931 in response to accusations by İsmail Hakkı Uzunçarşılı, a prominent historian of the interwar period and a member of the Turkish Historical

2 Leont'ev, " Solov'ev protiv Danilevskogo," 510.

3 Leont'ev, "Solov'ev protiv Danilevskogo," 511.

4 Calvin, *Institutes*, book 10: 11: 14.

Society. Uzunçarşılı implied that Köprülü had excessively emphasized the influence of Byzantine institutions on the Ottoman administration.[5] In the meantime, in 1934, he gave a series of lectures in Paris in an attempt to respond to an argument from Gibbon's scientific armory which seemed particularly dangerous: that the Ottoman state's core population in Asia Minor was in its majority comprised of Islamicized inhabitants who were not of Turkish origin. In reality, Gibbons's uncoupled the meanings of "Turk" and "Ottoman."[6] The Ottomans were the result of intermixing Turkish-descended nomads with Anatolia's Islamicized "native" populations (Greeks, Armenians, Laz, etc.).[7]

These two polemics in which Köprülü had become embroiled are crucial for understanding his stance. In response, Köprülü resorted to tried and tested, nineteenth-century historiographical formulations. In order to build a model of continuity, he could not avoid negotiating the Ottoman Middle Ages and, consequently, its relationship to Byzantium. Exactly as the Greek nationalist historiography of the nineteenth century had appropriated Byzantine Empire through its Hellenization, according to Köprülü, Turkish historiography should not allow the complete de-Turkification of the Ottoman Empire, although at the same time, he rejected the Ottoman past.

Köprülü, thus, attempted to follow the type of argument used by Marin Drinov in establishing the Bulgarian people's Slavic origins. Drinov had countered the claim that modern Bulgarians might have been descended from a small Turanic tribe. In the same way, Köprülü had to refute the position that the origins of the Ottoman Empire were to be found in the tents of some four hundred Turkish nomads.[8]

As already seen, Byzantium's influence had to be limited. Referring to the Sassanids was a method that had been tested for various reasons in the nineteenth century (Leont'ev–Gobineau). This point merits special attention. As has been seen, Köprülü chose to respond to Uzunçarşılı through an attack on Rambaud's school of Orientalist Byzantine scholars, and he

5 Behar "Ottoman Empire," 148.

6 Köprülü, *Origins*, 2–13.

7 Decades later, Spyros Vryonis tried to make the same argument in *The Decline of Medieval Hellenism in Asia Minor.*

8 Köprülü, *Origins*, 10, 13, 44.

attempted to reverse the derogatory image they articulated especially with regards to the Seljuk period.

Halil Berktay was one of the first historians to emphasize Köprülü's struggle against the stereotypes of Western Orientalism.[9] Berktay tried to highlight Köprülü's work as an effort to view the Ottoman Empire from a perspective shared with the West, that of feudalism.[10] Approaching Köprülü as the Turkish Marc Bloch, Berktay created a genealogy of Turkish historiography, from the cosmopolitan rebel Yusuf Akçura to the liberal nationalist Köprülü and the statist-nationalist Ömer Lütfi Barkan.[11]

Büşra Ersanlı correctly distanced herself from this analysis, with a reminder of the danger of shifting historical perspective from interpretation to evaluation.[12] But that is not all. If Köprülü sought to equate the Ottoman Empire's historical character with that of the modern Western states, this would constitute one more reason to view his attempt as a formation of a classical model of continuity. Berktay's assertion that Köprülü laid the foundations for the Ottoman Empire's feudal character constitutes a positive evaluation of his work precisely because it placed it in the grand scheme of continuity that Western historiographies had followed based on the theory of progress (ancient slave society, medieval feudalism, capitalist modernity).[13] However, alongside the empire, a way to legitimize its cultural core, religion, was required.

Köprülü understood that in addition to undermining the claim of Byzantine culture's primacy, he had to find a way to describe Islam's role. In order to support the cultural interaction between Byzantium and the Caliphates, he posed a rhetorical question in *Bizans müesseselerinin*: "Is the perception correct of those who claim an Islamic influence in the Iconoclast movement?"

---

9 Berktay, *Cumhuriyet* İdeolojisi, 12–20, and particularly, 22–23.

10 Berktay argued that the construction of Western historiography on feudalism as a *sui generis* socioeconomic system that could not be found anywhere outside Western Europe and with political decimation as its main characteristic did exist at the root of the Orientalist hermeneutical approaches to the Ottoman Empire (as also *sui generis*). Still, it is very interesting that Iorga, who found himself in Köprülü's crosshairs as the main representative of the Orientalist school, also shared the view that medieval feudalism in the West was not much different from that in the East, thus building a model of parity between the West and Byzantium with state centralization as the common denominator.

11 Berktay, "Search for the Peasant," 149.

12 Ersanlı-Behar, *İktidar ve Tarih*, 136.

13 Soviet historiography at the time followed the same route.

Byzantium did not fall to the Iconoclasts, of course, but it did fall to (Ottoman) Islam. Here, too, we must rethink the form of continuity for which Köprülü is attempting to provide a structure. Again, it was Halil Berktay who described this process in detail.

FIG. 1. Köprülü's continuity scheme of the Turkish nation, according to Halil Berktay (Berktay, *Cumhuriyet ideolojisi*, 21).

Arab invasion and Byzantine legacy	}	Arab-Islamic civilization and Ancient Persian legacy	}	Oghuz invasion and Iranian Islamic civilization	}	Great Seljuks
Great Seljuks	→	Anadolu Seljuks and Byzantine Legacy	→	Beyliks	→	Ottoman Empire

According to his description, Köprülü reconstructed two great schemes of continuity which, however, were based on Orientalist models. The first ran in a single line straight from Byzantium to the Ottomans and was faithfully served by Western historiography. The second ran from the Oghuz Turks to the Seljuks and from there to the Ottomans, and it would be sufficient for the defenders of an ethnocentric Turkish historiography (along racial lines, such as that of Afet Inan).[14]

The form Köprülü proposed was dialectical in its inception: two invasions were catalysts in the process of dissolving pre-existing cultural units and the appearance of new ones. The Arab invasion served as a catalyst for the dissolution (or better, the transformation) of Byzantine civilization and as a consequence for the emergence of Arab-Islamic culture. The Oghuz invasion served as a catalyst for the dissolution of the Irano-Islamic civilization leading to the Seljuks' appearance. The Ottomans as heirs of the Seljuks completed what the Arabs had left unfinished: the process of dissolving Byzantium. In this case, Islam became the link between the two processes. If Islam would be connected to Iconoclasm, then the problem appears to have two solutions. When Islam is considered a variation on

14 Ersanlı, however, also praises the "breadth" of Köprülü's vision with regards to his approach to Byzantium, without attempting to place it in a large interpretive framework by establishing a scheme of continuity with Orientalist extensions. See Büsra Ersanlı, "Ottoman Empire," 149.

monophysitism, then it was an "internal" cultural conflict that led to dissolution of Byzantium. But when Iconoclasm is viewed as a result of Islamic aniconic influence, then the same conflict becomes a reflection of the dominant role of Islam. Köprülü appears to have adopted the second alternative.

However, if Islam was necessary for the establishment of a scheme of continuity that transcended the old Orientalist dichotomies, Köprülü was particularly insistent on Byzantium's relationship with the heritage of ancient Persian civilization. The advantages of citing the Sassanids have been noted above. Berktay, however, who highlighted this dimension of Köprülü's work, avoided "censuring" its Orientalist versions. And this is because the image of a liberal thinker opposing the West's Orientalism would be stigmatized. Finally, the model of continuity was even stronger than dialectics.

3. Nicolae Iorga: The Iconoclasts as the Organizers of National Discourse

In the early 1920s, Nicolae Iorga would also face the issue of an interpretive approach to Iconoclasm.[15] A brief summary of his positions is useful for seeing how he built his case for continuity between the Byzantine and Ottoman Empires. Iorga reviewed the theories proposed for interpreting the causes of Iconoclasm, distancing himself from those with a conspiratorial bent. The most widespread theory in the texts of Iconophile writers such as Theophanes and Nikephoros supported the idea of a Jewish conspiracy against the Iconolaters.[16] Iorga doubted a possible Jewish influence on the empire's internal affairs and simultaneously noted that there was no need to seek secret conspiracies in order to explain the start

15 Iorga, *Origines de l'iconoclasme.*

16 According to a prophecy regarding the reign of Caliph Yazid II, a Jewish magus from Tiberias (or Laodicea) named Tessarakontapichus said that his reign would last thirty years if he would destroy all icons and representations of the divine in the Christian churches and censured the idolaters. Yazid II did indeed issue an edict in 721 but died immediately afterwards, in 724.Theophanes and other Iconophile chroniclers perceived his death as justification of the Iconolaters' views of a conspiracy. See Vasiliev, "Iconoclastic Edict," 23–47. The case was also mentioned in the proceedings of the Seventh Ecumenical Council of 787 and presented by presbyter Ioannis of Jerusalem, the representative of the Bishops of the East. See also Grunebaum's analysis "Byzantine Iconoclasm and the Influence of the Islamic Environment." Grunebaum retrospectively justifies Iorga's position that the Iconoclastic tendency was already strong in the Christianity, and it was not necessary to look for its roots in Islam or Judaism.

of the Iconoclastic movement, but rather its explanation was to be found in the weakening of the Christian populations of the Eastern provinces, who were facing demographic decline as a result of growing Arab expansion.[17] Moreover "person-centered" interpretations have been formulated to explain Iconoclasm.[18] However, the role of prominent personalities of the Arab Islamic world and the possible influence of the Paulicians in Asia Minor did not, for Iorga, offer sufficient reasons for the emergence of the Iconoclast movement.

Iorga also kept his distance from an interpretation that was common in the nineteenth century (as we saw in Gedeon, for example) and which had been reproduced by many writers in the early twentieth century: Iconoclasm's interpretation through Leo III's caesaropapist tendencies, his attempts to place the Church and those monasteries that disputed political authority under his control. Leo's caesaropapism was no more than an illusion.[19] On the contrary, Iorga tried to inject a sociological tone into his approach, describing Iconoclasm as the result of the gradual alienation of the Eastern provinces' populations from the center. Resistance on the part of the populations of Egypt, Syria, and Palestine to the "doctrinal centralization" of the "Chalcedoneans" of the Byzantine center as well as the Byzantine administration, which was "almost incomprehensible" to the Bedouins, had gradually rendered them foreign to the empire. Evading heavy taxation was certainly one reason for the mass conversions to Islam, yet Iorga also noted the allure of Islam's victorious dissemination for these populations. Islam appeared as a renewed version of the faith of the humble, and it was easily understood by those who viewed it as a renewed version of Christianity.

But there was also a further dimension. Iorga did not believe that Islam was the exclusive expression of the Arabs' "national" spirit. On the

17 Iorga, *Origines de l'iconoclasme*, 1–2.

18 For example, the supposed effect of Caliph Omar II, Yazid's successor, on his friend Emperor Leo III, whom he called on to destroy "the symbols that are counter to the true spirit of Christianity" (2). This interpretation rests mainly on the work of the Armenian chronicler Ghévond. According to his account, in a letter to Leo, Omar reminded him that it was the saints depicted who deserved the respect of the faithful and not the icon's "wood and colors." By another account, also mentioned by Theophanes, Leo had been influenced by a former Islamic apostate who had been arrested by the Byzantines, reconverted to Christianity, and became the Emperor's advisor.

19 Iorga, *Origines de l'iconoclasme*, 3.

contrary, he saw it as reflecting very ancient expressions of the Syro-Egyptian world, as he dubbed it, which influenced the development of the corresponding Arab-Islamic civilization. For him, this was the reason the Byzantine Empire's dissenters so easily assimilated Paulicians, Manicheans, and other expressers of the aniconic tradition, along with the heirs of Persian Mazdaism. These undercurrents in the Near East were the basis for official Iconoclasm. In this context, the importance of Leo III's Syrian origins should not be underestimated. This observation should be linked to Iorga's claim that Leo's policies did not exhibit caesaropapism. Leo III's iconomachic choices stemmed from deeper cultural underpinnings than a desire for the Church's subjugation by the state.[20]

We, thus, observe that Iorga used a similar argument, albeit in reverse, from the one employed by Köprülü later on. Just as Köprülü uses the reference to the Sassanids as an added influence, not denying the Byzantine contribution to shaping the Ottoman Empire (the Abbasids and Umayyads were not sufficient, despite Berktay's claims), Iorga cited the pre-Islamic cultural heritage of the Near and Middle East to mitigate the Islamic contribution to the emergence of Iconoclasm.

Iorga viewed the "dissenters" sympathetically, not unlike Paparrigopoulos' claim that reaction to monasticism's increasingly powerful place in Byzantine society was justified. But unlike the Greek historian who saw the Iconoclastic movement as an imperial choice for Reformation, Iorga insisted that it was a reaction by the lower social classes and by large landowners who saw their social status threatened by the unrestricted growth of monastic possessions. This, however, did not meant that Iorga overlooked the Iconoclast emperors' autocratic behavior. Although he absolved Leo III from the charge of caesaropapism, he recognized that the Iconoclast emperors, particularly in the tenth century, were excellent warriors. Yet, he could not forget whether the destruction of the icons had been as violent as the destruction of Catholic symbols by the Protestant reformers.[21] Like Paparrigopoulos, Iorga also compared Iconoclasm with the Reformation. He did not do this to praise attempts at civil reform before civil society had emerged but as a reminder of the violence of the

20 Ibid., 7.
21 Ibid., 8.

emperors chosen as political representatives of his favored "dissenters" of the East. Iorga would recall Paparrigopoulos (and Gibbon), drawing a parallel between Iconoclasm and the Protestant Reformation, but, like Zambelios, he would draw a distinction between the (dissident) People and the (violent) Monarchy.

A closer examination of this point is necessary here. Iorga's sympathy for the "dissenters" led him to make a number of comparisons. First, he brought to mind the monasteries' parasitic role in Romanian history, a reminder that may have been decisive for his approach to Iconoclasm. But Iorga went a step further. He drew historical comparisons between two other similar cases, comparing Byzantium's Iconoclast emperors with the reformist Habsburg emperors of the late eighteenth and early nineteenth centuries and the Chinese Emperors from the sixth to the ninth centuries. Here, however, his criterion was not social conduct, but the choices made by the political authorities.

The Habsburgs behaved harshly towards the Orthodox populations of Transylvania and Bukovina, inspired by the eighteenth-century centralist spirit of "enlightened monarchy." This was not aimed at their conversion to Catholicism; the Habsburgs themselves did not enjoy a good relationship with Rome. Rather the Habsburgs aimed at assimilating the Orthodox into the Uniate Church.[22]

The Chinese Emperors initiated a long persecution of the Buddhists in the fourth century that peaked (according to Iorga) with the dominance of Confucianist "Taoism" in the ninth century. In 849, some forty-five thousand Buddhist temples were destroyed, while oppressive measures were enforced similar to those suffered by their Byzantine counterparts a century later under the Isaurians.[23]

There was a paradox inherent to these comparisons, especially those between Maria Theresia and Joseph II with Leo III and Constantine V. The Habsburgs' persecutions, especially in Transylvania, targeted the core of what Iorga later described as "Byzantium after Byzantium," the Orthodox monasteries. The Orthodox monasteries in the broader Romanian space, those dedicated to the Orthodox Patriarchates of the East,

---

22 Ibid., 8–9.

23 Ibid., 10–12.

Mount Athos, the Sinai monastery and Meteora, constituted a living representation of the Byzantine heritage. Iorga carried out a delicate balancing act with regard to this point: he was not charmed simply by the post-Byzantine heritage but also by the secularization process which in the nineteenth century led to the seizure of monasteries. This was a process inspired by the 1789 French Revolution as much as by the enlightened Habsburgs' tough anti-Orthodox policies.

Iorga began his argumentation on this point with an historical analysis of the cause of Iconoclasm, an analysis that aimed to be objective in identifying neither with the Iconoclasts nor the Iconolaters but distinguished between Iconoclasm's social foundation and its political direction. He understood the autocratic characteristics of the Iconoclasts' political direction through comparisons with the Habsburgs (who, of course, were of greater interest to him) and the Chinese Emperors. This allowed him to view the Habsburgs' enlightenment project of limiting the role of religion in a modern secularized state with a measure of irony. Iorga paradoxically launched his argument with the "dissenting" Iconoclasts in order to conclude it with the "dissenting" Orthodox. In Transylvania, the dissenters were Orthodox and, in fact, Romanian. Iorga, thus, salvaged the essence of Eastern Romanity, Orthodoxy, which later became the basis for *Byzantium after Byzantium*.

Iorga was sympathetic to the "dissenters" precisely because he wanted to organize the era of the nation-state along a clash with an Empire with hybrid characteristics (traditional and modern). Köprülü wanted to organize the time of the nation-state along the lines of a reconciliation with the past of a traditional empire. The perspective from which they viewed Byzantium should not allow us to forget that they both based the final tone of their respective arguments on their interpretations of Iconoclasm. From the moment that both, for different reasons, effectively accepted the continuity of the Byzantine and Ottoman Empires, one would expect that their views of Iconoclasm would approximate those expressed by Gedeon. But, paradoxically, the opposite was the case.

Both Iorga and Köprülü adopted a friendly stance toward the Iconoclasts, just as Paparrigopoulos had done. Iorga because he believed the Iconoclasts opposed the center's tight controls, Köprülü because he believed Iconoclasm emerged from the indisputable influence of Islam. It is certain that Paparrigopoulos would not have concurred with either of these positions. But in all three cases, Iconoclasm as internal critique of the (Byzantine) Empire worked as a counterweight metonymy to (modern) empires: in Paparrigopoulos, at a moment when the (Greek) nation state was to adopt the types of reforms implemented by the (Ottoman) Empire (competitively); in Iorga at a moment when the (Romanian) nation-state had to complete itself territorially at the expense of the old (Habsburg) Empire (dismissively); and in Köprülü, at a moment when the (Turkish) nation-state had to reaffirm the structure of continuity that would reconcile it with its (Ottoman) imperial past (approvingly).

4. The Icon as the Hegemon's Representation

The following story about Saint John of Damascus (John Damascene) is quite well known: the Arab writer recreated his severed hand restored by a divine miracle—a punishment imposed by the Caliph of Syria Oualid for whom John was the consultant and after defamatory advice of the Iconoclast Emperor Leo III—as a third arm on the icon of the Virgin Hodegetria. The latter was transformed to Virgin Tricherousa. The icon of the Tricheroussa (Three-Handed Virgin) was moved from the Holy Lavra of Saint Sabbas in Palestine to the Hilandar Monastery on Mount Athos by Saint Sava, the patron saint of the Serbs. *Trojeručica* became an iconographical type particularly popular not only among the Serbs but generally among the Slavs of Eastern Europe. The symbolic expression of the trinity in its move from East to West would paradoxically become the imperial dreams of those who were the object of the Byzantine civilizing process.

Nonetheless, John of Damascus's work[24] has prompted contradictory interpretations of what is, in fact, an icon. Is an icon characterized by a substantial difference between the materials used and the person being depicted? Or does it represent the continuous presence of the Hegemon's

24 "If the image of the king is the king, the image of Christ is Christ, and the image of a saint the saint, and if power is not divided nor glory distributed, honouring the image becomes honouring the one who is set forth in image. Devils have feared the saints, and have fled from their shadow. The shadow is an image, and I make an image that I may scare demons." Or elsewhere "An image is a likeness of the original with a certain difference, for it is not an exact reproduction of the original" (John of Damascus, *Apologia of St John of Damascus*).

body in the space and time of the subjects and is it one of the foundations of his power? For John of Damascus, such a contradiction did not arise. The "difference" to which he referred was represented with two examples: it was the difference between the person of the Father and that of the Son,[25] the difference between God and Man.[26] In both cases, however, the icon suggested differences within the same substance (*homoousios*). The world of an Iconolater perceived the social relation composed not as otherness but as substance, which needs the Trinitarian scheme to ratify the relationship of the two *homoousios* persons through a third.

By contrast, Iconoclasm captivated those who wanted to compile a national historiography during the nineteenth and twentieth centuries because it suggested a fundamental moment of alienation distinct from a period when the earthly world was the mirror of the heavens and identified with the emperor's political body. This was the springboard for secularization and, at the same time, the point of distancing from the empire. Iconoclasm was the worship of the modern state; Iconolatry was the disengagement from state patriotism.

The discussion of Iconoclasm in reality reflected the duality and contradictory relationship between nation and state. And here, perhaps someone can trace the emergence of the latent clash between the model of origin and the model of continuity as it was described in most of the Balkan historiographies. The nation was formed on the model of "difference" (from other nations) that corresponds with the distance separating the icon/depiction from the depicted. But if the nation was a creation of state will, then it was the state that must speak in its name and the icon that must depict the state, the ruling power, and not the cultural difference.

The empire of the Iconolaters claimed the identification of the world with its representation. On the contrary the nation-state of the Iconoclasts, at the moment of its formation, debunked this relationship. This

25 "Thus, the Son is the living, substantial, unchangeable Image of the invisible God (Col. 1.15), bearing in Himself the whole Father, being in all things equal to Him, differing only in being begotten by the Father, who is the Begetter; the Son is begotten" (Ibid).

26 "I do not adore creation more than the Creator, but I adore the creature created as I am, adopting creation freely and spontaneously that He might elevate our nature and make us partakers of His divine nature. Together with my Lord and King I worship Him clothed in the flesh, not as if it were a garment or He constituted a fourth person of the Trinity—God forbid" (Ibid).

did not mean that it would not adopt its own symbols or that it would not produce a series of representations that would serve as indicators of the "discovery"/manufacture of its subjects' "national character." But this process was based on acceptance of the principle of rationalization, and this was inextricably linked to the principle of secularization. The reference to Iconoclasm cannot but have been a note of demystification of the past at the time when it acquired a linear and evolutionary character in its narrative that describes the nation's course.

5. Historiographical Divergences and the Empire's Memory

The divergences we examined in three different instances of Balkan national historiographies—Greek, Bulgarian, Albanian—and their metatheoretical heritage—Romanian, Turkish—seem to have destabilized the continuity structures on which the latter (the historiographies) were based. The historiographical divergences were not necessarily founded on discontinuities that every national historiography recognized—the medieval Slavic and Albanian settlements in the Greek, the oblivion of the medieval kingdoms in the Bulgarian, the gap separating Skënderbeu and the Frashëri brothers in the Albanian. But discontinuity certainly played a pivotal role in the national historiographies' emergence. Discontinuities referenced Historicism's scientific methodology as long as they obliged the historiographers to manage them by narrating their continuity schemes with logical cohesion; divergences were produced by the shadow cast by the empire of the *fin de siècle*, an historical possibility of the nation's survival in broader imperial entities. However, the former was feeding the latter.

Unavoidably, discontinuities and divergences were defined by the Orientalism-Occidentalism dipole. Discontinuities surfaced under the pressures of a nation's recognition by the West, and if the nation wished to be included in the Western imaginary, it had to continuously recognize its shortcomings in relation to the Western canon. Conversely, divergences were produced the moment that the continental empires of Eastern Europe emerged on the scene as equal players at the level of organizing the collective imaginary. Divergences produced new forms of continuity that were legitimizing for empires; they did not reject the nation, but they constrained it in the dominant paradigm of empire's unity and continuous reform which, in any case, the West did whatever it could to make comprehensible to the peoples of the East. In other words, the anti-Western arguments appeared when segments of the East joined the West.

On each occasion, the national historiographical canon tried to resolve specific problems, but one most of all: establishing the West's recognition of the nation and the introduction of the nation into the realm of "civilized" states. Paparrigopoulos assigned the task of legitimization to the West, with the French Academy playing the significant albeit risky role described earlier; Drinov assigned the task to Russia, and Frashëri assigned it to the Great Powers.

The historiographical approach that sought to legitimize the imperial perspective in reality activated the rift of discontinuities that might be considered the weakness of any historical national narrative to conclude, once and for all, the issue of its internal cohesion.

While seeking to adopt an imperial perspective, the "divergent" writers could not easily overcome the problem of the nation's legitimization. They were, therefore, forced to move in a landscape that was strictly defined by the basic axes of the national historiographical canon.

Gedeon responded to Paparrigopoulos's cultural criterion for reading Byzantium by adopting a type of cultural "anti-critique," juxtaposing the Iconolaters to the Iconoclasts and the anti-Unionists to the Unionists.

Krâstevich, in the theory of origin according to which the Bulgarians were members of the large Slavic family, contrasted another theory of origin that might include the Bulgarians in the Orient but simultaneously set different foundations for discussing a possible break from the Ottoman framework.

Sami, although he had constructed the model of cultural continuity with Islam as the bridge between Ancient Greece and Western Europe, finally replaced it with another one: the model of national continuity.

All appropriated the canon's code to achieve divergence. But when they attempted this, they activated what we called a rift—that is, a rift in the narrative's consistency—and created a latent tension between the two components of a theoretically uniform and homogenized model; origin and continuity became polarized and ended up comprising different interpretative narratives of the nation's historical formation.

To solve the problem of Byzantium's nature, Gedeon supplanted the continuity of nation with the continuity of the Byzantine and Ottoman empires. To solve the problem of compatibility of national and imperial, Krâstevich was ultimately forced to admit that his Huns were Slavs. To adopt the form of continuity of nation, Sami was to deny the dominant role of religion. Although in his case, this divergence (imperial choice) came before, or rather alongside, the canon's formation (national choice), one cannot but observe that the cost of abandoning Islam as continuity's connective tissue could only be managed by adopting a hyper-interpretative theory of origin. Thus, as Pelasgians, the Albanians could be compared only to Rakovski's Bulgarian Arians.

All resorted to the solution of what we described as Romantic reconstruction, which was proposed by Leont'ev's paradigmatic version of Byzantism. Not all offered equally satisfactory responses. Contrary to the intelligentsia of the "center" (Leont'ev), who proposed a common denominator where the two rival imperial discourses (Ottoman and Russian) could converge in the imperial hybrid that was both modern and traditional, the intelligentsia of the periphery (Balabanov) was faced with a schizophrenic situation. Balabanov served the same political aim, or at least did so until assuming specific roles within the national framework, but he could not provide a satisfactory legitimization of his political actions. He, thus, remained stuck at the level of theoretical comparison without being able to advance to a (Romantic) reconstruction of the national and imperial, as Leont'ev was to do at about the same moment.

The management of this problem involved an interpretation of the Middle Ages and their relationship with Antiquity. Approaches to Byzantium were central. The writers were compelled to take a position because the West had already posed the question of the Byzantine Middle Ages from an orientalist point of view. Aside from an argument made by conservative supporters of the monarchy in Europe, Byzantium stood for a special dominance of the Roman West over the semi-barbarian East. Byzantium constituted a bulwark against the barbarian raids and at the same time an underrated model of autocratic socio-political organization.

The "cultural" Orientalism of the early nineteenth century differed of course from the Orientalism combined with racial theory of the late nineteenth and early twentieth centuries. Byzantium's engulfment by the West allowed Paparrigopoulos to adopt a reading that inserted the Greek case into the Western canon (with the main argument that Iconoclasm heralded the Reformation). Conversely, Orientalism's racial variants favored the adoption of historical discourses focused on origins. The construction of the Bulgarian "medieval antiquity" as Slavic forced Drinov to view Byzantium as Greek and classify Paisius as a reference point for the entire Bulgarian renaissance. Similarly, abandoning the Islamic Middle Ages and replacing them with Skënderbeu forced Sami to view Byzantium as Roman. Drinov nationalized Byzantium because this legitimized the continuity from the medieval Bulgarian kingdoms to his contemporary Bulgarians. The medieval disputes were reignited in the nineteenth century. Sami de-nationalized Byzantium because its heritage could not be handed over exclusively to the Greeks. Of course, these differences in approach were not only differences of perspective but also temporality: at the time of Drinov's writings, the border of the Greek state was the Ambracian Gulf, while at the time of Sami's writings, the border of the Greek state had reached Mount Olympus.

During this same period, A. D. Xenopol shaped the canon of Romanian national historiography. The Latinized Daco-Getae never abandoned the Danube's northern banks but could not avoid the influence of Slavicization. Roesler (that is, Xenopol's Fallmerayer) allowed him to create a continuity scheme but one in which the Middle Ages were not a prelude to the Romanian nation's induction into the West—as was the case with Paparrigopoulos, who did not accept the Slavicization of the Greek Byzantine populations. The Daco-Getae's national identity was shaped in antiquity based on the influence of the First Rome, but their "slavicized" and also "dark" Middle Ages hampered their historical destiny.

Also around this time, and especially after the Young Turk Revolution, Turkish national identity rejected its medieval Ottoman period (Ziya Gökalp) and sought legitimization in its Central Asian past (Ayşe Afet İnan). This tendency was crystallized at the first Turkish History Conference, which adopted the old solution of a hyper-interpretive theory of origins to induct Turkey into the West by diving into a mythical, pre-Arian this time, East.

In neither the Romanian nor the Turkish instances were there any historiographical divergences of the type described with respect to other Balkan historiographies because the imperial perspective had been eclipsed or permanently delegitimized. Nonetheless, it is obvious that these two historiographies were built on weak solutions from earlier periods. Simply put, the structures of origin based on an idealized antiquity that had been chosen were obviously incapable of resolving the question of continuity. The five centuries separating the Daco-Getae from the appearance of the Vlachs in the written sources and the seven more centuries of the Ottoman Empire's dominance could not be brushed aside so easily. And without a resolution to the problem of the Middle Ages, there could not be a credible structure positing continuity.

In both the Romanian and the Turkish cases, the solution was sought in the ways in which the Byzantine period was managed. Nicolae Iorga solved the problem of Slavic influences by shifting the center of gravity from the First Rome to the Second Rome. Byzantium was not simply necessary for survival in an era when the Moldo-Wallachian rulers were subordinated to the Ottomans, but because it constituted a cultural paradigm that was never subjugated to the Slavs. On the contrary, Byzantium had a decisive influence on the Slavic world, which it inducted into its own cultural sphere. Linking the Romanians to Byzantium's Romans, therefore, was infinitely more useful than linking the Romanians to Rome's Romans. This suggests the true political content of his *Byzance après Byzance* thesis: if the Romanians were recipients of the great Byzantine cultural heritage, then they were untouched by the consequences of the Slavic flood. The Romanian Middle Ages acquired a radically different connotation, the negative being transformed into a positive.

The imperial perspective appeared legitimized anew by Iorga, hence the references to Eastern Romanity. A secret undercurrent connecting him to nineteenth-century divergent writers, especially on the issue of the continuity of the Byzantine and Ottoman Empires, might be posited. And yet, this would not completely correct: Iorga reconstructed the scheme of national continuity because his "imperial" reference was not to the traditional dissolved Southeastern European empires but to the imperial Orientalist discourses of the colonial empires (in which the French Academy once again played a leading role, albeit for reasons different than those that concerned Paparrigopoulos).

In Turkish historiography, Byzantium had been delegitimized because it was precisely the model on which the Ottoman Empire had been built.

In order for Köprülü to resolve the continuity problem—that is, to create distance from the dominance of the form of origins—he had to prove that Byzantium had not been a model for the Ottomans. Iorga's Romanians emerged as Byzantium's heirs; Köprülü's Ottomans had to do everything to prove the opposite. Köprülü took a critical stance towards the Second Rome in order to distance himself from a racial reading of Turkish history. This did not automatically imply a rejection of Byzantium. Köprülü's true adversary was not Afet Inan's hyper-interpretative origin theory but a body of institutionalized Western knowledge of Byzantium that sought new ways to subordinate the East culturally.

All the divergences in the late nineteenth century emerged as peripheral narratives for legitimizing the empire. The pivotal question raised regarding the relationship between canon and divergence is the degree to which the latter had a decisive role in legitimizing the former. Or rather, at what point in a nation's development was divergence's assimilation of the canon functional.

This is a difficult question to answer, and it requires further research, although we can formulate some basic hypotheses. In Gedeon's case, for example, the approach condemning Iconoclast Byzantium seems to have prevailed over Paparrigopoulos's suggestion of an Eastern Middle Ages that gestated what emerged in the West from the fifteenth century onward. This adaptation of the national historiographical canon appears to correspond to a progressive assimilation/subordination of the religious by the national. Gedeon's intervention, however, contributed to the dominance of an evolved interpretative construction for the relationship between Modern Hellenism and Byzantium—a construction whose seeds were also sown by Paparrigopoulos's work, but which acquired greater clarity in the work of Spyridon Lambros and, even more, of Apostolos Vakalopoulos. Modern Hellenism emerged from the ruins of the Byzantine Empire between the two falls of Constantinople. From 1204 to 1453, the neo-Hellenic national identity was constructed as a clash—or, in Marxist Nikos Svoronos's version, an act of resistance—against the Catholic West and the Ottoman East. The ethnogenetic process was placed precisely in the late Middle Ages, following a sort of resolution of the "historicity" of the nation that was particularly common in Western historiography. At the time, Gedeon's scheme when it had been formulated concerned the vital issue of the empire's survival. However, it was to become compatible with the national historiographical canon at that moment when it was able to provide arguments for a balanced relationship between the nation and the West, even if this meant a small divergence from the ideals of the Byzantine East.

Something similar occurred with Gavril Krâstevich's "Hunnic" divergence. It took roughly a century for the Proto-Bulgarian past (along with the Thracian) to be assimilated as a fundamental element of modern Bulgarian ethnic identity. Of course, several historians such as the "Thracologists" Wilhelm Tomaschek, Dimitâr Dechev, and even Gyula Moravcsik had adopted similar positions before Duychev. But perhaps it was not coincidental that these views rebounded dynamically at the end of World War I with the publication of Vasil N Zlatarski's three-volume *Istoriya na Bâlgarskata dârzhava prez srednite vekov*. A revisionist Bulgaria and the Russian Empire's collapse composed the political framework for the emergence of a different management of Bulgaria's "medieval antiquity," an antiquity which if did not disconnect from the variable of Slavic origin, it would relativize it. This effort may not have endured, but it did create the prerequisites for reshaping the national historiographical canon in a period when the Marxist model in Bulgarian historiography seemed all-encompassing.

Perhaps this management of the imperial past only lacked a visible consequence for the reconstruction of the national historiographical canon in Frashëri's case. This, however, can easily be explained through the simultaneous development of a discourse about nation where the hyper-interpretative dimension of Pelasgian origins corresponded to the cultural dominance of the Islamic Ummah. Finally, with regard to the historiography of the twentieth century, it may be superfluous to make detailed mention of the Romanian and Turkish cases. Iorga and Köprülü took on the task of historiographical orientation in a fundamental and self-conscious manner. But it is worth noting the endeavor's timing—interwar Romania in one instance and postwar Turkey in the other—and its final success. Iorga's form prevailed quite easily, although we should not overlook criticisms by historians such as Andrei Pippidi.[27] By contrast, Köprülü's adaptation of Turkish historiography remains at stake, although the growth of Ottoman Studies outside Turkey has favored the prevalence of at least one version of it.

27 Pippidi, *Tradiția politică bizantină*.

Bibliography

I. Unpublished archival sources

Genika Archeia tou Kratous (GAK) [General State Archives]. Manuel I. Gedeon Archive (Samos).

Elliniko Logotechniko kai Istoriko Archeio (ELIA) [Greek Literary and Historical Archive]. Manuel I. Gedeon Archive (Athens).

Başbakanlık Devlet Arşivleri – Genel Müdürlüğü (BDA-GM) [State Archive of the Office of the Prime Minister, General Administration] (Istanbul).
Y.PRK.ZB: File 3, Folder 17
Y.A.HUS: File 183, Folders 44, 127
Y.PRK.ASK: File 68, Foldern 43

Bâlgarska Akademiya na Naukite (BAN) [Bulgarian Academy of Sciences]. (Sofia).
File 26: Marko Dimitrov Balabanov (1837–1921)
File 144: Symeon, Metropolitan of Varna and Preslav (Odysseus Popnikolov, 1840–1937).

Narodna Biblioteka Kiril i Metodiy – Bâlgarski Istoricheski Arhiv (NBKM–BIA) [Cyril and Methodius National Library, Bulgarian Historical Archive]. (Sofia).
File 386: Marko Dimitrov Balabanov.

II. Published archival sources

Protokoli na Bâlgarski naroden sâbor v Tsarigrad prez 1871 [Proceedings of the Bulgarian National Assembly in Constantinople in 1871]. Sofia: Izd. Sv. Sinod na Bâlgarska Tsârkva, 1911.

Birinci Türk Tarih Kongresi [First congress on Turkish history]. Ankara: T. C. Maarif Vekâleti, 1932.

İkinci Türk Tarih Kongresi [Second Congress on Turkish History]. Istanbul: Kenan Matbaasi 1943.

III. Journals and Newspapers

Chitalishte. Istanbul, 1870–1874.

Ecclesiastiki Alitheia. Istanbul, 1880–1922.

Neologos. Istanbul, 1866–1897.

Pandora. Athens, 1849–1857.
Periodikon Ellinikou Filologikou Syllogou Konstantinoupoleos. Istanbul, 1861–1920.
Journal des débats politiques et littéraires. Paris, 1850–1853.
Revue des Deux Mondes. Paris, 1850–1858.
Vek. Istanbul, 1874–1876.

IV. Primary Sources

Afet İnan, Ayşe. *Aperçu général sur l'histoire economique de l'Empire Turc-Ottoman*. Istanbul: Türk Tarih Kurumu Yayınları, 1976.

———. *Türkiye Halkının Antropolojik Karakterleri ve Türkiye Tarihi* [Anthropological characteristics of the Turkish people and Turkish history], Türk Irkının Vatanı Anadolu (64.000 kişi üzerinde anket). Ankara: TTK Basımevi, 1947. First published as *L'Anatolie, le pays de la "race" turque: recherches sur les caractères anthropologiques des populations de la Turquie (Enquêtes sur 64.000 indivus)*. Preface by M. Eugène Pittard. Geneva: Publications de la Faculté des Sciences Économiques et Sociales de l'Université de Gèneve–Georg & Cie S. A., 1941.

Akçura, Yusuf. *Osmanlı Devletinin Dağilma Devri (XVII. ve XIX. Asırlada)* [The Ottoman State's age of dissolution, 18th–19th centuries]. Istanbul: Maarif Matbaası, 1940.

———. Üç *tarz-ı siyaset* [Three principles of politics]. Ankara: Türk Tarih Kurumu Basımevi, 1991 (1904).

Altay, Koymen Mehmed. *Büyük Selçuklu İmparatorluğu Tarihi* [History of the empire of the great Seljuks]. 5 vols. Ankara: Türk Tarih Kurumu Yayınları, 1991.

Anonymous. *Lettre d'un pieux orthodoxe russe au Patriarche Oecumenique sur l'action systématique poursuivie en russie contre les* églises *orthodoxes de l'orient*. Athens: Etaireia O Ellinismos. Imprimerie Anestis Constantinidis, 1899.

Balabanov, Marko. *Bâlgarskata Koloniya v Edin Ostrov* [A Bulgarian community on an island]. Sofia: Dârzhavna Pechatnica, 1910.

———. "Borbata mezhdu Gârtsi i Bâlgari." *Vek*, February 22, 1875.

———. *Filosofski i sotsiologicheski sâchinenia* [Philosophical and sociological essays]. Edited by Mihail Bâčvarov. Sofia: Izd. Nauka i Izkustvo, 1986.

———. *Gavril Krâstevich (naroden deec, knizhovnik, sâdija, upravitel)* [Gavril Krâstevich: National politician, writer, judge, administrator]. Sofia: Izd. Sv. Sinod na Bâlgarska Cârvka, 1914.

———. *Shto e Narodnost?* [What is nation?]. Sofia, 1888.

———. *Stranica ot Politicheskoto ni Vâzrazhdane* [A page from our political renaissance]. Sofia: Proshekov, 1904.

———. "Trite shkoli i napredâkât" [The three schools and progress]. In *Filosofski i sotsiologicheski sâchinenia* [Philosophical and sociological essays], edited by Mihail Bâchvarov, 86–94. Sofia: Izd. Nauka i Izkustvo, 1986.

Beron, Petâr. *Origine de l'unique couple humaine: Dispersion de Ses Descendants*. 7 vols. Paris: Gauthier-Villars, 1864.

———. *Panépistème, ou Ensemble des sciences physiques et naturelles et des sciences métaphysiques et morales, devenu possible par la découverte de l'origine du mouvement et de l'affinité*. 8 vols. Paris: Gauthier-Villars, 1864–1870.

———. *Slavyanska Filosofiya* [Slavic philosophy]. Sofia: Marin Drinov, 2000.

Boué, Ami. *La Turquie d'Europe, ou, Observations sur la géographie, la géologie, l'histoire naturelle, la statistique, les moeurs, les coutumes, l'archéologie, l'agriculture, l'industrie, le commerce, les gouvernements divers, le clergé, l'histoire et le'état politique de cet Empire.* 4 vols. Paris: A. Bertrand, 1840.

Burmov, Aleksandâr. "Marin Drinov kato istorik na Bulgariya" [Marin Drinov as historian of Bulgaria]. In *Izsledvaniya v chest na Marin S. Drinov* [Essays in honor of Marin Drinov]. Sofia: Izd. na Bâlgarskata Akademiya na naukite, 1960.

Burmov, Todor S. *Bâlgaro–grâchka tsârkovna raspra* [The Bulgarian–Greek Church conflict]. Sofia: Izd. Sv. Sinod na Bâlgarska Tsârkva, 1902.

———. "Brachko obyasnenie na Bâlgarin kâm bratyata mu Bâlgare" [A brotherly explanation of a Bulgarian to his brother Bulgarians]. Bucharest, 1876.

Calvin, John. *Institutes of the Christian Religion.* Philadelphia: Presbyterian Board of Christian Education, 1936.

Chamoudopoulos, Minas, and Christos Chamoudopoulos. *Istoria tis Othomanikis Aftokratorias* [History of the Ottoman Empire]. Vol. 1. Smyrna: Typois Proodou, 1874.

Christovasilis, Christos. *Ipeiros kai Alvania: politiki pragmateia* [Epirus and Albania: a political treatise]. Athens: Ek tou Typografeiou ton katastimaton Anesti Konstantinidou, 1904.

Collas, Louis Charles. *Histoire de l'Empire Ottoman et Coup d'Oeil sur la Turquie Actuelle.* Paris: Germer Baillière et cie, [1880].

Corrispondenza del Cavaliere Andrea Mustoxidi col suo amico Andrea Papadopulo Creto. Athens: Nella stamperia di G. Angelopulo, 1860.

Damascene, Ioannis (John of Damascus). *Apologia of St John of Damascus Against Those Who Decry Holy Images.* London: Thomas Baker, 1898.

de Gobineau, Arthur. *Histoire des Perses: d'après les auteurs orientaux, grecs et latins et particulièrement d'après les manuscrits orientaux inédits.* 2 vols. Paris, 1869.

de Guignes, Joseph. *Histoire générale des Huns, des Turcs, des Mogols, et des autres Tartares occidentaux, &c. avant et depuis Jesus-Christ jusqu'à present: précédée d'une introduction contenant des tables chronol. & historiques des princes qui ont regné dans l'Asie.* 4 vols. Paris: Desaint & Saillant, 1756–58.

Diehl, Charles. *Byzance: Grandeur et décadence.* Paris: Flammarion, 1919.

———. *Histoire de l'Empire Byzantin.* Paris: A. Picard, 1920

Dimopoulos, Charilaos. *Epitheorisis ton Anatolikon Ethnon. Istoriki Synopsis kai Ithiki kai Politiki Katastasi* [Review of eastern nations. Historical overview and moral and political conditions]. Vol. 1. Bucharest: Typois Theatou, 1863.

———. *Istoria ton Voulgaron: Meta tis dianoitikis kai ithikis katastaseos kai tis politikis afton theseos en ti Anatoli; Defteron meros tis Epitheoriseos ton Anatolikon Ethnon* [History of the Bulgarians: Including their intellectual and moral conditions and their political position in the East; second part of the review of Eastern nations]. Brăila, 1866.

Dorotheos of Monemvasia. *Vivlion istorikon periehon en synopsi diaforous kai exohous istorias: archomenon apo ktiseos kosmou, mechri tis aloseos Konstantinopouleos, kai ton akolouthon Soultanon* [History book with a synopsis of events and extraordinary stories: From the beginning of the world until the fall of Constantinople and the Sultans who followed]. Venice: Para Nikolaou Glykei to ex Ioanninon, 1798.

Driault, Édouard. *La Grande Idée: La renaissance de l'hellénisme.* Paris: Librairie Félix Alcan, 1920.

Drinov, Marin S. "Hunni li sme? Po povod na Istoriya Bâlgarska sochinena ot Gavril Krâstovich. čast I, Tsarigrad 1871" [Are we Huns? With regard to Gavril Krâstevich's *Bulgarian History,* part 1, Istanbul]. In *Sâchinenia na M.S. Drlnov* [Writings of M. S. Drinov]. Vol. 3, edited by V. N. Zlatarski, 189–217. Sofia: Dârzhavna Pechatnica, 1909.

———. "Istoricheski Pregled na Bâlgarska Tsârkva" (1869) [Historical research on the Bulgarian Church]. In *Izbrani Sâchinenia* [Selected writings]. Vol. 2, edited by Ivan Duychev, 9–165. Sofia: Naouka i izkustvo, 1971.

———. "Otec Paisi, negovoto vreme, negovata istoriya i uchenitsite mu" [Father Paisius, his era, his story, and his students]. *Periodichesko Spisanie* 1, no. 4 (1871): 3–25. In Marin Drinov, *Izbrani Sâchinenia* [Selected writings]. Vol. 1, edited by Ivan Duychev, 163–85. Sofia: Naouka i izkustvo, 1971.

———. "Pogled vârhu proizhozhdaneto na bâlgarskiya narod i nachaloto na bâlgarskata istoriya" (1869) [A look into the origins of the Bulgarian people and the beginnings of Bulgarian history]. In *Sâchinenia na M. S. Drinov* [Writings by M. S. Drinov], edited by V. N. Zlatarski, vol. 1, 1–69. Sofia: Dârzhavna Pechatnica, 1909.

———. "Zaselenie Balkanskogo Poluostrova Slavyanami" [Slavic settlements in the Balkan Peninsula] (1872). In *Sâchinenia na M.S. Drlnov* [Writings of M. S. Drinov]. edited by V. N. Zlatarski, vol. 1, 139–316. Sofia: Dârzhavna Pechatnica, 1909.

Droysen, Johann Gustav. *Geschichte Alexanders des Grossen.* Berlin: Verlegt bei G. Finke, 1833.

———. *Geschichte des Hellenismus.* Hamburg: Bei Friedrich Perthes, 1836–43.

Engel, Johann Christian von. *Commentatio de expeditionibus Traiani ad Danubium, et origine Valachorum.* Vienna, 1794.

———. *Geschichte der Moldau und Walachei.* Halle, 1804.

———. *Geschichte des ungarischen Reichs und seiner Nebenländer.* Vol I, *Bulgarien, Pannonien.* Halle, 1797.

———. *Geschichte von Bulgarien.* Vienna, 1796.

Freeman, Edward Augustus. *Oi Tourkoi en Evropi. Pragmateia* [The Turks in Europe: A treatise]. Athens: ek tou typografeiou Parnassou, 1883 [1877].

Gatterer, Johann Christoph. *Synchronistische tabellen der völkergeschichte hauptsächlich nach herrn hofrath Gatterer's Versvch einer allgemeinen weltgeschichte von m. Daniel Gotthold Ioseph Hübler.* 3 vols. Freyberg in der Crazischen buchhandlung, 1799–1804.

Gedeon, Manuel. *Ai Phaseis tou par'imin ekklesiastikou zitimatos* [Phases in our Church question]. Istanbul: Patriarhiko Typografeio, 1910.

———. "Anekdota simeiomata peri ton patriarchon Anthimou B, Dionysiou C, Ieremiou C" [Unpublished notes on patriarchs Anthimus II, Dionysius III, Joachim III]. *Ekklisiastiki Alithia* 2 (1881–1882): 601–9.

———. *Apantisis idiotou eis Diatrivas Rosson peri ton kath'imas ekklesiastikon pragmaton* [A citizen's reply to Russians' treatises on the situation of our Church]. Athens, 1902.

———. *Aposimeiomata Chronografou* [A chronicler's annotations]. Athens: Ekdoseis Foinikos, 1932.

———. *Chronika tis Patriarchikis Akademias: Istorikai eidiseis peri tis M. tou Genous Scholis* [Chronicles of the Patriarchal Academy: Historical news of the Great School of the Nation]. Istanbul, 1893.

———. *Engrafa patriarchika kai synodika peri tou Bulgarikou zitimatos (1852–1873) ekdidomena eulogia kai kelefsi tou panagiotatou Oikoumenikou patriarchou Ioakeim III* [Patriarchal documents and appendices on the Bulgarian Question, 1852–1873: Published with the blessing and bidding of his All Holiness Ecumenical Patriarch Joachim III]. Istanbul: Patriarhiko Typografeio, 1908.

———. *I pnevmatiki kinisi tou Genous kata ton 18o kai 19o aiona* [The spiritual movement of the "Genos" in the eighteenth and nineteenth centuries]. Edited by F. Eliou and S. Asdrachas. Athens: Ermis, 1970.

———. *I proti peri ton pronomion rixis ekklisias kai kratous* [The first confrontation between Church and State over privileges]. Istanbul: Patriarhiko Typografeio, 1909.

———. *Kanonikai diataxeis* [Canonical decrees]. 2 vols. Istanbul, 1888–89.

———. *Konstantinoupolis* [Constantinople]. Istanbul, 1882.

———. *Kyrillos Loukaris. Meleti peri tis meta tin Alosin Orthodoxou Ekklisias, 1454–1638* [Cyril I Lucaris: A study on the Orthodox Church after the fall]. Istanbul, 1876.

———. *Logos Eisagogikos eis tin Ekklisiastikin Istoria* [Introduction to Church history]. Istanbul, 1877.

———. *Mesaionika Analekta* [Medieval anthology]. Athens: Metatyposis Chronou, 1874.

———. *Mneia ton pro emou, 1800–1863–1913* [What I witnessed, 1800–1863–1913]. Athens: Ekdoseis Ta Hronika, 1936.

———. *O Athos: Anamniseis – engrafa – simeioseis* [Athos: Memoirs, documents, notes]. Istanbul, 1885.

———. *Paideia kai ptocheia par imin kata tous teleftaious aionas* [Education and poverty in recent centuries]. Istanbul: Typ. Neologou, 1893.

———. *Patriarchikis Istorias Mnemeia* [Milestones in patriachal history]. Athens: Ekdoseis Georgiou Vasileiou, 1922.

———. *Vracheia simeiosis peri ton ekklesiastikon imon dikaion* [Brief note on our church rights]. Istanbul: Patriarhiko Typografeio, 1910.

Germanos (Grigoras), Archimandrite. *I en Halki Theologiki Scholi: (1844–1898)* [The Theological School of Halki, 1844–1898]. Alexandria: Typografeion K. A. Fakou, 1907.

Gervinus, Georg Gottfried. *Geschichte des neunzehnten Jahrhunderts seit den Wiener Verträgen*. Leipzig: W. Engelmann, 1855–66.

Gibbon, Edward. *The History of the Decline and Fall of the Roman Empire*. Vol. 8. London: G. Cowie and Co. Poultry, etc., 1825.

Gibbons, Herbert Adams. *The Foundation of the Ottoman Empire: A History of the Osmanlis up to the Death of Bayezid I (1300–1403)*. Oxford: Clarendon Press, 1916.

Gökalp, Ziya. *Türkçülüğün Esasları* [Fundamentals of Turkism]. Eski Şehir: Anadolu Üniversitesi Yayınları, 2019 [1923]. English edition: Gökalp, Ziya. *The Principles of Turkism*. Leiden: Brill, 1968.

———. *Türk medeniyeti tarihi* [The history of Turkish civilization]. Ankara: Toker Yayınları, 1995 (1926).

Goldsmith, Oliver *History of Greece, Abridged for the Use of Schools*. London: Printed for J.F. and C. Rivington, L. Davis, T. Longman, B. Law, G.G.J. and J. Robinson, T. Cadell, J. Nichols, R. Baldwin, W. Goldsmith, and J. Hayes, 1787.

Guettée, Vladimir (René-François). *Exposition de La Doctrine de L'Eglise Catholique Or-*

thodoxe accompagnee des differences qui se reconntrent dans les autres Eglises chretienes. Paris: Librairie de l'Union Chrétienne, 1866.

Guizot, M. (François). *Histoire générale de la civilization en Europe depuis la chute de l'Empire romain jusqu'à la révolution française.* 6th ed. Paris: Didier, Perrin et cie, 1857 (1828).

Hahn, Johann Georg. *Albanesische Studien.* Vol. 2. Vienna, 1853–54.

Hammer-Purgstall, Joseph-Freiherr von. *Geschichte des osmanischen Reiches: Grossentheils aus bisher unbenützten Handschriften und Archiven.* 10 vols. Pest: C.A. Hartleben, 1827–35.

Hegel, Georg Wilhelm Friedrich. *The Philosophy of History.* Prefaces by Charles Hegel. Translation by J. Sibree. Kitchener, Ontario: Batoche Books, 2001.

Hopf, Carl Hermann Friedrich Johann. *Oi Slavoi en Helladi: anaskevi ton theorion tou Fallmerayer* [The Slavs in Greece: Reconstructing the theories of Fallmerayer]. Translated by Frangiskos Zambaldes. Venice: Il Tempo, 1872.

Hoxhaj, Enver. "Mythen und Erinnerungen der albanischen Nation: Illyrer, Nationsbildung und nationale Identität." *Tyche* 20 (2005): 47–76.

Hugo, Gustav. *Lehrbuch der Geschicte des romischen rechts, bis auf Justinian.* Berlin: A. Mylius, 1820.

Iorga, Nicolae. Byzance après Byzance: Continuation de l' "Histoire de la vie Byzantine." Bucharest: Institut d'Études Byzantines, 1935. Romanian edition: *Bizant după Bizant.* Translated by Liliana Iorga-Pippidi. Bucharest: Editura enciclopedică română, 1972.

———. *Eikones apo tin simerini Ellada kai pente dialexeis gia tin syncroni elliniki zoi* [Images from today's Greece and five lectures on contemporary Greece]. Translated into Greek by Marika Manescu. Athens: Flamma Editions, 1932.

———. *Formes byzantines et réalités balcaniques: leçons faites à la Sorbonne.* Paris: H. Champion, 1922.

———. *Geschichte des Osmanischen Reiches nach den Quellen dargestellt.* 4 vols. Gotha: F.A. Perthes, 1908–13.

———. *Histoire des États balcaniques jusqu'à 1924.* Paris: J. Gamber, 1925.

———. *Histoire des Roumains et de la romanite orientale.* [S.n], 1937–45.

———. *Les origines de l'Iconoclasme.* Académie Roumaine, Bulletin de la Section Historique, tome XI, Congrès de Byzantinologie de Bucarest. Bucharest: Cultura Nationala, 1924.

———. *Quelques mots sur les relations entre les roumains et le peuple turc: Conference faite aux hôtes universitaires turcs à l'Université de Bucarest, le 6/19 mai 1914.* Bucharest: Imprimerie "Minerva," 1914.

———. *Relations entre l'Orient et l' Occident; Conférences faites à la Sorbonne.* Paris: J. Gamber, 1922.

———. *Roumains et Grecs: au cours des siècles: à l'occasion des mariages princiers de MDCCCCXXI.* Bucharest: Imprimerie "Cultura neamului românesc," 1921.

———. "Y-a-t-il eu un moyen-âge byzantin?" *Académie Roumaine, Bulletin de la Section Historique.* Vol. 13. Bucharest: Académie Roumaine, 1927.

Jireček, Konstantin. *Dějiny bulharského národa* [History of the Bulgarian nation]. Sofia: V. Praze, 1876.

———. *Istoriya na Balgarite* [History of the Bulgarians]. Sofia: Izd. Koreni, 1999.

Ivanov, Yordan. *Marko Balabanov: biografska beležka* [Marko Balabanov: a biographical note]. Vol. 1, *Bâlgarskj periodecheski pechat ot Vâzrazhdenneto mu do dnes* [Bulgarian periodical press from the Bulgarian renaissance to the present]. Sofia, 1893.

Karamzin, Nikolay Mikhailovich. *Istoria tis rossikis Aftokratorias* [History of the Russian Empire]. Translated by Krokidas. Athens: Ek tou typogr. P. K. Panteli, 1855.

Karolidis, Pavlos. *Simeioseis tines peri tis Mikrasiatikis Arias omofylias* [Notes on the Asia Minor Race]. Athens: Perri Brothers Printing Press, 1886.

Katartzis, Dimitrakis. *Dokimia* [Essays]. Athens: Ermis, 1974.

Katselidis, Georgios. *Epitomos Istoria tis Othomanikis Aftokratorias* [A concise history of the Ottoman Empire]. Athens: Andreas Koromilas, 1882.

Kemal Namık. *Osmanlı Tarihi* [Ottoman history]. 2 vols. 2nd ed. Istanbul: Bilge Kültür Sanat, 2012.

———. *Renan Müdafaanamesi* [Renan's defense]. Ankara: Akčağ, 2014.

Kiril, Patriarch Bâlgarski. *Ekzarh Antim (1816–1888)* [The Exarch Anthimus I, 1812–1888]. Sofia: Izd. Sv. Sinod na Bâlgarska Tsârkva, 1956.

———. *Graf N. P. Ignatiev i bâlgarskiyat tsârkoven vâpros: Isledvanija i dokumenti* [Count N. P. Ignatiev and the Bulgarian ecclesiastical question: Studies and documents]. Sofia: Izd. Sv. Sinod na Bâlgarska Tsârkva, 1959.

Klaproth, Julius von. *Archiv für asiastische Litteratur, Geschiche und Sprachkunde.* St. Petersburg: Im Acadmischen Verlage, 1810.

Köprülü, Mehmed Fuad. *Bizans müesseselerinin Osmanlı müesseselerine tesiri hakkında bâzı mülâhazalar* [Some observations on the influence of Byzantine institutions on those of the Ottomans]. Ankara: Kaynal Yayınları, 2002. First published as "Bizans müesseselerinin Osmanlı müesseselerine tesiri hakkında bâzı mülâhazalar." *Türk Hukuk ve İktisat Tarihi Mecmuası*, vol. 1 (1931): 165–313.

———. *Les Origins de l'Empire Ottoman.* Paris, E. de Boocard, 1935. English-language edition *The Origins of the Ottoman Empire.* Edited and translated by Gary Leiser. New York: SUNY Press, 1991.

———. *The Seljucks of Anatolia: Their History and Culture According to Local Muslim Sources.* Translated and edited by Gary Leiser. Salt Lake City: University of Utah Press, 1992.

Korais, Adamantios. *Dialogos dyo Graikon: ti symferei eis tin elevtheromenin apo Tourkous Ellada na praxei eis tas parousas peristaseis, dia na min doulothei eis Hristianous tourkizontas* [A dialogue between two Greeks: Liberated from the Turks, it is not in Greece's interest to be encumbered by Turkish Christians]. Venice, 1805.

Kotwicz, Władysław. "Contributions aux études altaïques (1929–30)." *Rocznik Orientalistyczny/Yearbook of Oriental Studies* 7 (1929–30): 130–234.

Koumas, Konstantinos M. *Istoriai ton anthropinon prakseon, apo ton archaiotaton chronon eos ton imeron mas, ek palaion Germanon istoriografon eletheros metafrasthisai* [Histories of human activity: From antiquity to our times, freely translated by older German historians]. 12 vols. Vienna: Anton von Haykul, 1830–1832.

Krâstevich, Gavril. *Istoriya Bâlgarska* [Bulgarian history]. Vol. 1. Istanbul, 1869.

———. "Kratko izslidovanie na Bâlgarska Drevnost" [A brief study of Bulgarian antiquity]. *Bâlgarski Knizhitsi*, no. 10 (1859): 40–73; no. 11 (1859): 81–100; and no. 12 (1859): 125–46.

———. *Otgovor na G. Drinovâta kritika vârhu Bâlgarskata Istoriya na G. Krâstevich* [Response to Mr Drinov's criticism on G. Krâstevich's "Bulgarian History"]. Istanbul, 1873.

Lavisse, Ernest, and Alfred Rambaud. *Histoire générale du IVe siècle jusqu' à nos jours*. Paris: A. Colin, 1893–1901.

Le Goff, Jacques. *History and Memory*. Translated by Steven Rendall and Elizabeth Claman. New York: Columbia University Press, 1992.

Lelevel, Joachim. *Histoire de Pologne*. Paris: A la Librairie Polonaise, 1844.

Leont'ev, Konstantin. *Against the Current: Selections from the Novels, Essays, Notes, and Letters of Konstantin Leontiev*. Edited, with an introduction and notes by George Ivask. New York: Wybright and Talley, 1969.

———. *Vostok, Rossiya i Slavyanstvo: filosofskaya i politicheskaya publicistika; Duhovnaya proza, 1872–1891* [The East, Russia, and Slavdom: Philosophical and political publications; spiritual prose]. 2 vols. Moscow: Respublica, 1996.

———. "Vladimir Solov'ev protiv Danilevskogo" [Vladimir Solov'ev versus Danilevsky]. In *Vostok, Rossiya i Slavyanstvo: filosofskaya i politicheskaya publicistika; Duhovnaya proza, 1872–1891*, vol. 2, 466–511. Moscow: Respublica, 1996.

Leontiou, Leontios K. *To alvanikon zitima* [The Albanian Question]. Athens: Ek tou typografeiou adelfon Perri, 1913.

Machiavelli, Niccolò. *The Discourses*. London: Penguin, 1970.

Mai, Angelo. *Novae patrum bibliothecae*. 10 vols. Rome: Typis Sacri Consilii Propagando Christiano Nomini, 1852–1905.

———. *Scriptorum veterum nova collection e vaticanis codicibus edita*. 10 vols. Rome: Typis vaticanis, 1825–1905.

Maior, Petru. *Istoria pentru începutul românilor în Dachia* [History of the Romanians' origins in Dacia]. Buda: Crăiasca Tipografie a Universităţii Ungureşti din Pesta, 1812.

Meyer, Gustav. "Die stellung des albanesischen im kreise der indogermanischen sprachen." In *Beitrage zur kunde der indogermanischen sprachen*. vol. 8., no. 3. Gottingen, 1884.

Michaud, Joseph-François. *Histoire des croisades*. Paris: Chez Michaud Jeune, 1825.

Migne, J. P. *Patrologiae cursus completus omninum SS patrum, doctorum scriptorumque ecclesiasticorum*. Paris: J. P. Migne, 1857–87.

Miliopoulos, Ioannis P. *Epitomi tis Othomanikis Historias* [Concise Ottoman history]. Constantinople: Typografeio K. Vretou, 1883.

Misirkov, Krste, *Za Makedonskite Raboti* [On Macedonian affairs]. Skopje: Makedonska akademiya na naukite i umetnostite, 2003.

Müller, Max F. *La science du langage: Cours professé a l'Institut Royale de la Grande Bretagne*. Paris: Auguste Durand, 1864.

Nikolaos I Mystikos, Patriarch of Constantinople. *Letters*. Washington, DC: Dumbarton Oaks Center for Byzantine Studies, Trustees for Harvard University–Locust Valley, NY: J. J. Augustin, 1973.

Novaković, Stojan. *Balkanska pitanja i manje istorijsko-političke beleške o Balkanskom poluostrvu 1886–1905* [The Balkan Question and brief historio-political notes on the Balkan Peninsula, 1886–1905]. Belgrade: Zadužbina Ilije M. Kolarca, 1906.

———. "Balkansko Poluostrvo i Etnografski sporovi: srpski, grčki i bugarski" [The Balkan Peninsula and ethnographical disputes: Serbs, Greeks, and Bulgarians]. In *Balkanska pitanja*, 305–408.

———. *Carigradska patrijaršija i pravoslavlje u Evropskoj Turskoj: razmatranja u prilog raspravi crkveno-prosvetnog pitanja u Evropskoj Turkskoj*. [Ecumenical Patriarchate and

Orthodoxy in European Turkey: Considerations in favor of discussing the Church-educational issue in European Turkey]. Belgrade: U Državnoj štampariji Kraljevine Srbije, 1895.

———. *Srbi i Turci XIV i XV veka* [Serbs and Turks in the fifteenth century]. Belgrade: Srpska književna zadruga, 2001.

Onciul, Dimitre. *Teoria lui Roesler: Studii asupra stăruinței Românilor în Dacia Traiană de A. D. Xenopol.* Bucharest, 1885–86.

Papadopoulos-Vrettos, Andreas. *La Bulgarie ancienne et moderne; sous le rapport géographique historique, archéologique, statistique et commercial.* St. Petersburg: Impr. de l'Académie impériale des sciences, 1856.

Paparrigopoulos, Konstantinos. "Bibliografia" [Bibliography]. *Nea Pandora* 3, no. 65 (1852): 397–403.

———. "Bibliografia," [Bibliography], *Nea Pandora* 3, no. 65 (1852): 397–403.

———. "I Orthodoxos Anatoliki Ekklisia kai ta dyo alla megala christianika thriskevmata" [The Eastern Orthodox Church and two other great Christian religions]. *Nea Pandora* 4, no. 79 (1853): 162–74.

———. *Istorikai pragmateiai: kat'eklogin tou syggrafeos* [Historical treatises: Selected by the author]. Athens: Ekdotis Georgios Kasdonis, typois adelfon Perri, 1889.

———. *Istoria tou Ellinikou Ethnous apo ton archaiotaton chronon mechri ton neoteron* [History of the Greek nation from antiquity to the present]. Vol. 5. Athens: N. Passaris, 1865–77.

———. *Istoria tou Ellinikou Ethnous [I proti morfi: 1853]* [History of the Greek Nation; the first draft: 1853]. Edited by K. T. Dimaras. Athens: Ermis, 1970.

———. "Oi teleftaioi Eikonomachoi" [The last Iconomachs]. *Nea Pandora* 3 (1852–53): 15–21, 65–71, 130–137, 175–82.

———. *Peri tis epoikiseos Slavikon tinon fylon eis tin Peloponnison* [On the settlement of Slavic tribes in the Peloponnese]. Athens: E. Antoniadou, 1843.

Paschides, Thomas. *Oi Alvanoi kai to mellon afton en to Ellinismo, meta parartimatos peri ton Ellinovlachon kai ton Voulgaron* [The Albanians and their future in Hellenism, with an annex on the Greek and Bulgarian Vlachs]. Athens: ek tou typografeiou tou Ethnikou Pnevmatos, 1879.

Pingaud, Leonce. *Notice sur Alfred Rambaud.* Besançon: Typogr. et Lith. Jacquin, 1906.

Polylas, Iakovos. *Pothen i mystikophobia tou Sp. Zambeliou* [Whither S. Zambelios's mysticism]. Corfu: Ermis, 1860.

Poujoulat, M. (Jean-Joseph François). *La France et la Russie à Constantinople: La question des lieux saints.* Paris: Amyot, 1853.

Pulevski, Georgi. *Rechnik od tri jezika s. makedonski, arbanski i turski* [Dictionary of three languages: Macedonian, Albanian and Turkish]. Belgrade: U držacnoj štampariji, 1875.

———. *Slavyansko-Makedonska Opshta Historiya* [General history of Slav-Macedonians]. Skopje: Makedonska Akademiya na naukite i umetnostite, 2003 [1892].

Rajić, Jovan. *Istorija raznih slavjanskih narodov naipače Bolgarov, horvatov i serbov* [History of various Slavic peoples, mainly, Bulgarians, Croats, and Serbs]. Vienna: Ab Slavenno-Serbskoj, Valahiskoj i Vostočnih Jažikov Privileg Tipografija, 1794–1798.

Rakovski, Georgi Stojkov. *Avtobiografiya i memoari* [Autobiography and memoirs]. Sofia: Dărzhavna pechatnitsa, 1925.

———. *Bâlgarska starina* [Bulgarian antiquity]. Bucharest: Knigopechatnica te Stefana Rasideska, 1864.

———. *Kratko razsâzhdenie vârhu tâmniya i lâzhovniya nachala, na koih e osnovana starata povestnost vseh evropeyskih narodov* [Short discussion of the dark and false origins on which the ancient history of all European peoples was based]. Belgrade, 1860.

———. *Nekoliko pechi o Asen pârvomu, velikomu tsar bâlgarskomu i sinu mu Asen vtorom* [Some words on Asen I, the Great King of the Bulgarians, and his son Asen II]. Belgrade: Pečatano v kn. Sirb. Knigo-pečatnice, 1860.

———. *Pokazalec ili râkovodstvo, kak da sja iziskvat i izdirjat stari čerti našego bitija, jazika, narodopokolenija, starago ni pravlenija, slavnago ni prošestvija i pročee* [A guide for how to search and study the old customs of our life, language, national population, ancient history, as well as our glorious origin]. Vol. 1. Odessa: Tipografiya P. Franchova, 1859.

———. *Sâchinenia v chetiri toma, treti tom: Istoriografiya* [Essays in four volumes: Third volume: Historiography]. Selected and edited by Veselin Traykov. Sofia, 1984.

Rallidis, O. "Zoiros pasas, Alexandros." In *Megali Elliniki Enkyclopaideia* [Great Greek Encyclopedia]. Vol. 12, 120. Athens: P. G. Makris, 1927–1934.

Rambaud, Alfred. Études sur l'histoire byzantine. Paris: A. Colin, 1912.

———. *Histoire de la Russie: depuis les origines jusqu'à nos jours.* Paris: Hachette, 1900.

———. *L'Empire grec au dixième siècle: Constantin Porphyrogénète.* Paris: A. Franck, 1870.

———. *Le monde byzantin: le sport et l'hippodrome a Constantinople, d'après des publications recèntes.* Paris: Bureau de la revue des deux mondes, 1871.

Reinhold, Carl Heinrich Theodor. *Noctes pelasgicae: vel Symbolae ad cognoscendas dialectos graeciae pelasgicas* [Pelasgian nights: The symbols of the Pelasgian Greek dialects.]. Athens: S. Garbola, 1855.

Renan, Ernest. *Discourses et Conférences.* Paris: Calmann Levy éditeurs, 1887.

———. "Islam and Science." A lecture presented at La Sorbonne, Paris, March 29, 1883. Translated by Sally P. Ragep. Montréal: McGill University, 2011.

Renieris, Markos. *Kyrillos Loukaris: o oikoumenikos patriarchis* [Cyril I Lucaris: the Ecumenical Patriarch]. Athens: Typografeion D. A. Mavromati, 1859.

Roesler, Robert. *Romänische Studien.* Leipzig: Duncker & Humblot, 1871.

Robert, Cyprien. "Le Monde gréco-slave." *Revue des Deux Mondes* 29 (1842): 380–430.

———. *Türkei: nämlich Serbier, Montenegriner, Bosniaken, Albanesen und Bulgaren; oder Darstellung ihrer hilfsquellen, ihrer Tendenzen und ihrer politischen Fortschritte.* Stuttgart: Franckh'sche Verlagsbuchhandlung, 1844.

Šafárik, Pavel Jozef. *Geschichte der slawischen Sprache und Literatur nach allen Mundarten* [History of the Slavic language and literature in all dialects]. Pest: Kön. Ung. Universitäts-Schriften, 1826.

———. *Slovanski náropodis* [Slavic ethnology]. 3 vols. Prague: Nakl, 1842. Československé akademie věd, 1955.

———. *Slovanské starožitnosti* [Slavic antiquities]. Prague: Tiskem I. Spurného, 1837.

———. *Über die Abkunft der Slawen, nach Lorenz Surowiecki.* Buda, 1828.

Sami (Frashëri), *Şemseddin. İslâmiyetin yayılması için yapılan çalışmalar* [Studies about the spread of Islam]. 1885. Istanbul: Gündoğan Yayınları, 1997.

———. *Kamus-ı Fransevi* [French–Turkish dictionary]. Istanbul: Mihran, 1895–1905.

———. *Kamus'ul Alami* [Encyclopedia of general science]. 6 vols. Istanbul: Mihran Matbaas, 1889–1898.
———. *Kamus-ı Türki* [Turkish lexicon]. Edited by Ömer Faruk Akün. Istanbul: Alfa, 1998 (1899–1901).
———. *Medeniyyet-i Islamiyye* [Islamic civilization]. 1879. Istanbul: Gündoğan Yayınları, 1996.
———. *Shqipëria ç'ka qenë, ç'është e ç'do të bëhetë?* [Albania: what was it, what is it, and what will become of it?]. Bucharest, 1899.
Sauvageot, Aurélien. *Recherches sur le vocabulaire des langues ouralo-altaiques.* Paris: Champion, 1930.
Savigny, Friedrich Carl von. *Geschichte des Römanischen Rechts im Mittelalters.* 2. Ausg., 7 vols. Heidelberg: J. C. B. Mohr, 1834–51.
Snegarov Ivan. *Istoriya na Ohridskata Arhiepiskopiya* [History of Archbishopric of Ohrid]. 2 vols. Sofia: Akademično izd-vo Prof. Marin Drinov, 1925.
Sokolov, I. I. *Konstantinopolskaya tserkov v 19veka: Oput istoriocheskovo izsledovaniya* [History of the Church of Constantinople in the 19th century: An Attempt at a Historical Study]. St. Petersburg, 1904.
———. *O vizantinizme v tserkovno-istoricheskom otnoshenii: vstupitel'naya lekcia po katedre istorii greko-vostochnoi tserkvi* [Byzantinism in ecclesiastical–historical relations: The inaugural lecture of the Chair of History of the Eastern Greek Church]. St. Petersburg: Tip M. Merkusheva, 1903.
———. *Svyatjshiy Ioakim Tretiy, patriarh Konstantinopol'skiy* [His All Holiness Joachim III, Patriarch of Constantinople]. St. Petersburg, 1901.
———. "Konstantinopol, Palestina i Russkaya tserkov" [Constantinople, Palestine, and the Russian Church]. In *Russkaya tserkov i patriarkhaty Vostoka: Tri tscerkovno-politicheskie utopii XX veka* [The Russian Church and the Patriarchates of the East: Three ecclesiastical-political utopias in the 20th century], edited by N. N. Lisovoy, 156–96. Moscow: Nauka, 2002.
Soulis, H. I. "Iroklis Vasiadis." *Megali Elliniki Enkyclopaideia* [Great Greek Encyclopedia]. Vol. 6, 746–47. Athens: P. G. Makris, 1927–1934.
Spanoudis, Konstantinos. *Istorikes selides, Ioacheim o Tritos* [Historical pages, Joachim III]. Constantinople: Gerardoi Brothers, 1902.
Spyromilios, S. *Alvanoi kai Alvanistai* [Albanians and Albanianists]. Athens: Ekdoseis Gavrilidi, 1914.
Stambolski, Hristo T. *Avtobiografiya, dnevnichi i spomeni* [Autobiography, diary, and memoirs]. Sofia: Dârzhavna Pechatnica, 1927.
Strabo, *Geography.* Vol. 8, Cambridge, MA: Harvard University Press, 1923.
Sulzer, Franz Joseph. *Geschichte des transalpinischen Daciens, das ist: der Walachey, Moldau und Bessarabiens, im Zusammenhange der Geschichte des übrigen Daciens als ein Versuch einer allgemeinen dacischen Geschichte.* Vienna, 1781–82.
Thierry, Amédée Simon Dominique. *Histoire d'Attila, de ses fils et successeurs jusqu'à l'établissement des Hongrois en Europe.* 2 vols. Paris: Didier, 1856.
———. *Récits de l'histoire romaine au Ve siècle: la lutte contre les Barbares et les luttes religieuses; Derniers Temps de l'Empire d'Occident.* Paris: Didier, 1860.
———. *Tableau de l'Empire romain, depuis la fondation de Rome jusqu'à la fin du gouvernement impérial en Occident.* Paris: Didier, 1862.

Thomopoulos, Iakovos I. *Pelasgika, itoi, peri tis glossis ton Pelasgon: archaiai Pelasgikai epigrafai Limnou, Kritis, Lykikai, Karikai, Etruskikai, Hetitikai: erminevomenai dia tis simerinis Pelasgikis Albanikis kai tis Ellinikis* [About Pelasgians, that is, about the language of the Pelasgians: Ancient Pelasgian inscriptions from Lemnos, Crete, Lycia, Caria, Etrurscean and Hittite Kingdoms: Interpreted through the modern Pelasgian Albanian and the Greek]. Athens: Typois P. Sakellariou, 1912.

———. *Pelasgika, itoi, peri tis glossis ton Pelasgon, meros B: Pelasgika ellinika & albanika themata en tois panarchaiois soumerikois lexikois ermineonta pleasgika onomata ellinikon Theon nison kai mython; ou soumeriki archaia albaniki* [About Pelasgians, i.e., about the language of the Pelasgians: Pelasgian, Greek and Albanian themes in ancient Sumerian dictionaries interpreting Pelasgian names of Greek Gods, islands, and myths, or Sumerian Ancient Albanian Part II]. Athens: Typois P. Sakellariou, 1912.

Thunmann, Johann. *Unterschungen über die Geschichte der östitch-europäischen Völker.* Leipzig: Crucius, 1774.

Traikov, Veselin N. *Georgi Stoikov Rakovski: A bibliography.* Sofia: Izd-vo na Bilgarskata akademiya na naukite, 1974.

Ubicini, Abdolonyme. *Lettres sur la Turquie, ou, Tableau statistique, religieux, politique, administratif, militaire, commercial, etc., de l'Empire ottoman, depuis le khatti-cherif de Gulkhane (1839).* Paris: J. Dumaine, 1853–54.

Urbini, Mauro. *Il Regno degli Slavi, Hoggi corrottamente detti Schiavoni.* Pesaro: Girolamo Concordia, 1601.

Uspenski, F. I. *Istoriya na Bizantiyska Imperiya* [History of the Byzantine Empire]. Sofia: Izd. Lik, 2001.

Vasa, Pashko. *La vérité sur l'Albanie et les Albanais.* Paris: Impr. de la Société anonyme de publications périodiques, 1879.

Venelin, Yuriy I. *Drevniye i nyneshniye bolgary v politicheskom, narodopisnom, istoricheskom i religioznom ih otnoshenii k rossiyanam.* [The ancient and modern Bulgarians and their political, national, historical, and relations with the Russians]. Moscow, 1829.

Vyzantios, D. Skarlatos. *I Konstantinoupolis* [Constantinople]. 3 vols. Athens, 1869.

Xenopol, Alexandru Dimitrie. *Histoire des Roumains de la Dacie Trajane depuis les origins jusqu' à l' union des principautés en 1859.* 2 vols. Paris: E. Leroux, 1896.

———. *Teoria lui Roesler: Studii asupra stăruinței românilor în Dacia Traiană.* [Roessler's theory: Studies on the presence of Romanians in Trajan's Dacia] Iasi, 1884.

———. *Une énigme historique: les Roumains au moyen-âge.* Paris: E. Leroux, 1885.

Zambelios, Spyridon. *Asmata Dimotika tis Elladas ekdothenta meta meletis istorikis peri Mesaionikou Ellinismou* [Demotic songs of Greece published with a historical study of medieval Hellenism]. Corfu: Typografeion Ermes, 1852.

———. *Kathidrisis Patriarcheiou en Rossia* [The foundation of the patriarchate in Russia]. Athens: Bibliop. D. N. Karavia, 1983.

———. *Vyzantinai Meletai. Peri pigon neollinikis ethnotitos apo ogdois axri dekatis ekatontaetiridos m.X.* [Byzantine Studies. On sources of Neohellenic ethnicity from the 8th to 10th Century A.D.]. Athens, 1857.

Zinkeisen, Johann Wilhelm. *Geschichte des osmanischen Reiches in Europa.* 7 vols. Hamburg: F. Perthes, 1840–63.

Zlatarski, Vasil. *Istoriya na bâlgarskata dârzhava prez srednite vekove* [History of the Bulgarian state in the middle ages]. Sofia: Nauka i Izkustvo, 1970–72.

V. Secondary Literature

Abu-Manneh, Butrus. "The Sultan and the Bureaucracy: The Anti-Tanzimat Concepts of Grand Vizier Mahmud Nedim Paşa." *International Journal of Middle East Studies* 22 (1990): 257–74.

Akün, Ömer Faruk. "Hayati Eserleri, Türklüge Hizmetleri ve Kamus-i Türki ile Şemseddin Sami." In *Şemseddin Sami, Kamus-i Türki*, edited by Ömer Faruk Akün, 1–32. Istanbul: Alfa, 1998.

———. "Şemseddin Sami." In *İslam Ansiklopedisi.* vol. 11: 411–22. Eskişehir: Anadolu Üniversitesi Güzel Sanatlar Fakültesi, 1997.

Anagnostopoulou, Sia. *The Passage from the Ottoman Empire to the Nation-States.* Istanbul: Isis Press, 2003.

Anestides, Stavros. "I ethnarchiki paradosi tis Megalis Ekklisias kai o Manouel Gedeon" [The Ethnarchical Tradition of the Great Church and Manuel Gedeon]. PhD diss., University of Athens, 1993.

Aretov, Nikolay. *Bâlgarskoto Vâzrazhdane i Evropa* [The Bulgarian renaissance and Europe]. Sofia: Izd. Kralica Mab, 2001.

———. *Natsionalna Mitologiya i Natsionalna Literatura* [National mythology and national literature]. Sofia: Izd. Kralica Mab, 2006.

———. "Shto e Oksidentalizâm i ima li toy potsva u nas? Predvaritelni tezisi v târsene na literaturnite aspekti na problema" [What is Occidentalism and what are its roots in our country? Preliminary positions on research in literary perspectives on the issue]. *Literaturna Misâl* 1 (2005): 123–30.

Argyriou, Asterios. *Les exégèses grecques de l'Apocalypse à l'époque turque, 1453–1821: Esquisse d'une histoire des courants idéologiques au sein du peuple grec asservi.* Thessaloniki: Etaireia Makedonikon Spoudon, 1982.

Argyropoulos, Roxane D. *Les intellectuels grecs à la recherche de Byzance, 1860–1912.* Athens: Institut de Recherches Néohélleniques-Fondation Nationale de la Recherche Scientifique, 2001.

Asimakopoulou, Foteini. "Arthur de Gobineau kai Jakob Philipp Fallmerayer: Dyo Symmahoi" [Arthur de Gobineau and Jakob Philipp Fallmerayer: Two allies]. *Ta Istorika* 16, no. 31 (1999): 331–48.

Bakić-Hayden, Milica. "Nesting Orientalisms: The Case of the Former Yugoslavia." *Slavic Review* 54, no. 4 (1995): 917–31.

———. "What's So Byzantine About the Balkans?." In *Balkan as Metaphor: Between Globalization and Fragmentation*, edited by Dušan I. Bjelić and Obrad Savić, 61–78. Cambridge, MA-London: MIT Press, 2002.

Bakić-Hayden, Milica, and Hayden, Robert. "Orientalist Variations on the Theme 'Balkans': Symbolic Geography in Recent Yugoslav Cultural Politics." *Slavic Review* 51, no. 1 (1992): 1–10.

Bayraktar, Uğur Bahadır. "Mythifying the Albanians: A Historiographical Discussion on Vasa Efendi's 'Albania and the Albanians.'" *Balkanologie* 13, nos. 1–2 (2011), http://journals.openedition.org/balkanologie/2272.

Berdyaev, Nikolay. *Leontiev*. Orono, ME: Academic International, 1968.

Berger, Stefan. *The Past as History: National Identity and Historical Consciousness in Modern Europe*. Houndmills-Basington: Palgrave MacMillan 1999.

———, ed. *Writing the Nation: A Global Perspective*. Hampshire: Palgrave Macmillan, 2007.

Berktay, Halil. *Cumhuriyet ideolojisi ve Fuat Köprülü* [The ideology of the Republic and Fuat Köprülü]. Istanbul: Kaynak Yayınları, 1983.

———. "The Search for the Peasant in Western and Turkish History." In *New Approaches to State and Peasant in Ottoman History*, edited by Halil Berktay and Suraiya Faroqhi, 109–84. London: Frank Cass, 1992.

Berlin, Isaiah. *The Roots of Romanticism*. The A. W. Mellon Lectures in the Fine Arts. Edited by Henry Hardy. Princeton, NJ: Princeton University Press, 1965.

Besançon, Alain. *L'image interdite: une histoire intellectuelle de l'iconoclasme*. Paris: Fayard, 1994.

Biçoku, Kasem. "Aleksandri i Madh në kujtesën historike të Skënderbeut e të shqiptarëve" [Alexander the Great in the historical memory of Skënderbeu and the Albanian people]. *Studime Historike* 59, no. 1–2 (2005): 7–29.

Bilmez, Bülent. "Sami Frashëri or Şemseddin Sami? Mythologization of an Ottoman Intellectual in the Modern Turkish and Socialist Albanian Historiographies Based on 'Selective Perception.'" *Balkanologie* 7, no. 2 (2003): 19–46.

———. "Shemseddin Sami Frashëri (1850–1904): Contributing to the Construction of Albanian and Turkish Identities." In *We, the People: Politics of National Peculiarity in Southeastern Europe*, edited by Diana Mishkova, 341–71. Budapest: CEU Press 2009.

Birtek Faruk, and Dragonas Thalia, eds. *Citizenship and the Nation-State in Greece and Turkey*. New York: Routledge, 2005.

Bobchev, Stefan S. *Marko Balabanov*. Sofia: Letopis na Bălgarska Akademiya na Naukite, 1921–1922.

Bogdan, Ioan. *Istoriografia Română și problemele ei actuale* [Romanian historiography, problems and realities]. Bucharest: C. Göbl., 1905.

Bohun, Michal. "Nikolay Mikhailovski and Konstantin Leontiev: On the Political Implication of Herbert Spencer's Sociology." *Studies in East European Thought* 54, no. 1/2 (2002): 71–86.

Boia, Lucian. *History and Myth in Romanian Consciousness*. Budapest–New York: Central European University Press, 2001.

Boneva, Vera. *Gavril Krâstevich: Biografija* [Gavril Krâstevich: A biography]. Shumen: Izd. Helion, 2000.

———. "Gavril Krâstevich za pravnite, politicheskite i kanonicheskite aspekti na bâlgarskiya tsarkoven vapros (1856–1872)" [Gavril Krâstevich on the legal, political, and canonical aspects of the Bulgarian church question, 1856–1872]. *Duhovna Kultura* 9 (1992): 18–24.

———. *Hristomatiya po Istoriya na Bâlgarskoto Vâzrazhdane: Tsârkovno-nacionalno dvizhenie* [Chrestomatheia in the history of the Bulgarian renaissance. The Church-national struggle]. Shumen: Universitetsko Izdatelstvo "Episkop Konstantin Preslavski," 2002.

———. "Istorikât Gavril Krâstevich" [The historian Gavril Krâstevich]. *Istoricheski pregled* 4, no. 5 (1993): 182–209.

———. *Vâzrazhdane*: Bâlgariya i Bâlgarite v prehod kam novoto vreme [Renaissance: Bulgaria and Bulgarians in the transition to modern times]. Shumen: Universitetsko Izdatelstvo "Episkop Konstantin Preslavski," 2005.

Bozhinov, Plamen. "La mission diplomatique bulgare du 1876 et Dr Stoyan Tchomakov—un conflit sans alternative." *Bulgarian Historical Review* 31, no. 1–2 (2003): 68–98.

———. "Marko D. Balabanov: Obshtestveno-politicheski idei i deynost (do 1878 godina)" [Marko Balabanov: Socio-political ideas and action (through 1878)]. Phd diss., University of Sofia, 1996.

Breuilly, John. "Changes in the Political Uses of the Nation: Continuity or Discontinuity?" In *Power and the Nation in European History*, edited by Len Scales and Oliver Zimmer, 67–101. Cambridge: Cambridge University Press, 2005.

Brown, Keith, and Yannis Hamilakis. *The Usable Past: Greek Metahistories*. Lanham, MD: Lexington Books, 2003.

Brucciani, Giacomo. *La scrittura della nazione: storia, lingua e fede nel Risorgimento bulgaro, 18–19 sec.* Pisa: Plus, 2009.

Buruma, Ian, and Avishai Margalit. *Occidentalism: The West in the Eyes of Its Enemies*. New York: Penguin, 2004.

Çalık, Etem. *Şemseddin Sami ve Medeniyyet-i Islamiyye* [Şemseddin Sami and Islamic civilization]. Istanbul: Insan Yayınları, 1996.

Chanev, Dimităr. *Bâlgarskata Istoricheska knizhnina prez Vâzrazhdaneto* [Bulgarian historical literature during the Renaissance]. Sofia: Nauka i izkustvo, 1989.

Chasiotis, I. *Apo tin 'Anarrosin' stin 'Anapterigiași n' tou Genous: i Orthodoxi Ekklisia kai i diamorfosi tis neoellinikis ideologias kata tin Tourkokratia* [From recovery to the re-soaring of the Genos: The Orthodox Church and the shaping of modern Greek political ideology under Turkish rule]. Thessaloniki: Aristotle University of Thessaloniki, 1999.

Cioroianu, Adrian. "The Impossible Escape: Romanians and the Balkans." In *Balkan as Metaphor: Between Globalization and Fragmentation*, edited by Dusan I. Bjelić and Obrad Savić, 209–33. Cambridge, MA: MIT Press, 2002.

Clarke, James F. "Serbia and the Bulgarian Revival (1762–1872)." *American Slavic and East European Review* 4, no. 3–4 (1945): 141–62.

Clayer, Nathalie. *Aux origines du nationalisme albanais: La naissance d'une nation majoritairement musulmane en Europe*. Paris: Karthala, 2007.

Cloutier, H. Handley. "Leont'ev and Nationalism." *The Review of Politics* 17, no. 2 (1955): 262–72.

Comisso, Ellen. "Empires as Prisons of Nations versus Empires as Political Opportunity Structures: An Explanation of the Role of Nationalism in Imperial Dissolutions in Europe." In *Empire to Nation: Historical Perspectives on the Making of the Modern World*, edited by Joseph W. Esherick, Hasan Kayali, and Eric Van Young, 138–66. Lanham, MD: Rowman & Littlefield, 2006.

Copeaux, Étienne. *Espaces et temps de la nation turque: Analyse d'une historiographie nationaliste, 1931–1993*. Paris: CNRS, 1997.

———. "I efevresi tis Istorias" [The invention of history]. In *Turkia: thriskeia, koinonia kai politiki* [Turkey: Religion, society, and politics], 199–214. Athens: Ellinika Grammata, 2004.

Daldal, Aslı. "Afet İnan, Fuat Köprülü ve Birinci Turk Tarih Kongresi'nde tartışmalar" [Afet İnan, Fuat Köprülü, and the confrontations at the First Congress of Turkish History]. *Toplum ve Bilim* 24, no. 92 (2002): 234–48.

Danova, Nadya. "Arhivât na Ivan Dobrovsky kato iztochnik na informatsiya za Balkanskata Istoriya" [The archives of Ivan Dobrovsky as a source on Balkan history]. In *B. Bibliotekata: Minalo i Nastoyashte* [B Library: Past and present], 212–18. Sofia, 2005.

———. "Ivan Dobrovski à Vienne: Contribution à l'histoire de Vienne en tante que centre politique et culturel des peuples balkaniques au XIX siècle." *Études Balkaniques* 39, no. 2 (2003): 3–45.

———. "Ivan Dobrovsky v New York (1954–1855)" [Dobrovsky in New York]. In *Bâlgaro-amerikanski kulturni i politicheski vrâzki prez XIX–pârvata polovina na XX vek* [Bulgarian–American cultural and political relations, 19th–first half of 20th century], 176–89. Sofia: Universittetsko Izdatelstvo "Sv. Kliment Ohridski," 2004

———. "La bibliothèque de Pavel Šafárik et les relations culturelles bulgaro-grecques." *Études Balkaniques* 41, no. 4 (2005): 111–20.

———. "La traduction grecque de l'ouvrage de Juri Venelin 'Les Bulgares anciens et modernes.'" In *Relations des influences réciproques entre Grecs et Bulgares XVII–XXs*, 123–28. Thessaloniki: Institute for Balkan Studies, 1991.

———. "Les étudiants bulgares à l'Université d'Athenes." In *Actes du Colloque Internationall Université: ideologie et culture*, 257–69. Athens, 1989.

———. "Le voyage de Marco Balabanov en Grèce en 1891 et son journal." *Balkan Studies* 26, no. 2 (1984): 309–20.

———. "L'incorporation de la Thessalie à la Grèce et l'opinion publique bulgare." In *Actes du Symposium Historique International, La Dernière Phase de la Crise Orientale et l'Hellénisme (1878–1881)*, 165–83. Athens, 1983.

———. "Marko Balabanov i grâtskiyat kulturen i ideyno-politicheski zhivot prez XIX vek" [Marko Balabanov and Greek cultural and political life in the 19th century], *Istoricheski pregled* 3 (1986): 58–71.

———. "Otnovo za 'Oksidentalizma' kato obraz na Drugiya" [Revisiting Occidentalism as a form of the "Other"], paper presented at the colloquium *Kakvo stravnyava sravnitelonoto literaturoznanie?* November 16–17, 2006. Sofia: Institut za Balkanistika, 2007, issue 17, 18–28.

———. "Otnovo za Pavel Šafárik i Bâlgarite" [Revisiting Pavel Şafarík and the Bulgarians]. In *Restoriki na pameta: Jubileen sbornik v chest na 60-godishnitata na prof. d.i.n. Ivan Pavlov* [Festschrift in honor of the sixtieth anniversary of Prof. Ivan Pavlov], 323–34. Sofia: University St. Kliment Ohridski, 2005.

Daskalov, Rumen. *The Making of a Nation in the Balkans: Historiography of the Bulgarian Revival.* Budapest: Central European University Press, 2004.

Demetrakopoulos, Fotis. *Vyzantio kai Neoelliniki Dianoisi sta mesa tou 19ou aionos* [Byzantium and Neo-Hellenic intellectuals in the mid-19th century]. Athens: Kastaniotis Editions, 1996.

Deringil, Selim. *The Well-Protected Domains: Ideology and the Legitimation of Power in the Ottoman Empire, 1876–1909.* London: I.B. Tauris, 1999.

Detchev, Stefan. "Beltween Slavs and Old Bulgars: 'Ancestors,' 'Race' and Identity in Late Nineteenth-Century Bulgaria." In *Manufacturing Middle Ages: Entangled History of Medievalism in Nineteenth-Century Europe*, edited by Patrick Geary and Gábor Klaniczay, 347–76. Amsterdam–Leiden: Brill, 2013.

Dimaras, Konstantinos T. *Konstantinos Paparrigopoulos: I epochi tou—i zoe tou—to ergo tou* [Konstantinos Paparrigopoulos: His time, his life, his work]. Athens: MIET, 1986.

Dimitrov, Bozhidar. *Bâlgarite: Pârvite Evropeichi* [Bulgarians: the first Europeans]. Sofia: Universittetsko Izdatelstvo "Sv. Kliment Ohridski," 2002.

Ditchev, Ivaylo. "The Eros of Identity." In *Balkan as Metaphor: Between Globalization and Fragmentation*, edited by Dušan I. Bjelić and Obrad Savić, 230–50. Cambridge, MA: MIT Press, 2002.

Drace-Francis, Alex. *The Making of Modern Romanian Culture: Literacy and the Development of National Identity*. London: Tauris Academic Studies, 2006.

Duijzings, Ger. "Religion and the politics of 'Albanianism': Naim Frashëri's Bektashi writings." In *Albanian Identities: Myth and History*, edited by Stephanie Schwandner-Sievers and Bernd J. Fischer, 60–69. London: Hurst and Company, 2002.

Duţu, Alexandru. *Political Models and National Identities in "Orthodox Europe."* Bucharest: Babel, 1998.

Duychev, Ivan. *Protobulgares et Slaves: sur le probleme de la formation de l'Etat bulgare.* [s.l.]: Institut Kondakov, 1938

——— "La formation de l'État bulgare et de la nation bulgare." In *L'Europe aux IXe-XIe siècles. Aux origines des États nationaux [actes du Colloque international sur les origines des États européens aux IX-XI siècles, tenu a Varsovie et Poznan du 7 au 13 septembre 1965. Publies sous la direction de Tadeusz Manteuffel et Aleksander Gieysztor]*, 215–24. Warsaw: Państwowe Wydawnictwo Naukowe 1968.

———. "Les problème de la continuité dans l'histoire de la Bulgarie médiévale." In *Aspects of the Balkans: Continuity and Change; Contributions to the International Balkan Conference held at UCLA, October 23–28, 1969*, edited by H. Birnbaum and Spyros Vryonis, 138–50. Hague–Paris: Mouton, 1972.

Economou, Eleni. "Paisiou Hilandarinou: Slavovoulgariki Istoria." PhD diss., Aristotle University of Thessaloniki, 1999.

Eleftheriadis, Pavlos. "Political Romanticism in Modern Greece." *Journal of Modern Greek Studies* 17 (1999): 41–61.

Exertzoglou, Haris. *Ethniki taftotita stin Konstantinoupoli ton 190 ai.: o Ellinikos Filologikos Syllogos Konstantinoupoleos 1861–1912* [National identity in 19th-century Constantinople: The Greek Literary Society of Constantinople]. Athens: Nefeli, 1996.

Eraslan, Cezmi. *Abdülhamid ve Islam Birliği* [Abdul Hamid and Islamic unity]. Istanbul: Ötüken, 1995.

Ersanlı-Behar, Büşra. *İktidar ve Tarih: Türkiye 'de "Resmi Tarih" Tezinin Oluşumu (1929–1937)* [Political power and history: The shaping of the thesis on "official history" in Turkey]. Istanbul: AFA Yahınları, 1996.

———. "The Ottoman Empire in the Historiography of the Kemalist Era: A Theory of 'Fatal Decline.'" In *The Ottomans and the Balkans: A Discussion of Historiography*, edited by Fikret Adanir and Suraiya Faroqhi, 115–54. Leiden: Brill, 2002.

Firkatian, Mari. *The Forest Traveller: Georgi Stoikov Rakovski and Bulgarian Nationalism*. New York: Peter Lang, 1996.

Fleming, Katherine E. "Orientalism, the Balkans, and Balkan Historiography." *The American Historical Review* 105, no. 4 (2000): 1218–33.

Frashëri, Kristo. "Semseddin Sami Frashëri: Ideolog i Levizjes Kombëtare Shqiptare" [Semseddin Sami Frashëri: Ideologist of the Albanian national novement] *Studime Historike* 4, no. 2 (1967): 79–94.

———. "Semseddin Sami Frashëri – idéologue du mouvement national albanais." *Studia Albanica* 3, no. 1 (1966): 95–110.

Furst, Lilian R., *Romanticism in Perspective: A Comparative Study of Aspects of the Romantic Movements in England, France and Germany*. New York: MacMillan, 1969.

Gabrovski, Spyridon Jeroshimonah. *Istoriâ vo krattse o bolgarskom narode slavenskom* [Concise history of the Slavo-Bulgarian people]. Translated by Mincho G. Minchev. Gabrovo: Luna, 2000 (1792).

Ganev, Ginjo, ed. *Dârzhava i Tsârkva – Tsârkva i dârzhava v Bâlgarskata istoriya* [State and Church—Church and State in Bulgarian history]. Sofia: IK "Sv. Kliment Ohridski," 2006.

Gasimov, Zaur. "Transfer and Asymmetry: Turkological Dialogue between Russia and Turkey in the First Half of the 20th Century." *European Journal of Turkish Studies* 24 (2017). DOI: https://doi.org/10.4000/ejts.5432.

Gaut, Greg. "Can a Christian be a Nationalist? Vladimir Solov'ev's Critique of Nationalism." *Slavic Review* 57, no. 1 (1998): 77–94.

Gawrych, George W. *The Crescent and the Eagle: Ottoman Rule, Islam and the Albanians, 1874–1913*. London–New York: I.B. Tauris, 2006.

———. "Tolerant Dimensions of Cultural Pluralism in the Ottoman Empire: The Albanian Community, 1800–1912." *International Journal of Middle East Studies* 15, no. 4 (November 1983): 519–36.

Gazi, Efi. *Scientific National History: The Greek Case in Comparative Perspective (1850–1920)*. Frankfurt am Main: Peter Lang, 2000.

Genchev, Nikolay. *Bâlgarskoto Vâzrazhdane* [The Bulgarian Renaissance]. Sofia: Izd. Kasta, 1995.

Georgieva, Gergana. "V Ogledaloto na Zapadna Evropa" [In the mirror of Western Europe]. *Literaturna Misal* 8, no. 2 (2000): 78–87.

Gerd, Lora. *Konstantinopol' i Peterburg: Tserkovnaya Politika Rossii na Pravoslavnom Vostoke, 1878–1898* [Constantinople and Petersburg: Russian Church policy in the Orthodox East]. Moscow: Indrik, 2006.

———. "Russian Imperial Policy in the Orthodox East and its Relation to Byzantine Studies." In *Imagining Byzantium: Perceptions, Patterns, Problems*, edited by Alena Alshanskaya, Andreas Gietzen, and Christina Hadjiafxenti, 93–100. Byzanz zwischen Orient und Okzident 11. Mainz: Verlag des Römisch–Germanischen Zentralmuseums, 2018.

Goldsworthy, Vesna. *Inventing Ruritania: The Imperialism of the Imagination*. New Haven, CT: Yale University Press, 1998.

Gorski, Philip S. "The Mosaic Moment: An Early Modernist Critique of Modernist Theories of Nationalism." *Journal of American Sociology* 105, no. 5 (2000): 1428–68.

Gounaris, Basil. "From Peasants into Urbanites, from Village into Nation: Ottoman Monastir in the Early Twentieth Century." *European History Quarterly* 31, no. 1 (2001): 43–63.

———. *Ta Valkania ton Ellinon: apo ton Diafotismo eos ton Proto Pagkosmio Polemo* [The Greeks' Balkans: From the Enlightenment to World War I]. Athens: Epikentro, 2007.

Grunebaum, Gustave E. von. "Byzantine Iconoclasm and the Influence of the Islamic Environment." *History of Religions* 2, no. 1 (1962): 1–10.

Gbúrová, Marcela. *Slavdom in Europe, Europe in Slavdom: A Vision of the Modernization of Slavs by Stefan Launer*. Chisinau: LAP, 2015.

Habermas, Jürgen. *The Structural Tranformation of the Public Sphere: An Inquiry into a Category of Bourgeios Society*. Translated by Thomas Burger in collaboration with Frederick Lawrence. Cambridge, MA: MIT Press, 1989.

Haldon, John. "Res publica Byzantina? State Formation and Issues of Identity in Medieval East Rome." *Byzantine and Modern Greek Studies* 40, no. 1: 4–16.

Hanioğlu, M. Şükrü. *A Brief History of the Late Ottoman Empire*. Princeton, NJ: Princeton University Press, 2008.

Heyd, Uriel. *Foundations of Turkish Nationalism: The Life and Teachings of Ziya Gökalp*. London: Luzac–Harvill, 1950.

Hitchins, Keith. *The Romanians 1774–1866*. Oxford: Clarendon Press, 1996.

Hobsbawn, Eric J., and Terrence O. Ranger, eds. *The Invention of Tradition*. Cambridge: Cambridge University Press, 1984.

Hopkins, Anthony G. "Back to the Future: From National History to Imperial History." *Past and Present* 164 (1999): 198–243.

Hosking, Geoffrey A. *Russia: People and Empire, 1552–1917*. Cambridge, MA: Harvard University Press, 1997.

Hoxhaj, Enver. "Mythen und Erinnerungen der albanischen Nation: Illyrer, Nationsbildung und nationale Identitat." *Tyche* 20 (2005): 47–76.

Iliou, Filipos. "Pothos Martyriou: apo tis vevaiotites stin amfisbitisi tou M. Gedeon. Symboli stin istoria ton neomartyron" [Passion for testimony: From the certainties to disputation of M. I. Gedeon—a contribution to the history of neo-martyrs]. *Ta Istorika* 12, no. 23 (1995): 267–84.

Kaldellis, Anthony. *The Byzantine Republic: People and Power in New Rome*. Cambridge, MA: Harvard University Press, 2015.

Kariotoglou, Alexandros. *Islam kai christianiki chrismologia: apo to mytho stin pragmatikotita* [Islam and Christian divinations: From myth to reality]. Athens: Armos, 2000.

Karpat, Kemal. *The Politicization of Islam: Reconstructing Identity, State, Faith, and Community in the Late Ottoman State*. New York: Oxford University Press, 2001.

Katartzis, Dimitrios. *Dokimia* [Essays]. Athens: Ermis 1974.

Katsofska-Maligoudi, Yanna. *Oi Slavoi ton Balkanion: eisagogi stin istoria kai ton politismo tous* [The Balkan Slavs: An introduction to their history and culture]. Athens: Gutenberg, 2004.

Kepov, Ivan P. *Gavril Krâstevich: Zhivot, obshtestveno-tsârkovno i knizhovna deynost* [Gavril Krâstevich: His life and social-ecclesiastical and literary activity]. Sofia: Farkel, 1929.

Kiousopoulou, Tonia. *Vasilefs i oikonomos: politiki exousia kai ideologia prin tin Alosi* [King or *Oikonomos*: Political power and ideology before the fall]. Athens: Polis, 2007.

Kitromilides, Paschalis. "Imagined Communities and the Origins of the National Question in the Balkans." *European History Quarterly* 19, no. 2 (1989): 149–92.

———. "Oi dytikes piges ton antidytikon epiheirimatologion stin Elliniki Paideia" [The western sources of anti-Western argumentations in Greek Culture]. In *Evropi kai Neos Ellinismos* [Europe and modern Hellenism]. Athens: Idryma Moraiti-Etaireia Spoudon Neoellinikou Politismou kai Genikis Paideias 2001.

———. "On the Intellectual Content of Greek nationalism: Paparrigopoulos, Byzantium, and the Great Idea." In *Byzantium and the Modern Greek Identity*, edited by David

Ricks and Paul Magdalino, 25–33. London: Centre for Hellenic Studies–King's College, 1998.

Kofos, Evangelos. "Patriarch Joachim III (1878–1884) and the Irredentist Policy of the Greek State." *Journal of Modern Greek Studies* 4, no. 2 (1986): 107–20.

Konortas, Paraskevas. "I exelixi ton 'ekklisiastikon' veration kai to Pronomiako zitima" [The development of "Church" *berats* and the privilege issue]. *Ta Istorika* 5, no. 9 (1988): 259–86.

———. *Othomanikes theoriseis gia to Oikoumeniko Patriarheio, 17os–arhes 20ou aiona* [Ottoman views on the Ecumenical Patriarchate, 17th–early 20th century]. Athens: Alexandreia, 1998.

Konstantakopoulou, Angeliki. *I Elliniki glossa sta Balkania, 1750–1850: to tetraglosso lexiko tou Daniil Moschopoliti* [The Greek language in the Balkans, 1750–1850: the quadrilingual dictionary of Daniel of Moschopolis]. Ioannina: University of Ioannina, 1988.

———. "Mnimi Ellis Skopetea (1951–2002): Istoriografia kai afigimatikotita," In *I Dysi tis Anatolis kai i Anatoli tis Dysis: ideologikes antanaklaseis kai stereotypa (teli 18ou–arches 20ou ai.)* [The West of the East and the East of the West: Ideological reflections and stereotypes, late 18th–early 20th centuries]. *Egnatia*, Scientific Review of the School of Philosophy's Department of History and Archaeology, Appendix to vol. 9 (2005): 27–40.

———. *Politiki kai mnimi sta Balkania: oi ellinikes eikones tou Mavrovouniou (19os–A Pagkosmios polemos)* [Politics and memory in the Balkans: Greek images of Montenegro, 19th century to World War I]. Ioannina: University of Ioannina, 2004.

Korkuti, Muzafer, Islami Selim, Prendi Frano, Anamali Skënder, and Shukriu Edi. *Historia e Popullit Shqiptar* [History of the Albanian people]. 2 vols. Tirana, 1959 and 1965.

Koselleck, Reinhart. *Critique and Crisis: Enlightenment and the Pathogenesis of Modern Society*. Cambridge, MA: MIT Press, 1988.

———. *Futures Past: On the Semantics of Historical Time*. Cambridge, MA: MIT Press, 1985.

Kostis, Kostas. "The Formation of the State in Greece, 1830–1914." In *Citizenship and the Nation-State in Greece and Turkey*, edited by Frank Birtek and Thalia Dragonas, 18–36. New York: Routledge, 2005.

Koubourlis, Giannis. "I idea tis istorikis synecheias tou ellinikou ethnous stous ekprosopous tou ellinikou Diafotismou: i diamachi gia to onoma tou ethnous kai oi apopseis gia tous archaious Makedones kai Byzantinous" [The concept of the Greek nation's historical continuity for representatives of the Greek Enlightenment: The dispute over the nation's name and views of the ancient Macedonians and Byzantines]. *Dokimes* no. 13–14 (2005): 137–91.

———. *La formation de l'histoire nationale Greque. L'apport de Spyridon Zambélios (1815–1881)*. Athens: Institut de Recherches Néohelléniques–Fondation Nationale de la Recherche Scientifique, 2005.

Landau, Jacob M. *The Politics of Pan-Islam: Ideology and Organization*. Oxford: Clarendon Press, 1994.

Lanyi, Gabriel. "Debates on the Definition of the Romanticism in Literary France (1820–1830)." *Journal of the History of Ideas* 41, no. 1 (1980): 141–50.

Levend, Agâh Sırrı. *Şemsettin Sami*. Ankara: Türk Dil Kurumu Yayınları, 1969.

Liakos, Antonis. "Hellenism and the Making of Modern Greece: Time, Language, Space." In *Hellenisms: Culture, Identity and Ethnicity from the Antiquity to Modernity*, edited by Katerina Zacharia, 201–36. Aldershot: Ashgate 2008.

———. "'Pros episkevin olomeleias kai enotitas': I domisi tou ethnikou chronou" ["Towards repairing plenary and unity": Structuring national time]. In *Epistimoniki synantisi sti mnimi tou K. T. Dimara* [Scientific conference in memory of K. T. Dimaras], 171–99. Athens: Center for Neo-Hellenic Research–National Research Foundation, 1994.

Lieven, Dominic. "The Russian Empire and the Soviet Union as Imperial Politics." *Journal of Contemporary History* 30, no. 4 (1995): 607–36.

———. "Dilemmas of Empire 1850–1918. Power, Territory, Identity." *Journal of Contemporary History* 34, no. 2 (1999): 163–200.

Lovejoy, Arthur O. "The Meaning of Romanticism for the Historian of Ideas." *Journal of the History of Ideas* 2, no. 3 (1941): 257–78.

———. *The Revolt Against Dualism: An Inquiry Concerning the Existence of Ideas.* La Salle, IL: The Open Court Publishing Company, 1960.

Löwy, Michael, and Robert Sayre. *Romanticism Against the Tide of Modernity.* Translated by Catherine Porter. Durham, NC: Duke University Press, 2001.

Lukashevich, Stephen. *Konstantin Leontev, 1831–1891: A Study in Russian "Heroic Vitalism."* New York: Pageant Press, 1967.

Maciu, Vasile, St. Pascu, Dan Berindei, Miron Constantinescu, V. Liveanu, and P.P. Panaitescu. *Outline of Rumanian Historiography until the Beginning of the 20th Century.* Bucharest: Pub. House of the Academy of the Romanian People's Republic, 1964.

Madzharov, Mikhail Ivanov. *Iztochna Rumeliya (istoricheski pregled)* [Eastern Rumelia: A historical overview]. Sofia: S. M. Staykov, 1925.

Magdalino, Paul. "The History of the Future and Its Uses: Prophecy, Policy, and Propaganda." In *The Making of Byzantine History: Studies Dedicated to Donald M. Nicol*, edited by Roderick Beaton and Charlotte Roueché, 3–34. London: Variorum, 1993.

Mänchen-Helfen, Otto J. *The World of the Huns: Studies in Their History and Culture.* Edited by Max Knight. Berkeley: University of California Press, 1973.

Mango, Cyril. *Byzantium and Its Image: History and Culture of the Byzantine Empire and Its Heritage.* London, Variorum Reprints, 1984.

———. "Byzantinism and Romantic Hellenism." *Journal of the Warburg and Courtauld Institutes* 28 (1965): 29–43. Reprinted in *Byzantium and Its Image: History and Culture of the Byzantine Empire and Its Heritage.* London: Variorum Reprints, 1984.

Mardin, Şerif. *The Genesis of Young Ottoman Thought: A Study in the Modernization of Turkish Political Ideas.* Princeton, NJ: Princeton University Press, 1962.

Markova, Zina. *Bâlgarskata Ekzarhiya, 1870–1879* [The Bulgarian Exarchate]. Sofia, 1989.

Meininger, Thomas A. *Ignatiev and the Establishment of the Bulgarian Exarchate, 1864–1872: A Study in Personal Diplomacy.* Madison: University of Wisconsin Press, 1970.

Meyendorff, John. "Was There Ever a 'Third Rome'? Remarks on the Byzantine Legacy in Russia." In *The Byzantine Tradition after the Fall of Constantinople*, edited by John James Yiannias, 45–60. Charlottesville: University Press of Virginia, 1991.

Mishkova, Diana. *Beyond Balkanism: The Scholarly Politics of Region Making.* London: Routledge, 2019.

———. *Prisposobyavane na svobodata. Modernost-legitimnost v Sarbiya i Rumaniya prez XIX vek* [The discipline of freedom: Modernity and legitimation in Serbia and Rumania in the nineteenth century]. Sofia: Paradigma, 2001.

Moser, Charles A. *A History of Bulgarian Literature 865–1944*. Hague: Mouton, 1972.

Nanakis, Andreas "I hireia tou Oikoumenikou thronou kai i eklogi tou Meletiou Metaxaki 1918–1922" [The vacancy of the Ecumenical throne and the election of Meletius Metaxakis, 1918–1922]. PhD diss., University of Thessaloniki, 1988.

Nazârska, Zhorzheta Dimitrova. "Gavril Krâstevich: zhivot mezhdu staroto i novoto" [Gavril Krâstevich: Life between old and new]. *Minalo* 1 (1995): 49–62.

———. "Iztochnorumeliyskiyat dârzhavnik Gavril Krâstevich, 1879–1885 god" [Gavril Krâstevich, the politician of Eastern Rumelia, 1879–1885]. PhD. diss., University of Sofia, 1999.

Nelson, Dale Lawrence. *Konstantin Leontiev and the Orthodox East*. Minneapolis: University of Minnesota Press, 1975.

Obolensky, Dimitri. *The Byzantine Commonwealth: Eastern Europe, 500–1453*. London: Weidenfeld and Nicolson, 1971.

Özcan, Azmi. *Pan-Islamizm: Osmanlı Devleti, Hindistan Müslümanları ve Ingiltere (1877–1914)* [Pan-Islamism: The Ottoman State, the Muslims of India, and England]. Istanbul: ISAM, 1992.

Panagiotopoulos, "Vasilis I Viomichaniki Epanastasi kai i Ellada 1832–1871" [The Industrial Revolution and Greece]. In *Eksynchronismos kai Viomichaniki Epanastasi sta Balkania ton 190 aiona* [Reform and industrial revolution in the Balkans in the nineteenth century], edited by V. Panagiotopoulos, 216–35. Athens: Themelio, 1980.

Pantazopoulos, Nikolaos I. *Church and Law in the Balkan Peninsula during the Ottoman Rule*. Hidryma Meleton Chersonésou tou Haimou 92. Thessaloniki: Institut for Balkan Studies, 1967.

———. "Gustav Geib: Enas opados tis Istorikis Scholis tou dikaiou stin monarchiki Ellada (1833–1834)" [Gustav Geib: A follower of the historical school of jurisprudence in monarchist Greece]. In *Armos, Timimitikos Tomos ston kathigiti N. K. Moutsopoulo gia ta 25 chronia pnevmatikis tou prosforas sto Panepistimio* [Festschrift in honor of Professor N. K. Moutsopoulos's 25 years of spiritual service at the university]. vol. 3, 1377–89. Thessaloniki: Aristotle University of Thessaloniki, 1991.

Papoulides, Konstantinos. *To Rossiko Archaeologiko Instituto Konstantinopoleos (1894–1914)* [The Russian Archaeological Institute of Constantinople]. Thessaloniki: IMXA, 1987.

Parla, Taha. *The Social and Political Thought of Ziya Gökalp, 1876–1924*. Leiden: E. J. Brill, 1985.

Pippidi, Andrei. *Tradiția politică bizantină în țările roman în secolele XVI–XVIII* [Byzantine political tradition in the Romanian lands in the 16th–17th centuries]. Bucharest: Editura Academiei Române, 1983.

Poliakov, Leon. *The Aryan Myth: A History of Racist and Nationalist Ideas in Europe*. London: Chatto & Windus Heinemann for Sussex University Press, 1974.

Politis, Alexis. *Kataloipa Fauries kai Brunet de Presle: Analytikos katalogos* [Fauriel and Brunet de Presle residues. Analytical list]. Athens: Kentro Neoellenikom Ereunon E.I.E, 1980.

———. *Romantika chronia: Ideologies kai nootropies stin Elláda tou 1830–1880* [Romantic years: Ideologies and mentalities in Greece 1830–1880]. Athens: Mnimon, 1993.

Poulin, Francis. "Vladimir Solov'ev's Rossiia i Vselenskaya Tserkov', Early Slavophilism's Pneumatic Spirit and the Pauline Prophet." *Russian Review* 52, no. 4 (1993): 528–39.

Poulton, Hugh. *The Top Hat, the Grey Wolf, and the Crescent: Turkish Nationalism and the Turkish Republic*. New York: NYU Press, 1997.

———. "The Turkish State and Democracy." *The International Spectator* 34, no. 1 (1999): 47–62.

Prifti, Kristaq. "Koncepti i Lidhjes së Prizrenit për shtetin kombëtar shqiptar (1878–1881)" [The meaning of the League of Prizren for the Albanian state]. *Studime Historike* 57, no. 3–4 (2003): 43–59.

Psilos, Christophoros. "Albanian Nationalism and Unionist Organization, 1908–1912." *Mediterranean Quarterly* 17, no. 3 (2006): 26–42.

Pundeff, Marin V. "Bulgarian Nationalism." In *Nationalism in Eastern Europe*, edited by Peter F. Sugar and Ivo John Lederer, 93–165. Washington: University of Washington Press, 1994.

Randev, Nikolay. *M. Drinov i K. Ireček i prosvetnoto delo v Knyazhestvo Bâlgariya* [Marin Drinov, Konstantin Jireček, and education in the Bulgarian Kingdom]. Sofia, 1984.

Reichert Robert W. "Anti-Bonapartist Elections of the Academie Francaise during the Second Empire." *The Journal of Modern History* 35, no. 1 (1963): 33–45.

Roosevelt, Priscilla Reynolds. *Apostle of Russian Liberalism: Timofei Granovsky*. Newtonville, MA: Oriental Research Partners, 1986.

Rowland, Daniel B. "Moscow: The Third Rome or the New Israel?" *Russian Review* 55, no. 4 (1996): 591–614.

Sampimon, Janette. *Becoming Bulgarian: The Articulation of Bulgarian Identity in the Nineteenth Century in its International Context: An Intellectual History*. Amsterdam: Uitgeverij Pegasus, 2006.

Schelting, Alexander von. *Russland und der Westen im russischen Geschichtsdenken*. Berlin: Forschungen zur osteruropäischen Geschichte, 1989.

Schleicher August, *Compendium der vergleichenden Grammatik der indogermanischen Sprachen: Kurzer Abriss der indogermanischen Ursprache, des Altindischen, Altiranischen, Altgriechischen, Altitalischen, Altkeltischen, Altslawischen, Litauischen und Altdeutschen*. 2 vols. Weimar: H. Boehlau, 1861–62.

Secaattin, Tural. *Semsettin Sami*. Istanbul: Sule Yayinlar, 1999.

Sfetas, Spyridon. "Syniparxi kai sygrousi tis Dysis me tin Anatoli: Serbophilia kai Serbophobia stin Ethniki Ideologia ton Kroaton ton 190 aiona" [Coexistence and conflict between West and East: Serbophilia and Serbophobia in 19th-century Croatian national ideology]. In *I Dysi tis Anatolis kai i Anatoli tis Dysis: ideologikes antanaklaseis kai stereotypa (teli 18ou–arches 20ou ai.)* [The West of the East and the East of the West: Ideological reflections and stereotypes, late 18th–early 20th centuries]. *Egnatia*, Scientific Review of the School of Philosophy's Department of History and Archaeology, Appendix to Vol. 9 (2005), 139–54.

Sigalas, Nikos "'Ellinismos' kai exellinismos: o schimastismos tis neoellinikis ennoias ellinismos" ["Hellenism" and Hellenization: The formation of the neo-Hellenic concept of Hellenism]. *Ta Istorika* 18, no. 34 (2001): 3–70.

———. "Hellénistes, hellénisme et idéologie nationale: De la formation du concept d'"hellénisme" en grec moderne." In *L'Antiquité grecque au XIXème siècle: Un* exemplum *contesté?*, edited by Chryssanthi Avlami, 239–91. Paris: L'Harmattan, 2000.

Skendi, Stavro. *The Albanian National Awakening, 1878–1912*. Princeton, NJ: Princeton University Press, 1967.

———. "Beginnings of Albanian Nationalist Autonomous Trends: The Albanian League, 1878–1881." *American Slavic and European Review* 12, no. 2 (1953): 219–32.

Skopetea, Elli. "The Balkans and the Notion of the 'Crossroads Between East and West.'" In *Greece and the Balkans: Identities, Perceptions, and Cultural Encounters Since the Enlightenment*, edited by Dimitris Tziovas, 171–76. Aldershot: Ashgate, 2003.

———. *I Dysi tis Anatolis: Eikones Apo to Telos tis Othomanikis Aftokratorias* [The West of the East: Images from the end of the Ottoman Empire]. Athens: Gnosi, 1992.

———. "Oi Ellines kai oi Echthroi tous: i katastasi tou ethnous stis arches tou 20ou aiona" [The Greeks and their enemies: The state of the nation in the early twentieth century]. In *Istoria tis Elladas tou 20ou aiona: oi aparches 1900–1922* [The history of Greece in the twentieth century: the origins of 1900–1922]. Vol. A, edited by Christos Hatziiosif, 9–35. Athens: Bibliorama, 1999.

———. "O Konstantinos Paparrigopoulos tou K. T. Dimara kai merikes skepseis peri ethnikis historiographias" [Dimaras's Konstantinos Paparrigopoulos and some thoughts on national historiography]. *Synchrona Themata* 11, no. 35–37 (1988): 286–94.

———. *To "Protypo vasileio" kai i Megali Idea: Opseis tou ethnikou provlimatos stin Ellada (1830–1880)* [The "model kingdom" and the great idea: views on the national problem in Greece]. Athens: Polytypo, 1988.

Smith, Anthony D. *Chosen Peoples: Sacred Sources of National Identity*. Oxford: Oxford University Press, 2003.

———. *Myths and Memories of the Nation*. Oxford: Oxford University Press, 1999.

———. *Nationalism and Modernism: A Critical Survey of Recent Theories of Nations and Nationalisms*. London: Routledge, 1998.

Stamatopoulos, Dimitris. *The Eastern Question or Balkan Nationalism(s): Balkan History Reconsidered*. Vienna: Vienna University Press, 2018.

———. "Ecumenical Ideology in the Orthodox Millet (19th–20th c.)." In *Economy and Society on Both Shores of the Aegean*, edited by Lorans Tanatar Baruh and Vangelis Kechriotis, 201–47. Athens: Alpha Bank Historical Archives, 2010.

———. "From Cratylus to Herder: Dimensions of the Language Question in the Ottoman Empire (Late 19th Century)." In *Language, Society, History: The Balkans*, edited by Anastasios Foivos Christidis, Maria Arapopoulou, and Maria Chriti, 253–64. Thessaloniki: Center for the Greek Language, 2007.

———. "From Machiavelli to the Sultans: Power Networks in the Ottoman Imperial Context." *Historein* 5 (2005): 76–93.

———. "From the Vyzantism of K. Leont'ev to the Vyzantinism of I.I. Sokolov: The Byzantine Orthodox East as Motif of the Russian Orientalism." In *Héritages de Byzance en Europe du Sud-Est à l'époque moderne et contemporaine*, edited by Olivier Delouis and Petre Guran, 329–48. Athens: EFA, 2013.

———. "Hellenism versus Latinism in the Ottoman East: Some Reflections on the Decline of the French Influence in the Greek Literary Society in Istanbul." Études *Balkaniques* 14, no. 3 (2007): 79–106.

———. "I Ekklisia os Politeia: anaparastaseis kai metashimatismoi tou Orthodoxou millet stin Othomaniki Avtokratoria (devtero miso tou 19ou aiona" [The Church as state: Representations and transformations of the Orthodox millet in the Ottoman Empire (second half of the 19th century)], *Mnimon* 23 (2001): 183–220.

———. *Metarrhythmisi kai Ekkosmikefsi: pros mia anasynthesi tis Istorias tou Oikoumenikou Patriarcheiou ton 19o aiona* [Reform and secularization: Toward a reconstruction of the history of the Ecumenical Patriarchate in the nineteenth century]. Athens: Alexandria, 2003.

———. "O Manuil Gedeon kai i epanadiorganosi tou oikoumenikou modelou" [Manuel Gedeon and the restructuring of the Ecumenist model]. In *Mnimi Alkis Angelou: Ta afthona schmimata tou parelthontos; zitiseis tis politismikis istorias kai tis theorias tis logotechnias* [In memory of Alkis Angelou: The abundant forms of the past: research in the cultural history and theory of literature]. Conference proceedings, 8th Scientific meeting, 377–87. Thessaloniki: University Studio Press, 2004.

———. "The Splitting of the Orthodox Millet as a Secularizing Process: The Clerical–Lay Assembly of the Bulgarian Exarchate (Istanbul 1871)." In *Griechische Kultur in Südosteuropa in der Neuzeit: Beiträge zum Symposium in memoriam Gunnar Hering (Vienna, December 16–18, 2004)*, edited by Maria A. Stassinopoulou and Ioannis Zelepos, 243–70. Vienna: VÖAW, 2007.

Stamatov, Atanas, and Regina Raycheva. "Paradoxes in the Bulgarian Reception of European Philosophical Thought." *Studies in East European Thought* 53, no. 1–2 (2001): 3–19.

Stavridis, Vassilios T. *I Iera Theologiki Scholi tis Halkis* [The Holy Theological School of Halki]. Thessaloniki: Kyriakidis, 1988.

Stokes, Gale. *Three Eras of Political Change in Eastern Europe*. Oxford: Oxford University Press, 1997.

Tabaki, Anna. "Un aspect des Lumières néo-helléniques: l'approche scientifique de l'Orient: Le cas de Dimitrios Alexandridis." *Ellinika* 35, no. 2 (1984): 316–32.

Temelski, Hristo, ed. *Tsârkovno-Narodniyat Sâbor 1871 g: Dokumentalen sbornik no sluchay 130-godişninata ot Pârviya-Tsârkovno-Naroden Sâbor* [The Clerical–Lay Assembly of 1871: A collection of documents on the occasion of the 130th anniversary of the meeting of the First Ecclesiastic National Assembly]. Sofia: Universittetsko Izdatelstvo "Sv. Kliment Ohridski," 2001.

Thompson, Edward A. *A History of Attila and the Huns*. London: Oxford University Press, 1948.

Todev, Ilia, ed. *Dr. Stoyan Chomakov (1819–1893): Zhivot, Delo, Potomtsi* [Dr. Stoyan Chomakov, 1819–1893: life, works, descendants]. Sofia: Akademitčno Izdatelstvo Prof. Marin Drinov, 2003.

Todorova, Maria. "Bulgaria." *The American Historical Review* 97, no. 4 (1992): 1105–17.

———. *Imagining the Balkans*. Oxford: Oxford University Press. 1997.

Trautmann, Thomas R. *Aryans and British India*. Berkeley: University of California Press, 1997.

Trifonov, Yordan, *Istoriya na grad Pleven do Osvoboditelnata Voyna* [History of the city of Pleven during the liberation war]. Sofia: Dârzhavna Pechatnica, 1933.

Trix, Francis. "The Stamboul Alphabet of Shemseddin Sami Bey: Precursor to Turkish Script Reform." *International Journal of Middle East Studies* 31, no. 2 (1999): 255–72.

Türköne, Mümtaz'er. *Siyasi Ideoloji olarak Islamcılığın Doğuşu* [Political ideology as the dawn of Islamism]. Ankara: Lotus Yayinevi, 2005.

Vaio, John. "George Grote." In *Classical Scholarship: A Biographical Encyclopedia*, edited by Ward W. Briggs and William M. Calder, 119–26. New York: Garland Press, 1990.

Vasiliev, Alexander A. "The Iconoclastic Edict of Caliph Yazid II, A.D. 721." *Dumbarton Oaks Papers* 9–10 (1956): 23–47.
Veloudis, Georgios. *O Jakob Philipp Fallmerayer kai i gennisi tou Ellinikou istorismou* [Jakob Philipp Fallmerayer and the birth of Greek historicism]. Athens: EMNE-Mnimon, 1982.
Vryonis, Spyros. *The Decline of Medieval Hellenism in Asia Minor and the Process of Islamization from the Eleventh through the Fifteenth Century.* Berkeley: University of California Press, 1971.
———. "*Prior tempore, fortier ure:* Ethnogenetikes theories sti NA Evropi kata ton 200 aiona" [Ethnogenetic theories in Southeastern Europe in the 20th century]. *Egnatia* 4 (1993–1994): 189–220.
White, Hayden V. *Metahistory: The Historical Imagination in Nineteenth-Century Europe.* Baltimore: Johns Hopkins University Press, 1975.
Wolff, Larry. *Inventing Eastern Europe: The Map of Civilization on the Mind of the Enlightenment.* Stanford, CA: Stanford University Press, 1994.
Xholli, Zija. *Sami Frasheri.* Tirana: Mihal Quri, 1978.
Yazıcı, Nevin. *Osmanlılık Fikri ve Genç Osmanlılar Cemiyeti* [Ottoman thought and the Young Ottomans]. Ankara: Türk Tarih Kurumu Basımevi, 2002.
Yonkov, Hristo M. *Georgi Stoykov Rakovski.* Sofia: Izd. Sibiya, 2005.
Zaimova, Raia. "Po vâprosa za zapadnoevropeyskata istoriografiya i 'Istoriya Slavyanobâlgarska'" [The issue of Western European historiography and Slav-Bulgarian history]. *Literaturna Misal* 1, no. 2 (1991): 44–54.
Zannouvios, Nikandros. *I Rosia kai to Voulgariko Zitima* [Russia and the Bulgarian Question]. Athens: Ekdoseis I. Kouvellou kai A. Trimmi, 1878.
Zavalani, Tajar. "Albanian Nationalism." In *Nationalism in Eastern Europe,* edited by Peter F. Sugar and Ivo John Lederer, 55–92. Washington: University of Washington Press, 1994.
Zhechev, Toncho. *Bâlgarskiyat Velikden ili Stratstite Bâlgarski* [The Bulgarian Easter or the Bulgarian Passions]. Plovdiv: Hristo G. Danov, 1985.
Zub, Alexandru. "En quête d'une synthèse: l'historiographie roumaine au XIXe siècle." *Nouvelles études d'histoires* 9 (1995): 97–102.
———. *L'historiographie roumaine à l'âge de la synthèse: A. D. Xenopol.* Bucharest: Editura Ştiinţifică şi Enciclopedică, 1983.

Index

C

D

P

T

U

V

Lightning Source UK Ltd.
Milton Keynes UK
UKHW021258281022
411258UK00005B/116

9 789633 863077